MEETING MYSTERY

THEOLOGY IN GLOBAL PERSPECTIVE SERIES

Peter C. Phan, General Editor
Ignacio Ellacuría Professor of Catholic Social Thought,
Georgetown University

At the beginning of a new millennium, the *Theology in Global Perspective* series responds to the challenge to reexamine the foundational and doctrinal themes of Christianity in light of the new global reality. While traditional Catholic theology has assumed an essentially European or Western point of view, *Theology in Global Perspective* takes account of insights and experience of churches in Africa, Asia, Latin America, Oceania, as well as from Europe and North America. Noting the pervasiveness of changes brought about by science and technologies, and growing concerns about the sustainability of Earth, it seeks to embody insights from studies in these areas as well.

Though rooted in the Catholic tradition, volumes in the series are written with an eye to the ecumenical implications of Protestant, Orthodox, and Pentecostal theologies for Catholicism, and vice versa. In addition, authors will explore insights from other religious traditions with the potential to enrich Christian theology and self-understanding.

Books in this series will provide reliable introductions to the major theological topics, tracing their roots in Scripture and their development in later tradition, exploring when possible the implications of new thinking on gender and sociocultural identities. And they will relate these themes to the challenges confronting the peoples of the world in the wake of globalization, particularly the implications of Christian faith for justice, peace, and the integrity of creation.

Other Books Published in the Series

Orders and Ministry: Leadership in the World Church, Kenan B. Osborne, O.F.M.
Trinity: Nexus of the Mysteries of Christian Faith, Anne Hunt
Spirituality and Mysticism: A Global View, James A. Wiseman, O.S.B.
Eschatology and Hope, Anthony Kelly, C.Ss.R.

THEOLOGY IN GLOBAL PERSPECTIVE SERIES
Peter C. Phan, General Editor

MEETING MYSTERY

Liturgy, Worship, Sacraments

NATHAN D. MITCHELL

ORBIS BOOKS

Maryknoll, New York 10545

Founded in 1970, Orbis Books endeavors to publish works that enlighten the mind, nourish the spirit, and challenge the conscience. The publishing arm of the Maryknoll Fathers
and Brothers, Orbis seeks to explore the global dimensions of the Christian faith and mission, to invite dialogue with diverse cultures and religious traditions, and to serve the cause
of reconciliation and peace. The books published reflect the opinions of their authors and
are not meant to represent the official position of the Maryknoll Society. To obtain more
information about Maryknoll and Orbis Books, please visit our website at www.mary-
knoll.org.

Library of Congress Cataloging in Publication Data

Mitchell, Nathan D.
    Meeting mystery : liturgy, worship, sacraments / Nathan D. Mitchell.
        p. cm.
    Includes bibliographical references and index.
    ISBN-13: 978-1-57075-674-0 (pbk.)
    ISBN-10: 1-57075-674-0
    1. Public worship. I. Title.
    BV15.M58 2006
    264—dc22

                                                2006017581

Contents

PART 2
POLYPHONY: THE LANGUAGES OF LITURGY

Foreword

by Peter C. Phan

Liturgy or divine worship, as Vatican II teaches, is "an exercise of the priestly office of Christ . . . an action of Christ the priest and of his Body which is the Church" (*Sacrosanctum Concilium* 7). It occurs, however, as Nathan Mitchell reminds us, at the intersection of three distinct but interdependent liturgies: the "liturgy of the world," the "liturgy of the church," and the "liturgy of the neighbor."

But how is liturgy to be celebrated today, in postmodernity, when the meanings of these three realities—world, church, and neighbor—have changed radically? What shape will liturgy take when the world is no longer Europe and America, when even Earth itself is no longer the center of the universe, when the "globe" has become truly global? With what rituals will Christians worship God when the church is no longer the church of the West but when more than two-thirds of Christians will live in the so-called third world—in Africa, Asia, and South America—amid non-Christians? How will Christians meet God when their neighbor is no longer an SUV-driving, Starbucks-consuming, Internet-surfing suburb-dweller but the hungry, the naked, the thirsty, the sick, the imprisoned, and the poor?

Meeting Mystery helps us find answers to these troubling questions that our postmodern, multicultural, multireligious, globalized world poses to the heart of the Christian life. It begins by reflecting on the meaning of ritual as rhythmic and repetitive action. R seems to be Nathan Mitchell's favorite letter in his discussion of not only the "rhythm" and "repetition" but also the "roots," "roles," "risks," "rules," and "realm" of ritual. Under each of these categories, Mitchell shows how the reality of Christian worship has been challenged by the changes in our understanding of the trinity of world, church, and neighbor. Throughout the first part of his book, Mitchell urges us to reimagine ritual, for it is the imagination that needs expansion and perhaps even healing in order to understand that the liturgy is not a finished set of rites but a continuing bricolage constructed with both the world's material things and humanity's technologies; that the world we live in today is more like a rhizome growing every which way on the ground than a vertical tree with a sturdy trunk and nicely trimmed branches; that celebrating the liturgy is hazardous to our mental and spiritual health because it will turn our world topsy-turvy; that the goal of worship is the growth of the reign of God and not of the church; and that liturgy has less to do with saying what we are doing than with doing what we are saying.

All these things happen in the liturgy because it is polyphonous, as Mitchell argues in the second part of the book. Authentic worship requires the competence of a "polyglot" because the worshiper must be able to "speak" in several languages, verbal and nonverbal, with God and with others. The basic language of the liturgy, however, is not words but the body or, more precisely, the movement of the body through time and space, since the liturgy is primarily action. Furthermore, when it uses speech, the liturgy privileges metaphor rather than descriptive language, because it is essentially doxology. It is only in this context of polyphony that the worshiping community is "touched by fire" and can perform faithfully the four actions commanded by Jesus: take, bless, break, give.

Ritual, writes Mitchell in conclusion, "is principally about *connections*, about discovering what links us to God, to one another, to space, time, and history, to world and planet, to memory, desire, and expectation." Indeed, "connections," and plenty of them, are what readers of this marvelous book will find, connections with all those realities Mitchell lists above, but also with anthropologists, contemporary French philosophers, Zen Buddhism, biblical scholars, poets and novelists, mystics and artists. *Meeting Mystery* is not only a feast for the mind but also a delight for eyes and ears, replete as it is with sparkling wit and stylistic elegance.

Prologue

About ten years ago, Richard Gaillardetz published an essay in the journal *Worship* in which he noted that the Catholic community in North America is increasingly polarized between those who seek "community without transcendence" and those who seek "transcendence without community."[1] More than a decade later, Professor Gaillardetz's analysis remains an apt way to name the disagreement that has given rise to what pundits call "the liturgy wars," a subspectacle of those larger "culture wars" that roil church and society. As Gaillardetz pointed out, the solution to these conflicts must surely lie in the direction of "both . . . and," not "either . . . or." Proponents and opponents of liturgical renewal can come to common ground only if they acknowledge *both* God *and* community as awesome yet homely, homely yet awesome. Community is another name for that interhuman fellowship whose source is God's own inner life, where "personhood" exists as self-giving relationship. "Our relationship with God and our human relationships," writes Gaillardetz, "are not in competition with one another, they are two sides of the same coin."[2] Similarly, transcendence is a pseudonym for Otherness, where "Other" attempts to name an irreducible reality that is incomprehensibly *beyond*, yet utterly *near* to us—as visible and as audible as the hungry, the naked, the thirsty, the sick, the imprisoned, and the poor.

Meeting Mystery offers an introduction to Christian liturgy in its many dimensions: ritual, social, and sacramental. My goal has been to write a book that is accessible to nonspecialists—thoughtful without being too technical, informed yet not esoteric, clear but imaginative. While written from a Roman Catholic perspective, *Meeting Mystery* is, I hope, enriched by conversation with other cultures and religious traditions. It is not a work of liturgical history. Readers interested in studying the historical evolution of Christian worship—its rites, its books, and their history—are advised to consult reference works such as Anscar J. Chupungco, ed., *Handbook for Liturgical Studies*; Oxford University Press's *The Study of Liturgy*; Cyrille Vogel's classic *Medieval Liturgy: An Introduction to the Sources*; and Eric Palazzo's *A History of Liturgical Books*. A recent and very accessible introduction to the fundamentals of Christian symbols in their ritual, celebratory contexts may be found in Bernard Cooke's and

---

1. Richard Gaillardetz, "North American Culture and the Liturgical Life of the Church: The Separation of the Quests for Transcendence and Community," *Worship* 68, no. 5 (September 1994): 403-16.
2. Ibid., 412.

Gary Macy's *Christian Symbol and Ritual.* For studying the most important of the liturgies of Eastern Christendom, one can do no better than to begin with Robert Taft's *The Byzantine Rite: A Short History.*[3]

While historical details are occasionally discussed in *Meeting Mystery*, the book's goal is to promote an understanding of Christian ritual and liturgical prayer within its broader contexts—contexts that are simultaneously global and "postmodern" (a word I will examine in chapter 1). It is increasingly clear, for example, that we can no longer understand the West without seeking to understand the East; we can no longer discuss tenets of Christian theology in isolation from interreligious dialogue; we can no longer interpret the arts of ritual apart from those of music, sculpture, painting, and architecture; we can no longer interpret ritual *verba et gesta* (words and deeds) apart from the languages and gestures of pluralist, postmodern societies. Without denying the distinctiveness of the Christian liturgical tradition, *Meeting Mystery* seeks to situate that tradition within the larger framework of "faiths and cultures."

This book assumes, therefore, that readers engage ritual not only as participants in Christian liturgy but as agents in an evolving human history, as citizens of a world—a universe—whose magnitude and complexity challenge many of our traditional (and comforting) conjectures about the relation between God, people, and planet. Today, for example, we know

- that the universe probably began as a mass with almost no physical size, its density and temperature approaching the infinite—and that the expansion of the universe from almost no dimension continues even now;
- that there are nearly fifty billion galaxies in the universe, each having, on average, two to four billion stars;
- that our known universe is approximately fifteen billion light years "across," though its "edges" aren't really edges at all;
- that it is expanding at a tremendous rate of speed, yet subatomic particles on one side of this vastness appear to be able to communicate instantly with their partners on the other side; indeed, that there may be subatomic particles that literally bilocate, that is, inhabit two different places at once;
- that our own sun, a star of average size and intensity, consumes over four

3. Anscar J. Chupungco, ed., *Handbook for Liturgical Studies* (5 vols.; Collegeville, Minn.: Liturgical Press/A Pueblo Book, 1997-2000); Cheslyn Jones, Geoffrey Wainwright, et al., eds., *The Study of Liturgy* (rev. ed.; New York: Oxford University Press, 1992); Cyrille Vogel, *Medieval Liturgy: An Introduction to the Sources,* trans. and rev. William Storey and Niels Rasmussen (NPM Studies in Church Music and Liturgy; Washington, D.C.: Pastoral Press, 1986); Eric Palazzo, *A History of Liturgical Books: From the Beginning to the Thirteenth Century,* trans. Madeleine Beaumont (Collegeville, Minn.: Liturgical Press/A Pueblo Book, 1998); Bernard Cooke and Gary Macy, *Christian Symbol and Ritual: An Introduction* (New York: Oxford University Press, 2005); Robert F. Taft, *The Byzantine Rite: A Short History* (American Essays in Liturgy; Collegeville, Minn.: Liturgical Press, 1992).

million tons of its own matter every second, yet will survive for another six billion years;

- that an ant can lift fifty times its own weight;
- that each human adult body has about one hundred trillion cells, yet each cell is as complex as the city of Los Angeles;
- that jet aircraft need almost three miles of runway for safe takeoff, while most birds are airborne instantly, after a tiny jump (and you almost never hear of a bird crash-landing).

Just as Thomas Aquinas, in the thirteenth century, recognized that Christian theology needed the wisdom of the Greek philosophers—as interpreted by medieval Islamic translators—so contemporary theology needs "global perspective." As I suggested in a recent essay, we know today that Europe and America are

> not the center of Earth, and Earth is not the center of anything, whether one thinks of the solar system, galaxy, or universe. We know that the planet's resources are not inexhaustible and the human future could be altered, suddenly and irreversibly, by global warming, an errant meteor, or a moment of nuclear madness. So, while we human . . . theologians take pride in our species as the summit and crown of creation, modern astronomy and cosmology offer a far more sober assessment of our place in "the great scheme of things."[4]

Meeting Mystery thus invites readers to remember, on every page, that Christian ritual, prayer, and sacrament occur at the confluence of three distinct—yet essentially interdependent—liturgies: the "liturgy of the world," the "liturgy of the church," and the "liturgy of the neighbor." That is one reason why a *sacramental* rite such as the eucharist can never be understood apart from economics and ethics. The Christian community never celebrates its liturgies for itself; it celebrates them in and for the world, for "the life of the world." In this, believers are simply following the lead of the Creator. "World," writes Aidan Kavanagh, "is the fundamental mode in which their Creator manifests himself, infesting it with himself all the while."[5] God's life is a contagion whose host is the world. Or, as the great twentieth-century German theologian Karl Rahner reminded us:

> Christ is already in the midst of all the poor things of this earth, which we cannot leave because it is our mother. He is the wordless expectation of all

---

4. Nathan D. Mitchell, "Theological Principles for an Evaluation and Renewal of Popular Piety," in Peter C. Phan, ed., *Directory on Popular Piety and the Liturgy: Principles and Guidelines: A Commentary* (Collegeville, Minn.: Liturgical Press, 2005), 59-76, here, 61.

5. Aidan Kavanagh, *On Liturgical Theology* (Collegeville, Minn.: Liturgical Press/A Pueblo Book, 1992), 14.

creatures which, without knowing it, wait to share in the glorification of his body. He is in the history of the earth . . . transforming all things. . . . He is in the beggar to whom we give, as the secret wealth which accrues to the donor. He is in our powerlessness as the power which can allow itself to seem weak, because it is unconquerable. He is even in the midst of sin as the mercy of eternal love patient and willing to the end. . . .

He is with us like the light of day and the air which we do not notice. . . . [H]e is there, the heart of this earthly world and the secret seal of its eternal validity.[6]

Liturgical prayer is, then, a social transaction, something human between us and God. Reduced to its simplest components, liturgy is (1) *ritual* action, rhythmic and repetitive, that is also (2) *polyphonic* (able to speak in several voices simultaneously). These two components frame the two parts of *Meeting Mystery*. Part 1 ("The Hyper-Reality of Worship") explores ritual's roots (chapter 1), ritual's roles and risks (chapter 2), ritual's rules (chapter 3), and ritual's realm, a "reimagined world" (chapter 4). Moreover, liturgy is a polyglot; it speaks several vernaculars simultaneously. These polyphonic vernaculars shape part 2 ("Polyphony"), which explores "the book of the body" (chapter 5), "ritual speech and the logic of metaphor" (chapter 6), and "parts and participation (ministry, assembly, sacrament)" (chapter 7).

Working their way through these chapters will, I hope, acquaint readers with the basics of liturgical theology in a postmodern mode. As I suggested above, in my comments about the intersection of three liturgies (world, church, and neighbor), Christian worship is worldly by definition. It uses not only the world's bounty (water, wine, bread, oil, salt, light, fragrance) but also the world's technologies (sound stretches to speech and song, seeing swells to image and icon, space aspires to architectural form and structure, movement expands to procession and dance). Over more than two millennia, of course, Christian worship has coalesced into identifiable forms; but it all began as bricolage, constructed from whatever was near at hand in the world's ritual repertoire (meeting, marrying, birthing, burying, washing, anointing, dining). No liturgy's pedigree is produced by parthenogenesis. Even Jesus' cross (his death liturgy) spoke the technologized language of Roman, state-sponsored capital punishment, with its ingeniously devised vocabulary of torture, humiliation, and depersonalization.

Thus, though liturgical historians like to trace genealogies and ritual family trees, the fact is that worship is never fully aware of its own sources, its

---

6. Karl Rahner, "Easter: A Faith That Loves the Earth," in *The Great Church Year*, ed. Albert Raffelt, trans. Harvey D. Egan (New York: Crossroad, 1994), 192-97; here, 196.

own ancestry. We cite Jesus' "Last Supper," his farewell meal with his friends, as the charter and origin of the Christian eucharist—yet we recognize that Jesus' own table ministry was linked to his experience as a marginal Jewish layman and to food practices in the ancient Mediterranean world, where meals were maps, and "who ate what with whom" reinforced (or damaged) one's social standing.[7] Hence, the eucharist is linked to the whole history of human hunger, a history that takes us back to the very origins of our species. For what helped make us was our gradual ability to make four life-sustaining realities portable: food, fire, water, and experience embedded in language and remembered as story.[8]

At the end of the day, then, a liturgical theology begins not with historical reconstruction or even with our "experience of worship's symbols, rites, and texts," but with the sober recognition that *we don't know what we're doing*. This may sound strange, but as Louis-Marie Chauvet points out in his important study *Symbol and Sacrament*, the first effect of using vernacular languages in Roman Catholic worship after the Second Vatican Council was to make the congregation "understand that they did *not* understand." As Chauvet observes, the "basic law of liturgy is 'Do not say what you are doing; do what you are saying.'"[9] That comment could well serve as an overarching motto for *Meeting Mystery*. Liturgy's most fundamental purpose is not to install us as "masters of the universe" but to *deprive* us of our desire for power, mastery, and control. Liturgical rites work primarily "before and beneath the advent of meanings"[10] (a point we will discuss in much greater detail in chapter 2). In a nutshell, liturgies have no other content than the body itself in prayer, the body-as-prayer, and though we often heap them high with meanings, the fact remains that we don't "mean" (control, determine) rites; rites "mean" *us*.[11] They are older than we are.

Liturgies are, finally, about *connection*; about *being* connected and *making* connections—to God, people, and planet; to space, time, culture, and history; to difference and otherness; to memory and expectation. As Catherine Bell notes, societies often have

---

7. The description of Jesus as a marginal Jewish layman is derived from the work of John P. Meier. See his three-volume (so far) study, *A Marginal Jew: Rethinking the Historical Jesus* (Anchor Bible Reference Library; New York: Doubleday, 1991–). We will discuss aspects of Meier's work (as they relate to Jesus' attitudes toward ritual prayer and worship practice) in chapter 3.

8. See my *Eucharist as Sacrament of Initiation* (Chicago: Liturgy Training Publications, 1994), 47-57.

9. Louis-Marie Chauvet, *Symbol and Sacrament*, trans. Patrick Madigan and Madeleine Beaumont (Collegeville, Minn.: Liturgical Press/A Pueblo Book, 1995), 328 (emphasis added).

10. Ibid., 326.

11. See chapter 5, "The Book of the Body."

more than just one ritual system; usually, multiple systems overlap, sometimes in tension with each other, sometimes in complementary harmony. At times, the Christians of China and Africa have felt caught between two ritual systems deemed incompatible—traditional rites to the ancestors on the one hand, and Christian rites that explicitly forbid the "idolatry" of worshipping other gods, on the other hand. . . .

Some cultures, such as traditional Hawaiian society, appear to have had a relatively neat ritual system that explicitly integrated, however loosely, multiple and sometimes competing subsystems. . . . Chinese religion . . . has long demonstrated a complex interaction among any number of levels of ritual life, including the local level of village religion . . . and various regional levels defined by the practices of any number of Taoist, Buddhist, sectarian or lineage associations.[12]

Rituals rarely arise in isolation, therefore; they travel in packs and form large systems (whether complementary or competitive). They are, as I will argue in chapter 1, "rhizomal," networks characterized not by a single "root," but by multiple—and often random—interconnections. Rites resemble crabgrass more than they do trees. A tree ("family trees," genealogies, any rooted structure) is concerned with "origins, foundations, ontologies, beginnings and endings—roots. The rhizome is concerned with . . . connections, lines of flight, with the 'and.'"[13]

Our study of Christian ritual and liturgical prayer will be, then, a study of connections—of the endlessly variable fabric that links the liturgy of the world, the liturgy of the church, and the liturgy of the neighbor. As I mentioned above, there are already available any number of good introductions to Christian liturgy, worship, and sacraments. This book means to introduce the reader to what is *not* said in them. I want to help both students of liturgy and general readers to question the assumption that they already "know what worship is all about," and to spend some time in conversation with me about the way liturgy beckons us *to meet God in Jesus Christ and the Spirit*, not to produce "meanings" or "meaningfulness." Such meetings with the living God are bound to be harrowing. We should probably leave our churches limping, rather than congratulating ourselves on a "job well done." We are, then, about to embark on a journey whose destination we can never reach: to put into words experiences that are beyond the capacity of speech to mediate.

---

12. Catherine Bell, *Ritual: Perspectives and Dimensions* (New York: Oxford University Press, 1997), 174-75.
13. Jim Powell, *Postmodernism for Beginners* (New York: Readers and Writers Publishing, 1998), 111.

Part 1

The Hyper-Reality of Worship

1

Ritual's Roots

Rhizome, Web, Word, and World

"ALWAYS LEARN, NEVER TEACH." This Native American aphorism captures, in four short words, the great gift that students give their teachers. Wisdom is not something "haves" impart to "have-nots"; it arises from mutuality, from dialogue and exchange, from *listening*, as the prologue of the sixth-century *Rule of St. Benedict* puts it, "with the ear of the heart." Like polyphony, wisdom requires the simultaneous presence of many voices, combining, recombining, and sometimes *challenging* one another in their search for beauty and truth. For the process of learning is never a done deal; it requires an abiding willingness to *renegotiate* and to *reimagine* what one has long regarded as settled.

This chapter invites readers to ponder the significance of Christian liturgy and sacramental worship by reimagining its structure, its sources in human life and experience, and its changing cultural contexts. Almost forty-five years ago, *Sacrosanctum Concilium*, the Second Vatican Council's Constitution on the Sacred Liturgy, recognized that liturgy is *communal ritual action* embodied in a variety of living, historical *cultures* (SC 14, 23, 37). Most simply defined, a "culture" is the sum total of all the ways human persons interact and live together. It includes their social contacts, contracts, conventions, and covenants; their shared language and literature; their arts and artifacts, their science and technology; their meanings and memories, beliefs and behaviors, icons and images; and not least, their religious convictions and values transmitted in song and story, and rehearsed in ritual actions. Culture is thus not merely the inevitable context within which Christians celebrate the liturgy; it is the indispensable means by which they recognize and respond to God's action among them.[1] Pope John Paul II made this point clearly in his encycli-

---

1. For a summary of debates among contemporary social scientists about the meanings and significance of culture, see my discussions in the "Lexicon" section of *Liturgy Digest* 3, no. 2 (1996): 63-107, esp. 94-97. See also my *Liturgy and the Social Sciences* (American Essays in Liturgy; Collegeville, Minn.: Liturgical Press, 1999).

cal *Redemptoris Missio* (1990): "The Spirit is at work in the heart of every person, through the 'seeds of the Word,' to be found in human initiatives," and hence "the Spirit's presence and activity affect not only individuals but also *society and history, peoples, cultures, and religions*" (no. 28).

We cannot, therefore, talk about Christian faith—and still less about Christian liturgy—without speaking about *culture*. Culture is the basic *site* where the Spirit's presence and activity are known, named, and celebrated in word and sacrament. John Paul's words expand a theme that had begun to emerge a quarter-century earlier, especially in the Second Vatican Council's Declaration on the Relation of the Church to Non-Christian Religions, *Nostra Aetate*, and in its Pastoral Constitution on the Church in the Modern World, *Gaudium et Spes*. This latter document proclaimed the church's "solidarity with the whole human family" and invited Catholics to participate in a dialogue with peoples of "every nation, race and culture," a dialogue that "excludes nobody" and includes, especially, those who "respect outstanding human values without realizing who the author of those values is, as well as those who oppose the Church" (GS 92). In short, the council insisted, "We must be aware of and understand the aspirations, the yearnings, and the often dramatic features of the world in which we live," the world in which a "real and cultural transformation" is taking place (GS 4).

Modernity was not, of course, a creation of the twentieth century. Its origins reach back at least to the sixteenth century, when printing presses began to revolutionize people's access to information, and when humanist scholars began calling for closer attention to the classical sources of Western civilization (now available in print!)—a move that led to a deeper appreciation of human history, its origins, evolution, and vicissitudes. During the European Enlightenment of the eighteenth century, modernity took still another turn, toward the thinking human subject and that subject's vital role in the construction of reality. The Enlightenment's attention to subjectivity embodied an increasing optimism about the power and range of human reason. Both philosophers and scientists became increasingly confident in the ability of thinkers and researchers to discover, measure, and analyze the forces at work both within human beings and outside them, in the larger universe.

By the mid-twentieth century, then, "modernity" was no longer very modern. The world's increasing complexity raised new questions about the power of "clear and distinct ideas" to penetrate the mysteries of life and the universe. Scientists began talking about "relativity" (Einstein), "indeterminacy" (Heisenberg), and "randomness" (Prigogine) as essential factors governing the structure of reality and the sometimes erratic behavior of its building blocks. And while science continued to make enormous progress, the price was high. As William Butler Yeats wrote in "The Second Coming," a famous poem published in 1921, "Things fall apart; the centre cannot hold; / Mere anarchy is loosed upon the world . . . / And what rough beast, its hour come round at last,/ Slouches toward Bethlehem to be born?"[2] Many felt that the horrors of the Second World War—with its systematic genocide of Jews and its unleashing of nuclear weapons on Hiroshima and Nagasaki—proved that Yeats's words were prophetic.

Ironically, then, just as the Roman Catholic Church was opening a dialogue with modernity in *Gaudium et Spes*, the world itself had moved in a different direction. It has become customary among philosophers and social scientists to call this new direction "*post*modernity." "Postmodern" is a broad term used to describe a wide variety of social patterns, artistic and intellectual movements, and technological innovations.[3] Its exact definition need not detain us here, since its features are obvious and surround us everywhere. As Jim Powell describes it in his entertaining primer, *Postmodernism for Beginners*, postmodern cultures are notable for their eclecticism and fragmentation, for their preoccupation with image and pastiche. Postmodern city-dwellers, writes Powell, live in "an exhilarating blur . . . fixated on commodities, on products, on images, like the explosion of Andy Warhol's pop art"; all is "surface . . . with no link to any reality; . . . masses of spectators abandoned to a gaze of image addiction; TV images stripped of reality, leaving only a surface, a simulacrum, schlock, kitsch, B-movies, pulp fiction, advertising, motels, *Readers Digest* culture; the merely decorative, superficial, gratuitous."[4] In a nutshell: cell phones; video games; "reality TV"; *Desperate Housewives;* and people "connected" to each other 24/7, while feeling utterly isolated and alone.

But postmodernism isn't just about surfaces, fragmentation, isolation, and bad news. Here, I hope to highlight its positive aspects. In chapter 1, I thus invite readers to think imaginatively about postmodern cultures, especially—though not exclusively—those of late-capitalist, industrialized Western societies such as that of the United States. Accordingly, the first part of this chapter invites readers to a conversation about the "postmodern condition" and suggests that postmodern cultures create networks of "interconnected differences" that closely resemble the technologies that flourish within them (e.g., the information technologies of Web, Internet, iPods, and cellular

---

2. *The Collected Poems of W.B. Yeats* (New York: Macmillan, 1956), 184-85.

3. On the relation between postmodernism and consumer cultures, see the classic essay of Fredric Jameson, "Postmodernism and Consumer Society," in Hal Foster, ed., *The Anti-Aesthetic: Essays on Postmodern Culture* (Port Townsend, Wa.: Bay Press, 1983), 111-25. See also Jameson's "Postmodernism, or the Cultural Logic of Late Capitalism," in Michael Hardt and Kathi Weeks, eds., *The Jameson Reader* (Oxford: Blackwell, 2000), 188-232.

4. Jim Powell, *Postmodernism for Beginners* (New York: Readers and Writers Publishing, 1998), 36-37.

phones). In the second part of the chapter, I will show how postmodern technologies such as the Web may shed light on Christian understandings of Word (God's self-communication to humankind) and world (the place where God's Word chose to "pitch its tent" and dwell among us [John 1:14]). We begin our study of Christian liturgy, then, by trying to reimagine ritual in light of our postmodern experience of life, culture, and technology.

THE POSTMODERN CONDITION

Trees versus Crabgrass: Reimaging Liturgy in Postmodern Cultures

In her elegant collection *Chosen by the Lion*, American poet Linda Gregg writes of a God who "lies dreaming in the lap of the world," a God who "knows the owls will guard the sweetness / of the soul in their massive keep of silence," a God who "thinks about / poetry all the time, breathes happily," and whispers, "There are fish in the net, / lots of fish this time in the net of the heart."[5] A God who "lies dreaming in the lap of the world," is, of course, incomprehensibly *near* yet elusive; a God whose *presence* may feel more like *absence*, whose truth grows mute when spoken, whose wide grace seeps through a woefully narrow gate.

Perhaps without intending to, Gregg calls our attention to an experience of God that many people who live in postmodern cultures may recognize. Postmodernity has, in fact, become an inescapable condition that shapes much of our twenty-first-century experience, at least in Western industrialized cultures.[6] As British theologian Graham Ward has written,

> If thinking in modernity (a period roughly inaugurated by the rapid development of capitalism, technology, and the cult of the individual in the late sixteenth century) is dominated by highly determined forms such as the circle, the cube, the spiral, even the double helix, then postmodernity (not a period . . . but more a condition) finds expression in indeterminate forms such as . . . the rhizome. As a form the "rhizome" is reducible neither to the One nor the multiple. . . . It is composed not of units but of dimensions, or rather directions in motion. It has neither beginning nor end, but always a middle . . . from which it grows and which it overspills.[7]

---

5. Linda Gregg, *Chosen by the Lion* (St. Paul: Greywolf Press, 1994), 30.
6. The notion that postmodernity is better understood as a "condition" rather than a movement, historical period, or episode has been developed in David Harvey's *The Condition of Postmodernity* (Oxford: Blackwell, 1990).
7. Graham Ward, "Postmodern Theology," in David F. Ford, *The Modern Theologians* (2nd ed.;

Writers like Ward suggest that during the second millennium (1000-2000 C.E.), the cultural climate of Western societies changed—slowly at first, then more rapidly—from *traditional* to *modern* to *postmodern*. *Traditional* cultures value stability, regularity, order, and repetition; *modern* cultures emphasize innovation, novelty, and dynamism.[8] Yet traditional and modern cultures have something crucial in common: *both of them value determined structures and forms.* Thus, for example, America's "Founding Fathers" were political innovators deeply influenced by the eighteenth-century European Enlightenment. They prized human reason as a God-given antidote to superstition and stressed human intelligence as the proper basis for social and scientific progress. (The late eighteenth century, after all, marked the advent of the Industrial Revolution, a key moment in the development of modern capitalist societies such as those of Great Britain and the United States.) So while men like John Adams and Thomas Jefferson endorsed the colonies' revolt against British imperialism, they abhorred anarchy. Following the colonists' military success in the War of Independence, these founders moved quickly to establish order through a *written* Constitution and a representative form of government in which each branch (legislative, judicial, executive) reined in the others (the system of "checks and balances"). Revolutionary though it was, American "freedom" and "democracy" still prized political institutions and proposed the "rule of *law*" to replace the arbitrary whims of human agents. The founders were "modern," but they shared traditional culture's fondness for form and structure.

But the postmodern cultures that began to emerge in the mid-twentieth century challenged modernity's confidence in the world's coherence and in reason's ability to analyze nature. Postmodernity favored indeterminacy, process, and motion over modernity's structure and stability. That is one reason why, in the text quoted above, Graham Ward draws our attention to the difference between the determined forms of modern cultures (e.g., the circle, the cube, the pyramid, the spiral) and the indeterminate fluidity of postmodern cultures, where structures seem to exist merely on the surface (and hence, e.g., can be deleted with the single click of a computer's mouse). Ward and others thus use contrasting images to illustrate the basic differences between

---

Cambridge, Mass.: Blackwell, 1997), 585. Not everyone would share Ward's rather negative assessment of modernity. Thus, for example, many historians would argue that modernity is best understood in distinction from "traditional societies." Where traditional societies value stability, regularity, order, and repetition, modernity values "innovation, novelty, and dynamism." See Steven Best and Douglas Kellner, *Postmodern Theory: Critical Interrogations* (New York: Guilford Press, 1991), 2.

8. Powell, *Postmodernism for Beginners*, 111. The image of postmodern cultures as "rhizomatic" is derived from the work of two French thinkers, Gilles Deleuze and Félix Guattari, *Rhizome: Introduction* (Paris: Éditions de Minuit, 1976). See also Kevin Hart, *Postmodernism: A Beginner's Guide* (Oxford: Oneworld, 2004), 6.

modernity and postmodernity. As Ward suggests, postmodern cultures can be described as "rhizomatic" (a horizontal network of randomly connected roots) rather than "arboreal" (vertical, treelike structures with firm root systems, trunks, and branching extensions).

Simply put, postmodern cultures resemble crabgrass more than a grove of majestic maples. Anyone who has ever tried to rid a lawn of crabgrass by pulling it up soon learns that its root system resembles a mole's maze of tunnels. Instead of a single, central root, crabgrass, Powell says, "has zillions of roots, none of which is central—and each off-shoot interconnects in random, unregulated networks in which any node can interconnect with any other node." A "crabgrass culture" is thus a culture in constant motion, flowing, darting in every direction at once without ever forming a coherent pattern. "Arboreal" cultures, by contrast, are concerned about "origins, foundations, ontologies, beginnings and endings—roots."[9] My main goal in this chapter will be to analyze the shift from late-modern "arboreal" cultures to postmodern "rhizomatic" ones, because this shift has begun to reshape our understanding of liturgy and sacrament in the industrialized West.

The distinction between cultures that resemble trees and those that resemble crabgrass was developed in the second half of the twentieth century by two French thinkers, Gilles Deleuze and Félix Guattari, who collaborated on a number of influential works, among them *Anti-Oedipus, Rhizome*, and *A Thousand Plateaus: Capitalism and Schizophrenia*.[10] The great value of their work lies in what they tell us about the intimate relation between images and our understanding—indeed, our *lived experience*—of the world. Deleuze and Guattari pointed out that an image is never a mere figure of speech or a colorful example; an image is an optic, a lens through which we simultaneously perceive and interpret reality as it *shows* itself, *gives* itself to us. Use the wrong lens, and your vision is distorted. Use the wrong image, and your grip on reality slackens. From the sixteenth through the twentieth centuries, Deleuze and Guattari argue, the image that dominated our understanding of the world—its peoples and cultures, its parts and their relationship—was the tree, a firmly rooted, hierarchically arranged unity whose individual parts constitute an organic whole, a single plant. In such a world, these writers noted, everyone has a place—and knows it. Like actors on a stage, everyone stays "in role," in

---

9. Powell, *Postmodernism for Beginners*, 111.
10. Gilles Deleuze and Félix Guattari, *Anti-Oedipus: Capitalism and Schizophrenia*, trans. Robert Hurley, Mark Seem, and Helen Lane (Minneapolis: University of Minnesota Press, 1983); *Rhizome*, translated by John Johnston, in Deleuze and Guattari, *On the Line* (New York: Semiotext[e], 1983) and by Brian Massumi, in Deleuze and Guattari, *A Thousand Plateaus: Capitalism and Schizophrenia* (Minneapolis: University of Minnesota Press, 1987), 3-25.

character. Leaders lead; inventors invent; writers write; painters paint; scientists discover; warriors fight. But change the image—the lens, the optic—and the world is suddenly a very different place. In their work, Deleuze and Guattari asked, "What if the world shows and gives itself to us not as a tree, but as crabgrass, as a network of interconnected differences?"

Deleuze and Guattari thus raised startling new questions about how we perceive, experience, and interpret the world. They set out to challenge two currents of thought that had come to dominate European philosophy, political science, and psychoanalysis during the 1960s and 1970s. One of these was *structuralism*, as represented by the work of the influential French anthropologist Claude Lévi-Strauss, whose ideas about archaic (premodern, traditional) cultures were widely followed in both Europe and the United States; the other was "State philosophy," a term Deleuze and Guattari used to describe the ideological foundation on which most modern nation-states are based, including the liberal democracies of Europe and North America. [11] A closer look at each of these currents of thought will help us understand why postmodern thinkers reacted so strongly against them.

To begin, let's examine the way Deleuze and Guattari analyzed "State philosophy," which, they argued, favors thought about human persons and their social relationships that is heavily hierarchical, dominated by determined forms, structures, and images. Take the image of a "tree," for instance. Such an image encourages the concept of cultures as an organic whole that springs from a single taproot. The resulting plant—the tree—is a botanical symphony of *dominance and subordination, superiority and inferiority* that suggests a world, a culture, of orderly regulation. In the West, Deleuze and Guattari argued, such arboreal thinking has been applied to everything from philosophy (e.g., Plato's notion of a material world whose myriad manifestations stem from a unified realm of ideal forms), to psychoanalysis (e.g., the Freudian tendency to trace all psychological processes back to an originary, unresolved Oedipal conflict), to statecraft (e.g., totalitarian ideology of a superpower that views its political moxie as universal and absolute).

But the mistake of modern "State philosophy," Deleuze and Guattari

---

11. The phrase "State philosophy" is used by Deleuze and Guattari to refer to "the representative thinking that has characterized Western metaphysics since Plato, but has suffered an at least momentary setback during the last quarter century at the hands of Jacques Derrida, Michel Foucault, and poststructuralist theory generally." Brian Massumi, "Foreword," in Deleuze and Guattari, *A Thousand Plateaus*, xi. As we shall see, the critique of "classical metaphysics" found in the work of Deleuze and Guattari is also a prominent theme in postmodern philosophers like Jacques Derrida and in postmodern theologians as diverse as Louis-Marie Chauvet and Jean-Luc Marion (both of whom critique metaphysics on their way to establishing the foundations for a new Roman Catholic approach to sacramental theology).

charged, is that it "talks the talk" of benign order, structure, and respect for individual persons, their liberty and uniqueness, but it doesn't "walk the walk." State philosophy takes a one-size-fits-all approach to cultures and the structures they create. It assumes, moreover, that all persons everywhere, in all times and places, share a common genealogy, "attributes of sameness and constancy," a "shared, internal essence," rooted (there's the tree metaphor, again!) in a common identity.[12] Under such conditions, the real differences between people—the real differences between cultures—are ignored or neglected. More ominously, persons and their cultures are seen as little more than the tool (note the image!) by which the state—itself depersonalized and abstract—incarnates itself and implements its intentions in the world. It becomes progressively harder for thinking citizens to free themselves from political propaganda and to reclaim their essentially critical function in the realm of public discourse (e.g., by *voting*). In effect, the State annexes its citizens as a "wholly owned subsidiary," so that they are no longer free and independent critics but patriotic cheerleaders for their government's policies, goals, and social programs. The *reasonable, thinking, compliant* person is the ultimate "good citizen," while the State "defines itself in principle as '*the rational and reasonable organization of a community*,'" of *any* community, of *all* communities. If sound reason and the State are siblings—twin branches produced by a common parent—one can sense how strongly an *image* (tree) promotes certain actions, and why even modern liberal democracies place such emphasis on *social compliance* and *obedience*: "Always obey. The more you obey, the more you will be master, for you will only be obeying pure reason, in other words yourself."[13]

Such, Deleuze and Guattari argued, is the ideology advanced by State philosophy and its network of supporting publics (social, political, ecclesiastical, academic). It is an archaizing, totalizing ideology that, as they wrote in *Anti-Oedipus*, has grown out of touch with the everyday conditions of Western life, for "we live today in the age of partial objects, bricks that have been shattered to bits, and leftovers. . . . We no longer believe in a primordial totality that once existed, or in a final totality that awaits us at some future date."[14] Ours is no longer a tidy, hierarchically organized world of form and structure, but an age of fragmentation, bits and pieces, leftovers. Yeats was right; the "center cannot hold." In an age of relentless consumerism and intense competition for scarce resources, polarization among peoples, cultures, and even religious communities escalates. Thus, even though economists and politi-

---

12. Brian Massumi, "Foreword," in Deleuze and Guattari, *A Thousand Plateaus*, xi.
13. Deleuze and Guattari, *A Thousand Plateaus*, 374, 375 (emphasis added), 376.
14. Deleuze and Guattari, *Anti-Oedipus*, 42.

cians today speak about globalization, and cultural analysts confidently predict a shrinking world in which distance and differences are overcome by the wonders of information technology, real divisions continue to grow, driven sometimes by economic conditions (e.g., the gap between the world's rich and its poor), and at other times by ideological or religious factors (e.g., the impact of fundamentalism in virtually every region of the world, including North America).

By challenging us to change our *image*—our lens, our optic—for perceiving, experiencing, and interpreting the world, Deleuze and Guattari help us see that postmodernism is less a philosophy than a cultural condition that arises when the modernist project—dominated by "tree-centered" thinking—falls victim to its own pretensions. Our world is not, in fact, a coherent whole whose parts can be analyzed with precision and whose peoples share a common genealogy, a "shared internal essence" rooted in a common identity. *Gaudium et Spes*, the Second Vatican Council's Pastoral Constitution on the Church in the Modern World, was surely right to point out the common vocation and the common destiny of all humankind (GS 22), but to say this is not to deny the *real differences* that separate rich from poor, haves from have-nots, the powerful from the powerless, and those with influence from those without it. Deleuze and Guattari were trying to show that if we allow the metaphor of the "tree" to dominate our thinking, we will fail to grasp what *really* separates—and connects—one individual to another, one culture to another in the world of today.[15] Ours is not a monocultural world that rises, treelike, from a single, unified root, but a multicultural one that erupts everywhere at once, like crabgrass in a lawn. In such a world, unity results not from denying cultural differences, still less from "homogenizing" them, but from recognizing their importance, their distinctiveness, and their indelibility. As Deleuze and Guattari put it, we have to be prepared to celebrate not "arboreal unity," but "counter-principles of difference and multiplicity in theory, politics, and everyday life."[16]

This is not easy task, because the image of the tree shapes and dominates virtually *all* Western thought, "from botany to information science to theology."[17] And it is precisely to oppose the sclerotic, hierarchical, totalizing tenor

---

15. Best and Kellner, *Postmodern Theory*, 76. Best and Kellner provide a lucid account of the significance of Deleuze and Guattari's work, pointing out similarities to and differences from the theories of other important French thinkers such as Michel Foucault and Jacques Derrida.

16. Ibid.

17. Ibid., 98. Note that the image of "body" as the preferred metaphor for understanding who and what the church is, has had a similar impact. The body, too, is a hierarchically arranged organism, with clear lines of command and subordination. Thus, when the Second Vatican Council shifted the lens—by using the image of the "people of God" in its Dogmatic Constitution on the Church (*Lumen Gentium*)—some church leaders began to feel uneasy.

of this arboreal philosophy that Deleuze and Guattari proposed an alternative analysis of social life and culture that flows from "rhizomatic" or "nomadic" models.[18] To say that the difference between these models resembles the difference between trees and crabgrass is to affirm Deleuze's and Guattari's point that *multidimensional images* offer a better way for us to understand human cultures, behaviors, experiences, thought, art, and relationships.

A CULTURE OF INTERCONNECTED DIFFERENCES: BEYOND STRUCTURALISM

The second current of thought that Deleuze and Guattari challenge us to reimagine—to *re-image*—is that of *structuralism*. Like their critique of State philosophy, their critique of structural anthropology (and its consequences for understanding diverse cultures) is based on a shift of image, from "tree" to "crabgrass." Both *Rhizome* and *A Thousand Plateaus* are rich in such images, and anyone who has a nodding acquaintance with computer technology and its connection to the Internet will instinctively grasp how Deleuze and Guattari imagine rhizomatic thinking and cultures. Several factors shape their views about rhizomes and the way they illumine our understanding of human experience and relationships. The first two factors flow from what Deleuze and Guattari call the "principles of connection and heterogeneity." These twin principles require that *any point within a rhizome system be capable of direct connection any other point*—which means, from the get-go, that rhizomes resemble a Google search much more than a hierarchical chain-of-command. Indeed, rhizomes are exuberantly *anti*-hierarchical, having the characteristics of burrows or pack animals. "Rats are rhizomes. Burrows are too, in all of their [diverse] functions of shelter, supply, movement, evasion,

---

18. As Best and Kellner point out, Deleuze and Guattari use a variety of terms for their proposed alternative to "aborescent thinking": schizoanalysis, rhizomatics, pragmatics, diagrammatics, cartography, micropolitics, "vagabond" or "nomad" science, as opposed to the "royal science" of State philosophy (see *Postmodern Theory*, 98). Such a diverse vocabulary is meant "to prevent their position from stabilizing in [or hardening into] an ideology, method, or single metaphor" (ibid.). Thus, in their seminal work *A Thousand Plateaus*, Deleuze and Guattari use "avant-garde writing techniques." The book's very *form*, for example, becomes continuous with its "content"—or rather, as Best and Kellner observe, the distinction between form and content breaks down altogether. This means, among other things, that Deleuze and Guattari ignore the conventions of traditional literary "narrative" in favor of writing that resembles "collage" or "bricolage." They abandon "any semblance of narrative or argument exposition in favour of a random, perspectival juxtaposition of chapters, or 'plateaus' (Gregory Bateson's terms), comprised of complex conceptual flows. These plateaus range promiscuously across diverse topics, time frames, and disciplinary fields" (*Postmodern Theory*, 98). The chapters of *A Thousand Plateaus* may thus be read in any order, "with the proviso that the 'conclusion,' a 'dictionary' of terms, is to be read last" (ibid.).

and breakout. The rhizome itself assumes very diverse forms . . . when rats swarm over each other. The rhizome includes the best and the worst: potato and couchgrass, or the weed. Animal and plant, couchgrass is crabgrass. . . . [A]ny point of a rhizome can be connected to any other, and must be."[19] The image of "rhizome" thus suggests a world of "endlessly interconnected *differences*," not a hierarchical, homogeneous structure.

Take language as an example. A chain of words, even if organized by grammar and syntax, is not really a hierarchy (sentence diagrams notwithstanding); instead, it resembles

> a tuber agglomerating very diverse acts, not only linguistic, but also perceptive, mimetic, gestural, and cognitive: there is no language in itself, nor are there any linguistic universals, only a throng of dialects, patois, slangs, and specialized languages [e.g., argots]. There is no ideal speaker-listener, any more than there is a homogeneous linguistic community. Language is . . . an essentially heterogeneous reality. There is no mother tongue, only a power takeover by a dominant language within a political multiplicity. Language stabilizes around a parish, a bishopric, a capital. It forms a bulb. It evolves by subterranean stems and flows, along river valleys or train tracks; it spreads like a patch of oil. . . . A language is never closed upon itself, except as a function of impotence.[20]

Ultimately, Deleuze and Guattari argue, language is not about prescribed order, sequence, and power (the power, for instance, that accrues to those who use language well) but about *innovation* (saying something *new*) and multiple *connections*.[21]

Multiplicity (or "multidimensionality") is, indeed, the third notable quality of rhizomes, a quality that puts rhizomatic thinking on a collision course with the structuralism that dominated much of Western philosophy during the mid-twentieth century.[22] French structuralism of the sort espoused by the brilliant anthropologist Claude Lévi-Strauss sought to identify and index the basic architecture of the human mind (and of human societies) by analyzing fundamental distinctions ("binary oppositions") found everywhere in human life—distinctions between nature and culture, the raw and the cooked, male and female, endogamy and exogamy, insiders and outsiders. In the very first

---

19. Deleuze and Guattari, "Introduction: Rhizome," in *A Thousand Plateaus*, 7-8.
20. Ibid.
21. In their "Conclusion" to *A Thousand Plateaus*, Deleuze and Guattari admit that language may often seem to possess a treelike structure, but they add that inevitably, "the trees of language are shaken by buddings and rhizomes. So that rhizome lines oscillate between tree lines that segment and even stratify them, and lines of flight or rupture that carry them away" (506).
22. Ibid., 8.

volume of his monumental *Introduction to a Science of Mythology*, Lévi-Strauss announced his program clearly:

> The aim of this book is to show how empirical categories—such as the categories of the raw and the cooked, the fresh and the decayed, the moistened and the burned, etc., which can only be accurately defined by ethnographic observation and, in each instance, by adopting the standpoint of a particular culture—can nonetheless be used as conceptual tools with which to elaborate abstract ideas and combine them in the form of propositions. . . .
>
> I intend to carry out an experiment which, should it prove successful, will be of universal significance, since I expect it to prove that there is a kind of logic in tangible qualities, and to demonstrate the operation of that logic and reveal its laws.[23]

In short, Lévi-Strauss proposed that "universals" common to all human cultures really exist, and that they appear *not* at the level of multiple details—that is, not at the microlevel of customs surrounding diet, food preparation, marriage laws, tribal authority, and so on—but only "at the [macro-]level of *structure*."[24] This search for cultural "universals"—codes or laws that apply to all peoples in all times and places—was rooted in the science of linguistics as it had developed in the first half of the twentieth century, especially in the semiotic theories of Ferdinand de Saussure (1857-1918).[25] Saussure argued, first, that language can be accurately analyzed *according to the present laws that govern its usage*, without reference to its historical qualities and evolution, and second, that every linguistic sign (or word) has two integrated parts: "an acoustic-visual component, the *signifier*, and a conceptual component, the *signified*."[26] Language, for Saussure, is thus a "system of signs [*signifiers*] that expresses ideas [*signifieds*]," and the interaction between signifier and signified gives rise to *meanings*. Moreover—and this would have crucial consequences not only for comprehending language but, as we will see later in this book, for understanding ritual and sacramental signification as well—Saussure understood that linguistic signs (speech, words) are arbitrary, that there is no natural link between signifier and signified, but only "a contingent cultural" connection.[27] At the same time, he insisted that linguistic signs belong to a

---

23. Claude Lévi-Strauss, *The Raw and the Cooked: Introduction to a Science of Mythology*, volume 1, trans. John and Doreen Weightman (New York: Harper Torchbooks, 1969), 1.
24. Edmund Leach, *Claude Lévi-Strauss* (New York: Viking Press, 1970), 22 (emphasis added).
25. Ibid., 23: "Lévi-Strauss sets about deriving his cultural generalizations from his linguistic base."
26. Ibid., 19.
27. Ibid. The Saussurian denial of any real or essential relation between "sign" and "signified"—between what scholastic theology called *signum et significatum*—was not itself new. Such a rupture

system of meanings in which "words acquire significance only by reference to what they are *not*," that is, only in relation to their "opposites."[28] Thus, structuralism embraced a linguistic theory that derived language itself from the culturally constructed, binary relation between signifier and signified, and it derived significance or "meaning" in language from the polarity between words and what they are *not*.

It is not surprising that Lévi-Strauss applied linguistic analysis to his studies of cultures—their mythology, kinship systems, ritual performances, and culinary customs.[29] He had come to believe that thinking about *language* is a good way to think about *social relations*, for there is, he insisted, a link between the *unconscious* codes or rules that govern social structures (e.g., dietary laws or regulations that govern who eats what with whom at a formal meal) and similarly unconscious codes at play in speech and story (e.g., the rules that determine how cultures form and transmit their mythological narratives). In both cases, unconscious but effective codes establish meaning "through a differential set of binary opposites."[30] Thus, speech yields its meanings through the polarity inherent in the play between signifier and signified, while traditional stories (myths) disclose their significance in a way similar to musical variations on a theme, where "meanings" flow *not* from surface-level similarities but from deeper (and often unconscious) *contradictions* and *contrasts*.[31]

As Lévi-Strauss wrote in *Structural Anthropology*, myth's basic purpose is "to provide a logical model capable of overcoming a contradiction,"[32] that is, to create a story that lets hearers think the unthinkable, imagine the unimaginable, and reconcile themselves to the irreconcilable. Myths do this by proposing a series of opposites (young vs. old, fertility vs. infertility, parent vs.

---

was already well under way in the West during the late medieval and early modern periods, and it would result in a severe challenge to traditional Catholic understandings of the *real* relation between "signs" and "things signified" in sacramental rites (the basis for the assertion that signs "really contain and impart" what they signify). See Thomas M. Greene, "Ritual and Text in the Renaissance," *Canadian Review of Comparative Literature /Revue Canadienne de Littérature Comparée* 15 (June/September 1991): 179-97.

28. Leach, *Claude Lévi-Strauss*, 19.

29. As Lévi-Strauss wrote: "[E]verybody will agree that the Saussurean principle of the arbitrary character of linguistic signs was a prerequisite for the accession of linguistics to the scientific level" (*Structural Anthropology*, trans. Claire Jacobson and Brooke Grundfest Schoepf [Garden City, N.Y.: Doubleday Anchor Books, 1963], 204). Earlier in the same book, Lévi-Strauss had noted that "although they belong to *another order of reality*, kinship phenomena are *of the same type* as linguistic phenomena."

30. Best and Kellner, *Postmodern Theory*, 18.

31. On the complexity of mythic structures and their variants, see Lévi-Strauss's chapter "The Structural Study of Myth," in *Structural Anthropology*, 202-28. "Myth" does not mean "falsehood." Myth is a form of speech used to express experiences and realities that exceed the ordinary power of language to communicate.

32. Lévi-Strauss, *Structural Anthropology*, 226.

child) that help hearers crack the codes that conceal the unconscious infra-structure of the story itself. Thus, for example, the Oedipus myths embedded in classical Greek drama allow hearers to imagine the unimaginable—viz., that "if society is to go on, daughters must be disloyal to their parents and sons must destroy (replace) their fathers."[33] In other words, the myth gives hearers permission to consider actions that are taboo (incest, parricide), strictly prohibited by both personal ethics and public law. Nevertheless, while these stories permit "thinking about the unthinkable," they do not resolve every conflict. As Edmund Leach observes, commenting on Lévi-Strauss's analysis of the Oedipus stories:

> Here then is the irresolvable unwelcome contradiction, the necessary fact that we hide from consciousness because its implications run directly counter to the fundamentals of human morality. There are no heroes in these stories; they are simply epics of unavoidable human disaster. The dis-aster always originates in the circumstances that a human being fails to fulfill his or her proper obligations toward a deity or a kinsman, and this, in part at least, is what Lévi-Strauss is getting at when he insists that the fundamental moral implication of mythology is that "Hell is ourselves," which I take to mean "self-interest is the source of all evil."[34]

Few would deny that Lévi-Strauss's work offers great insight into human behavior and social structure. Indeed, in *A Thousand Plateaus*, Deleuze and Guattari cite, approvingly, Lévi-Strauss's notion that "the world begins to sig-nify before anyone knows *what* it signifies; the signified is given without being known." In other words, the world "means" long before we attribute any "meanings" to it. Here one can discern a theme dear to postmodern philoso-phers: viz., that "every sign refers to another sign, and only to another sign, ad infinitum," that "all signs are signs of signs," and hence that the "world of signs" (the world of words and speech, stories and myths, icons and symbols) is not a logically structured, hierarchically arranged universe—as the "tree" metaphor would have it—but an amorphous continuum, a rhizome thriving as riotously as crabgrass. "Not only do signs form an infinite network," write Deleuze and Guattari,

> but the network of signs is infinitely circular. The statement survives its object, the name survives its owner.... [T]he sign survives both its state of things and its signified; it leaps like an animal or a dead person to regain its place in the chain and invest a new state.... There is a whole regime

---

33. Leach, *Claude Lévi-Strauss*, 83. See Lévi-Strauss's own synopsis of the Oedipal cycle in *Struc-tural Anthropology*, 209-13.
34. Leach, *Claude Lévi-Strauss*, 83.

of roving, floating statements, suspended names, signs lying in wait to return and be propelled by the chain. . . .

But what counts is less this circularity of signs than the multiplicity of the circles or chains.[35]

Cultures as Multiple, Interacting Plateaus

We can begin to see, then, why "postmodernism"—as a recognizable philosophical movement—first emerged as "poststructuralism," a repudiation of the structuralist project. Ultimately, structuralism was felt to be reductionistic, for it organizes and condenses human thinking and behavior into predictable patterns and units and thereby defies (or simply erases) the inevitable messiness and multidimensionality of real life. In other words, structuralism tries to turn crabgrass into trees. To counter such a move, thinkers like Deleuze and Guattari argue that we can understand the richness and diversity of human experience only if we avoid moving too quickly to generalizations—the common structure, the code, the "universal rule" valid in "all times and places"—and learn, instead, to value the *differences*, the rhizome-like multiplicity of peoples, cultures, and their activities. Neither word nor world, neither speech nor story signifies simply by means of logical, linear discourse; *all signification (and hence, all meaning) is inescapably multiple.* That is one reason why philosophers and theologians today speak of the multidimensionality, the "polyvalence," of symbols. Symbols are polyglot; they speak several languages simultaneously—and their meanings (like their speech) are multiple.

Thus, the world really does begin to show and give itself—to signify—long before anyone knows *what* it signifies. And when it signifies, it does so by speaking several languages simultaneously—much like the Pentecost scene in Acts 2:5-13 where people from all over the ancient world, "Jews and converts to Judaism, Cretans and Arabs," hear the apostles speaking as though "in our own tongues" of the "mighty acts of God." The world's cultures are better understood as simultaneously interacting plateaus—thus the title of Deleuze's and Guattari's magnum opus, *A Thousand Plateaus.* It is no accident that one chapter (or "plateau") of this book is introduced by a reproduction of Fernand Léger's Cubist painting *Men in the Cities.* Cubism delights in the simultaneous presence of multiple perspectives that have neither hierarchical arrangement nor an approved order of eminence and subordination. At the same time, Cubist painting points to the inevitable *segmentation* of human

---

35. Deleuze and Guattari, *A Thousand Plateaus*, 112-13.

life and activity. Structuralists like Lévi-Strauss were right, Deleuze and Guattari comment, to speak about the "binary" segmentation of humanity, about dualist divisions, the "great major ... oppositions: social classes ... men-women, adults-children, and so on" that inevitably appear in mythic stories and social structures. After all,

> the human being is a segmentary animal. . . . Dwelling, getting around, working, playing: life is spatially and socially segmented. The house is segmented according to its rooms' assigned purposes; streets, according to the order of the city; the factory, according to the nature of the work and operations performed in it. We are segmented in a binary fashion. . . . We are segmented in a circular fashion, in . . . ever wider disk . . . my neighborhood's affairs, my city's, my country's, the world's. . . . We are segmented in a linear fashion . . . as soon as we finish one proceeding we begin another. . . . School tells us "You're not at home anymore"; the army tells us, "You're not in school anymore." . . . But these figures of segmentarity, the binary, circular, and linear, are bound up with one another, even cross over into each other, changing according to the point of view [like a Cubist painting!].[36]

So yes, the early poststructuralists said, human life is segmented, organized into units that assign us to specific and limited social locations ("You're in the *army*, now, recruit!"). *But that isn't all.* What structuralism seemed to forget was the messy, ineradicable presence of the *human*—what Chilean poet Pablo Neruda once called the "confused impurity of the human condition ... footprints and fingerprints, the abiding presence of the human engulfing all artifacts."[37] Ultimately, the human is an "organism" that is *unorganizable.* Human persons and their cultures are a chaotic circulation of energies, movements, relations, changing directions, inconsistencies, an "amorphous continuum" that finally defies definition and will not submit (without protest) to limiting codes, rules, structures, "universals," or hierarchies. People, in short, prefer to relate to one another as crabgrass rather than as trees. That is why Neruda celebrated "a poetry impure as the clothing we wear, or our bodies, soup-stained, soiled with our shameful behavior, our wrinkles and vigils and dreams ... [t]he holy canons of madrigal, the mandates of touch, smell, taste, sight, hearing, the passion for justice, sexual desire, the sea sounding . . . the deep penetration of things in the transports of love."[38]

In sum, structuralism had focused so resolutely "on the underlying rules

---

36. See ibid., 208-9.
37. *Selected Poems of Pablo Neruda*, trans. Ben Belitt (New York: Grove Press, 1961), 39.
38. Ibid.

which organized phenomena into a social system" and on its own description of "social phenomena in terms of linguistic and social structures, rules, codes, and systems" that it threatened to reject "the humanism which had previously shaped the social and human sciences."[39] In the structuralist model, the human subject "was dismissed, or radically decentred, as merely an effect of language, culture, or the unconscious"; it was "denied causal or creative efficacy." To a degree, the poststructuralists shared with structuralism this "dismissal of the concept of the autonomous subject."[40] Yet they also sought to reclaim the human, to reassert the real presence of a human face against structuralism's tendency to treat persons as mere "social and linguistic constructs," the by-products of unconscious drives and impersonal forces.

So the early postmodernists—Deleuze and Guattari among them—resisted the structuralist argument that the mind has some "innate, universal structure," and hence that human nature is invariable, the same across all cultures. People's cultures, they insisted, really do *differ* from one place to another and from one time period to another. They form a world of real, though interconnected, *differences*. Postmodernism thus favored "a thoroughly *historical* view which sees *different* forms of consciousness, identities, signification, and so on as historically produced and therefore varying in *different* historical periods."[41] As we will see over the course of this book, it was this respect for historical change and consequent cultural variability that helped to shape the Second Vatican Council's approach to the liturgy. Thus, *Sacrosanctum Concilium* affirms that "in the liturgy the Church does not wish to impose a rigid uniformity," but seeks to "respect and foster" the different, indigenous "qualities and talents of the various races and nations" (37).

Speaking, Writing, and Meaning

Postmodernism did not, then, arise as simply a repudiation of structuralism. For instance, Saussure's theory of *the arbitrary relation between "signifier" and "signified"* continued to exert an influence, especially in the thought of thinkers such as Jacques Derrida.[42] As Derrida notes, the meaning of our words (especially when they are in the process of being written) is never "precanned." We literally do not know what our writing *means* until we've actually written it. (Musicians often say the same thing; we do not know what a musical score "means" until we play or sing it.) "Meaning must await being

---

39. Best and Kellner, *Postmodern Theory*, 19.
40. Ibid., 19-20.
41. Ibid., 20.
42. Ibid., 21.

said or written in order to inhabit itself," writes Derrida, "in order to become, by differing from itself, what it is: meaning."[43] That is why, as Maurice Merleau-Ponty once observed, "Communication in literature is not the simple appeal on the part of the writer to meanings which [are] . . . part of an a priori [content] of the mind; rather, communication arouses these meanings in the mind through enticement and a kind of oblique action. The writer's thought does not control his language from without; the writer is himself a kind of new idiom, constructing itself." As a result, "my own words take me by surprise and teach me what I think."[44]

Notice that both Derrida and Merleau-Ponty make a connection not only between *speaking* and meaning but, more especially, between *writing* and meaning. This may seem odd, because most of us assume that when it comes to the communication of meaning, *speech* is primary, while writing is secondary. Ever since Plato, Western philosophy has shown a preference for the spoken word and a suspicion of writing as a kind of "false memory."[45] Speech, after all, seems much more directly linked to the speaker. When *I* speak, *I* seem to be in firm control of what *I* mean; I create a covenant between my words and the meaning I intend by them, and this bond is guaranteed by my physical presence. (The swearing of oaths in a court of law is based on precisely this assumption—namely, that there is a solemn bond between my *word* and *me*.) Writing, by contrast, seems to drive a wedge between me and my words. After all, written words won't sit still; they squirm and wiggle, migrating well beyond the borders of my body, consciousness, and thought. (Just ask anyone who's ever written a letter they wish they'd never sent!) Written words take on a life of their own, a life of unintended connotations. Indeed, my writing survives my death and makes my words available to be read by others long after I'm in my grave. That means that written words can be interpreted in unexpected—and perhaps inaccurate—ways. Once words take flesh as writing, *signifiers* (the words themselves) are no longer bound to their *signifieds* (their references and meanings); they begin to point beyond themselves and become something *I* neither created nor intended.

All this is undoubtedly why Derrida speaks of writing not only as "inaugural" (having the characteristics of a fresh beginning) but as "dangerous and anguishing." Writing, he notes, "does not know where it is going, no knowl-

---

43. Jacques Derrida, *Writing and Difference*, trans. Alan Bass (Chicago: University of Chicago Press, 1978), 11.

44. Maurice Merleau-Ponty, *The Primacy of Perception*, as cited in Derrida, *Writing and Difference*, 11; see also p. 302 n. 31.

45. See Catherine Pickstock, *After Writing: On the Liturgical Consummation of Philosophy* (Oxford: Blackwell, 1998), 25. Pickstock presents a sustained critique of Derrida's notion of the primacy of writing and argues, instead, for reclaiming the Platonic preference for speech (pp. 3-46).

edge can keep it from the essential precipitation toward the meaning that [is] . . . its future. . . . There is thus no insurance against the risk of writing."[46] (Again, ask any student who's ever written a "brilliant" essay for "Freshman Comp," only to get an F from the prof!) Writing is risky because it reveals that meanings are not only *announced* (by live speakers), but must then be *discovered* and *read* by a diverse community of readers. Writing reminds us that, at the end of the day, authors often have little control over the "meaning" of what they produce. Rather, meanings arise from a complex series of interactions between speakers and hearers, writers and texts.

Meanings, therefore, cannot be self-willed, self-produced, and self-proclaimed. They emerge, sometimes slowly, from the give-and-take between reader and text, from the reader's discovery of an "other" (another person) in the written text. "[D]oes not meaning present itself as such," asks Derrida, "at the point at which the other is found, the other who maintains both the vigil and the back-and-forth motion, the work, that comes between writing and reading, making this work irreducible? Meaning is neither before nor after the act."[47] Strangely, writing has more to do with *meeting* (another person) than with meaning. Surely it is no accident that the Word not only became *flesh* (John 1:14) but *writing*—and thereby guaranteed that the historical process of God's self-revelation would continue indefinitely as new communities of readers encountered the body of the text. For as most Christian readers of the Bible would affirm, *God* is always that "other person" who is met in that physical body we call the Bible. The Bible is, above all, a site—a meeting place—that implicates both Speaker and readers in a common quest for "the other." When the Scriptures are read, especially in the church's liturgy, God's search for us meets our search for God.

"The meaning of meaning is infinite implication," says Derrida, and his comment leads us back to the "rhizomatic" thought and images of postmodern thinkers like Deleuze and Guattari. Here again we can begin to see the great value of their challenge to change our *image*—our lens, our optic—for perceiving, experiencing, and interpreting the world and its multiple cultures. Consider, for instance, what happens when the Internet is perceived not as a branching "tree" but as a species of flourishing, electronic crabgrass—a "hypertextual" rhizome, if you will Any node on the Internet may connect with any other node to create a virtually limitless maze of connections and

---

46. Derrida, *Writing and Difference*, 11. When Derrida speaks about "writing," he is referring not only to the act of writing as a technological tool or to inscribed texts but to an intrinsic component of *all* language, because every "grapheme" (letter)" is essentially "testamentary," a promissory sign meant to endure in the absence of the writer. See Derrida, *On Grammatology*, trans. Gayatri Chakravorty Spivak (Baltimore: Johns Hopkins University Press, 1974), 69.
47. Derrida, *Writing and Difference*, 11.

launch a chain reaction of multiple, unpredictable meanings. Paradoxically, the meanings found in hypertexts arise not from individual words but from the empty spaces *between* words. A hypertext's meanings are not limited to the "original author's intention," but multiply as new readers interact with them—rewriting or co-writing them. Here we can sense the mobility and mutability that Derrida assigns to the risky act of writing. As anyone who's ever placed a text on a Web site knows, once that's done, the author is no longer in control. For the electronic word has no palpable author, no discernible point of origin, no "innate" meaning lurking behind it as it makes its way across the Web. Meanings are not "in" or "behind" hypertexts, but "ahead" of them, in that "future event" when "words take me by surprise and teach me what I think."[48]

APPLIED RHIZOMATICS

I have spent time discussing the postmodern distinction between "trees" and "crabgrass" because, as I have suggested, when we change our images, our perception and experience of the world change. Moreover, it is the rhizomal image of crabgrass (rather than tree) that dominates the *theory* that drives the *technology* that is reshaping both the world of the twenty-first century and the ways we experience (think, feel, and speak about) that world. A change of image can indeed change the world—and nowhere is this more evident than in the development of the World Wide Web and the Internet. What we sometimes fail to notice, however, is that this same change of image has begun to impact our religious faith and practice, our liturgies and rituals. The Western Christian experience of Word and worship is being profoundly reshaped by information technology, just as the invention of printing reshaped both Catholic and Protestant worship in the sixteenth century.

Many people regard such technology as frightening, and perhaps for good reason. Information technology, after all, often affects us without our ever being aware of it. Under such conditions, great mischief—as well as great benefit—may result. Yet before we reject the "Information Revolution" in righteous Luddite horror, we would do well to reflect on a far more fundamental—and potentially more devastating—revolution in human history, the invention of writing itself. Writing, notes Denise Schmandt-Besserat, was

---

48. One should note that there are strong resemblances between writing (as Derrida and Merleau-Ponty understand it) and liturgical rites. For in the case of liturgies, too, we do not know what the actions mean until we actually *do* them. That is one reason why, in ancient Christianity, the "mystagogic" instruction of neophytes *followed*—and did not precede—their experience of the liturgy of initiation.

"the first technology to make the spoken word permanent"—to make it, that is, *independent* of the speaker(s).[49] Not only did writing make data retrieval possible in a way that orality alone could not, it also allowed people to communicate with each other without ever having to meet face to face. Writing, moreover, permitted a person to "capture" thoughts or ideas as soon as they arose, even if no one else was present to share the discovery. Beyond that, one could, on the spot, revise or edit one's ideas, alter or embellish them, prepare different versions of them—one for private, another for public consumption. People who complain today about the isolating effects of computer technology—about our penchant for sitting alone in studies or offices, communing with a flickering screen instead of talking to real, live people—should not forget that writing, too, may be (and usually is) an intensely solitary activity.

Word, World, and Web

My point here is that new technologies, like the new images proposed by Deleuze and Guattari, not only reshape cultures; they reshape religious experience (including ritual and liturgy) as well. The situation in which Catholic worshipers find themselves today is hardly unprecedented. Indeed, the technological revolution that is now reconfiguring Western thought and experience in postmodern cultures is simply the latest in a series of revolutionary changes that have been going on since the beginning of the second millennium. Three such earlier revolutions in technology may be identified:

1. The intellectual and artistic renaissance that blossomed in late-twelfth-century Europe, stimulated in part by Christian contact with other cultures during and after the Crusades;
2. The artistic, scientific, and technological revolutions of the late fifteenth century—those of Renaissance artists in Italy (and eventually in northern Europe), of Copernicus in the field of astronomy, and of Gutenberg in the field of printing and movable type; and
3. The Industrial Revolution, which began in mid-eighteenth-century England and quickly spread to the European continent and to the New World.

During the second millennium, these three revolutions radically reorganized Western thinking, art, commerce, politics, religion, and economics—to

49. Denise Schmandt-Besserat, *How Writing Came About* (Austin: University of Texas Press, 1996), 1.

say nothing of production methods and hence the relation between workers and their products. But the roots of these revolutions reach back much further, at least into the early centuries of the first millennium. Indeed, the rhizomal characteristics of the Internet may also be found in the Jewish Talmud, as Jonathan Rosen has pointed out. "[W]hen I look at a page of Talmud and see all those texts tucked intimately and intrusively onto the same page, like immigrant children sharing a single bed," writes Rosen, "I . . . think of the interrupting, jumbled culture of the Internet. For hundreds of years, response, questions on virtually every aspect of Jewish life, winged back and forth between scattered Jews and various centers of Talmudic learning. The Internet is also a world of unbounded curiosity, of argument and information, where anyone with a modem [or wireless connection] can wander out of the wilderness for a while, ask a question and receive an answer."[50]

To highlight some of the similarities between Internet and Talmud, Rosen recounts his own frustrating search for the source of a frequently quoted line from John Donne ("Never send to know for whom the bell tolls"). Rosen's first impulse was to check academic Web sites, especially those of research libraries, but he kept drawing a blank, largely because much of Donne's poetry and prose had not yet been digitized and made available electronically. Serendipitously, he finally found the quotation he was looking for "not as part of a scholarly library collection but simply because someone who loves John Donne had posted it on his home page."[51] Here, Rosen suggests, is a case where the Internet provided a rapid connection between reader and writer that more traditional methods of bookish research could not easily match. A first-rate scholarly index or "Donne concordance" might eventually have led him to the line, "for whom the bell tolls," but that could have meant hours of travel to and from libraries, plus additional time slogging through Donne's *opera omnia*.

Rosen admits he felt guilty about switching from traditional research tools (printed books) to digital ones (Internet searches). Like most dedicated readers and writers, he values the bond between book and body and fears its loss. Is it, he asks, "out of the ruined body of the book that the Internet is growing"? Perhaps, but Rosen believes that he can find within his own religious tradition a link between Internet and Talmud, because both, he suggests, were born out of loss. "The Talmud," he suggests, "offered a virtual home for an

---

50. Jonathan Rosen, *The Talmud and the Internet: A Journey between Worlds* (New York: Farrar, Straus & Giroux, 2000), 10–11. The Talmud, which exists in Babylonian and Palestinian versions, represents collections of law and lore that embody both the text of the Mishnah (the oral teaching of rabbis codified about 200 C.E.) and later rabbinic debate about the mishnaic text, the Gemara. Both versions of the Talmud were compiled during the fifth century C.E.

51. Ibid., 12.

uprooted culture [the Jewish people of the Diaspora], and grew out of the Jewish need to pack civilization into words and wander out into the world." Once the Romans had destroyed the Temple in 70 C.E., its liturgy—"those bodily rituals of blood and fire and physical atonement"—ceased. Jews lost their home, and "God lost His [the Temple]"; from then on, "Jews became the people of the book," no longer the "people of the Temple or the land." This physical loss meant that home and Temple had to become Torah and Talmud. Israel's physical space shrank to *writing*, to inscription, to the textual space of "the Book." "That bodily loss is frequently overlooked," writes Rosen, "but for me it lies at the heart of the Talmud. . . . The Internet, which we are . . . told binds us all together, nevertheless engenders in me a similar sense of Diaspora, a feeling of being everywhere and nowhere. Where else but in the middle of Diaspora do you *need* a home page?"[52]

In a word, the rabbis whose words are inscribed in Mishnah and Talmud (the codifications of oral law that accompanied and commented on Torah) had "created a virtual Temple after the real one was destroyed." The Talmudic tractate *Shabbat*, for example, discusses the many works forbidden on the Sabbath, and all of them, Rosen notes, stem from the kind of labor that had been required by the Temple's construction. In rhizomal fashion, the rabbis argued that Jews are forbidden to drag a heavy piece of furniture "across an earthen floor on the Sabbath because it might inadvertently create a furrow"; a furrow suggests the sowing of seeds; and plant life hints at the production of vegetable dyes used, for example, for the vestments of the officiating priests and for the Temple's furnishings. This rhizomal, chain-link argument points to a mazelike metaphor that connects God's house—and God—to Jewish homes and Jews. As a result, Rosen comments, "The Temple lives and does not live in the mysterious, intermediate space of the Talmud. The creation of that space was one of the tricks of Jewish survival. You could be scattered and still be at home, banished and still at the center of things."[53]

It may be, Rosen concludes, that the Internet is our postmodern Western way of dealing with the loss of a center, "a response to changes that have already taken place, to losses we have not yet begun to acknowledge."[54] But it is also true that the Web's crabgrass-like connections create "vast democratizing networks of information" that have the potential to realign cultures and societies globally. Technology spreads much more rapidly and pervasively than virtually any other human phenomenon. When it comes to the basic

---

52. Ibid., 14.
53. Ibid., 105-6.
54. Ibid., 109.

know-how needed for the production of food or the sharing of information, technology eventually rules. John Deere tractors can be found almost anywhere on the planet, and so, increasingly, is the Web. Even premodern cultures such as that of the Clovis peoples in North America developed technologies (carved spear points) that spread rapidly across great distances, hundreds of miles away from the rock source originally used to make these tools. If there is a global lingua franca that connects diverse cultures today, its name is surely "information technology."[55]

Technological revolutions succeed, therefore, not so much because they are theoretically or intellectually innovative, but because they reshape how people interact and live together and how they *do* basic tasks.[56] One may argue that the rapidly evolving "information revolution" has already begun to reshape cultures—and the church—in ways that affect five fundamental human interactions:

1. *Power and authority.* Perhaps information technology's most obvious consequence is that it offers access to people who might otherwise be kept "out of the loop." A knowledgeable fifteen-year-old hacker with a bit of chutzpah can break into classified Pentagon files without ever leaving the security of his suburban home. That such acts are possible and even routine signals a radical dispersal and realignment of any culture's structures of power and authority. Traditionally centralized social, political, economic, moral, and religious power begins to move *away from the center and toward the margins.* In premodern cultures (e.g., ancient Israel's after the establishment of the Davidic dynasty), power and authority coalesced around a focal center—an urban community, a royal dynasty, a temple, a priesthood—and eventually, a *book* (the Torah, the Tanakh). But in the postmodern world of the Web, as we have seen, authority is "rhizomally" dispersed, and access to power operates on many plateaus simultaneously, thanks to multiple crabgrass connections that cannot easily be controlled "from the top down." The Internet is blissfully "nonhierarchical" and "horizontal"; its nodes "intersect in random, unregulated networks in which any node can interconnect with any other node."[57]

---

55. To say this is not to ignore the perils of technologies, especially those emerging in late-capitalist, industrialized cultures. For a critique of such technologies and their possibly damaging effects on liturgy, see Richard Gaillardetz, *Transforming Our Days: Spirituality, Community and Liturgy in a Technological Culture* (New York: Crossroad, 2000).

56. There may of course be alliances between philosophical movements and technological innovation, a point I have tried to show in this chapter by noting the similarities between Deleuze and Guattari's poststructural "rhizomatics" and the crabgrass conditions that connect people and information on the Web.

57. Powell, *Postmodernism for Beginners*, 114.

2. *Belonging.* Our experience of what it means to "belong" (to anything or anyone) is being altered; For example, the church's liturgy has long relied on a seat-of-the-pants principle: "Bring your body; your mind will follow." That is, if believers get themselves to church regularly, repeatedly, the light will slowly dawn. Understanding and change result from repeated *action*: people act their way into new ways of thinking; they don't think their way into new ways of acting. This principle has been the bedrock of the Roman Catholic ritual system for more than two millennia. Liturgical acts first address the *body*, the sensorium, not the neocortex. *Caro cardo salutis,* wrote Tertullian; "the flesh is the hinge of salvation." Thus, we baptize bodies, not brains: we immerse shivering skin in water; smear chrism on flesh aquiver with desire and emotion; and finally lead hungry neophytes to food and drink at the Lord's table. In a word, our ritual system presupposes that we belong to God's *people* precisely by belonging to a corporate *body.* And so, at eucharist, the ecclesial body of Christ gathers *at* and *around* the table to receive the body of Christ that is *on* the table.

So we believe. But Internet access can connect us, virtually, with prayer and praying communities worldwide, without the need for body to meet body. An old Zen proverb says there are some things that can be learned "only by rubbing two people together," and, as the preceding paragraph argues, a similar principle underwrites the Catholic tradition of sacramental worship. Indeed, "God's Word at the mercy of the body" is a short and apt definition of sacrament.[58] The body is not only the condition but the *site*—the very *place*—of the liturgy, "a living body, a singular body of desire where the threefold body—cosmic, social, and ancestral—is collected and interconnected . . . a body where the liturgy becomes world."[59] In Catholic sacramental practice, body is the aboriginal Internet, our species' first, indispensable, rhizomally connecting Web.

Can that Body-Web compete with the World Wide Web of our evolving information technology? Some would answer yes, noting that the Web is simply a digital extension of the skin, much as telescopes extend the eye's range of vision and loudspeakers amplify the ear's auditory powers. Yet there seem to be crucial differences. The Internet's connections are virtually instantaneous; a mere nanosecond separates the body's *desire* (for image, for information) from fulfillment. Yet experience teaches us, paradoxically, that instant

---

58. See Louis-Marie Chauvet, *The Sacraments: The Word of God at the Mercy of the Body* (Collegeville, Minn.: Liturgical Press/A Pueblo Book, 2001).

59. Louis-Marie Chauvet, *Symbol and Sacrament: A Sacramental Reinterpretation of Christian Existence,* trans. Patrick Madigan and Madeleine Beaumont (Collegeville, Minn.: Liturgical Press/A Pueblo Book, 1995), 309.

satisfaction is in fact the *death* of desire, for human desires live only by being endlessly *deferred* in an "indefinite process of incompletion."[60] To be human, as Louis-Marie Chauvet says, "is precisely to be opened by an *unsealable breach* and thus to look for quiet without ever being able to find it."[61] Restlessness and deferral are what define us humans as "creatures of desire," and Christian ritual respects that condition. As I will argue later, liturgies are beginnings, not endings, and their verification happens beyond the space of worship—in embodied ethics, in the "liturgy of the neighbor." The body's role in "how we belong"—to humankind, to church—seems indispensable. In contrast, information technology often seems impatient, even resentful, of corporality. The challenge facing us is whether we can reconcile the liturgical principle of materiality (flesh as the necessary "condition of possibility" for our spiritual meeting with God[62]) with a technology whose way of connecting may bypass the body and minimize the need for "face-to-face" behavior.

3. *Private and public.* A third challenge arises from the blurring between "private" and "public" in all sectors of human life. Readers may recall, for example, how, during Bill Clinton's presidency, the contents of Special Prosecutor Kenneth Star's impeachment referral to the U.S. House of Representatives (along with Clinton's own four-hour testimony before a grand jury) were dumped, complete and uncensored, onto the Internet. Aside from the ethical and legal questions such an unauthorized release raised, the action made it clear that privacy, as a "constitutionally protected right," is no longer a foregone conclusion for *anyone*, in *any* circumstances. In a flash, millions of Internet users learned more about the private sex lives of public figures than they probably wanted to know.

The Internet, of course, makes no firm distinction between fact and fiction, truth and falsehood, virtue and vice, good and bad, public persona and private peccadillo. The computer screen is a great homogenizer. One click, and you can devoutly read the text of the Torah in Hebrew or the prayers of Isaac the Blind; another click, and your screen is flooded with "adult entertainment." Moreover, while you are watching your screen, others are watching you, unobserved and unannounced—tracking your credit card

---

60. Chauvet, *Symbol and Sacrament*, 368.
61. Ibid.
62. As twentieth-century theologians like Karl Rahner pointed out, "flesh" and "spirit" are not polar opposites in Christian theology. On the contrary, human persons are a unity, and hence, the more I become my body, the more I become spirit, just as the more I become spirit, the more I become my body. It is "only through this actual bodily quality that the spiritual nature [of human persons] comes to be." Jörg Splett, "Body," in *Encyclopedia of Theology: The Concise Sacramentum Mundi*, ed. Karl Rahner (New York: Seabury Press, 1975), 106.

transactions, analyzing your buying habits, monitoring your investment portfolio. Several years ago, for instance, *The Chronicle of Higher Education* ran a short essay on the use of "cookies" in computer-based research.[63] Cookies are "small computer files that can imperceptibly track a user's travels on the Web." One researcher, Oren Etizioni of the University of Washington, described himself as "pro-cookies," arguing that cookies are a good thing for research purposes. Others, however, objected to the whole idea of doing research on people without their informed consent.

Public and private—on the Internet the difference is often negligible, despite the proliferation of so-called secure servers. And of course the blurring of this fundamental distinction raises enormous questions for a religious tradition that, for more than two millennia, has considered the "private sanctuary of conscience" the supreme moral authority and has prized the "seal of confession" as sacrosanct.

4. *Content and access.* Evolving information technology shows how difficult it is today for religious authorities to control the content of (or access to) information about belief and behavior. The *Catechism of the Catholic Church* (no. 890) insists that "it is . . . the Magisterium's task to preserve God's people from deviations and defections and to guarantee them the objective possibility of professing the true faith without error." But anyone who has spent time surfing the Internet knows that what one finds posted on "Catholic" Web sites as "official teaching" may or may not bear any resemblance to the real core of our tradition. The *Catechism*'s conviction that it is "the Magisterium's task to preserve God's people from deviations and defections" may be a laudable goal, but it is very difficult to achieve in an intensely competitive cybernetic environment.

Is this a "new situation"? Not entirely. After all, St. Paul devoted a significant chunk of his Second Letter to the Corinthians to complaining that "super-apostles"—slick, first-century spin doctors whose eloquence seemed to guarantee the authenticity of their teaching—were in fact charlatans, not to be trusted as teachers of the truth (see 2 Cor 10-13). Significantly, the only antidote Paul could offer against these sleek celebrities was his *body*—his weak flesh and "contemptible" speech, his beatings, his brushes with death, his shipwrecks, his sleeplessness, his dangers, his hunger and thirst, his cold and exposure (see 2 Cor 11:16-33). Paul's answer to his critics—the ultimate defense of his gospel—was not a theological proof but a *body*—his own and that of the crucified One (2 Cor 13:3-4). Here again, the challenge is to overcome the Internet's impression that its contents are internally self-authenti-

---

63. September 25, 1998, pp. A 31-32.

cating (and hence true). As I noted in the prologue to this book, Christian ritual practice requires "exteriority" for verification; the liturgy of the church must be validated in the liturgy of the neighbor.

5. *Community.* Finally, our understanding of what constitutes "community" is being profoundly reshaped by the technologies that surround us. For instance, until about the middle of the last century, Catholic identity in the United States was often mediated through *immigrant, ethnic* identity. My own family's ethnic heritage was rooted in the Great Hunger that afflicted nineteenth-century Ireland and caused waves of immigration to the United States and elsewhere. Under such conditions, Catholic identity was as closely connected to rituals of ethnic affiliation as it was to the rituals of Word and sacrament celebrated in church. Or perhaps it would be more accurate to say the two were virtually indistinguishable. Indeed, that was Catholicism's strength as it migrated west across the Atlantic in the late nineteenth and early twentieth centuries. It had an amazing ability to promote membership in a *global* religious community by promoting its members' allegiance to *ethnic particularity.*[64]

But that time may now have passed. Thanks largely to the impact of information technology, Catholics who have arrived in this country as a result of more recent immigrations—for example, from Mexico, Vietnam, or the Philippines—are assimilated to American culture far more rapidly than their predecessors were. In significant ways, the Web and the Internet act as *solvents* upon traditional, ethnic understandings of community. But this technology-assisted pattern of assimilation may raise as many questions as it resolves. Twenty years ago, Mark Searle argued that "American Catholics are in process of becoming more characteristically American than characteristically Catholic . . . [and] cultural assimilation appears to be occurring at the expense of a distinct Catholic identity. . . . Where liturgy is concerned, this means a growing alienation from precisely that sense of collective identity and collective responsibility which the liturgy might be thought to rehearse."[65] Perhaps true; perhaps not. In any case, Searle raises, from another angle, the issue of "belonging" noted in point 2 above. What does it mean to belong to the Catholic community—and does the liturgy contribute decisively to that belonging?

To help answer this question, let us explore more thoroughly the connection between the Web and the Word.

---

64. For an illuminating analysis of this phenomenon, see Colleen McDannell, *Material Christianity: Religion and Popular Culture in America* (New Haven: Yale University Press, 1995).

65. Mark Searle, "The Notre Dame Study of Catholic Parish Life," *Worship* 60, no. 4 (July 1986): 333.

Word as Web

If we turn now to the history of the Bible in Christian contexts, a connection similar to the one Rosen sees between Internet and Talmud emerges. As Edward Mendelson notes, the hyperlink system on which the Internet depends had already begun to appear, arguably, in handwritten, illuminated Bibles that Christian monks, East and West, produced in their scriptoria. The Bible was in fact the first book to be interconnected by a system of cross-references—"marginal notes that directed a reader from one biblical passage to another, perhaps to a passage written at a distance of hundreds of years from the first. . . . The marginal references to the Bible and the hyperlinks of the World Wide Web," Mendelson argues, "may be the only two systems ever invented that give concrete expression to the idea that everything in the world holds together, that every event, every fact, every datum is connected to every other."[66]

That is perhaps the most obvious benefit offered by Internet technology: connections are everywhere, and they are accessible by everyone (at least everyone with access to a computer). And liturgy, as I noted in the prologue, is about connections, about being connected to God, people, planet, space, time, culture, and history. Modern information technology gives us an unprecedented capacity to connect people to people; people to history; and people to an inexhaustible stream of ideas, information, images, cultures, arts, and products. Hyperlinks have unimaginable potential for reshaping our personal and public life. But the bad news, as we've seen, is that this same system of hyperlinks may introduce us to "a world where connections are everywhere but are mostly meaningless, transient, fragile and unstable."[67] A few clicks and you can create your own Web page; a few more clicks, and you can destroy it—or change it into something quite different. Like Jonathan Rosen, Edward Mendelson suggests that the Internet may be built around a loss—not only the loss of homeland and worship center (as happened when Israel was dispersed in the Diaspora) but a deeper loss. "In a world without tangible bodies or enduring memories," Mendelson observes, "no one can keep promises, and yet the Bible is, above all, a book of oaths, covenants that a personal God has already kept and promises that will be kept in the future."[68]

---

66. See Edward Mendelson, "The Word & the Web," in *The New York Times*, June 2, 1996 ("Bookend" in the *New York Times Book Review*). This article was accessed on May 17, 2005, at http://www.columbia.edu/~em36/wordweb/bookend.html.

67. Ibid.

68. Ibid.

The presence of a promise thus presupposes the presence of *bodies*. The body is, after all, our primary mode of connecting with self, world, others, and God. The Bible's "hyperlink system" was thus an *incarnate* one; it told the history of salvation in terms of the history of a people on the move. Moreover, for most of the first millennium, the encounter between believer and Bible was intensely physical, for Scripture (like other written sources) was read *aloud* and not only with the eyes.[69] Hence reading was an embodied *motor* activity, a *social* transaction within a community of other readers, a physical fact of flesh and saliva, mumbling lips, moving tongue and teeth. Reading aloud was a way to connect *meaning* and *memory* to *movement*. The same principle influenced instruction in medieval (and modern) Qur'anic schools. Moreover, to read aloud—even if alone—was to call and invite reading partners, and thus to imply that meanings are socially constructed, that they flow from *communal* discoveries based on a shared humanity.

Connecting meaning and memory to movement helped give the Bible its enormous power to transform social structures. Mendelson argues, for example, that the abolition of slavery in the United States resulted not merely from mid-nineteenth-century socioeconomic pressures but also (and more importantly) from the fact that Quakers and other devout readers of the Bible understood the inescapable *connection* between Exodus 13:21 (where God marches before the people in a pillar of cloud by day and a pillar of fire by night) and 1 Corinthians 10:1-4, where Paul parallels the liberating work of Moses and the liberating work of Christ. For the abolitionists, this connection and its consequences were utterly clear: *Christians are morally obligated to repeat in their own time and place the liberating work of Moses.* As long as any people or any individual person is enslaved, God's promised act of liberation remains unfinished. To *accept* slavery (whether one is its victim or its perpetrator) is to enroll in Pharaoh's army; to *fight* it is "to obey the same imperatives that Moses [and Jesus] obeyed."[70]

This example is important because it shows how hyperlink connections—whether the Bible's or the Web's—can reshape a community's behavior. As tangible, physically inscribed realities, both the Bible and the human body make and keep promises. Christian liturgical traditions, East and West, thus treat Bibles and bodies (especially, but not only, Christ's eucharistic body) in the same way: both are reverenced, held, touched, lifted, greeted with acclamations, swathed in light and perfume.[71] For all public prayer, as Laurence

---

69. That is why the *Rule of Benedict* famously instructed monks to read "so as not to disturb others."

70. Mendelson, "Word & the Web."

71. One should properly speak of an "elevation" of the Gospel book at Mass much as one speaks of the elevation of the consecrated bread and wine at the end of the eucharistic prayer. (Technically,

Paul Hemming notes, "is worded—which means that all prayer is my being inscribed into the Word of prayer, which through the Spirit returns to the Father. In so much as I am of Christ, my prayer is of the body, and so takes for granted the assembly, the *ecclesia*, the body of Christ."[72] Because God's Word inscribes itself in human speech and sacrament, in body and Bible, the Christian's prayer and promises are *physical* realities, written on the body, carried on breath and blood, carved in the bone.

We are now in a better position to understand why, as French symbolist poet Stephane Mallarmé once wrote, "*the world exists in order to become a book.*" The biblical Word, like the Web, is a rhizomal *reading* of the world's crabgrass-text. As Jews and Christians understand it, Scripture is not human beings reading God's mind, but God reading the world's mind, probing its meanings in creation and covenant, story and song, deed and desire, hunger and history. Because the Bible is itself an inscribed body (the displaced homeland of a people), it can read the world's body, much as lovers read one another's flesh. If writing is the act by which "my own words take me by surprise and teach me what I think," then the Bible ("God's writing") is the Word taking the world by surprise and teaching it what it thinks.

Word as Polyphony, "Nomad Space"

When Word reads world, in short, the result is polyphony, a rhizomal multiplicity of meanings sounding simultaneously. What Word sees in world is crabgrass, not a "root-book" built on strict principles of organic order or logical sequence.[73] (Anyone who still believes the universe runs on logic hasn't

---

the "elevations" after the words over bread and cup are "showings" rather than elevations properly speaking.) Both book and body are greeted with joyful acclamations by the people: "Alleluia" (at the Gospel procession) and "Amen" (at the end of the eucharistic prayer).

72. Laurence Paul Hemming, "The Subject of Prayer: Unwilling Words in the Postmodern Access to God," in *The Blackwell Companion to Postmodern Theology*, ed. Graham Ward (Malden, Mass.: Blackwell, 2001), 445.

73. Deleuze and Guattari begin their work "Rhizome," with reflections on the changed character and status of books and book-making: "A book has neither object nor subject; it is made of variously formed matters, and very different dates and speeds. To attribute the book to a subject is to overlook this working of matters, and the exteriority of their relations. . . . A book is an assemblage . . . and as such is unattributable. It is a multiplicity—but we don't know yet what the multiple entails." See "Introduction: Rhizome," in *A Thousand Plateaus*, 3-4. In this "rhizomal" account, books are a reality quite different from the "root-books" of the past, which were written on the model of a tree (root, trunk, branches), and which assumed that "the book imitates the world as art imitates nature" (p. 5). The rhizomal book "ceaselessly establishes connections between semiotic chains, organizations of powers, and circumstances relative to the arts, sciences, and social struggles" (p. 7). Like writing and like language itself, rhizomal books no longer assume an "ideal speaker-listener" and no longer assume that "a homogeneous linguistic community" exists (p. 7).

been paying attention.) The antistructural layout of Deleuze and Guattari's *A Thousand Plateaus* is, paradoxically, a far more accurate image of the "world as book" and of "Word reading world" than the orderly compositions college profs teach freshmen to write. The Bible is like *A Thousand Plateaus*, and that is one reason why neither Jewish nor Christian liturgy reads it in strict order, from beginning to end. On the contrary, liturgy reads the Bible rhizomally, polyphonically, with many systems working at once.[74] Through the sheer diversity of its arrangements for reading the Bible, Christian liturgy implies that Scripture is an open system—"nomad space," to use Deleuze and Guattari's phrase).[75] Nomad thought is "smooth space" that resists reduction to treelike structures, closed systems, or single meanings; it resembles not the linear, cause-and-effect, sedimentary narratives favored by historians (*this* happened; then *that* ...), but the polyphonic textures of the Bible.[76] One can jump into a nomad text at any point and find a connection to any (or every) other point. Liturgical lectionaries treat the Bible as nomad space, as an assemblage of mobile texts that can be placed in "conversation" with each other, even if they are not united by theme, structural similarity, or authorship. The "logic" behind such choices lies in the conviction that each biblical "passage" (itself a nomadic image) connects to every other, and hence any combination of texts opens a space where the Word may "take the world by surprise and teach it what it thinks."

So nomad space is "smooth," that is, open-ended; it lets one "rise up at any point and move to any other."[77] It spreads itself out "in an open space (hold the street), as opposed to entrenching itself in a closed space (hold the fort)."[78] Deleuze and Guattari borrow the notion of "smooth space" not from geology or geography, but from music—and more particularly, from the work of the distinguished contemporary composer and conductor Pierre Boulez. Nor is their appeal to music a mere flourish. Musical works offer the best insight not only into nomad space and thought but into the way Web and Word read world, as I will try to show in the paragraphs that follow.

For centuries—even before the invention of printing—books and their

---

74. A look at the lectionaries of Christian churches will demonstrate this point. Among Roman Catholics, since the reforms of the Second Vatican Council, at least three distinct systems of reading the Bible function simultaneously: the one-year cycle of biblical readings assigned in the Liturgy of the Hours; the two-year cycle of readings assigned for use at eucharistic celebrations on weekdays; and the three-year cycle of readings assigned for Sunday eucharist.

75. See Deleuze and Guattari, *A Thousand Plateaus*, section 12, "Treatise on Nomadology—The War Machine," 351-423.

76. See *A Thousand Plateaus*, 553-54 n. 20.

77. Massumi, "Translator's Foreword," to *A Thousand Plateaus*, xiii.

78. Ibid.

pages have been imagined largely as warehouses for the storage and retrieval of data. Such a model implies that reading is simply scanning, the taking of inventories. To read is to take stock, to "tally the contents" of the warehouse. But suppose pages, whether printed or electronically digitized, are not primarily storage systems but *tablature*. (Note the change of image!) As defined today, tablature may refer, broadly, to *any* musical notation, but at an earlier period it signified notation for instrumental music that indicates rhythm and fingering, *but not the actual pitches to be produced by the player.* There was a great deal of *indeterminacy* in such a notation system. Moreover, musical tablature (in both broad and narrow senses) never actually stores or retrieves musical data at all; it merely furnishes cues and clues about the music's "realization" or performance—structure, rhythm, dynamics, phrasing, clefs, and (perhaps, though not always) keys and pitches. The visual image that introduces the section entitled "Rhizome" in *A Thousand Plateaus* is the opening page of Sylvano Bussotti's *Five Piano Pieces for David Tudor* (1959).[79] To classically trained pianists, this score looks a little bewildering, because, though it has familiar elements (staves, clefs), much of the notation resembles a Jackson Pollock painting. Bussotti's score looks scattered, "thrown together," without including clearly organized pitches or "key signatures." The score looks maddeningly rhizomal, nomadic, indeterminate; it's an inkblot graphic that leaves the player wondering just how the piece is supposed to "sound." And of course that's the point. David Tudor (1926-1996), the performer to whom Bussotti's composition is dedicated, was well known as both a virtuoso pianist and an exponent of what is called "live electronic music." He and other American musicians, notably John Cage, elevated indeterminacy to a compositional principle (or "anti-principle"). For these artists, the success of a work depends on the indeterminate interplay between the composer's cues (in the score), the performer's imagination, and, often, the active presence of other media (e.g., film, video, laser projections, dance, mobile loudspeaker sculptures, etc.). The goal is a performance both flexible and complex, with sound materials unfolding unpredictably through large gestures (some acoustic, some visual) in space and time.

What the "indeterminate" scores of Bussotti and others reveal is that *all* music is meta-notational; it happens *beyond* the score (not behind it)—or not at all. Ultimately, performance is less about the meticulous observance of the

---

79. Deleuze and Guattari, "Introduction: Rhizome," in *A Thousand Plateaus*, 3. There, Bussotti's name is spelled with one *t*, though the preferred spelling requires two. David Tudor was a distinguished American pianist and composer (1926-1996).

composer's cues—necessary as that may be—than about creating *music*. Moreover, the postmodern principle of indeterminacy—promoted in the twentieth century by the likes of Sylvano Bussotti, John Cage, David Tudor, Pierre Boulez, Stefan Wolpe, and a host of others—is actually not as radical as it might first appear. Everyone knows that the earliest "scores" of the Gregorian Chant repertoire in the West were little more than graphic cues scratched above the words of liturgical manuscripts, with the actual sound left largely to the skill and imagination of performers, working within the parameters of a tradition that was primarily oral. If you wanted to know for certain how a bit of Roman (or Gallican, or Mozarabic) chant sounded, you had to send for one of that rite's cantors. Similarly, the vast variety of ornamentation employed in Baroque music (e.g., that of J. S. Bach), though shaped by convention, was largely left to an individual performer's skill and spontaneity.

Historically, Christian ritual reads liturgical "pages" the way musicians read scores—as tablature. A ritual text is not a warehouse for storing data or retrieving dogma. Nor are ritual meanings sedimentary and immobile; they do not lie "embedded," awaiting arousal, in either texts or nonverbal gestures. Like music, liturgical meaning is performed "beyond the text," or not at all. That is why, as the work of Louis-Marie Chauvet shows, Christian worship, like its Jewish antecedent, is not—and can never be—*self*-verifying, *self*-authenticating. Israel's rites for offering firstfruits were not internally self-legitimating, because "recognition of God and thankfulness toward God . . . can be true only if they are veri-fied [*sic*] in recognition of the poor: it is in the ethical practice of *sharing* [of divestiture, dispossession] that the liturgy of Israel is thus accomplished."[80]

Similarly, Christian liturgy has to be verified outside itself, exteriorly, in what Emmanuel Levinas called "the liturgy of the neighbor."[81] Eucharist, for instance, cannot exist apart from ethics—and the reasons for this are both *theo*logical (in the precise sense of that word) and philanthropic. Paul clearly affirms that each time we celebrate the Lord's Supper we "proclaim the death of the Lord until he comes" (1 Cor 11:26)—and as Chauvet says, "God crucified in the form of a slave does not tolerate being mastered by a science. Its Word can be expressed only as an . . . *imperative* of life and action." The ethical action that flows from eucharist "gives body to God" and "gives privilege of place to the exercise of justice and mercy where we have recognized the 'liturgy of the neighbor.' . . . The ethics of 'living-in-grace,' primarily with

---

80. Chauvet, *Symbol and Sacrament*, 238 (emphasis and material in brackets added).
81. Quotations in this paragraph are from Chauvet, *Symbol and Sacrament*, 238, 535.

regard to those whom humans have reduced to the state of slaves, is the place of veri-fication [*sic*], the *veritas*, of the filial 'giving thanks' of the Eucharist."

Word, Rite, and the Discourse of the Body

We can understand, then, why, for Christians, ethical practices like the preferential "option" for the poor are *not*, in fact, optional. The obligation of ethical action flows precisely from *God's own act* of self-emptying, self-erasure, self-outpouring (Phil 2:7-8). Jesus' act of self-abasement ("he *emptied* himself, taking the form of a slave" [Phil 2:7]) was not merely exemplary; for the cross "can be interpreted only as the renunciation by God of God's very self," and hence it is "only as the action of the Trinitarian God that the scandal of the cross can be endured by the believer."[82] On the cross, God subverts all we know of "God." Such a searing scandal cannot be grasped *conceptually*; it "requires the passage *from discourse to body* . . . where the body of our desire, our history, and our society becomes the place of the truth of our *word*."

Liturgical *discourse* must, then, inevitably give way to the *body*, to the embodied action of ethical performance. To say this is not to deny the emphasis, in Catholic tradition, on sacramental worship as intrinsically efficacious *ex opere operato* ("from the very doing of the deed"); still, that much-maligned phrase must be parsed accurately. To the words *ex opere operato* one must always add *Dei* ("of God") or *Christi* ("of Christ"). The guarantee of efficacy (i.e., grace will truly be offered and bestowed whenever this action is performed) flows from God-in-Christ, who acts as the sacrament's "principal agent" or "final cause," to use traditional scholastic language. This obviously does *not* mean that sacraments "say what they do and do what they say" simply or solely because the rite has been validly celebrated by an assembly (ministers + people) having the required intentions. *Ex opere operato* is not a defiant assertion that sacraments "work" mechanically, despite the minister's disposition; it is, rather, a stern reminder that Christian worship is not self-legitimating. Even if one views sacraments as "self-actualizations" or "self-expressions" of the *church* (defined as God's "eschatologically triumphant grace," as Christ's abiding presence and availability in our world), one must still remember that the church's identity as "sacrament of salvation" in and for the world is not self-produced or self-bestowed. Chauvet is unquestionably right when he insists that in liturgy and sacrament the church does not "invent" its own identity, but receives it from a God who is incomprehensi-

---

82. Quotations in this section are from Chauvet, *Symbol and Sacrament*, 532, 535, 375, 409; Chauvet quotes both Hans Urs von Balthasar and Walter Kasper.

bly near yet irreducibly Other. Sacraments are thus acts of "submission" to the Other; in them, the church puts itself "at the disposal of the Other," and hence it "lets the Other act by performing a gesture which is not from itself, by saying words which are not its own, by receiving elements which it has not chosen." In a word, it is only "by *receiving itself* from [Christ], its Lord, that the Church attains its identity. The sacraments . . . are the *instituting* mediation of this identity." And thus, whenever it celebrates sacramental liturgy, the church confesses its radical dependence on Christ as the very condition of its existence and its freedom.

Rule of Prayer, Rule of Faith, Rule of Life

I am arguing, then, that Christian ritual is best understood as tablature or musical score—and that liturgical scores are "rhizomal, nomadic," limitlessly multiple in meaning and internally "indeterminate," that is, capable of verification only through the *exteriority* of ethical action.[83] Christian liturgy begins as ritual practice but ends as ethical performance. Liturgy of the neighbor verifies liturgy of the church, much as a composer's score makes *music* only through the risk of performance.

Hence, the ancient, binary formula *lex orandi, lex credendi* ("the rule of prayer is the rule of faith")—though often invoked to assert the priority of doxology over doctrine[84]—is in fact something of a red herring. The formula is flawed from the get-go, because its reasoning is circular: "We *believe*," it asserts, "that the church's public prayer shapes what (and how?) we believe." But such a statement *already expresses* fundamental convictions—*beliefs*— about the nature of both Christ and church, beliefs that make liturgy possible (and obligatory) in the first place. There is a sense, of course, in which it is quite true to say that liturgy is where theology is born—where the church

---

83. I use the term "ritual" here and throughout this book in much the way Ronald Grimes understands it. *Ritual*, Grimes argues, is the "general idea," the formal "definition or characterization," while *rites* are what people actually enact (see Ronald Grimes, "Emerging Ritual," in *Proceedings of the North American Academy of Liturgy* [Valparaiso, Ind.: NAAL, 1990], 16). The term "ritual" is thus broader; it implies a "convergence of several kinds [of action] we normally think of as distinct. It is an 'impure' genre. Like opera, which includes other genres—for example, singing, drama, and sometimes even dancing—a ritual may include all these and more" (see Ronald Grimes, *Ritual Criticism* [Columbia: University of South Carolina Press, 1990], 192). For a detailed and technical discussion of ritual as a fusion of thought and action, theory and culture—as well as of the relation between definitions of ritual and understandings of culture—see two books by Catherine Bell: *Ritual Theory, Ritual Practice* (New York: Oxford University Press, 1992) and *Ritual: Perspectives and Dimensions* (New York: Oxford University Press, 1997).

84. See, e.g., Aidan Kavanagh, *On Liturgical Theology* (Collegeville, Minn.: Liturgical Press/A Pueblo Book, 1984/1992), 3: "Worship conceived broadly is what gives rise to theological reflection, rather than the other way around."

is "caught in the act of being most overtly itself as it stands faithfully in the presence of the One who is both object and source" of its faith—and hence that liturgy alone deserves the moniker *theologia prima*.[85] Still, the *lex orandi, lex credendi* formula suffers from the same limitations that beset all such closed-circuit, binary oppositions. If doxology checks doctrine, might not the reverse be true as well, viz., that doctrine checks doxology?

That, certainly, was the opinion of Pope Pius XII, who argued in his apostolic constitution *Munificentissimus Deus* (1950), that "the liturgy of the church does not engender Catholic faith, but rather springs from it, in such a way that the practices of sacred worship proceed from the faith as the fruit comes from the tree."[86] (Old images die hard!) Three years earlier, the same pope had disputed the idea that "the sacred liturgy is a kind of proving ground for the truths of faith, meaning . . . that the Church is obliged to declare such a doctrine sound when it is found to have produced fruits of piety and sanctity through the sacred rites of the liturgy, and to reject it otherwise."[87] Such words suggest that Pius XII was more concerned about doctrinal control of the liturgy than about promoting Prosper of Aquitaine's dictum, *legem credendi lex statuat supplicandi* ("let the rule of prayer establish the rule of belief"). While he admitted that Prosper's adage could be understood as "perfectly correct" if "one desires to differentiate and describe the relationship between faith and the sacred liturgy in absolute and general terms," he still insisted that the "entire liturgy . . . has *the Catholic faith for its content.*"[88]

The slogan *lex orandi, lex credendi* does not, then, offer as much light as it may seem to promise. In spite of the tension between them, doxology and doctrine remain a cozy *ménage à deux*, each partner in the pair defining itself in terms of the other. But the deeper question is not whether faith controls worship, or vice versa, but whether either of them can be verified in the absence of a *lex agendi* (a rule of action or behavior), an ethical imperative that flows from the Christian's encounter with a God who is radically "un-God-like," a God who, in the cross of Jesus and in the bodies of the "poor, the hungry, the thirsty, the naked, the imprisoned," has become everything we believe a God is *not*. The ethical imperative implied by the phrase *lex agendi* breaks apart our comfortable "faith and worship" duo by introducing that subversive element of *indeterminacy*.

85. Ibid., 74, 75.
86. Pius XII, *Munificentissimus Deus* (November 1, 1950), 20. Latin text in *Acta Apostolicae Sedis* 42 (1950): 760. Note the use of the arboreal metaphor to express the relation between liturgy and faith.
87. Pius XII, *Mediator Dei* (November 20, 1947), 46. Latin text in *Acta Apostolicae Sedis* 39 (1947): 540.
88. *Mediator Dei*, 48, 47. Latin text in *Acta Apostolicae Sedis* 39 (1947): 540-41.

Christian liturgy, moreover, gives this indeterminacy an unsettling theological twist. Indeterminacy destabilizes; it de-centers—and that is salutary, even if discomfiting. The God who is "beyond all forms of being, of wisdom, and of power," the God who acquires a Self only through those "little ones who do not exist" (i.e., the marginalized have-nots whose poverty, hunger, and misery count for nothing in the world's eyes) can be met and worshiped only within the "body of the world and of humanity"—more specifically, of suffering humanity. Christian liturgy always speaks the Word of the cross, and it is "a rupturing Word."[89] It was surely not mere rhetoric that prompted Paul to remind the Corinthians (and us) that "as often as you eat this bread and drink the cup, you proclaim the *death* of the Lord until he comes" (1 Cor 11:26).

The rupturing Word of the cross proclaims that God has become what we customarily believe God *is* not and *should* not be. As Stanislas Breton puts it,

> It is precisely because [God] is nothing of that which is that he must become. But this "becoming" necessarily passes through the face of the other. Nothing is more disconcerting ... than the last judgment according to St. Matthew (25.31-46). At the hour of truth that sounds the final decline of the idols, in that flash of lightening [*sic*] that concentrates a life upon the one thing necessary, what we would have thought essential is not what finally matters. The last day is ... the triumph of the everyday. The "blessed of the Father" hear ... the revelatory Word: "I was hungry and you gave me to eat; ... thirsty ... a stranger ... a prisoner." Those awaiting the sentence make no appeal to those things that common religious sense would have deemed indispensable: cult, adoration, absolute submission to a transcendent Truth. The elect themselves seem not to understand. ... Would the most distant also be the most near? Or is it that we know neither near nor far? Are not the poor, in their non-being, the shadow on our earth of that kenosis Paul celebrates [cf. Phil 2.5-11] as that yet unseen future?[90]

The last day is the triumph of the everyday; God's becoming passes *through the face of the other*. Surely Stanislas Breton is right to insist that "the history of the Cross is defined by the humblest gestures: dress, nourish, shelter, quench. In such banality, it is not surprising that the irresponsible faithful fear that the economy of faith has been reduced to vulgar materialism. Indeed, the

---

89. Stanislas Breton, *The Word and the Cross*, trans. Jacquelyn Porter (New York: Fordham University Press, 2002), 120-22.
90. Ibid., 121-22.

intransigent paradox [of the parable in Matthew's Gospel] signifies the necessity of giving, to that which has no face."[91]

The judgment scene in Matthew 25 has all the characteristics of a heavenly liturgy, to which all nations have been summoned and invited to participate. Worshiping angels are present (a sign of cultic context); the eschatological "Son of Man" presides, speaking and blessing; and a kind of "dialogue homily" precedes the just ones' entry into eternal life, imaged earlier in Matthew as a royal "wedding feast" (Matt 11:1-14). But at the heart of this "heavenly liturgy" lies a subversive indeterminacy. Those who sincerely believed they "dressed, nourished, sheltered, and quenched" are shocked to learn they *didn't*; those who didn't seem to realize they were "dressing, nourishing, sheltering, and quenching" are shocked to learn they *did*. Like Matthew's parable, liturgical indeterminacy ruptures our "complacent equilibriums"[92] and forces us to deal with radical Otherness (the *Other* who is God, *others* who are human). To do so means forgetting the imperious, autonomous self so that "the wound of an Otherness . . . always beyond our grasp" may leave on us "its trace in the humble call of the neighbor."[93] In a word, God's hiddenness is not merely a consequence of "godless relativism, humanism, materialism, and modernity" (the usual suspects); it is a fundamental fact of Christian experience. Always, Christian theology is staurology, a science of the cross, "the study of a God whose divinity is effaced in a humanity crushed *to the point of* requiring of us this body of world and humanity without which God cannot come among us in truth."[94]

To celebrate liturgy on the blissful assumption that we *know* the God we worship is thus a dreadful mistake. For one thing, liturgy (*opus Dei*) is less "our work for God" than God's work for us. Moreover, God's coming among us always passes through the face of the other and through the banality of the humblest gestures: dress, nourish, shelter, quench. Such considerations should give us pause, yet, as American novelist and poet Annie Dillard writes, Chris-

---

91. Ibid., 123.

92. Ibid.

93. Chauvet, *Symbol and Sacrament*, 75. Emmanuel Levinas's "liturgy of the neighbor" is based on precisely such an understanding about the inescapable demands of Otherness. Ordinarily, "the I dominates the Other," and hence "total self-knowledge is total immanence and sovereignty." But the presence of the Other (and here Levinas means the *human* other) calls the "I" into question. "Before the Other [the human other], the I is infinitely responsible. The Other is the poor and destitute one, and nothing which concerns this Stranger can leave the I indifferent." See E. Levinas, "Transcendence and Height," in *Emmanuel Levinas: Basic Philosophical Writings*, ed. Adriaan Peperzak, Simon Critechley, and Robert Bernasconi (Bloomington: Indiana University Press, 1996), 18. Here, Levinas (like other postmodern philosophers) opposes the classical metaphysical notion of Being ("impersonal, anonymous, violent reducer of otherness to the totality of the same") by invoking the Other ("pure eruption and rupture bursting, through the 'Face,' the unifying pretensions and the ultimately totalitarian essence of [traditional Greek philosophy's] *logos*." See Chauvet, *Symbol and Sacrament*, 46.

94. Chauvet, *Symbol and Sacrament*, 75.

tian worshipers often "come at God with an unwarranted air of professionalism, with authority and pomp, as though they knew what they were doing."
Confident in their long and hallowed traditions of public worship, commu-
nicants in such churches often seem to "saunter through the liturgy like
Mohawks along a strand of scaffolding who have long since forgotten their
danger. If God were to blast such a service to bits, the congregation would be,
I believe, genuinely shocked."[95]

The Call to Conversion

To forget the liturgy's danger is to resist or ignore its call to conversion. It is
entirely possible, as Anglican theologian Urban Holmes noted a quarter-
century ago, for religious belief to use its loud affirmations of orthodoxy in
order to insulate itself from the God who "lies sleeping in the lap of the
world," who lives "hidden in the darkness."[96] Nor is liturgy immune from this
temptation. When worship no longer hears the rupturing Word of the cross,
when it forgets that Christian doxology and doctrine are *both* staurology (a
"science of the cross"), when it closes its eyes to the God whose divinity is
effaced in a crushed humanity, it may wind up serving ideology rather than
"the dark mystery to which liturgical symbols would point."[97] Those who fear
that if liturgy "pays too much attention" to the human it will forget the divine
should remember that "*God is nowhere more divine than in the humanity—the
sub-humanity—of the Crucified.*"[98] Whether we place ourselves on the left
wing or the right wing of an increasingly polarized Christianity, we err if we
approach the liturgy expecting to have our lives *a*ffirmed and our ideas *con*-
firmed. We should not underestimate the sovereign "I's" eagerness to erase
the Other, to forget that in the presence of this Other, I am *responsible.*
Emmanuel Levinas put the point perfectly: "The Other [here, the *human*
Other] is the poor and destitute one, and nothing which concerns this
Stranger can leave the I indifferent."[99] In a nutshell, no one gets into heaven
without a letter of recommendation from the poor.
    "Good liturgy," Urban Holmes wrote, "borders on the vulgar . . . leads us
to the edge of chaos, and out of that experience will come a theology different from any previous theology." Commenting on Holmes's point in his clas-

---

95. Annie Dillard, *Holy the Firm* (1977; paperback, New York: Bantam Books, 1979), 60.
96. Urban T. Holmes, "Theology and Religious Renewal," *Anglican Theological Review* 62, no. 1 (1980): 18.
97. Ibid., 19.
98. Chauvet, *Symbol and Sacrament*, 493.
99. See n. 93 above for full reference to this citation from Levinas.

sic study *On Liturgical Theology*, Aidan Kavanagh observes that the immediate post-traumatic result of our brush with chaos is "deep change in the very lives of those who participate in the liturgical act."[100] Indeed, the history of Christian worship is less the chronicle of its ritual texts and forms than the cumulative impact of changed lives on all participants. Take that away, and one has ideologically driven ritualism rather than worship of a God whose glory is seen in the disfigured body on the cross, a "laughable caricature of a body, a body so wasted, so liquefied, so melted away that it is already treated as dead by those who divide his clothing."[101] That is why Kavanagh insists that liturgies "grow" only when the assembly is "brought regularly to the brink of chaos in the presence of the living God," for it is precisely *change—* radical *adjustment* in living—that makes liturgy "theological." Such change is a process "partly conscious and partly unconscious . . . long term and dialectical," its agents "more likely to be charwomen and shopkeepers than pontiffs and professors."[102]

We cannot, in other words, worship God without consenting to God's command that we "*recognize others as like us in their very otherness.*"[103] The price of such consent, writes Louis-Marie Chauvet, is very high indeed; it is "nothing less than the choice of a freedom that is responsible for the others . . . an inescapable responsibility from which no others . . . can relieve me."[104] Liturgies "grow"; they have "meaningful histories," precisely (and only) to the degree that they chronicle the unfolding of conversion in a real, live, quivering community. Kavanagh is quite right to argue that

> the liturgical assembly's stance in faith is vertiginous, on the edge of chaos. Only grace and favor enable it to stand there; only grace and promise brought it there; only grace and a rigorous divine charity permit the assembly . . . to come away whole from such an encounter, and even then it is with wounds which are as deep as they are salutary.[105]

We leave the liturgy limping and sore from wrestling with the Stranger (see Gen 32:23-33). For we cannot acknowledge God's victory in Jesus' cross, we cannot acknowledge the crucified One as "the Other who is like the Father," without "ourselves being called into question."[106] In liturgy, as in life, our confession of God's glory

---

100. Kavanagh, *On Liturgical Theology*, 73.
101. Chauvet, *Symbol and Sacrament*, 501, 500.
102. Kavanagh, *On Liturgical Theology*, 74-75.
103. Chauvet, *Symbol and Sacrament*, 506.
104. Ibid.
105. Kavanagh, *On Liturgical Theology*, 75.
106. Chauvet, *Symbol and Sacrament*, 506, 501.

goes hand in hand with the unveiling of our own sin. . . . How can we . . . speak of God on the basis of the cross without being ourselves implicated down to the very marrow of our desire? A reversal of desire is demanded here, a reversal that would not only confess our own injustice in the very place we arrogated to ourselves the authority . . . to condemn the Just One, but also simultaneously confess a God completely Other than our infantile desire's God of Marvels.[107]

Liturgy leads us to the brink of chaos in order to tutor our desire, to reverse its triumphalism and megalomania.

CONCLUSION

This chapter has explored the relation between ritual's roots and the postmodern condition that shapes Western industrialized cultures and deeply influences our self-understanding, our experience of others and world, our faith, our religious practice, and especially our connection to liturgical word and worship. When all is said and done, we can speak about a *theology* of liturgy not because doxology and doctrine are old allies that feed off each other's triumphs, but because, as I have argued throughout this chapter, worship is "applied rhizomatics." Its indeterminacy opens *ethical* space (the space of *lex agendi*) that requires us to deal with radical Otherness (the *Other* who is God, *others* who are human) and allows us to verify the legitimacy of the church's public worship only through the "liturgy of the neighbor," only by passing through the face of the Other. Thus I have insisted that liturgy's mazelike, connective, crabgrass condition resembles music more than textbook, syllabus, or doctrinal definition.

Moreover, making use of the work of Deleuze and Guattari, I have suggested that a change of image—of optic—changes our perception, experience, and interpretation of the world. Ritual may thus be thought of "rhizomally," as a technology for "reading" the world. For, as our discussion of the connections between "rule of prayer, rule of faith, and rule of life" revealed, ritual does not abandon the world, but rearranges it as "rehearsal" for God's kingdom, as practice for that Supper of the Lamb where God and humankind meet at table. For Christians, the liturgy of the church can be verified only in the liturgy of the neighbor. But to say this is to confess that a celebrating community must open its doors to others, to *the* Other, who calls us by name. As theologians like Louis-Marie Chauvet remind us, the "name"

---

107. Ibid., 501 (slightly altered).

we are called is not self-assigned. At liturgy, we do not invent or assert our
own identity; we *receive* it. That is why Christian worship begins only after
all participants agree to act as impersonators, traveling to a "strange land"
under assumed identities, on another's passport: "In the name of the Father,
and of the Son, and of the Holy Spirit."[108] The liturgy's first words do not
announce who *we* are, but inscribe us in Another.

There is thus a kind of ventriloquism at work in ritual; *our* mouths open,
but Another speaks. Here, too, ritual resembles music. Both are audible arts
that make inaudible gestures. In his illuminating essay "Music, Music," postmodern philosopher Jean-François Lyotard notes that music's enigma lies not
in what it says but in what it lets us hear beyond the audible. Music is partu-
rition—it *labors* giving birth, struggling to open "a passageway through which
something can happen that has not yet happened, a child, one's past, . . . a
musical phrase." The musician's task is to open the passage. For ultimately,
music's source isn't a sound—an engine's roar, or breath passing through an
ebony tube, or a column of air vibrating in a lead pipe—but a "gesture" made
before and beyond sound, a language beneath and beyond words.[109] Is it T. S.
Eliot's "Music heard so deeply / That it is not heard at all, but you are the
music / While the music lasts"?[110]

Perhaps, then, music's source—and ritual's—is that inaudible Other whose
"word" is the discourse of the body, with what Pablo Neruda called its
"impure speech," its vigils and wrinkles and dreams. For the body is how we
listen most deeply to the world—it is, indeed, the "eye" through which we
read the world. Perhaps, as Pascal Quignard suggests, the ultimate, inaudible
source of both music and ritual may be *lamentation*, that primal cry of terror
we utter whenever we are threatened by nullity and loss—the cry with which
we first greet the world.[111] Ours is, after all, a species deeply and inescapably
afraid, haunted by fears carried on our breath, carved on bone and body.
Could it be that music and ritual both arise from a fear that borders awe?
Does not music often begin as a rattling, a drumming, a beating, a moaning?
Perhaps beyond these acoustic banalities lies lamentation, a deep sadness, a
cry of loss and abandonment, the ruptured Word of the Crucified: *Eli, Eli,
lema sabachtani?*

Music and ritual do not express this dereliction directly, yet it is always
heard, an ever-present "mute" within our music, sorrow's shadow in the bright

---

108. Pickstock, *After Writing,* 181, 184.
109. Jean-Francois Lyotard, "Music, Music," in *Postmodern Fables,* trans. Georges van den Abbeele
(Minneapolis: University of Minnesota Press, 1997), 218, 221.
110. T. S. Eliot, "The Dry Salvages," section V, in *Four Quartets* (New York: Harcourt Brace
Jovanovich, 1971), 44.
111. See Lyotard, "Music, Music," 221-26, for an extended quotation from Quignard's work.

joy of Mozart. And there is something more. Beyond the loss and lamentation that breathe in all our music and ritual, there lives *affect*, the ability not merely to have emotions but to *feel* them. Affection, as Aristotle noted, is what animals *do*. If lamentation is our music's mute source, affection is what propels us forward. As Lyotard writes, "Music labors to give birth to what is audible in the inaudible breath. It strives to put it into phrases. . . . Every sonorous phrase, even the simplest, announces that there will be another phrase, that it is not yet over. . . . Every phrase asks to be honored by [another] . . . phrase. [So] [t]he phrase goes out toward you and asks you for a phrase"— a *response*, not an "answer" but a moving forward. And what happens? "A community is born, polyphonic even in plainsong, enchanted by sonorous apparitions even within the war of counterpoint. The community forgets the anonymous horde moaning with the terror of [loss, extinction]. [Still,] [t]he community . . . does not efface the horde."[112]

All music—and all ritual—are perhaps cries against extinction, against the body's bondage, the ending of the waltz, the fading of the rose, the dying of the light. Despite all our bravado, our claims of autonomy and control, our confidence in the mutuality of doctrine and doxology, ritual makes *us* well before we make it. That is why learning to *do* liturgy requires not knowledge of ritual but conversion, deep change met at the brink of chaos. Such learning, as Chauvet suggests,

> amounts to the slow work of apprenticeship in the art of "un-mastery," a permanent work of *mourning* where, *free of resentment,* a "serene" consent to the "*presence of the absence*" takes place within us little by little. In gospel terms, this is a work of conversion to the presence of the absence of a God who "crosses himself out" in the crushed humanity of this crucified One whom humans have reduced to less than nothing, and yet where, in a paradoxical light, faith confesses the glory of God.[113]

QUESTIONS FOR REFLECTION

1. What images would you use to describe the culture(s) in which you live? What images best describe your experience of "church"? In what ways are these images different? similar? compatible? reconcilable? irreconcilable?
2. How does your experience of contemporary information technology impact your experience of the world? of relations with others? of God's Word? of ritual action and liturgical prayer?

---

112. Ibid., 229.
113. Chauvet, *Symbol and Sacrament*, 74.

3. This chapter listed five ways that information technology is presently reshaping culture and church (see pp. 26-30 above). What would you add to or subtract from that list?

4. A central theme of this chapter is that Christian liturgy can be "verified" only through the "liturgy of the neighbor." How would you describe the relation between liturgy ("the rule of prayer"), belief ("the rule of faith"), and ethical action ("the rule of life")?

5. Do you regularly (or ever) experience sacramental liturgy as a "call to conversion"? Why or why not?

SUGGESTIONS FOR FURTHER READING

Best, Steven, and Douglas Kellner. *Postmodern Theory: Critical Interrogations.* New York: Guilford Press, 1991. The authors provide a clear and critical guide to the significance of thinkers such as Deleuze and Guattari, while pointing out similarities to and differences from the theories of other important French thinkers such as Michel Foucault and Jacques Derrida.

Chauvet, Louis-Marie. *The Sacraments: The Word of God at the Mercy of the Body.* Collegeville, Minn.: Liturgical Press/A Pueblo Book, 2001. A good guide to understanding liturgical prayer and sacramental worship as postmodern theology understands them.

Hart, Kevin. *Postmodernism: A Beginner's Guide.* Oxford: Oneworld, 2004. A clear and excellent guide to postmodern thought, especially as it shapes Christian philosophy and theology.

Mitchell, Nathan D. *Liturgy and the Social Sciences.* American Essays in Liturgy. Collegeville, Minn.: Liturgical Press, 1999. A brief study that examines and assesses the many ways research in the social sciences (e.g., sociology, anthropology, cultural studies) has impacted thinking about ritual and liturgical prayer since Vatican Council II (1962-65).

Pecklers, Keith, ed. *Liturgy in a Post-Modern World.* New York: Continuum, 2003. A collection of papers from a symposium held in Rome in 2002; each paper addresses a specific aspect of liturgical prayer and celebration.

2

Ritual's Roles and Risks

How Symbols Mean

THE FIRST CHAPTER OFFERED a preliminary sketch of ritual's roots—its sources in culture, technology, and Christian tradition. We explored not only the impact of information technology on the relation between Word and world, but also postmodern interpretations of human existence from both philosophical (e.g., Gilles Deleuze and Félix Guattari) and theological (Louis-Marie Chauvet, Stanislas Breton) perspectives. Christian liturgies, we saw, are not linear, sequential, logical structures; they have "crabgrass-like (rhizomal)" characteristics similar to those of musical scores (tablature), which can be realized only through the risks and indeterminacies of performance.

In this chapter, our challenge is to reimagine the roles and risks ritual brings to human life and behavior. I say "reimagine," because, until rather recently, many persons working in the field of liturgical studies had assumed that the meanings and definitions of ritual were more or less "settled." As I noted in my study *Liturgy and the Social Sciences*, a kind of "orthodox consensus" about what and how ritual "means" had emerged by the 1970s and early 1980s. That consensus held that "ritual is essentially a way to regulate social life; to shape personal and corporate identity; to review and renew values; to express and transmit meaning in symbolic word and act; to preserve tradition; and to insure cultural cohesion" and to guarantee social continuity. This prevailing, "orthodox consensus" further assumed that rituals are not "utilitarian," but characteristically symbolic in structure, as well as "ambiguous, septic, and multiple" in meaning. They are, in short, nonverbal deeds, not texts—performances "done by heart, without intrusive explanation or commentary," and they are normative for participants' belief (doctrine) and behavior (ethics).[1]

While many of these characteristics can still be affirmed, the study of

---

1. Nathan D. Mitchell, *Liturgy and the Social Sciences* (American Essays in Liturgy; Collegeville, Minn.: Liturgical Press, 1999), 25-26.

human ritual by anthropologists, sociologists, and social historians has opened up new perspectives over the past quarter-century.[2] We in the West have slowly begun to learn what other cultures—especially those of Asia—have to tell us about ritual, ritual symbols, and ritual spaces. In Buddhism, for example, after the Buddha's death, or "final *nirvana*,"[3] disciples

> cremated his body, distributed his ashes as relics, and enshrined them in funerary mounds, or *stupas*. The veneration of these remains provided the model for the tradition of Buddhist worship, which came to be directed not only at relics but also at other objects, images, and sites sanctified through their association with events in the Buddha's life. In Buddhist tradition, these constitute the Buddha's "Form Body," while his teaching is known as his "Dharma Body." In the two types of "body" (often understood differently in different parts of the Buddhist world), the Buddha continues to be a presence in the wider Buddhist community.[4]

Other burial places—those connected with bodhisattvas,[5] for example—also became pilgrimage sites. *The Journey to the West*, a sixteenth-century novel that narrates the travel experiences of Xuanzang, a Chinese monk, shows "the connection between the *bodhisattva* Guanyin and the pilgrimage site at Mount Putuo, an island off the coast of southern China."[6] In the novel, Guanyin is celebrated for her serene beauty, wisdom, and compassion:

> With brows of new moon shape
> And eyes like two bright stars,
> Her jade-like face beams natural joy,
>
> . . . .
>
> She redeems the multitude;
> She has great compassion;
> Thus she rules on T'ai Mountain
> And lives in the South Sea.
> She saves the good, searching for their voices,
> Ever heedful and solicitous,

---

2. I summarize several of these newer perspectives in *Liturgy and the Social Sciences*, 63-93.

3. The Sanskrit word *nirvana* literally means "extinction," but as the term is ordinarily used in Buddhism, it signifies a state of absolute bliss or felicity, characterized by freedom from passion, desire, and suffering.

4. Malcolm David Eckel, "Buddhism," in *Eastern Religions: Hinduism, Buddhism, Taoism, Confucianism, Shinto,* ed. Michael D. Coogan (New York: Oxford University Press, 2005), 120-21.

5. In Buddhism, a bodhisattva is one who has attained a degree of enlightenment that qualifies for Buddhahood, but who declines out of compassion for others. A bodhisattva may thus be regarded as a "future Buddha."

6. Eckel, "Buddhism," 181.

Ever wise and efficacious,
Her orchid heart delights in great bamboos;
Her chaste nature loves the wisteria.[7]

Indeed, one of the earliest legends connected with the foundation of Mount Putuo as a Buddhist shrine tells of Egaku, a Japanese monk who was sailing home, accompanied by an image of Guanyin. His ship ran aground, and after praying to the bodhisattva, he found safety in a cave near shore, where the grateful monk built a shrine for Guanyin, "who refused to leave."[8]

This story and its related rituals of pilgrimage help us understand the pervasive human impulse to link sacred places of worship with important burial sites. Christians from earliest times, for example, venerated the spot where Jesus' body was interred after his crucifixion. Indeed, it was when the spice-bearing women went to the tomb to anoint Jesus' body "very early on the first day of the week" that they were met by a radiant "young man" who told them the startling news, "You seek Jesus of Nazareth, the crucified; he has been raised, he is not here" (Mark 16:2, 5-6). In the centuries that followed, Christian churches were often built at or near the tombs of the martyrs, the witnesses who gave their lives after the example of Jesus, "the Faithful Witness, the Firstborn of the dead" (Rev 1:5).

Our second chapter, then, will begin with a new look at ritual's roles as seen through the eyes of a Western thinker (Roland Barthes) whose encounter with Zen led him to suggest that ritual activity may have less to do with the *accumulation* of meaning than with its banishment and *loss*. Ritual, in other words, may focus less on the "social management of meaning" than on the emptiness that opens participants to radically new revelations, to fresh meetings with Mystery. This, surely, was the experience of those women who gathered at Jesus' tomb on the first Easter (see the preceding paragraph). To embrace ritual as "loss" is, of course, a risky enterprise. So our chapter will discuss not only ritual's roles, but its risks as well.

RITUAL'S ROLES

Often today it is said that we live in a culture that resists ritual, that is anti-ritualistic, that regards ritual behavior as neurotic or meaningless. To my way of thinking, this is precisely the wrong analysis. Our problem is not that we

---

7. The text is taken from *The Journey to the West*, trans. Anthony C. Yu (4 vols.; Chicago: University of Chicago Press, 1977), 1:185.
8. Eckel, "Buddhism," 181.

expect too little of ritual, but that we expect too much of it. We seek to inflate its significance.

One of the most insightful and entertaining interpretations of ritualized human behavior appears in Roland Barthes's brief book *Empire of Signs*. A careless reader might assume that the goal of Barthes's study was ethnographic—to write a succinct "ritual history" of Japanese life, from its cuisine to its codes of public politeness. But nothing could be further from the truth. Although the word "Japan" appears on virtually every page of *Empire of Signs*, the reference cannot be taken too literally. In his book, Barthes used familiar features of *real* Japanese life (chopsticks, flower arranging) in order to think about *something else*—namely, the way human persons seek significance and meaning through ritual means. "What is presented here," writes Barthes, "does not appertain . . . to art, to Japanese urbanism, to Japanese cooking," even though all these matters come in for comment. In fact, he suggests, no Westerner can write a book "about" Japan, for at least two reasons. First, our ignorance of Asia is so profound that writing about any of its peoples or cultures will merely "manifest the density of our narcissism" and result in a book about ourselves.[9] Second, a Western book "about" Japan will inevitably seek to assign "meanings" to its symbols, art, architecture, rituals, landscapes, urban environments, and so on. So intense is our Western preoccupation with "what *things* mean," that we bloat meanings as much as we overfeed pets. And, writes critic Edmund White, it was precisely Barthes's "repulsion for the 'overfed' meanings . . . the 'diseased' signs of our petit-bourgeois culture with its advertising, glossy theatrical spectacles, agony columns and child prodigies" that prompted him to write *Empire of Signs* in the first place.[10]

One might say, then, that Barthes's purpose was not to write "about" Japan, but simply to write Japan—or, better, to let a fictive Japan write us, subverting our "overfed" pop-culture images. Echoing Derrida's dictum that "the meaning of meaning is infinite implication"[11] rather than a fixed, immovable center, Barthes suggests that *writing*—the method we ordinarily use for "getting at" or "unpacking" complex meanings—has, in fact, the opposite purpose. Writing doesn't feed or accumulate meaning; on the contrary, it deflates and empties language:

> Writing is, in its way, a *satori: satori* [the experience of enlightenment] . . . is a more or less powerful . . . seism which causes knowledge, or the sub-

9. Roland Barthes, *Empire of Signs*, trans. Richard Howard (New York: Hill & Wang, 1982), 4.

10. Edmund White, review of Roland Barthes's *Empire of Signs* and *A Barthes Reader* (edited by Susan Sontag), in *The New York Times*, September 12, 1982, Sunday, Late City Final Edition, section 7, page 1, column 2; Book Review Desk.

11. See above, chapter 1, "The Postmodern Condition."

ject, to vacillate: it creates *an emptiness of language.* And it is also an emptiness of language which constitutes writing; it is from this emptiness that
derive the features with which Zen, in the exemption from all meaning,
writes gardens, gestures, houses, flower arrangements, faces, violence.[12]

Thus, as White notes, *Empire of Signs* "might more properly be called "The
Empire of *Empty* Signs." In this, Barthes was not trying to be cleverly obscu-
rantist or nihilistic. For him, "emptiness" is not an evacuation but a tear, an
almost imperceptible slit, a slender, luminous thread, a sudden opening, a
"flash of light." The purpose of such emptiness is not to arouse panic or cause
us to look for fatter, "more meaningful" symbols elsewhere, but to focus our
attention on the tear, the "fissure" that splits *every* symbol, that belongs to the
very definition of symbols.[13] Symbols crack; that is ultimately the source of
their power. So what Barthes is resisting in *Empire of Signs* is the reduction
of symbols to "meanings," for when that happens, symbols become dead
coals, producing neither light nor warmth. As White notes, Barthes often
said,

> "A named meaning is a dead meaning." . . . One might say that Barthes,
> contradicting Aristotelian Nature, abhorred everything that wasn't a vac-
> uum. He was far too elegant and tentative . . . to feel entirely at home in
> the West with its looming unmistakable pregnancies of meaning. To me
> Barthes has always been unexpectedly funny, never more so than in the
> superficially sober and meticulous "S/Z," his line-by-line analysis of a
> short story by Balzac. Barthes decodes and deflates the pretensions to
> meaning present everywhere in Balzac's "realistic" text, which he ends up
> by treating as a sort of grand computer stocked with clichés and chatter-
> ing away to itself. Behind this chatter, this cultural yammering, Barthes
> detects a terrible anxiety in Western society, an unarticulated fear that lan-
> guage itself means nothing, that it is merely an automaton's gesture flag-
> ging down the void.[14]

In *Empire of Signs*, therefore, Barthes puts his finger directly on an anxiety
that afflicts not only Western cultures generally but Western religions specifically. Barthes did not pretend, of course, to be a cultural diagnostician, and
he would surely have denied any direct connection between his thought about
the "emptiness" of signs and the symbol-strewn stories and deeds that shape
the ritual repertoires of Christian communities. Nor does his curiosity about

---

12. Barthes, *Empire of Signs*, 4.
13. Ibid., 83, 4. Recall that the original image of the word "symbol," in its Greek roots, is a coin
whose two halves must be brought together (*synballein*).
14. White, review of Roland Barthes's *Empire of Signs*, p. 1, col. 2.

Zen and its experience of *satori* as "*loss* of meaning" signify a "religious interest," as Westerners would understand that phrase, even though he sometimes
mentions analogies with Western mysticism.[15] Barthes' point is that symbols
(like *satori* itself) are important not for what they say but for what they *don't*
say, for their "loss," their "emptiness." Symbols do not *expand* language (with
its endless system of referents); they suspend it, bring it to a screeching halt.
Like *satori*'s silent enlightenment, symbols offer "breathing room"; they open
up space, create a desert emptied of meanings and hence fertile for the revelation of the genuinely *new* and *different*, the *unexpected*, the completely *other*.
As we will see, this notion of symbol as empty space that allows "the new . . .
the unexpected . . . the other" to appear is vital for understanding how rituals
yield meanings.

What Do Slot Machines, Flowers, Puppets, Chopsticks, and Haiku Have in Common?

Barthes's playful approach to symbols and their "emptiness" did not, then, signify a cynical lack of concern for the ethical or spiritual conditions of modern life. On the contrary, he was sharply critical of the Western compulsion
to replace transcendence with cults of personality and to displace the *real*
with "semantic prattle . . . marked by the excessive fear of failing to communicate meaning."[16] *Empire of Signs* is, in fact, Barthes's antidote to our neurotic habit of finding meanings where there are none or putting them where
they don't belong. Paradoxically, our Western impulse to overfeed symbols, to
load them with stacks of meaning they cannot sustain, makes us miss their
real power to reveal and disclose the new, the unexpected, the *other*. Symbols
(and the rites that deploy them) are indeed thick and layered, polyvalent and
multiple in their meanings. But, as I will argue throughout this book, these
characteristics flow not from a symbol's fullness but from its *emptiness*. Five
examples drawn from Barthes's work will help us see why the "emptiness" of
ritual symbols is essential to their capacity for signification.

   In a brief chapter on the slot machine (*pachinko*), Barthes writes that its
Western version

   sustains a symbolism of penetration: the point is to possess, by a well-
   placed thrust, the pinup girl who, all lit up on the panel of the machine,

---

15. Barthes, *Empire of Signs*, 74. Barthes notes, for instance, that Zen appears to be "an enormous
praxis destined *to halt language*"—to jam those constantly yammering radio signals that surround us,
and "to empty out . . . stupefy . . . dry up the soul's incoercible babble."
   16. Roland Barthes, *S/Z*, trans. Richard Miller (New York: Hill & Wang, 1974), 79.

allures and waits. In pachinko, no sex (in Japan—in that country I am call-ing Japan—sexuality is in sex, not elsewhere; in the United States, it is the contrary; sex is everywhere, except in sexuality).[17]

Just as pachinko has to do with gaming skill, not "symbolism," so flower arranging (*ikebana*) is *gesture*, rather than the rigorous construction of a "meaningful" product. What *ikebana* offers is not artistic "symbol" or "state-ment" but simply "the circulation of air, of which flowers, leaves, branches . . . are only the walls, the corridors."[18] In this way, *ikebana* confronts us once more with Zen's unsettling "emptiness." The point of flower arranging (if it has to have a point) is not to create a symbolic cosmos of meanings and ref-erents but to let the hand move naturally through space, tracing a trajectory from blossom to branch, to leaf, to stem. The "naturalness" of flower arrang-ing arises from its *spareness*. Only when cut and arranged—only, in other words, when their utter finitude and mortality are plain for all to see—do flowers achieve "naturalness," for it is precisely the nature of vegetation to wither, to die. In contrast, the West seems to believe that nature is undying profligacy, profusion. Consider, for instance, the conventions of seventeenth-century Dutch still-life painting, with its masses of flowers and fruit spilling beyond the picture's plane. Not so in *ikebana*; there, all is spareness and econ-omy of gesture.

Dennis Hirota draws attention to the historic roots of Zen aesthetics, which shape not only the practice of *ikebana* but also the arts of haiku and tea ceremony (*chanoyu*).[19] According to the fifteenth-century Buddhist mas-ter Shinkei (1406-1475), whose thought still influences Zen aesthetics, beauty manifests itself only

> when the glittering surface of the world has lost all appeal and when per-sons have authentically awakened to their finitude. At that point, where deep-seated attachments to an imagined self fall away, the ordinary things of the natural world disclose a beauty pervaded by a profound sense of pathos and mystery. This beauty [Shinkei] expressed as "withered" (*kare*), "chill" (*hie*), and "meager" or "gaunt" (*yase*).[20]

For Shinkei, the withered, the chill, and the lean (gaunt, meager) are not principles of ascetic denial but images "rooted in Buddhist awakening to real-ity."[21] They resist the aggrandizing self, with its noisy plans and assertions, its

---

17. Barthes, *Empire of Signs*, 28-29.
18. Ibid., 44.
19. Dennis Hirota, *Wind in the Pines: Classic Writings of the Way of Tea as a Buddhist Path* (Fre-mont, Calif.: Asian Humanities Press, 1995), 40.
20. Ibid.
21. Ibid., 41. As Hirota notes, "chill" is not the quality of being cold but is rather "spareness and solitude" (p. 43). This is why Shinkei thought of ice and winter as beautiful. "Nothing is more exquis-

grandiosity, its specious claims to meaning and truth, and they point to a sense of the world "in which expectations of the future and selfish grasping after life have fallen away."[22] Zen seeks to let the world speak for itself—to reveal its own nature, on its own terms, in its own way. Commenting on the way *ikebana* makes use of withered, chill, and lean principles, the modern Japanese philosopher Nishitani Keiji (1900-1990) observes that "flowers in the field 'pollinate in order to procreate,'" and they thereby express the "natural will or desire of life."[23] Hirota explains that planted in gardens or meadows, flowers "put down roots in a struggle to survive; they seek to 'deny time' and conceal their fundamental rootlessness." However, flowers *cut* and *arranged* can finally point to their true nature:

> To be shifted from the world of life into the world of death is, for the flower, a kind of transcendence. The flower made to stand upon death has been cut off from the constructs of time that occur in life, and it is just as though it stands in the timeless present; its evanescent existence of several days becomes a momentary point in which there is no arising or perishing. ... [Hence] the flowers exist with solemnity, floating in emptiness, just as though they have emerged from nothingness.[24]

Paradoxically, it is flowers grown in fields and gardens that occupy unnatural, time-denying habitats; only the "artificiality" of arrangement finally lets them *be* what they *are*. They abandon desire, with its pretense of an infinite deferral of time, and open up a world "divested of causality and instrumentality."[25] Chilled, lean, and withered, they are at last "*in* the world but not *of* it."

In a similar vein, the famous *Bunraku* puppet theater resists the conventions we in the West ordinarily attribute to effective drama. It "is superb because of its reserve, its avoidance of the hysteria of the Western theater, its delegation of 'the whole cuisine of emotion' to the speaker who sits to one side of the stage."[26] Western theater embellishes the human voice, makes it a trumpeting mouthpiece for meanings, the symbol of our uniqueness (and implied indispensability) on the planet. In contrast, *Bunraku limits the voice*:

> Without being eliminated (which would be a way of censuring it, i.e., of designating its importance), the voice is thus set aside. ... *Bunraku* gives

---

ite than ice," he wrote. "The stubbled fields of early morning, with needles of ice formed where sleet has glazed the cypress bark on the roof, or the dew and hoarfrost frozen upon the withered grasses and trees of the meadow—what is there to match this loveliness, this beauty?" (cited in Hirota, 43). Spareness and solitude lead to an intense awareness of actuality, akin perhaps to what the Victorian Jesuit poet Gerard Manley Hopkins called "inscape," the radical "suchness" of things.

22. Hirota, *Wind in the Pines,* 49.
23. Text cited in Hirota, *Wind in the Pines,* 50.
24. Ibid.
25. Ibid.
26. White, review of Roland Barthes's *Empire of Signs,* p. 1., col. 2.

the voice a counterpoise . . . a countermove: that of gesture. . . . In our theatrical art, the actor pretends to act, but his actions are never anything but
gestures: on stage, nothing but theater, yet a theater ashamed of itself.
Bunraku . . . separates action from gesture; it shows the gesture, lets the
action be seen, exhibits simultaneously the art and the labor, reserving for
each its own writing. The voice . . . is accompanied by a vast volume of
silence, in which are inscribed, with all the more finesse, other features,
other writings. . . . Language . . . [is] collected to one side of the acting, all
the importunate substances of Western theater are dissolved: emotion no
longer floods, no longer submerges, but becomes a reading, the stereotypes
disappear . . . the spectacle collapsing into originality.[27]

In *Bunraku* the voice embodies silence rather than speech, just as in *ikebana*
flowers gesture spareness and solitude rather than fertility.

Finally, consider the experience of a meal in the "fictive Japan" of Barthes's
Empire of Signs. There, dinner begins as a "motionless tableau," a space for *seeing* that gradually yields to a space for *doing* (choosing, cooking, eating). One
begins the meal in a picture frame, where objects used in dining are displayed
against a dark background: "bowls, boxes, saucers, chopsticks, tiny piles of
food, a little gray ginger, a few shreds of orange vegetable, a background of
brown sauce." Slowly, the frame is broken, and the "tableau at the start
becomes a workbench or chessboard, the space . . . of *praxis* or play . . . [in]
which you are . . . taking up here a pinch of vegetables, there of rice, and over
there of condiment, here a sip of soup, according to a free alternation." A
space for seeing becomes a space for doing. The event is ritually formal, but
not scripted; there is order without protocol. As Barthes comments, "you
yourself make what it is you eat; the dish is no longer a reified product" whose
preparation occurs in advance, in secret, apart from us (as in a Western-style
restaurant).[28]

This contrast is heightened when one considers that in the "Japanese"
meal, everything is *small*. Writes Barthes:

Occidental food, heaped up, dignified, swollen to the majestic, linked to a
certain operation of prestige, always tends toward the heavy, the grand, the
abundant, the copious; the Oriental follows the converse movement, and
tends toward the infinitesimal: the cucumber's future is not its accumulation or its thickening, but its division, its . . . dispersal.[29]

---

27. Barthes, *Empire of Signs*, 49, 54.
28. Ibid., 11, 12.
29. Ibid., 15.

Not only is Western food heaped up and "swollen to the majestic," but its eating requires sharp, pronged cutlery—knives, forks—which are easily confused with weapons. Small wonder that at a Western meal, diners are always in danger of becoming dinner. It is difficult to divorce knives and forks from actions that are violent, destructive, disfiguring. But blunt chopsticks are another matter. Their purpose is not only utilitarian (to carry food to the point); as Barthes points out, they are also "deictic." A chopstick "*points* to the food, *designates* the fragment, *brings into existence by the very gesture of choice.*" Because they are used not merely to *eat* but to point and *choose*, chopsticks introduce an element of caprice into the framed formality of a meal. Each diner may choose—freely, even indolently—without disrupting the ritualized social structure of the event. Freedom coexists comfortably with formality. Besides "pointing" and "choosing," chopsticks allow diners to divide food nonviolently, by discovering its natural fissures. Chopsticks do not mutilate, cut, or pierce; they unravel, gently probe and prod, letting the food find its own way to divide itself.[30]

In Barthes's fictive Japan, therefore, items as diverse as slot machines, flowers, puppets, food, and chopsticks are not fat, bloated into self-importance or "swollen to the majestic"; rather, they are characterized by "leanness," "absence," and "emptiness." In this, they resemble the quintessential Zen poetry form, haiku. But here too caution is needed. To us in the West, haiku's attraction lies in its ability to condense deep meaning in concise form. We are inclined to think of haiku as a genial, indulgent host who "lets you make yourself at home with all your preferences, your values, your symbols intact." We thus imagine haiku whispering to us: "You are entitled . . . to be trivial, short, ordinary; enclose what you see, what you feel, in a slender horizon of words, and you will be interesting; you . . . are entitled to establish your own notability; your sentence, whatever it may be, will enunciate a moral, will liberate a symbol, you will be profound."[31]

In fact, of course, haiku is the antithesis of Western self-indulgence, of the self's covetousness for meaning, profundity, and notability. Far from blessing our home-grown "preferences, values and symbols," haiku (like the famous koans of Zen monastic training) incinerates them. It renounces the metaphor, symbolism, and commentary that usually accompany poetry writing in the West. Its purpose, as Barthes writes, "is to suspend language, not to provoke it."[32] Haiku distances itself from commentary, from what George

30. Ibid., 16 (emphasis added), 17-18.
31. Ibid., 69, 70.
32. Ibid., 72.

Steiner calls "the parasitic secondary."[33] As Basho (1644-1649) wrote in one
of his travel notebooks:

> How admirable he is
> Who does not think "Life is ephemeral"
> when he sees a flash of lightning.[34]

Basho knew how *not* to give sermons. For haiku does not homilize; it simply
"lets" and "lets be," while the West "moistens everything with meaning, like
an authoritarian religion which imposes baptism on entire peoples" because it
assumes that the purpose of language is to make "converts."[35]

Slot machines, flowers, puppets, food, chopsticks, haiku: none of them
needs a homily, because the real needs no commentary. Freedom does not
threaten formality; the spontaneous coexists comfortably with the scripted;
honoring the free choice of participants never endangers communal actions
(e.g., those of a meal). To us Westerners, all this may seem baffling. Our anxiety about meaning—our insistence that symbols yield predictable "referents"
that have precise (or at least predictable) significances—is perhaps the last
gasp of a post-Enlightenment modernity that prized both reason's order and
order's reasonableness. That is surely one reason why Roland Barthes
regarded Voltaire, the Enlightenment sage par excellence—as the West's last
happy writer. "He meant," as White says, "that Voltaire was the last writer
who could cheerfully assume that the whole planet, both the known and the
unknown parts, reflected principles that were perfectly grasped."[36] Enlightenment optimism—its confidence in science and reason, in the perfectibility
of human nature, in the ability of citizens to create "more perfect unions"—
imagined a world as reasonably ordered as a Haydn symphony. Order is a
coefficient of reason, and reason's main task is to figure out what things mean,
how and what they "signify." Barthes's project was to bulldoze such optimism,
such confidence in our human ability to assign (or discover) "the meaning of
things." Thus, for Barthes in the *Empire of Signs*, "Japan is a test, a challenge
to think the unthinkable, a place where meaning is finally banished."[37]

The Risks of Ritual

To speak of "a place where meaning is finally banished" will surely sound puz-
zling to most Christians. The Christian imagination, after all, is crowded by

---

33. See George Steiner, *Real Presences* (Chicago: University of Chicago Press, 1989), 3-50.
34. Quoted in Barthes, *Empire of Signs*, 72.
35. Ibid.
36. White, review of Barthes's *Empire of Signs*, p. 1., col. 2.
37. Ibid.

meanings: biblical, doctrinal, doxological, catechetical, moral, and ethical. "Saying what matters of faith and morals *mean*" is, in fact, what Roman Catholics expect as the chief function of the church's magisterium (the authoritative teaching of its bishops, pastors and theologians). Moreover, one thing that progressive and traditionalist combatants in the post–Vatican II "liturgy wars" appear to agree on is that Christian worship is (or is supposed to be) profoundly *meaningful* in both its symbols and its substance. Many would define liturgical rites as the church's public, repeated rehearsal of its deepest identity, unity, values, convictions, and *meanings*. The "General Instruction of the Roman Missal" (GIRM) does not hesitate, in fact, to describe the liturgical assembly—people and ministers gathered to celebrate eucharist—as *the* place par excellence where the church's belief and behavior are best revealed: "In the local Church, first place should certainly be given, because of its significance, to the Mass at which the Bishop presides, surrounded by his presbyterate, deacons, and lay ministers, and in which the holy people of God participate fully and actively, for it is there that the preeminent expression of the Church is found."[38] What could be more basic and "meaningful" than that?

Yet my central contention in this chapter is that the purpose of liturgical rites is *not* to "produce meanings." Liturgy's goal isn't meaning but *meeting*. And meetings are always risky. Christian worship is not doctrine disguised in ritual shorthand but action that draws us into the dynamic, hospitable, yet perilous space of God's own life. For as Christians understand God, the "persons" of the Trinity (Father, Son, Spirit) are not discrete, individuated, incommunicable "centers of consciousness" (as we humans are). Rather, the persons in God *exist only by giving themselves to one another in mutual self-surrender*. To speak of persons in God is to speak of God, *given*: given to, given away, given over, poured out, each person to the other in endless exchange and communion. In God, therefore, personhood arises only from self-gift and self-surrender, not from clinging to "identity" or asserting "personality" (as it is among us).

To use a biblical word, God's interpersonal life—as revealed by Jesus' death and rising and by the sending of the Spirit—is "kenotic." *Kenosis* is the Greek word Paul uses in his Letter to the Philippians to describe how Jesus, "though he was in the form of God, did not regard equality with God something to be grasped. Rather, he emptied [*ekenōsen*] himself, taking the form of a slave . . ." (Phil 2:6-7). As Paul's text shows, *kenoun* means "to empty," "to make empty," that is, to erase, to nullify, to abase to the point of nothingness. As the

---

38. GIRM 112; the phrase translated into English as "the preeminent expression of the Church" is, in Latin, *praecipua manifestatio ecclesiae*.

renowned French sacramental theologian Fr. Louis-Marie Chauvet, notes, Paul's theology of Jesus' death thus implies a radical "revolution in the image of God." God's "glory" is revealed not in magnitude and eminence but, paradoxically, "in the disfigured face of him whom humans have reduced to nothing." In the crucified One—whose form, Paul says, is that of a slave—God is "crossed out," and "the humanity of the divine God . . . is revealed to us."[39]

This crossing out—this self-emptying and erasure—has crucial significance for us and for God. Walter Cardinal Kasper, the eminent ecumenist and theologian, has written:

> The Bible makes unavoidable the question of the suffering of God. The Bible tells us over and over that God is affected by the action and suffering of human beings. . . . The New Testament continues this line of thought by telling us of the anger of Jesus (Mark 3:5), his compassion (Mark 6:34), and his weeping over Jerusalem (Luke 19:41). Fundamental in this context are the words of Jesus about being abandoned by God (Mark 15:34; Matt 27:46). . . . It is impossible to dismiss all this as simple anthropomorphism, or to ascribe it solely to the human nature of Jesus, while leaving his divinity untouched by it. For the kenosis [that Paul describes] is that of the pre-existent Son of God (Phil 2:7), and it is the humanness of God that has made its appearance (Titus 3:4). *In his humanness, then, and in his living and dying Jesus Christ is the self-interpretation of God.*[40]

If Jesus is God's "self-interpretation," then we must conclude that in the self-emptying of Christ's cross, something quite unexpected and perplexing about God's inner life—and about us—is revealed. When, as both Mark and Matthew attest, the dying Jesus cried out in the words of Psalm 22, "My God, my God, why have you forsaken me?," he was calling

> not just on the God of the Old Testament, but on the God he called Father in an exclusive sense, the God with whom he felt uniquely linked. In other words, *he experienced God as the one who withdraws in his very closeness,* who is totally other. Jesus experienced the unfathomable mystery of God and his will, but he endured this darkness in faith. This extremity of emptiness enabled him to become the vessel of God's fullness. His death

---

39. Louis-Marie Chauvet, *Symbol and Sacrament: A Sacramental Reinterpretation of Christian Existence*, trans. Patrick Madigan and Madeleine Beaumont (Collegeville, Minn.: Liturgical Press, 1995), 508.

40. Walter Kasper, *The God of Jesus Christ*, trans. Matthew J. O'Connell (New York: Crossroad, 1984 [paperback, 1994]), 190 (emphasis added).

became the source of life. . . . *This death is the form in which the Kingdom of God exists under the conditions of this age, the Kingdom of God in human powerlessness, wealth in poverty, love in desolation, abundance in emptiness, and life in death.*[41]

In Jesus—God's self-interpretation hanging on a cross—we see God manifesting God's self by withdrawing, and

> it is precisely at this moment when the absence of God is most acute in this Crucified One that the Church acknowledges him to be *the Other who is like the Father.* . . .
>
> In dying as the "Abandoned of God," Jesus is *left to himself,* delivered over to his irreducible finitude of being-for-death, to his world, to his enemies, without God intervening to save him, him the Just One. Now, it is in the experience of this total letting-God-be-God, of this *radical difference* of God, so other that God recedes into God's silence—it is there that his [Jesus'] likeness with the Father is fully revealed.[42]

All this signifies that something utterly unexpected has happened within the life of God—and that something decisive has happened within humanity as well, something we call "salvation," something "which concerns God as much as the world." As Louis-Marie Chauvet says this "something" could occur only if a unique person were to burst upon the scene and overturn our "idolatrous misunderstanding of God," a misunderstanding deepened by our overconfident theological discourse, by our pretense of living justly and ethically, by our self-justifications. "But what descendant of Adam," asks Chauvet, "could carry out such a subversion? It was necessary, 'according to the Scriptures,' for God's very self to get involved. Jesus, the Christian faith confesses, . . . did not regard equality with God as something to be exploited, but emptied himself . . . to the point of death' (Phil 2:6-11), so that humans, finally recognizing their injustice, could enter into a conversion which is their salvation."[43]

In Christ's passion and cross, a "ritual to end all rituals," humankind discovers not a meaning but a *meeting*: the meeting between a self-deceived humanity and *a God whose self-interpretation is One who dies on the cross "abandoned by God!"* In the desolation of the cross, Jesus meets the radical Otherness of God—and (more startling still) *is identified precisely with that*

---

41. Walter Kasper, *Jesus the Christ* (new ed.; paperback, Mahwah, N.J.: Paulist, 1977), 118-19 (emphasis added).
42. Chauvet, *Symbol and Sacrament*, 506 (emphasis in original).
43. Ibid., 507.

Otherness, as the church confesses: "Because of this, God greatly exalted him and bestowed on him the name that is above every name, that at the name of Jesus every knee should bend, of those in heaven and on earth and under the earth, and every tongue confess that Jesus Christ is Lord to the glory of God the Father" (Phil 2:9-11).

That is why I have spoken of the daunting risks of ritual. Meaning, after all, is filtered, processed through human intelligence and reason that shape and massage our messages even as we transmit them. But real meetings are not "planned events" filtered first through reason; they are eruptions, raw and unscripted. The sheer suddenness of meeting exposes us (as it exposed Jesus on the cross) to the peril of a radical Otherness. Embraced first by God, that peril must also be embraced by us if we hope to experience the "something" that the Bible calls "salvation":

> To become a child . . . is to learn . . . *to recognize others as like us in their very otherness;* and, simultaneously, it is to learn to consent to this radical otherness, outside of which there is no likeness. The price of such a consent is high: nothing less than the choice of a freedom that is responsible for the others, the brothers and sisters, an inescapable responsibility from which no others . . . can relieve me.[44]

This childlikeness, this learning to recognize others as *like us in their very otherness* is precisely what Jesus manifested on the cross, and it is what led the church to acknowledge him as precisely "*the Other who is like the Father,*" the "image of the invisible God" (Col 1:15). This is the "meeting" that Christian ritual tries to open up to participants in the liturgy. Paradoxically, we meet the mystery of this Otherness in the liturgy only by meeting what is most simple and most real about our lives, our bodies, and our world. *Both* the Otherness of God *and* the otherness that comes from *recognizing others as like us in their very otherness* are met and acknowledged at worship in acts of walking, standing, kneeling, touching, taking, tasting, breaking (bread), pouring (wine), lifting, carrying, singing, saying, swinging (censers), smearing (oil on skin), seeing, showing, telling, listening. God is met in bodily acts whereby we enact the choice of a freedom that is responsible for others. That is why liturgy is not merely meaningful commentary, and why the "liturgy of the church" must be verified in the "liturgy of the neighbor."

---

44. Ibid., 506 (emphasis added).

RITUAL: FROM FAITH TO MEETING

Risky ritual, understood this way, is an act of faith, where faith is experienced as assent to loss, consent to "the presence of absence."[45] Like the slot machines, flowers, puppets, chopsticks, and haiku of Roland Barthes's fictive Japan, Christian ritual is animated by a letting-go, an emptying-out, rather than by the wantonly majestic covetousness that drives our Western mania for meaning. Consider, for a moment, the famous story about two dejected disciples who are making their way toward the village of Emmaus in the aftermath of Jesus' passion and death (Luke 24:3-35). These two disappointed seekers are beset by a problem that bothers (or should bother) every thoughtful person of faith. How can God still be God if God's anointed Servant has been condemned by God's law and has died forsaken? What kind of God remains silent when his Son cries out in dereliction, "My God, my God, why have you abandoned me?" What God would let his Anointed One *die*, only to raise him up in vindication, *contrary* to God's own law, which plainly says that "God's curse rests on him who hangs on a tree" (Deut 21:23)? Why would God permit his Christ to "become a curse for us," as Paul puts it (Gal. 3:13)? As the dejected disciples ponder these questions, a stranger joins them and tries to show the pair the "meaning" of Scriptures that speak about God's Suffering Servant. The disciples seem to remain skeptical, unconvinced by the stranger's commentary, yet as evening comes on, they invite their unidentified companion to stop and have dinner with them. At table, the ritual flashpoint suddenly occurs: they recognize the stranger's identity "in the breaking of the bread" (Luke 24:35). Yet the moment their eyes "were opened . . . he vanished from their sight" (Luke 24:31).

The disciples' eyes open not on splendor but on *absence* and *emptiness*. Instead of receiving reassurances about God's plan and its meaning, instead of regaining possession of their lost friend, they are led to a *meeting* that ends in *loss* and *dispossession*: "He vanished from their sight" (Luke 24:31). The central challenge of faith, Luke's narrative suggests, is to assent to this loss, to consent to "the presence of this absence." The risen One, Luke further insists (see Acts 1:6-12) has "ascended," that is, *departed*: we must not only "agree to this loss if we want to be able to find him," but we can find him only in that rag-tag community of congenital doubters and misfits known as the church.[46]

---

45. These themes—the "consent to loss" and the "presence of absence"—are central to Chauvet's sacramental theology; see *Symbol and Sacrament*, 62-63, 74, 98, 170, 177, 307, 404-5, 534.

46. Ibid., 177.

The church is thus the historical, embodied community that mediates—to, for, and in the world—the presence of the absence of that stranger who, breaking bread among his disciples, "vanished from their sight." The church thus

> radicalizes the vacancy of the place of God. To accept its mediation is to agree that this vacancy will never be filled. . . . But it is precisely in the act of respecting his radical absence or otherness that the Risen One can be recognized [ritually and] symbolically. For this is the faith; this is Christian identity according to the faith. *Those who kill this sense of the absence of Christ make Christ a corpse again.*[47]

Faith is thus an assent to loss, a consent to absence and dispossession, a making peace with emptiness and vacancy. We may mourn this loss, but we cannot resent it. It is, after all, the "condition of possibility" for that faith first born among spice-bearing women who "went to anoint Jesus very early when the sun had just risen on the first day of the week" (see Mark 16:1-2). As Thomas Sheehan wrote in his provocative study *The First Coming*, these women—the first witnesses to Jesus' resurrection—were confronted by a *double* absence. Not only had Jesus *died*; now even his tomb was empty and his corpse gone. Jesus had become altogether "unfindable," and hence what these women discovered that Easter morning was both an utter absence and the futility of their continued search for him among the dead.[48] In a nutshell, Easter began as a question, not an answer. It began not with trumpets and lilies and shouts of "Alleluia" but with terror. The Greek words that conclude the original ending of Mark's Gospel (16: 8) are *ephobounto gar*, "for they [the women] kept on being afraid."[49] Moreover, no explanations are given (in Mark, at any rate) that might ease the women's consternation. Their early-morning ritual brought them not meanings but a meeting with a messenger. This young man tells them what they already know: Jesus is not here. Instead of finding a body to anoint, the women meet emptiness, absence, and loss.

In short, these women had to face the full fury of ritual's inherent riskiness. For in the absence of a body, the rite of anointing was deprived of any

---

47. Ibid., 178.

48. Thomas Sheehan, *The First Coming: How the Kingdom of God Became Christianity* (New York: Random House, 1986; Vintage paperback, 1988), 168-69. A revised edition of this book is forthcoming from Polebridge Press.

49. The Greek verb ἐφοβοῦντο (from φοβέομαι) is in the imperfect tense. The Greek imperfect, like the Latin, denotes an action in the past that "keeps on" and *continues*. For 16:8 as the original (or "shorter") ending of Mark's Gospel, see Daniel J. Harrington, "The Gospel According to Mark," in *The New Jerome Biblical Commentary*, ed. Raymond E. Brown et al. (Englewood Cliffs, N.J.: Prentice-Hall, 1990), 41:108-9, pp. 628-29.

meaningful religious significance. No wonder the women trembled and "kept on being afraid." They were staring at emptiness, vacancy, at the possibility that ritual itself—*any* ritual, *all* ritual, and the religious beliefs that sanctioned it—was a vacuous waste of time. In her groundbreaking study of elderly Jews (most of them immigrants from Eastern Europe) living in a seniors' center in Venice, California, Barbara Myerhoff puts her finger on precisely this disturbing dilemma:

> All rituals are paradoxical and dangerous enterprises, the traditional and improvised, the sacred and secular. Paradoxical because rituals are conspicuously artificial and theatrical, yet designed to suggest the inevitability and absolute truth of their messages. Dangerous because when we are not convinced by a ritual we may become aware of ourselves as having made them up, thence on to the paralyzing realization that we have made up all our truths: our ceremonies, our most precious conceptions and convictions—all are mere invention, not inevitable understandings about the world at all but the results of mortals' imaginings.[50]

Another fine example of how ritual risks *meeting* and resists retreating into predictable meanings may be found in Myerhoff's short piece entitled "Chicken Foot Stew," part of the research she later included in her study *Number Our Days*:

> Being so rooted in their Judaism helped the old people in their struggles and celebrations. They were sufficiently comfortable with it to improvise upon it and adapt it freely as needed, for small requirements and large. Basha [an elderly woman] exemplified this when she described her dinner preparations. She ate alone in her tiny room. Over an electric hot plate, she cooked her chicken foot stew (chicken feet were free at the supermarket). Before eating, she spread a white linen handkerchief over the oilcloth covering the table, saying:
>
> "*This my mother taught me to do. No matter how poor, we would eat off clean white linen, and say the prayers before touching anything to the mouth. And so I do it still. Whenever I sit down, I eat with God, my mother, and all the Jews who are doing these same things even if I can't see them.*"
>
> Such a meal is a feast, superior to fine fare hastily eaten, without ceremony, attention, or significance. Because of such things, I came to see the Center elderly as in possession of the philosophers' stone—that universally sought, ever-elusive treasure, harboring the secret that would teach us how

---

50. Barbara Myerhoff, *Number Our Days* (New York: Simon & Schuster, 1978; Touchstone Books paperback, 1980), 86. Myerhoff's book later became an Oscar-winning documentary.

to transmute base metals into pure gold. The stone, like the bluebird's feather of happiness, is said to be overlooked precisely because it is so close to us, hidden in the dust at our feet.[51]

"Whenever I sit down, I eat with God, my mother, and all the Jews who are doing these same things even if I can't see them." Basha's experience couldn't be clearer. Her "chicken foot stew" ritual risks *meetings*: she eats with God, with her mother, with "all the Jews who are doing these same things even if I can't see them." These ritual actions—cooking the stew, spreading the fair white linen cloth on her table, eating with God and unseen others—affirm the "presence of absence." There seems to be a similarity between Basha's ritual experience and that of the frightened women at Jesus' empty tomb. Peering into the emptiness of a space formerly occupied by a beloved body, those women conceive

> a unique form of seeking: the desire for that which can never be had. This unique kind of seeking is the experience that makes human beings different from any other kind of entity. . . . Such seeking is not something we occasionally get caught up in; rather, it is what makes us human, constitutes us as the futile passion, the unfulfilled and presumably unfulfillable desire that we are. If we were not this endless eros, either we would be God, who cannot seek because he has already found everything, or we would be animals, those living entities that . . . never have a desire that exceeds the possibility of being fulfilled.[52]

We can say, then, that to risk ritual —to risk *meeting* its "emptiness"— makes us uniquely human. In this respect, ritual is closely linked to the Easter faith that first gripped those spice-bearing women as they stood bewildered before Jesus' burial place. Such faith is fundamentally *desire*, a restless reaching out, a ceaseless seeking that essentially shapes our human nature. "Beyond all our seeking for things that can be found," writes Thomas Sheehan, "we find ourselves still directed to a 'more.' . . . We remain, fundamentally, an act of questioning to which there is no answer."[53]

I have been saying that faith and its ritual embodiment require "assent to loss" and "consent to the presence of absence." This may sound shocking, but it is important to note that the phrase "presence of absence," is not negative; it does not mean "the absence of presence." Rather, it alerts us to the distinc-

---

51. Jewish Women's Archive, "JWA—Barbara Myerhoff—Chicken Foot Stew," http://www.jwa.org/exhibits/wov/myerhoff/stew.html (June 15, 2005).
52. Sheehan, *First Coming*, 172.
53. Ibid.

tion Christians commonly make between "seeing with the eyes of flesh" and "seeing with the eyes of faith." Faith *is* vision, but it is not vision in the natural, organic, or biochemical sense. Nor is "absence," as I am using the word here, an absolute denial, for *absolute* absence would simply annul itself: it would not and could not *be*.[54] The phrase "presence of absence" thus points to the tension that exists within every ritual or symbolic activity: the tension between concealing and revealing, between hiding and showing. Every ritual, every symbol, reveals by concealing and conceals by revealing. Or as Thomas Aquinas once put it, *sacramenta dantur hominibus quorum est per nota ad ignota pervenire* ("sacramental symbols are given to human persons, who come to *know* by moving from what is familiar [*nota*] to what is unknown and unfamiliar [*ignota*]"). Symbols, Aquinas held, are heuristic; they trigger a process of invention, of discovery. They begin in ignorance (*ignota*) and end in knowledge (*nota*). That is what gives rituals and symbols their power to point to an inexhaustible "surplus" of truth and reality that it is impossible for reason alone to discern. That is also why rituals and symbols invite *faith*. To speak of the "presence of absence" *affirms*—it does not deny—the Christian conviction that God both reveals and bestows God's self within our history and our embodied humanity. God reveals by concealing and conceals by revealing. Consenting in faith and ritual to the "presence of absence" thus amounts to what Louis-Marie Chauvet calls

> the slow work of apprenticeship in the art of "un-mastery," a permanent work of mourning where, free of resentment, a "serene" consent . . . takes place within it little by little. In gospel terms, this is a work of conversion to the presence of the absence of a God who "crosses himself out" in the crushed humanity of [the] crucified One whom humans have reduced to less than nothing and yet where, in a paradoxical light, faith confesses the glory of God.[55]

In a word, meeting emptiness and absence in faith means learning the art of *letting*: *letting go* of our compulsion to control or master people, places, and things; *letting enter* the God who is moving toward us "into presence," without violence and manipulation on our part. For God is always a giver, and this "movement of donation can only be welcomed graciously in an attitude of 'letting-enter-into-presence,' where the accent falls not on the presence itself but on the letting as '*letting* the coming-into-presence.'"[56] So the distress of

---

54. See ibid.
55. Chauvet, *Symbol and Sacrament*, 74.
56. Ibid., 61. Chauvet is using the language of Heidegger here.

absence to which we assent in faith is not nothing; it is "the presence of a hidden plentitude," what "the Hebrew prophets and Jesus named 'the divine.'"[57] Hence, absence is not a conclusion but a starting point, as Easter itself is. It is the "open place" where we suspend the search to master reality through reason's calculations in order to learn the art of "un-mastery." We assent to absence by recognizing, to our distress, that faith is not *grasping* something (a person, a belief, a value, a meaning) but *letting oneself be grasped* by an Unknown that eludes our knowledge but is indispensable. To remain in a "mature proximity to this absence" is a daunting but essential task.[58] For that is how there is kept alive within us "the wound of an Otherness which, always beyond our grasp, nonetheless leaves its trace in the humble call of the neighbor." As the Jewish philosopher Emmanuel Levinas said, "an invisible God signifies not only an unimaginable God but also a God *accessible* through justice."[59] Paradoxically, absence holds the key not only to mature faith but to the concrete practice of justice and mercy "for the life of the world."

CONCLUSION

We began our chapter by reimagining ritual's roles through the "Zen" eyes of Roland Barthes's "fictive Japan." We saw that, whereas we in the West tend to "overfeed" and "fatten" ritual symbols with multiple meanings, a Zen perspective is comfortable with loss and absence, with emptiness. Such a perspective, I suggested, may also be valuable when it comes to analyzing the roles and risks of Christian ritual. As the work of theologians such as Louis-Marie Chauvet has shown, absence asks us to abandon our infantile covetousness for mastery over meaning, and to *let* God come toward us in a gracious—indeed kenotic—movement of self-donation. To insist that faith and ritual risk meeting absence and emptiness has nothing to do, therefore, with atheism (which proclaims God's death) or with indifferentism (which says the question of God is of no consequence to humanity or its future). But it has everything to do with the conditions that make mature faith (and its embodiment in ritual acts) possible in the first place. In this connection, we have much to learn from much-maligned deconstructionists like Jacques Derrida. Derrida makes no claim to be a theologian, yet he well understands that "faith and its theology grow like desert flowers in a desert place, bloom-

---

57. Ibid., 62.
58. The phrase "mature proximity to absence" comes from J. Greisch, "La contrée de la sérénité et l'horizon de l'espérance," in *Heidegger et la question de Dieu* (Paris: Grasset, 1980), 184.
59. Ibid., 75; Levinas quoted by Chauvet.

ing when all the elements conspire against it . . . [l]ike an experience of something that will, in a manner of speaking, knock us dead."[60] He knows that any search for the God who is "totally *Other*" (and not a figment of the imagination, a conclusion reached by reason, or an alibi for our behavior) will lead straight to the desert, the place of absence and emptiness. "The essence of faith *par excellence*," Derrida writes, is that it "can only ever believe in the unbelievable."[61] Faith begins not as "content" but as conversion, a saying yes to "the stranger to come, . . . yes to the stranger to whose shores" we may espy "without attempting to land . . . to explore . . . or . . . to conquer."[62]

The proper correlative of "the presence of absence" is thus not doubt, denial, or despair but the unquenchable desire of faith, a desire born when the spice-bearing women arrived at the tomb and found it, precisely, *empty*. Faith is desire for that *utterly* Other, desire whose goal is not possession (grasping God on *our* terms) but dispossession (saying yes to the Stranger whose shores can finally be neither reached nor conquered). It is desire that "renounces the momentum of appropriation," desire that is not "driven by the passion of a [human] subject for possession . . . for something determinable, but by the passion for the impossible." Faith, finally, is what drove Christian mystics to "pray God to rid us of God," to "seek God without God," to insist that God is met not within the reassuring economy of familiar truths and platitudes, but in the heart's desert and the soul's dark night.[63]

QUESTIONS FOR REFLECTION

1. Chapter 2 suggests that ritual is "risky" because it resists our schemes to "master the meanings" (of life, self, world, God, others) and invites us, instead, to let God move toward us as a Mystery we can neither elude nor control. What items would be on your own list of "ritual's risks"?
2. "Every ritual, every symbol, reveals by concealing and conceals by revealing" (above, p. 67). How would you express, in your own words, Thomas Aquinas's notion that ritual symbols (such as sacraments) are "heuristic," triggering a process of discovery?
3. French theologian Louis-Marie Chauvet speaks often of "the presence of absence" as a basic aspect of ritual symbols (sacraments). What is the relation

60. John D. Caputo, *The Prayers and Tears of Jacques Derrida* (Bloomington: Indiana University Press, 1997), 61.

61. Jacques Derrida, *Specters of Marx: The State of the Debt, the Work of Mourning, and the New International*, trans. Peggy Kamuf (New York: Routledge, 1994), 143.

62. Caputo, *Prayers and Tears of Jacques Derrida*, 64.

63. Ibid., 62.

between this "oscillation" (presence as absence, absence as presence) and Christian faith?

4. The "General Instruction of the Roman Missal" (GIRM, 112) affirms the "local church gathered for liturgy as the place where Christian belief and behavior are best revealed" (see p. 59 above). Does this affirmation match your own experience? Is liturgy the best place to find "Christian faith in action"?

5. "In God, personhood arises only from self-gift and self-surrender" (see p. 59 above). How are God's persons (Father, Son, Spirit)) both like and unlike human persons? What does it mean to say human persons are "created in God's image and likeness"?

SUGGESTIONS FOR FURTHER READING

Barthes, Roland. *Empire of Signs.* Translated by Richard Howard. New York: Hill & Wang, 1982. A modern classic that offers a new way to think about the relation between "signs" and "meanings."

Chauvet, Louis-Marie. *Symbol and Sacrament: A Sacramental Reinterpretation of Christian Existence.* Translated by Patrick Madigan and Madeleine Beaumont. Collegeville, Minn.: Liturgical Press, 1995. This difficult but important study of how Christian identity is formed stresses the role of Word, Sacrament, and Ethics in that formation.

Kasper, Walter. *The God of Jesus Christ.* Translated by Matthew J. O'Connell. New York: Crossroad, 1984; paperback, 1994. A challenging but rewarding study of Christology that emphasizes the humanness of God as revealed in the life, death, and resurrection of Jesus.

3

Ritual's Rules

Rehearsing the Kingdom of God

IN THE PREVIOUS TWO CHAPTERS, we have considered ritual's roots and risks. In each case, we have seen how a willingness to "reimagine" ritual from new perspectives (postmodernism, Asian cultural and religious traditions) can enrich and illumine our understanding of Christian liturgy and its ritual symbols. This chapter turns to a more explicitly biblical source: Jesus' own life and ministry, as it was linked both to the practice of Jewish ritual and to "readiness for the kingdom of God." As this chapter will emphasize, Jesus did not repudiate ritual, but reinterpreted it as practice—rehearsal—for God's arriving reign or kingdom.

My principal goal in this chapter, therefore, is to show how Jesus immersed himself thoroughly in the social (Galilean) and religious (Jewish) cultures of his day in order to become "a worshiper of the Father in spirit and truth" (see John 4:23). As I hope to show, Jesus himself was a person of prayer, devoted, though not uncritically, to the worship practice of his people. He became a participant in liturgy through a life that was historically specific, concrete, and particular: by worshiping, in Temple and synagogue, as a devout Jewish layperson from Galilee. In so doing, Jesus revealed that the way that leads to the God whom *all* seek is through the *particularities* of each community's life and liturgy. That is why, as I noted in the introduction to chapter 1, Pope John Paul II insisted that "the Spirit's presence and activity" reach beyond the confines of Christianity and touch "not only individuals but also *society and history, peoples, cultures, and religions,*" especially in their life of prayer and worship (see *Redemptoris Missio* 28).

This is one reason why Christians today must learn to pray and worship "globally." As John D. Witvliet has written, Revelation 21:24-26 describes the full, final coming of God's kingdom as a global ingathering, when "the 'glory and honor of the nations' will be brought into the Holy City of God. In this place of perfect worship and the immediate experience of God's presence, the culturally particular gifts of nations find a natural home."[1] C. Michael Hawn uses the phrase "polyrhythmic worship" to describe liturgy that celebrates the multiple perspectives that arise from "differences in gender, vocation . . . generations, socioeconomic position, and cultural orientation." Learning to worship polyrhythmically means not only being willing to learn new repertoire, but being willing to become participant observers, "self-conscious and culturally displaced." It means learning how *not* to be "in charge," culturally, and how to become "vulnerable in areas of inexperience."[2]

Take, for example, the liberation hymnody of South Africa, especially the work of the prophet Ntsikana, the first Christian from the Xhosa tribe (of which Nelson Mandela was a member).[3] Ntsikana is best known for his "Great Hymn" (*Ahomna, homna*), which includes lines such as these:

> You are the Great God who dwells in the heavens,
> . . . .
> You created life, you created on high,
> . . . .
> A Star flashed forth, bringing us your message.
> You created the blind—did you not create them for a purpose?
> . . . .
> You are the hunter who hunts souls.
> You gather together flocks rejecting each other.
> You are the Great Blanket with which we are clothed.
>
> Your hands are wounded.
> Your feet are wounded.
> Your blood—why is it streaming?
> Your blood was poured out for us.[4]

God the Hunter, Gatherer; God the Great Blanket! North American Anglos who have never known the experience of apartheid may find the

---

1. John D. Witvliet, "Series Preface," in C. Michael Hawn, *Gather into One: Praying and Singing Globally* (Grand Rapids: Eerdmans, 2003), x.

2. Hawn, *Gather into One*, 274, 276. Hawn gives the example of Anglo North Americans who may feel uncomfortable participating in liturgies that include dance. To worship polyrhythmically, Anglos must let themselves be culturally displaced, becoming vulnerable to the experience of others. For there are many persons in the world, especially in African nations, for whom worship "cannot take place, cannot be meaningful, without dance." Hawn is citing the work of Barbara Browning, *Samba: Resistance in Motion* (Bloomington: Indiana University Press, 1995).

3. Hawn, *Gather into One*, 128-37.

4. Text in Hawn, *Gather into One*, 133-34; quotations in the remainder of this section are from Hawn, 135-36.

images and theology of Ntsikana's Great Hymn strange and even suspect. They may wonder whether the hymn adequately expresses Christian teaching in African terms. But this reaction reveals less about African theology than about our Anglo discomfort at being culturally displaced. "In African theology . . . it is not necessary to trace the sources and discover how this text came to be. This is a Western analytical process. From the African perspective one accepts the text as a gift of God through one of God's prophets."

The wideness of God's mercy, celebrated in song and ritual, is reached only through the "narrow door" of a culture's native "qualities and talents" (*Sacrosanctum Concilium* 37). During one of the sessions of the South African Truth and Reconciliation Commission, Archbishop Desmond Tutu recounted his experience with a black South African woman who wanted to know exactly "who had tortured and killed her husband." Tutu replied by asking what possible good such information would serve. The woman's answer "stunned the TRC panel. 'I must know who did these terrible things,' she said, 'so that I can forgive him.'"

Polyrhythmic worship does not mean "homogenized" worship, nor does it mean liturgy that ransacks the ritual traditions of other peoples in an effort to become "trendy" and "multicultural." We do not, for example, honor Jesus' injunction to "worship the Father in spirit and truth" by trying to figure out precisely what went on, ritually, in first-century Palestinian synagogues in Galilee or in the Second Temple during the period of the Herodian monarchy. We can and must study such things, of course—as we will be doing in this chapter—but not for the sake of imitation. Rather, we strive to learn how, in each age, through the cultural distinctiveness and religious practice of diverse peoples, God's mercies are "new every day," extending from "pole to pole" and from "age to age."

JESUS' RESPONSE TO RITUAL

It is true, of course, that in their sacraments, Christians often claim to "do what Jesus did." Yet their literature has often presented him as an antiritualist who disputed or despised the liturgies of Temple and synagogue. Recent scholarship, however, resists the conclusion that Jesus' religious attitude was one of antiritualism. On the contrary, there is good reason to think that a Jewish male of Jesus' background (the northern Galilean countryside, where the uncomplicated "basics" of Jewish faith and life were emphasized) would have taken regular participation in the synagogue for granted.[5] But what of

---

5. See John P. Meier, *A Marginal Jew: Rethinking the Historical Jesus*, vol. 2, *Mentor, Message, and Miracles* (Anchor Bible Reference Library; New York: Doubleday, 1994), 1040.

his attitude toward the Jerusalem Temple? Three of the four Gospels include stories that suggest Jesus' preference for "mercy" over "sacrifice," for compassion toward sinners over the ritual observances of the righteous (see Matt 9:9-13; Mark 2:14-17; Luke 5:27-32). All four Gospels, moreover, recount the episode of Jesus' "cleansing the temple" (Matt 21:12-13; Mark 11:15-19; Luke 19:45-46; John 2:14-16). Until fairly recently, commentators have assumed that Jesus toppled "the tables of the money changers and the seats of those who were selling doves" (Mark 11:15) because trading within the Temple precincts polluted the place where God is worshiped and "compromise[d] its religious function."[6] Jesus' action has thus been interpreted, traditionally, as a restoration of the Temple liturgy's purity.

Over the past two decades, however, Scripture scholars have made a concerted effort to appreciate Jesus' Jewishness and to interpret the "cleansing" episode "within a context of actual first-century Jewish practice."[7] An example of such scholarly reorientation may be found in the work of the distinguished Roman Catholic exegete John P. Meier. Temple and Torah were not only, Meier argues, the pivotal religious symbols of Palestinian Judaism in Jesus' time; "they were also the two great battlefields for power and control," symbols of unity that had become "major sources of division." Opposition to and withdrawal from the Temple by members of the Qumran ("Dead Sea Scrolls") community is well known, though as Meier points out "Qumran's ultimate objection to the temple was that Qumranites did not control it and run it according to their rules." (Liturgy wars have a long history among Jews and Christians!) The Qumranites had a love-hate relationship with the Temple; on one hand, its priesthood and liturgy were central to their theology; on the other, its practices, in their view, had become defiled, unclean.[8]

Although Jesus, like the Qumranites, represented a distinctive "religious renewal movement" in first-century Palestine, his own attitudes toward the Temple were complex and are not easy to reconstruct. For one thing, it is probable that Jesus emerged from the prophetic movement associated with John the Baptist. It is likely, indeed, that John was the single most significant influence on Jesus' career, and that Jesus never completely left John (or his

---

6. Paula Fredriksen, *Jesus of Nazareth, King of the Jews: A Jewish Life and the Emergence of Christianity* (New York: Knopf, 1999), 208.

7. Ibid.

8. For material in this and the following section ("Jesus, Jewish Layman"), see John P. Meier, *A Marginal Jew: Rethinking the Historical Jesus*, vol. 1, *The Roots of the Problem and the Person*; vol. 2, *Mentor, Message, and Miracles;* vol. 3, *Companions and Competitors* (Anchor Bible Reference Library; New York: Doubleday, 1991, 1994, 2001), 1:8, 345, 347, 499; 2:55, 100-177, 291, 1039-41; 3:498-501, 577n. 39. For a more detailed discussion of the Qumran community, its beliefs, and its similarities and contrasts to Jesus and his teaching, see 3:488-532.

teaching) behind.[9] The prophetic focus of John's ministry was God's "imminent fiery judgment, from which sinful Israelites could escape only by repentance," while its ritual focus was "a baptism which pointed forward to the outpouring of the holy spirit" by a still greater prophet (a "stronger one") who was still to come. In short, John seems to have believed that baptism enacted "the candidate's repentance and pledge of new life" while "proclaiming, anticipating, and assuring the cleansing from sin that the holy spirit would effect on the last day when it was poured out like water on the repentant sinner by the stronger one."

Luke's Gospel portrays John's family as closely connected to the Temple; it describes his father Zechariah as a priest whose ministry in the Temple was the immediate occasion for the announcement of John's birth (Luke 1:5-25). But John's own connection (if any) to the Temple, its priesthood, and its liturgy is not described in the Christian Scriptures. After John's birth, Luke says, "the child grew and became strong in spirit, and he was in the desert until the day of his manifestation to Israel" (1:80). In contrast, Jesus' relation to the Temple is prominent in John's Gospel, and it figures, as well, in the Synoptics' account of Jesus' final ministry in Jerusalem near the end of his life. In addition, Luke 2:41-52 recounts the episode of a preteen Jesus interacting with "teachers" in the Temple, while his parents frantically search out his whereabouts. As Meier observes, such a scene, as we now have it, is almost certainly the result of later Christian theology and not a reliable historical record.[10] Still, it shows that the Gospel traditions saw "nothing problematic in Jesus' presence at and participation in temple activities," and there is "no known countervailing tradition that can be considered historical." Meier's conclusion thus seems well justified:

> In all the Gospels, the fact that Jesus goes up to the temple, teaches in the temple, and—in the Synoptics—celebrates the Passover with a lamb slain in the temple according to the temple's ritual is taken for granted as an obvious datum that needs no explanation and generates no dispute. In this, Jesus stood with "mainstream" Palestinian Jews, who, no matter what they thought of the particular reigning high priest, revered the temple as the one sacred place chosen by God for lawful sacrifice.

Thus, Jesus' summary statement of his own ministry in John's Gospel—"I have always spoken publicly to the world. I have always taught in a synagogue

---

9. As Meier says, "The public ministry of the marginal Jew named Jesus takes its beginning from the public ministry of another marginal Jew, John the Baptist" (*Marginal Jew*, 1:1041).

10. There is "no reliable historical tradition," writes Meier, that Jesus himself "was of levitical or priestly descent" (*Marginal Jew*, 1:345).

or in the temple area"—appears to affirm his acceptance of the liturgical institutions of his time.[11] There is no reason, then, to believe that Jesus was an antiritualist who shunned Temple and synagogue, rejected the liturgical calendar, or complained about the illegitimacy of worship practice among first-century Palestinian Jews. "Unlike the Qumranites," notes Meier, "the historical Jesus . . . regularly went up to the temple, joined in the temple feasts, and used the temple as a solemn auditorium for addressing large numbers of his fellow Jews." In this, the adult Jesus may simply have continued the pattern of worship familiar from his childhood, a ritual pattern Paula Fredriksen has imaginatively reconstructed in her book *Jesus of Nazareth, King of the Jews.*[12]

Despite its limits and failings, obvious to the Qumranites and implied by the story of Jesus' "cleansing" it, the Temple—as a place of pilgrimage, prayer, instruction, and sacrifice—was, in Jesus' view, a perfectly legitimate institution "willed by God for the supreme acts of worship by all Jews." This is the case even if we accept Meier's portrait of Jesus as a "marginal Jew" from the Galilean countryside whose family milieu "shared in the reawakening of Jewish national and religious identity in Galilee" and "longed for the restoration of Israel in all its glory." Such families, though living in a heavily hellenized cultural context, were imbued, as Meier suggests, with a rather uncomplicated piety that reaffirmed the "basics" of traditional Jewish religion as "spelled out in the Mosaic Law: circumcision, observance of the Sabbath, observance of kosher food laws, and pilgrimage to the Jerusalem temple, whose sacrificial ritual during the great feasts was the high point of the annual cycle of their religious life."

But while Jesus clearly accepted the Jerusalem Temple as part of "the present order of things," he also seemed to believe that its days were numbered, that it "belongs to and is doomed to disappear with this present age." In short, Jesus seems to have expected a new age of salvation to dawn, a future that would come to pass through God's initiative at work in human agents. Whether, in Jesus' view, the Temple—reformed, restored, or ruined—would continue to play a role in Israel's religious life is unclear. For Jesus, the Temple liturgy was neither fatally flawed nor irrelevant; but it was *provisional*— it was destined to be supplanted by something else. What that "something" was—a new ritual pattern, a new and improved earthly sanctuary—cannot be described with certainty, though later Christians, such as the author of the Letter to the Hebrews, believed that the "heavenly sanctuary," which Jesus

---

11. It is of course possible that Jesus' statement to Annas in John 18:20 does not come, historically, directly from him (see Meier, *Marginal Jew*, 3:500).

12. Fredriksen, *Jesus of Nazareth*, 42-50.

had entered carrying his own blood, definitively surpassed the Jerusalem Temple, its priesthood, and its ritual (see Heb 5-10).

Jesus, Jewish Layman

Still, the Christian Scriptures themselves lend little support to the view that Jesus was an aggressive antiritualist whose main focus was promotion of a social program in opposition to the principal religious institutions (Torah, Temple) of his day. It would nevertheless be a mistake to imagine that Jesus was uncritical of contemporary religious practice or that he had no views at all about ritual or liturgical matters. For one thing, as the title of Meier's massively documented three-volume (so far) historical study demonstrates, Jesus was "a marginal Jew." Since he came from a pious family, lived in a relatively peaceful rural area, belonged to an honorable profession (woodworking) that provided a "modest but average standard of living," and was well connected to the "basics" of Jewish life and faith, Jesus could easily have "chosen to live out his days in the small-town tranquility and obscurity of Nazareth." But he didn't. Instead, he marginalized himself from mainstream Jewish social life, never marrying (as far as we can tell), and eventually embarking on a career as "an itinerant celibate layman proclaiming the imminent arrival of the kingdom of God," a choice that marginalized him further still.

It is this point—Jesus' life as a marginal Jewish layperson—that has special relevance to the topic of this book. *Jesus' relation to the rituals of his religious community was that of a layman, not that of a priest, a cleric, or a "liturgical professional" of any kind.* This too was a significant part of Jesus' marginalization, for among other things, it distanced him from the privileged aristocracy of old-money families (e.g., the Sadducean aristocracy of Jerusalem), who controlled the Temple, its liturgy, its priesthood, its jobs, its markets, its income, its ideologies, and its public relations. Because he did not belong—by choice, apparently—to a "power elite," still less a "liturgy elite," Jesus would have impressed most of his Jewish contemporaries as insufferably ordinary. He was a nobody from nowhere; at best, a minor celebrity, a peripheral phenomenon, rather uninteresting and certainly unimportant. His work was largely ignored also by the larger cultural elites of the Hellenistic and Roman worlds. Jewish historians such as Josephus and Romans such as Tacitus preferred to ignore him. To the Roman occupiers of first-century Palestine, Jesus' torture, trial, and execution were simply the just if grisly death that awaited *any* slave or rebel. To his co-religionists, Jesus' fate—death on the wood of the cross—was a certain sign that he had been *cursed* by God, for according to the

Torah, *anyone* hanged on a tree is cursed (see Deut 21:23). But Jesus' marginalization didn't stop there. As Meier writes, it wasn't

> only historians and politicians who marginalized Jesus. To a certain
> degree, Jesus first marginalized himself. At the age of roughly thirty, Jesus
> was an ordinary carpenter in an ordinary hill town of lower Galilee, enjoy-
> ing at least the minimum of economic necessities and social respectability
> required for a decent life. For whatever reason, he abandoned his liveli-
> hood and hometown, became "jobless" and itinerant in order to undertake
> a prophetic ministry, and not surprisingly met with disbelief and rejection
> when he returned to his hometown to teach in the synagogue. In place of
> the "honor" he once enjoyed he was now exposed to "shame" in an honor/
> shame society, where the esteem of others determined one's existence
> much more than it does today. Relying basically on the goodwill, support,
> and economic contributions of his followers, Jesus intentionally became
> marginal in the eyes of ordinary working Jews in Palestine, while remain-
> ing very much a Palestinian Jew himself.

Jobless, homeless, a vagrant, a grown man with no visible means of support, unemployed and perhaps unemployable, an uninvited "house guest"
who relied on the kindness of strangers: this is not a pretty picture. And it
gets worse. Jesus lived—deliberately and voluntarily it seems—*outside* the
institutions of marriage, parenthood, and family. Indeed, Jesus *may* have been
describing his own life choice in the shocking metaphor found in Matthew
19:12: "Some are incapable of marriage because they were born so; some,
because they were made so by others; some, because they have renounced
marriage [the Greek says they have *eunuchized*, castrated, themselves] for the
sake of the kingdom of heaven." Far from being a poster child for family values, Jesus chose a life on the margins of respectable society, highly irregular
and suspect. Although John the Baptist was probably the major figure in his
adult religious formation, Jesus apparently strayed from prominent features of
John's program of asceticism (e.g., fasting, abstention from wine, the harsh
life of the wilderness). He showed frustration toward his own family of origin (see Matt 12:46-50) and suggested that what binds people into families
is shared spiritual vision, not blood, genes, wedding vows, or children.

More shocking still, Jesus staunchly rejected a passel of patriarchal privileges—for example, the right claimed by Jewish *men* to divorce their wives
(the men could often remarry; the women usually could not). Jesus seems to
have "radically redefined the role of wom[e]n in marriage" by seeking to protect them from arbitrary dismissal by their husbands.[13] In Jesus' own time,

---

13. On Jesus' views about divorce as they are presented in Matthew's Gospel, see Douglas R. A.

this would not have been an insignificant matter. Women *needed* protection because, in the Jewish culture of the period, divorce meant economic ruin; women often found that they could survive only by becoming prostitutes or by entering into an adulterous relationship. Arguing from *within* the Torah, not against it, Jesus denounced and dismissed male claims of privilege and special treatment within the marriage covenant. In doing this, of course, Jesus was simply claiming the right of any Jewish teacher to interpret Torah, but he was also playing a dangerous and potentially deadly game. Almost certainly, as Meier notes, Jesus' status as a "lay Jewish teacher" was ridiculed by his opponents. He was, after all, a marginal nobody, and his vulnerability was "increased by the fact that, as a poor rural Galilean, he had never attended any scribal school" or been the talented student of "a noted teacher." In other words, Jesus lacked credentials. And yet he dared to question and challenge religious rules accepted by many Jews of his day. Moreover, he "proclaimed his own teachings with a sovereign authority whose basis was by no means clear to his opponents."

But perhaps the greatest scandal was simply Jesus' status as a *layman* who, for reasons that were and remain unclear, chose to remain single and presumably celibate. "Jesus was born a Jewish layman, conducted his ministry as a Jewish layman, and died a Jewish layman." That, in a nutshell, is the record of his life. "He belonged," writes Meier, "to the category of 'laity' at a time in Israel's history when, whether in Jerusalem or at Qumran, *priests*, and not the laity, controlled the levers of power. Simply by being a layman from an obscure town in the countryside of Lower Galilee, Jesus was already [suspect] . . . to the holders of religious power." On one level, Jesus' marginal status left him free and unencumbered; he owed no ostensible debts to "the powers that be," and owed his "job" to no one. On another, he probably struck many of his contemporaries as a kind of "loose cannon," without credentials and hence without credibility. Meier sums up Jesus' marginal status well:

> [Jesus] was a no-account Galilean in conflict with Jerusalem aristocrats; he was . . . a poor peasant in conflict with the urban rich; he was a charismatic wonderworker in conflict with priests very much concerned about preserving the central institutions of their religion and their smooth operation; he was an eschatological prophet promising the coming of God's kingdom in conflict with Sadducean politicians [who had] a vested interest in the status quo. But underneath many of these conflicts lay another conflict: he was a religiously committed layman who seemed to be threat-

Hare, *Matthew* (Interpretation: A Bible Commentary for Teaching and Preaching; Louisville: John Knox Press, 1993), 219-23; quotation from p. 226.

ening the power of an entrenched group of priests. That, as well as the other facets of his background, contributed to the final clash in Jerusalem. In short, that Jesus was a layman was not a neutral datum; it played a role in the development and denouement of his drama.

The Prayer of Jesus: Hallowing God's Name

Anything we say about Jesus' attitudes toward liturgy and ritual or about his teaching on prayer must take his marginalized lay status into account. This applies to perhaps the most famous of Jesus' prayers, the "Our Father" or "Lord's Prayer." Although its original context was not cultic, it has certainly been shaped, in the form we find it in the Gospels (e.g., Matt 6:9-13; Luke 11:2-4), by Christian liturgical traditions.[14] At the same time, there is good reason to believe that in this beloved prayer we catch something of the prayer life of the historical Jesus himself.[15]

The Christian liturgical use of the Lord's Prayer has a long history.[16] Here I will draw attention only to what this prayer may tell us about Jesus' own attitude toward the subject explored in the previous chapter, viz., the risks of ritual, of public worship. Consider, for example, the prayer's first petition: "Hallowed be thy name." The theme of "sanctifying" God's name has its roots in Jewish literature and liturgy, though it is largely ignored in the Christian Scriptures.[17] As Hal Taussig remarks, "It would have been nearly impossible for Jesus not to have prayed that God's name be revered and honored as holy. This sentence [in the Lord's Prayer] belongs to a number of traditional prayers that almost every Jew in Galilee said regularly."[18] The hallowing of God's name is, moreover, an action performed by both us and God. For humans, it consists in "believing God's word, trusting his promises, standing in awe of his majesty, praising him in worship, and observing his precepts in cult and ordinary life."[19] But more fundamentally, hallowing the name is

---

14. Meier, *A Marginal Jew*, 2:291.
15. See ibid., 293, where Meier suggests that the prayer may have arisen "among the disciples of the historical Jesus when they were still a loose band gathered around him." Moreover, "a number of considerations argue that the earliest form of the prayer comes from Jesus himself" (p. 294). For an accessible guide to how the various "fragments" (or "petitions") of the Lord's Prayer may have originated and been redacted by the gospel writers (Matthew and Luke especially), see Hal Taussig, *Jesus before God: The Prayer Life of the Historical Jesus* (Santa Rosa, Calif.: Polebridge, 1999), 35-66.
16. For the liturgical history of the Lord's Prayer, especially its use at the eucharist, see Joseph A. Jungmann, *The Mass of the Roman Rite: Its Origins and Development*, trans. Francis A. Brunner (2 vols.; 1955; repr.,Westminster, Md.: Christian Classics, 1992), 2:277-94.
17. An exception may be Jn 12: 28, where Jesus prays, "Father, glorify your name." See comments in Meier, *A Marginal Jew*, 2: 295.
18. Taussig, *Jesus before God*, 75.
19. Meier, *Marginal Jew*, 2:295.

something *God* does "by manifesting his power, glory, and holiness," that is, "his 'transcendence,' his 'otherness,' his 'God-ness' in the blazing light of a theophany that can bring either salvation or condemnation."[20] Here we meet once more a theme discussed in chapter 2: the risks ritual takes when it seeks to meet *otherness*—the utterly "Other," God, who is accessible only in those others for whom we are responsible in mercy and justice. For the God who is beyond names, who is "the name that cannot be named," is visible only in the eyes of the stranger, the hungry, the thirsty, the naked, and the imprisoned, and audible only in the cries of the poor (see Matt 25:31-46).

The sanctification of God's name—whether viewed as *our* liturgical act or *God's* salvific deed—cannot, then, be separated from the work of justice in the world. In the Hebrew Bible, God's sanctification of his own Name was a prominent theme in exilic and postexilic prophecy. Ezekiel announced that God *will* act, eschatologically (i.e., fully, finally, definitively), to "bring the scattered people of Israel out from among the Gentile nations and back home to their own land—through no merit of their own."[21] When God so sanctifies his Name, a new people—cleansed, reunited, and endowed with a new heart and a new spirit (Ezek 3:25-26)—will emerge; then, Israel's desolate homeland will blossom like a garden (Ezek 36:35).

When God hallows his Name, moreover, people are transformed. So radical is this transformation that it resembles nothing short of a new creation. "I will give you a new heart and place a new spirit within you, taking from your bodies your stony hearts and giving you natural hearts. I will put my spirit within you and make you live by my statutes. . . . You shall be my people, and I will be your God" (Ezek 36:26-27). Perhaps that is why, earlier in his prophecy, Ezekiel exotically reimagined—indeed, rewrote—the Hebrew Bible's earlier accounts of creation (e.g., those in Gen 1-2). Ezekiel 28:1-17 presents a "creation poem" addressed not to devout Jews but to a *pagan* ruler, the prince of Tyre, one of Israel's ancient enemies. Ezekiel imagines God speaking directly to this prince and saying to him:

> You were stamped with the seal of perfection,
>   of complete wisdom and perfect beauty.
> In Eden, the garden of God, you were,
>   and every precious stone was your covering. . . .
> Of gold your pendants and jewels were made,
>   on the day you were created.

---

20. Ibid., 295-96.
21. Ibid., 296; see, e.g., Ezek 36:23.

With the Cherub I placed you; you were on the holy
   mountain of God,
  walking among the fiery stones.
Blameless you were in your conduct from the day you were
   created,
Until evil was found in you, the result of your far-flung
   trade;
  violence was your business, and you sinned.
Then I banned you from the mountain of God;
  the Cherub drove you from among the fiery stones.
You became haughty of heart because of your beauty;
  for the sake of splendor you debased your wisdom.
(And) I cast you to earth, so great was your guilt.

Ezekiel's poem contains elements from both of the creation narratives in Genesis, but it imaginatively rewrites them. Gone, for instance, is the wily serpent who seduced human beings into sin. Ezekiel reimagines the "fall" as an inside job. "Complete wisdom and perfect beauty" were ours from the beginning, the prophet tells us, but we lost them because of our violence and hubris. The problem did not flow from God's bountiful gifts of beauty and wisdom, nor even from the slick seductions of a snake-in-the-grass; the problem arose from how we humans used God's generosity in dealing with others. The poem evokes an urban metaphor—Tyre, a city whose business was *business*—to portray humanity's fall not from a primal "innocence" (as in Genesis) but from the wisdom and beauty that were our native endowments, gifts of God's creating hand. The city of Tyre had become rich and powerful through international trade and through its innovations in the shipping business. Yet despite its entrepreneurial savvy, Tyre fell—not because it was fatally attracted by beauty or wisdom, but because its citizenry had become dishonest, arrogant, and violent. "The dishonesty of your trading—your busy trading—has filled you with violence and sin," says Ezekiel's poem (conflating Ezek 28:16+18, in the *Jerusalem Bible* translation).

The prophecy of Ezekiel 28 thus shows us *the sanctification of God's name in reverse*. When God hallows his own Name, the result is a people transformed (Ezek 36:23-28). But when divine gifts (beauty and wisdom) become mirrors for self-contemplation or excuses for self-absorption, humanity suffers. What ruined us humans, the poem in Ezekiel 28 suggests, was not a tree, an apple, a snake, or a bad case of indigestion, but overweening greed and egoism. Rapaciousness, dishonesty, and violence made us act *inhumanly* toward others, without justice and without mercy, and *that* is what brought us to ruin. Instead of begetting generosity, mercy, and justice, beauty begat bondage: "You became haughty of heart because of your beauty," Ezekiel imagines God saying, "for the sake of splendor you debased your own wisdom. Because of your guilt, your sinful trade . . . I have brought out fire from your midst which will devour you . . . reduce you to dust. . . . You have become a horror" (Ezek 28:17-19).

Echoes of Ezekiel's prophecy can perhaps be heard in John the Baptist's preaching, with its dual emphasis on interior renewal (repentance, conversion) and on the coming eschatological act by which God will sift humanity, separating wheat from chaff: "His winnowing fan is in his hand. He will clear his threshing floor and gather his wheat into his barn, but the chaff he will burn with unquenchable fire" (Matt 3:12). Clearly, then, the first petition of the Lord's Prayer ("hallowed be thy name") has roots in classical Jewish prophecy. But is it also linked to the rites of Temple and synagogue—and does its appearance in this prayer suggest that Jesus himself was deeply imbued and influenced by the public liturgical prayer of his people?

Scholars have long seen a parallel between the language of the first petition of the Lord's Prayer and the text of the *Qaddish* (or *Kaddish*), the Aramaic word for "holy."[22] The *Qaddish* is an ancient prayer that became "the doxology *par excellence* of the synagogue liturgy" and focused on the sanctification of God's Name.[23] An early version of this prayer reads as follows:

> Exalted and hallowed be His great name
>   in the world which He created according to his will.
> May He establish His kingdom in your lifetime and in
>   your days,
>   and in the lifetime of the whole household of Israel,
>   speedily and at a near time.[24]

The *Qaddish* explicitly links "hallowing the name" and "establishing God's kingdom," a connection also made in the opening phrases of the Lord's Prayer.

Nevertheless, there are problems that prevent us from saying with certainty that Jesus knew and used this *Qaddish* prayer or that it shaped his own understanding of public worship and ritual. Though the *Qaddish* prayer itself is most certainly ancient, our versions of it date largely from sources that appeared after Jesus' death, that is, during the Common Era.[25] And apart

---

22. Aramaic was the ordinary language Jesus himself would have spoken, though he was also acquainted with Hebrew from hearing the Scriptures read and explained at the synagogue service; he may have known a bit of Greek as well. See Meier, *Marginal Jew*, 2:1040.

23. Baruch Graubard, "The *Kaddish* Prayer," in *The Lord's Prayer and the Jewish Liturgy*, ed. Jakob Petuchowski and Michael Brocke (New York: Seabury Press/A Crossroad Book, 1978), 59.

24. Ibid., 37. For a slightly different version, see Meier, *Marginal Jew*, 2:297.

25. On the problems connected with dating the *Qaddish* prayer, see Meier, *Marginal Jew*, 2:297, and esp. 361-62 n. 36.

from problems of dating, there is the question of its actual role in the synagogue service (or *seder*). "The original function of the *Kaddish*," writes Baruch
Graubard, "does not seem to have been as much liturgical as it was homiletical, i.e., the congregation responded with this doxology as to the preacher's
homiletical discourse." Moreover, notes Graubard, "the language of the Kaddish itself is a somewhat Hebraized form of Aramaic, the language of the
common people, rather than Hebrew, the language of the liturgy."[26] We cannot assert conclusively, then, that the *Qaddish* was always—or ever—a part of
the liturgy in Galilean synagogues during Jesus' lifetime.

In spite of its long association with synagogue usage the *Qaddish* probably
did not enter the synagogue *seder* "until the end of the Talmudic period in the
fifth century CE," and thus "it can hardly be considered an example of 'Jewish norms of prayers' in the first century."[27] It is possible, too, that the gradual creation of the *Qaddish* prayer was less the result of liturgical practice than
of mystical speculation. Lawrence Hoffman has noted that both *Qaddish* and
a related prayer, the *Qedushah*, may well have been influenced by discussions
among Jewish mystics about God's "throne of glory" (*merkavah*). Worship's
purpose, these mystics argued, was

> to praise God . . . and to escape the fetters of worldly habitation in order
> to break through the barriers of the various heavens and see God in His
> splendor. . . . It was not petition, then, or even prayers of thanksgiving that
> were the hallmark of the mystic's liturgy. Praise was all. Like the angels in
> Isaiah's vision, the human worshipper was intent on praising God, while
> ascending through heaven after heaven in search of the ultimate throne of
> glory. Moreover, it was not the content of the words that mattered so much
> as the manner in which they were pronounced. Like mantras, they were a
> means by which a worshipper could transfer his mind from cognitive con-
> siderations to affective alteration of one's total perspective.[28]

In Hoffman's view there can be little doubt that mysticism (especially of
the *merkavah* variety) influenced the evolution of Jewish worship. But evidence for such mystical interpretations of the liturgy comes from well within
the Common Era and cannot be traced back to Jesus' own time, still less to
Jesus himself or the circle of his earliest disciples. What, then, might Jesus' use
of the famous phrase "hallowed be thy name" signify? The petition has often

---

26. Graubard, "*Kaddish* Prayer," 59. See also Lawrence A. Hoffman, *The Canonization of the Synagogue Service* (University of Notre Dame Center for the Study of Judaism and Christianity in Antiquity 4; Notre Dame, Ind.: University of Notre Dame Press, 1979), 56-65.
27. Joseph Heinemann, "The Background of Jesus' Prayer in the Jewish Liturgical Tradition," in
Petuchowski and Brocke, eds., *The Lord's Prayer and Jewish Liturgy*, 81.
28. Hoffman, *Canonization of the Synagogue Service*, 60.

been interpreted as moral advice or pragmatic exhortation—as though Jesus were saying, "Praise and hallow God because it is proper for a creature to honor the Creator." But this interpretation, Meier suggests, misses the point. Given its roots in Hebrew prophecy (e.g., Ezekiel)—and its continued evolution in Jesus' own time (e.g., among the Essenes at Qumran)—the theme of sanctifying God's Name connects to what we have said earlier in this chapter about God's radical Otherness. The distinctive theological trajectory of Jesus' prayer becomes clearer: it is "both God-centered and eschatological." That is,

> God alone can rightly and fully manifest himself in all his power and glory, . . . God alone can sanctify his name, which, it is hoped, he will do soon. This interpretation is supported by the close connection between the first and second "you petitions." Certainly only God can make his kingdom come; the tight parallelism between the two petitions would seem to argue that the same is true of sanctifying the name.[29]

If the Lord's Prayer is a reliable guide to Jesus' own practice and thought about public prayer—and there are good reasons to believe it is—then we must say that Jesus understands the rituals of worship not as manipulative techniques for "getting God to see things our way and giving us what we want," or as opportunities to assert our triumphant hold on truth, but as acts of radical "dispossession." The basic ritual gestures that shaped the liturgy of Jesus' own people were acts of *receiving* rather than taking, of *divesting* rather than possessing. The biblical commands to offer God the "unblemished best," the "firstfruits" of fields and flocks (see Exod 12; Deut 26), mean that God's people *have* only what they *receive*. These offerings are ritualized, symbolic acts of *dispossession* (surrender) through which Israel *receives* its land, precisely and only as *gift promised and bestowed by the God of creation and covenant*. Israel's identity is not chosen autonomously; it is neither self-generated nor self-bestowed, but God-given. The ritual acts of dispossession—of offering God the best of field and flock—thus have a double meaning. On one hand, it roots Israel's identity in a generous, unexpected act of God (who liberated an insignificant tribe from bondage in Egypt); on the other, it reveals that Israel can maintain its identity as God's "elect," *only by giving its best away*, only by divesting itself of the finest goods its land and livestock can produce, by sharing them with those who have nothing, especially the "alien, the orphan and the widow" (see Deut 24:6-22).

The idea that the liturgy of a religious community can be verified only in

---

29. Meier, *Marginal Jew*, 2:297-98.

"the liturgy of the neighbor" thus goes back to the earliest stages of Israel's cultic history. Ritual acts of dispossession, of receiving rather than taking, of sharing bounty with "the alien, the orphan, and the widow" (i.e., with society's most vulnerable persons), thus became basic "boundary symbols" that sustained and reinforced Israel's identity—and its land—as "God's own." Ritual not only "means" for Israel; it *makes* Israel by bringing her to *meet* that Other who bestows her identity, her memory, and her mission.

The petition "hallowed be thy name" in the Lord's Prayer summarizes this rich ritual history. If, as suggested earlier, Jesus the marginal Galilean grew up embracing a Jewish piety that emphasized "the basics" of Torah (including its ritual prescriptions) and adhering stubbornly to the "boundary symbols" that reinforced Jewish identity,[30] then we must conclude that Jesus affirmed ritual's importance not so much as a repository of "meaning" but as an occasion of *meeting* and *making*. In ritual, Israel abandons the fiction of self-autonomy, the pretense that it can create itself; it acknowledges that the land and all it gives belong to God alone. Israel offers the best of field and flock *to* an Other, *for* others (aliens, orphans, widows), acknowledging thereby that its own identity is *given from* that Other, *received from* the God whose land Israel occupies merely "on loan." These rites, as Louis-Marie Chauvet observes,

> remind Israel, from deep within itself, of its identity: even after having entered into possession of the land, Israel can live as Israel only by continuing, generation after generation, to receive it from Yahweh's gracious hand. . . .
>
> *The offering of firstfruits is the figure where object and sign, non-possession and possession, attainment and expectation, heaven and earth, God's grace and the human work intersect each other.* It is the figure of the history Israel must live to be true to its identity.[31]

RITUAL'S MEMORY

Such, in my view, is the ritual past—the "prehistory"—that lies behind the petition that opens the Lord's Prayer. Yet Jesus did not believe that Israel had merely a past; he thought it also had a future—or better, that *God* had a future *for* it. One of ritual's major risks is its memory, its endangered and dangerous memory. Memory can, after all, be hollowed out, robbed of its future. A

---

30. See Meier, *Marginal Jew*, 2:1039-40.
31. Louis-Marie Chauvet, *Symbol and Sacrament: A Sacramental Reinterpretation of Christian Existence*, trans. Patrick Madigan and Madeleine Beaumont (Collegeville, Minn.: Liturgical Press, 1995), 237 (emphasis in original).

familiar strategy of totalitarian political regimes is their habit of erasing the memory of peoples and cultures by outlawing their languages (and hence disrupting the transmission of their native narratives). Yet humankind has a future only because it has a memory; it lives from and for (i.e., *toward*) its memory. For memory has more to do with the future than with the past. Memory is the future, posing as the past and living in us without our knowing it. That is why "the dead are everywhere," as Lawrence Durrell wrote in his novel *Clea* (part of the *Alexandria Quartet*):

> They cannot be so blindly evaded. One feels them pressing their sad blind fingers in deprivation upon the panels of our secret lives, asking to be remembered and re-enacted once more in the life of the flesh—encamping among our heartbeats, invading our embraces. We carry in ourselves the biological trophies they bequeathed to us by their failure to use up life—alignment of an eye, responsive curve of a nose; or in still more fugitive forms like someone's dead laugh, or a dimple which excites a long-buried smile. The simplest of these kisses we exchanged had a pedigree of death. In them we once more befriended forgotten loves which struggled to be reborn. The roots of every sigh are buried in the ground.[32]

Our desire, our longing ("every sigh") is movement toward a future in whose every nook and cranny we meet the arriving past, "encamping among our heartbeats, invading our embraces." For part of what makes memory so dangerous is its habit of sleepwalking. The "memory as somnambulist" metaphor appears near the end of Eudora Welty's novel *The Optimist's Daughter*. Laurel McKelva Hand, the novel's chief protagonist, has returned to her childhood home in Mississippi to sort through family papers after the death of her father. While there, Laurel, widowed when she was quite young, finds letters that vividly recall her brief marriage to Phil, killed in action during the Second World War. Unexpectedly, she discovers that her emotions have been, all along, quite unaware of the passage of time. As she reads the letters, she "put her head down on the open lid of the desk and wept in grief for love and for the dead. She lay there with all that was adamant in her yielding . . . at last. *Now all she had found had found her.* The deepest spring in her heart had uncovered itself, and it began to flow again."[33]

Until that moment, Laurel thought her love for her late husband had long ago been sealed away, locked in its own perfection, consigned to the past. Now, suddenly, and "by her own hand, the past had been raised up, and *he*

---

32. Lawrence Durrell, *Clea* (New York: E. P. Dutton, 1960), 229-30.

33. Eudora Welty, *The Optimist's Daughter* (New York: Random House Vintage Books, 1972), 181 (emphasis added).

looked at her, Phil himself—here waiting, all the time, Lazarus." Laurel discovers that danger lies not in the past, but in memory. The past, she reflects, "is no more open to help or hurt than was [her] Father in his coffin. The past is like him, impervious, and can never be awakened." But memory is another matter. "It is memory that is the somnambulist. It will come back in its wounds from across the world . . . calling us by our names and demanding its rightful tears. . . . The memory can be hurt, time and again—but in that may lie its final mercy. As long as it's vulnerable to the living moment, it lives for us, and while it lives, and while we are able, we can give it up its due."[34]

With memory's danger in mind, let us return to the opening petitions of the Lord's Prayer: "Hallowed be thy name; thy kingdom come." What Meier calls the "God-centered, eschatological orientation" of Jesus' prayer has already been noted. For Jesus to pray "hallowed be thy name" is for him to ask that the God whose special name is *Abba*, "my own dear Father," act once and for all to reveal his holiness in humanity.[35] Yet here too we meet a paradox. Jesus has instructed his disciples to call God *Abba*, "my own dear Father," yet *Abba* was not—as every Jew knew—the proper Hebrew name for the Almighty. "*Abba*" was never God's official, personal name (a name so sacred it could not be pronounced in public prayer). *Abba* was an Aramaic word, familiar in every family and household—and yet *it is this "familiar God" whom Jesus asks to manifest the divine holiness in humanity once for all.*[36] There is no small irony in the link between "*Abba* in heaven" and "hallowed be thy name." "This ironic association of a familiar word for father with the revered name of God," writes Hal Taussig,

> was certainly jarring. . . . Just as Jesus' association of blessedness or happiness with the poor and hungry was shocking, so was the prayer "*Abba*/Father, your name be revered." The unexpected combination surprised people into rethinking what was and was not holy. As a prayer, it called upon people to put God and reverence in a much broader perspective. . . . This two-sentence prayer—like Jesus' parables and aphorisms—expanded people's vision of what was important and holy.[37]

In Jesus' prayer, the risks of ritual and the dangers of memory come to a

---

34. Ibid., 181 (emphasis in original), 207.

35. Meier, *Marginal Jew*, 2:297.

36. More than forty years ago, the distinguished scholar Raymond E. Brown noted that Jesus' use of "*Abba*," without modifier was not only distinctive, but already gave the Lord's Prayer an eschatological tonality, because it looked toward a time when the notion of a "national covenant with God" would be expanded to include all those who enter into a relationship with God in an intimate, personal way, as Jesus himself did (see "The Pater Noster as an Eschatological Prayer," in *New Testament Essays* [Milwaukee: Bruce, 1965], 217-53, here 225-26).

37. Taussig, *Jesus before God*, 76.

head. Jesus' co-religionists would have been fully familiar with the memory of God's acting as Mighty Ruler, especially in the liberating events of exodus, ritually rehearsed in the Passover liturgy (see Exod 12:24-27; 15:1-17; Num 15:37-41). In the Lord's Prayer, however, Jesus deliberately connects his opening cry, "*Abba*," to a central expectation of Jewish eschatology, that of "the glorious manifestation of God's power in the end time, when God comes to rule fully as king."[38] Jesus audaciously juxtaposes realities that might seem to cancel one another. The word *abba* was properly used for one's *human* father; it never designated God in Jewish liturgical prayer during Jesus' time.[39] Moreover, Jesus' strategy in the Lord's Prayer seems deliberately parabolic, aimed at provoking a clash that would overturn ordinary assumptions about who God is and how God acts in the world.[40]

Making People Think Twice: Jesus as Cultural Critic

"By calling God 'Father' [i.e., *Abba*]," writes Taussig, "Jesus made people think twice."[41] For us, thinking tenderly about God as "father of a family" is so familiar, so conventional, that it causes no comment. But Jesus' own contemporaries in the religiously conservative society of rural Galilee would have heard something disturbing in his *abba* language. Traditional piety taught devout Jews to rely on the *basics*, the conventional values of Torah, Temple, family, clan, nation, wealth, and economic success (sure signs of God's blessing on human work). Yet Jesus boldly challenged many of these conventions, and he brought that challenge directly into the gestures and practices of public prayer.

Recall the collection of anti-anxiety sayings in the sixth chapter of Matthew's Gospel (Matt 6:25-34). "Do not worry about your life, what you will eat, or about your body, what you will wear. . . . Look at the birds in the sky; they do not sow or reap, they gather nothing into barns, yet your heavenly Father feeds them. . . . Why are you anxious . . . ?" Such sayings seem to be "companion pieces" to Jesus' teachings about reliance on the wrong things: for example, wealth (Luke 6:20), family connections (Matt 12:48-50), "scholarly prestige" (Mark 12:38-39), or even religion and its rituals (Mark 2:27-28; Lk 18:10-14).[42] Benedict Viviano points out that Jesus' teaching in Matthew

---

38. Meier, *Marginal Jew*, 2:300.

39. Ibid. One must recognize that the contrast between God and the *abba* of a family in first-century Mediterranean societies such as the one Jesus knew would not have been as dramatic as it would be in twenty-first-century North America.

40. Jesus' strategy of parable and its relation to ritual as "reimagining the world" will be discussed more fully in the next chapter.

41. Taussig, *Jesus before God*, 67.

42. See ibid., 68, for this list.

6:25-34 "presupposes Galilean prosperity" and may even show some "insensitivity" toward the desperately poor and destitute; perhaps it reflects "a young person's interest in discovering the limits of human existence, the real necessities and true values of life." Also important is the Greek verb *merimnaō*, used throughout the passage and usually translated by English verbs such as "worry" or "be anxious." More accurately, *merimnaō* means to "be preoccupied" or "be absorbed by" something. In this light, Jesus' teaching seems to comment on "basic human needs, eating, drinking, clothing . . . insofar as they can become idols or fetishes."[43] Jesus seems to be saying that his *abba* is "not a God . . . enmeshed in and allied to systems of wealth," commerce, trades, markets, entrepreneurship, good-ole-boy networks—or even the more "reliable" systems of family and religion.[44] More shocking still, perhaps, Jesus seems to base his teaching about "not letting yourself be absorbed by these things" on simple observations about everyday experience, rather than on the Bible (e.g., the natural order of goodness depicted in the priestly poem of Gen 1:1-2:4a).[45]

Or consider Jesus' attitude toward "family values." In the first century C.E., according to Taussig, the "Galilee family was the primary form of 'social security,'" the bond that "provided a safety net for the needy and the aged," especially if they "suffered health or business disasters." It may thus surprise us to learn that Jesus was not exactly a poster child for either the "nuclear" or the "extended" family. In fact, he appears to have regarded "reliance on traditional family ties" as an "impediment to a lifestyle that trusts in the God beyond family conventions." Hence, "Jesus' core sayings regularly criticized dependence on these conventions, and invoked trust in the more basic fabric of life that God provides."[46]

Jesus' rather complex attitude toward the family may thus be part not only of his distinctive vision of God (*abba*) but also of his critique of culture. Novelist Mary Gordon draws our attention to the way Jesus interacts with children in Mark's Gospel (9:30-37; 10:2-16). The Victorians, she reminds us, were the first modern folk to "fall in love with childhood," a phenomenon especially evident in the novels of Charles Dickens. Jesus, Gordon suggests, was not a Victorian sentimentalist, but "was interested in children in a way that was really original"; he seemed to care about children *in themselves*—and

---

43. Benedict T. Viviano, "The Gospel According to Matthew," in *The New Jerome Biblical Commentary*, ed. Raymond E. Brown et al. (Englewood Cliffs, N.J.: Prentice-Hall, 1990), 42:45, p. 646.
44. Taussig, *Jesus before God*, 69.
45. See Viviano, "Gospel According to Matthew," 42:45, p. 646.
46. Taussig, *Jesus before God*, 68-69.

not as possessions, as markers of immortality, or as "future economic opportunities."[47]

Jesus' attitude is astonishing, if one recalls that in first-century Mediterranean societies, scant attention was paid to *individuals* at all—especially if they were children. Children were literally nobodies; they had no rights and (often enough) no real value except "potential." Among gentiles, an unwanted child (especially a girl) could be abandoned and left to die. Jesus lived within a social structure characterized by a "*groupism* based on kinship and gender."[48] Family honor mattered, connections mattered, patronage mattered, males mattered, politics mattered—but women and small children did not.

It may shock us to discover, therefore, that in a society that placed so much emphasis on the network of family ties, Jesus had some fairly harsh things to say about traditional "family values." "Do you think I have come to establish peace on earth?" Jesus asks in Luke 12:51; "No, I tell you, but rather division . . . a father will be divided against his son and a son against his father; a mother against her daughter and a daughter against her mother. . . ." And earlier in Luke's Gospel, when a woman from the crowd shouts, "Blessed is the womb that bore you and the breasts you sucked," Jesus fires back: "No! Blessed are they who hear God's word and keep it!" (see Luke 11:27-28). Here is evidence that Jesus refused to buy into the "family values" rhetoric of his own time and place. When someone declares, in "splendid Mediterranean fashion," that Mary is "blessed" because she mothered "a famous son," Jesus snaps back, rejecting the patriarchal chauvinism that values a woman *only* if she produces male offspring. Instead, Jesus says, God, his *abba*, is now offering *all* people *a new kind of blessedness*—a blessedness based not on fertility or family ties, a "blessedness open to *anyone who wants it*," even the most ordinary person, "without distinction of sex or gender."[49] In the world of "business as usual," Jesus claimed, family life is based on competitive power (who gets it, who uses it, and who's subject to it). But where God reigns or rules— that is, in the "kingdom" or world as it will be when God is directly and immediately in charge—things are different, *so* different that traditional family arrangements break down.

---

47. See Mary Gordon, "The Gospel According to Saint Mark: Parts of a Journal," in *Incarnation: Contemporary Writers on the New Testament,* ed. Alfred Corn (New York: Penguin Books, 1990), 19-20. On Dickens's portrayal of children, see Vladimir Nabokov, *Lectures on Literature,* ed. Fredson Bowers (New York: Harcourt Brace Jovanovich, 1980), 65-69, 83-94. Nabokov was analyzing Dickens's novel *Bleak House.*

48. John Dominic Crossan, *Jesus: A Revolutionary Biography* (San Francisco: HarperCollins, 1994), 58.

49. Ibid., 59 (emphasis added).

Jesus' Critique of the Rituals of Family Life

Jesus grew up in a religious culture that valued the many rites that mark transitions and guard the boundaries of personal and family life—rites surrounding sex, birth, marriage, planting and harvest, illness and recovery, contracts and covenants, meals, diet, dishes, and death (see, e.g., Lev 11-16, the laws regulating purity in personal and family life). As we have seen, however, the Gospels sometimes portray Jesus as sharply critical of the ritualized pieties proper to family life. Indeed, Mark's Gospel records a sharp exchange between Jesus and members of his own family. Told that his "mother and brothers" are outside asking for him, Jesus almost denies that he knows them. "Who are my mother and brothers?" he asks. "And looking around at those seated in the circle he said: 'Here are my mother and my brothers. For whoever does God's will is my brother and sister and mother" (Mark 3:31-35). Jesus' brusque response suggests a rather unsentimental relationship with his "family of origin." Indeed, Jesus claims to have a *new* family, one based on choice and intention rather than blood—on kith (friends, acquaintances, associates) rather than kin. To the people of his time, Jesus' words may well have sounded rash, even indefensible. After all, "in a society in which family relationships were extraordinarily important, the idea of a spiritual family had the effect of relativizing other relationships."[50] Moreover, salvation itself depended on one's continued *membership in a divinely chosen group* (the family bond reflected the larger covenant between God and Israel). By rejecting his natural family, Jesus would have done the unthinkable—placing himself "beyond the pale," *outside* the circle of salvation!

More troubling still are Jesus' words about wreaking havoc in families. "From now on, a household of five will be divided: three against two and two against three" (Luke 12:52). Here Jesus calls attention to a typical Palestinian "party of five," an extended family of five persons living under one roof: father, mother, (married) son, (unmarried) daughter, and daughter-in-law. We expect, of course, that Jesus will say something *nice* about the extended family (e.g., younger members showing respect, obedience and care for their elders). We expect him to applaud such arrangements as examples of God's goodness, care, and blessing, as signs of God's favor. Instead, Jesus says he intends to tear such families apart!

Because Jesus' words cause embarrassment to those who "focus on family," some commentators suggest that Jesus' vehement reaction stems from his

---

50. See Daniel J. Harrington, "The Gospel According to Mark," in *The New Jerome Biblical Commentary*, ed. Raymond E. Brown et al., 41:23, pp. 604-5. Harrington notes that the "central saying" of Mark 3:33 "contains at least a harsh note about Jesus' natural family."

knowledge that *some* family members will believe him, while others will *not*. But this explanation misses the point. The family isn't split over *faith;* it's split by a struggle over *power.* What Jesus rejects here isn't the "extended family" as such, but dysfunctional, manipulative families where fathers and mothers rule the roost, dominating even their adult sons, daughters, and daughters-in-law—bossing them, controlling them, treating them as inferiors rather than as equals. Jesus recognized that adult relationships based on competitive power—on who can boss, dominate, control, and manipulate all the others—are not only unhealthy but unstable. "The family," Jesus understood, "is society in miniature, the place where we first learn how to love and be loved, hate and be hated, help and be helped, abuse and be abused." Because it involves power—as well as the risky rituals of negotiating that power—a family is not only a "center of domestic serenity" and security; it also "invites the abuse of power," and it is "at that precise point that Jesus attacks it."[51]

In the kingdom—in that world where God is directly and immediately in charge—a new pattern of human relationships becomes possible, Jesus insists. This new pattern is not the "traditional family," Jesus says; rather, it's a whole new society, where the least and littlest are on equal footing with the best and brightest; where the have-nots sit at table elbow-to-elbow with the haves; where the unwanted and the unwashed are always welcome; where the hungry are fed, the naked clothed, the thirsty refreshed, and the prisoner visited. *These*, Jesus suggests, are the relationships that reveal the kingdom (reign, rule) of God. It isn't the *family* that models what God's *kingdom* is like; it's God's *kingdom* that models what *families* are meant to be. For that reason, Jesus believed that God's reign belongs not to the powerful—for example, not to manipulative parents who treat their adult offspring like disobedient children—but to the nobodies, to the children themselves. Recall the powerful scene in Mark 10:13-16:

> People were bringing children to him that he might touch them, but his disciples rebuked them. When Jesus saw this he became indignant and said to them, "Let the children come to me; do not prevent them, *for the kingdom of God belongs to such as these. Amen, I say to you, whoever does not accept the kingdom of God like a child will not enter it."* Then he embraced them, and blessed them, placing his hands on them.

These verses are sometimes read as a Victorian greeting card, a sentimentalized portrait of "Jesus, sweet friend of little children." We forget that in the sometimes horrific circumstances of first-century Mediterranean family life,

---

51. Crossan, *Jesus: A Revolutionary Biography*, 60.

a child was chattel, at the mercy of a father who could, freely and without any
punitive sanction, reject his own flesh and blood. Crossan explains that a
child could be sold to an "unscrupulous adult to be reared as a slave." Jesus, in
contrast, takes the side of those who have no power; he values the children in
and for *themselves*—not because of their social or economic "potential." Mark
says he touched, embraced, and blessed them. These are precisely the rituals,
the "official bodily actions of a father designating a newly born infant for life
rather than death, for accepting it into his family rather than casting it out
with the garbage."[52] Jesus places himself squarely on the side of life—he
accepts as *God-given* the *child's* right to live, grow, and flourish. For Jesus, the
kingdom of God is a kingdom of *children*, a kingdom of *nobodies*.

Nobodies. These are precisely the people Jesus calls to liturgy, to communion with God, to life as God's people, to feasting at God's table. The world
as it will be when God reigns, Jesus said, isn't about power—it's about vulnerability and need, about *justice*. In Luke's Gospel, especially, God's "kingdom" is closely connected to meals and table companionship. In Luke, writes
Eugene LaVerdiere, a meal "is not so much about food as it is about people.
In all meals it is the guest list, not the menu, that matters. Blessings and
prayers, liturgical and non-liturgical, have to do with the people who have
come together to share the meal."[53] Bread is always about bodies, and bodies
are always about justice. Unquestionably that is a primary reason why the
Christian eucharist has for centuries been the central icon, the sacrament par
excellence, of our faith. It is what "family" (as radically redefined by Jesus) is
about. "We must," writes Crossan, "keep together flesh and spirit, body and
soul, religion and politics, theology and economics. God's Law always
embraces those dichotomies together; . . . food is about justice and justice is
about God. The kingdom of God is about food and drink—that is, above
divine justice for material bodies here on material earth. We do not live by
bread alone. But bread is never alone."[54]

Jesus thus replaced "focus on the family" and its rituals (some good, some
bad) with the vision of a new human community initiated and sustained by
God's reign, rule, or kingdom. In such a community, "calling out to God as
'*Abba*/Father' replaced one's reliance on the family systems of privilege, inheritance, and honor. . . . Those listening to [Jesus'] '*Abba*' prayers were no doubt
aware that he was replacing tangible family security with a much more intan-

52. Ibid., 64.
53. Eugene LaVerdiere, *Dining in the Kingdom of God: The Origins of the Eucharist According to Luke* (Chicago: Liturgy Training Publications, 1994), vii.
54. John Dominic Crossan, *The Birth of Christianity* (San Francisco: HarperCollins, 1998), 422.

gible 'reign of God.'"[55] Jesus thus preached the wisdom of insecurity. God's reign is not a comfortable sinecure, but a people, a new community in which, as Juan Mateos notes,

> there is no one on top or beneath, but all are last and first at the same time (Mt 19:30), children with one father, servants with one Lord, disciples with one master, poor people whose only riches and security are in God . . . (Mt 6:19-21; 19:21). Here there is not mine or thine (Acts 32). It is a group filled with perfect joy (Jn 15:11; 16:24), mutual affection (Rom 12:10, Col 3:12), swift and unlimited pardon (Mt 18:21-22, Col 3:13), where no rivalry or partisanship exists, but all are united in love (Col 3:14) and reciprocal support (Mt 5:7). Each one shoulders the burden of the others (Gal 6:2), the qualities of each are at the service of all (Rom 12:3-8, 1 Cor 12:4-11, Eph 4:11-13), and authority means greater service, not superiority (Lk 22:26-27).[56]

Obviously, this portrait of a new community may have more to do with eschatological hope than with present fact. Still, Jesus himself did not underestimate the difficulty of replacing reliance on religious conventions (including the rituals of family life) with a new understanding of how persons could and should live together. He understood that "the root of the troubles of humanity lies in the very foundations of the institutions it has created: in the striving for money, desire for prestige and thirst for power; in the threefold ambition of 'holding,' 'climbing,' and 'commanding' that spurs people on to rivalry, hatred, and violence." Holding, climbing, commanding: the voluntary renunciation of these three addictions is the condition for creating "a new society in which people could be free and happy (Mt 5: 3-10)." When people reject "the three false values: money (thirst for riches), glory (ambition for recognition), and power (desire to dominate)," Jesus' vision can begin to take hold.[57] Bread is about bodies, and bodies are always about justice. Yet, compared to Israel's ancient prophets, the Christian scriptures seem sometimes much less passionate in their calls for justice. Mateos suggests a reason why:

> The radicalism of Jesus makes us understand why in the gospel we do not find the plea for justice as commonly as in the prophets. The prophets were reformers too, and they demanded justice because they believed in

---

55. Taussig, *Jesus before God*, 69.
56. Juan Mateos, "The Message of Jesus," *Sojourners* 6, no. 7 (July 1997): 8-16, here 15. Mateos wrote this essay as an introduction to a new Spanish edition of the New Testament. It was translated for *Sojourners* by Sister Kathleen England.
57. Ibid., 12.

the validity of the institutions. Jesus did not come to ask for justice, but to offer a final solution to the injustice of the world.[58]

Jesus' solution lay not in institutional or liturgical reform, but in a far more radical act that involved his own body and the bodies of those who believed with and in him. "The cross of Jesus is the radical condemnation of an unjust world," writes Mateos.

> There is no escape from the cross; you have to stay with the one crucified or stand with the crucifiers; there is no middle way. All that God values is hated and killed by the world, and what the world esteems, God abhors. Through Jesus, God offered the world equality, solidarity and mutual help, freedom, love, life, and happiness with God as its king and father [abba]. But domination, violence, injustice, the religious and civil power, the ruling class and the people seeking their security in institutions, hate life and give death. They prefer Caesar for king.[59]

The Rituals of a God Who Doesn't Act Like One

The Lord's Prayer, as our discussion earlier in this chapter has shown, hints that the God whose name Jesus prays might be hallowed is One prepared to act in surprisingly "un-Godlike" ways. Like Laurel McKelva Hand's late husband, Phil, Israel's God had seemed safely sealed in the past, impervious to change. Yet memory breaks the seals and so frees God to glide through Jesus' prayer like a somnambulist, resisting assigned roles, refusing to "stay in character," disrupting the perfection of the past. The "stark juxtaposition of the single, intimate word '*abba*' . . . with the powerful symbol of God as king coming to rule in the end time"[60] is a clue that, for Jesus, God's final act for the world (i.e., God's "eschatological" deed) will *not* be "business as usual." Meier summarizes this point well:

> Jesus teaches his disciples to pray for the longed-for coming of God as king, the king who would manifest his power and glory by regathering Israel in the end time. Yet this transcendent, almighty king of creation and history is addressed by the disciples as their own dear father. *Measureless divine might, about to explode in the final act of human hsitory, is accessible*

---

58. Ibid.
59. Ibid., 15. By "world," in this text, Mateos is referring not to the natural order of creation or to the world as an embodiment of God's will to save humankind, but to the world as John's Gospel sometimes uses it: the "world" as the collective focus of all that is opposed to God and to God's reign.
60. Meier, *Marginal Jew*, 2:300.

even now in prayer by those who enjoy intimacy with the diivne king, who is also their loving father. This union of opposites in a few tight words encapsulates in miniature a good deal of Jesus' message.[61]

Small wonder that early Christian writers referred to the Lord's Prayer as a brief "compendium of the whole gospel." Jesus may not have been an anti-ritualist, but neither did he believe that memory—even memory hallowed by communal prayer and scripture—could prevent God from acting *now*, as tender *Abba*, to "do a new thing," to bring salvation to the unsuspecting and the unlikely: "Amen, I say to you, tax collectors and prostitutes are entering the kingdom of God before you. When John came to you in the way of righteousness, you did not believe him, but tax collectors and sinners did" (Matt 21:31-32). The surprising accessibility of God as *Abba*—even (or especially) among those whom "religious" folk might wish to shut up or shut down—seems central to Jesus' understanding of prayer, ritual, and the new humanity whom God's grace and favor will establish in the end time.

In sum, Jesus' language in the Lord's Prayer, Taussig explains, does not easily fit into "the normal patterns of economy or social convention." In Jesus' prayer, Israel's ritually rehearsed memory of God—a transcendent, victorious warrior who acts "with mighty hand and outstretched arm"—begins to arrive from the future not as YHWH of hosts, potent LORD of armies, but as "my own dear Father," *Abba*. Moreover, *Abba's* "kingdom" (reign, rule, domain), whose coming Jesus prays for, seemed to transgress the very values that devout, "right-minded religious people" held dear. Thus, for instance, "to a society where having as many sons as possible was a sure sign of God's favor, Jesus saluted men who 'castrated themselves because of Heaven's imperial rule'" (Matt 19:12). Similarly, in a culture where "wealth was seen as a sign of God's blessing, Jesus pressed the *differentness* of God's reign"[62] by warning his hearers "how hard it is for those who have wealth to enter the kingdom of God" (Mark 10:23). And as we saw in the preceding section of this chapter, a society that relied on family as a fundamental form of "social security" may well have rejected Jesus' critique of family life as both disloyal and dangerous. To hear and take to heart such startling reversals of long-held religious expectations requires drastic change. Perhaps that is why Jesus remarked that "it is easier to pass through the eye of a needle than for one who is rich to enter the kingdom of God" (Mark 10:25). In any case, the risks involved in receiving Jesus' teaching were considerable. "Taking internalizing and spiritual steps to allow for and maintain this openness," writes Taussig,

---

61. Ibid., 300-301.
62. Taussig, *Jesus before God*, 82.

was the rationale for Jesus' prayer that the comprehensive, elusive, and surprising reign of God come. Many would be taken aback by someone praying, "let your [kingdom] come" in the middle of social situations in which
workers, families, and guardians of the economy were expecting a conventional order. Such an invocation challenged the hearers and those praying
to re-situate their own allegiances toward God *by changing the ways they
acted toward one another.*[63]

By teaching others to pray "*Abba*, . . . thy kingdom come," Jesus was invit-
ing them to begin experiencing, even now, that "new human community" that
would come to exist with the eschatological arrival of the kingdom—not a
warrior kingdom of soldiers, generals, and military exploits; not a family-
friendly kingdom of "business as usual"; not an economic juggernaut promis-
ing progress and prosperity; but a kingdom of the persecuted, the poor in
spirit, mourners, the meek, peacemakers, people hungry and thirsty for righteousness (see Matt 5:3-10).[64] The community of Jesus' *Abba* prayer is thus
not limited to the people of Israel but embraces all "the poor, the sick, and the
needy who accept Jesus' preaching of the kingdom, a kingdom prepared by
the Father through Jesus" and "already incipient" in Jesus' ministry.[65] This is
a kingdom—a realm, a reign—that manifests itself not in wealth, wars, or
weaponry, but in an itinerant prophet who "hobnobbed with the religious low
life of Palestine and traveled around the countryside with a strangely mixed
entourage of men and women 'on leave' from their spouses."[66]

More shocking still, perhaps, the "kingdom of God" for whose coming
Jesus prayed was not to be a community of priests but a community of *laypersons*. Despite the centrality of Temple and Torah in the religion of his time,
despite his own reverence, as a Galilean peasant, for the Temple's rituals of
priestly sacrifice, tithing, and pilgrimage, Jesus' own religious commitment—
from his birth in Bethlehem to his death outside the city of Jersualem—was
that of a devout, deeply engaged *layperson*. Theoretically, given his family
background in isolated, rural Galilee, and given the prevailing religious ethos
of that region in the first century C.E., one would expect Jesus' attitude toward
priesthood and Temple liturgy to be conservative, traditionalist.[67] Yet it seems
quite clear that "Jesus the Galilean peasant layman, who *claimed charismatic*

---

63. Ibid., 83 (emphasis added).
64. See Brown, "Pater Noster as an Eschatological Prayer," 227.
65. Ibid.
66. Meier, *Marginal Jew*, 1:344.
67. On the preponderance of conservative attitudes toward the Temple in Galilee, see Sean
Freyne, *Galilee from Alexander the Great to Hadrian, 323 B.C.E. to 135 C.E.* (Wilmington, Del.:
Michael Glazier, and University of Notre Dame Press, 1980), 259-60.

religious authority outside the recognized channels" eventually came into conflict with "the high priestly families of Jerusalem, whose power depended on controlling the sacred center of Jerusalem, the temple."[68]

One might ask how such a conflict could have happened since, as we have seen earlier in this chapter, Jesus was fundamentally a devout layman who respected the religious institutions of his people. No doubt part of this conflict was cultural, rooted in deep differences between rural poor and urban rich, between lay prophecy (with its eschatological emphasis on a "new order of things to come") and priestly bureaucracy (eager to keep the liturgical status quo). Yet this cultural conflict does not explain everything. We know, for example, that as the Synoptic Gospels portray him, Jesus also disputed with *lay* religious leaders (e.g., scribes, Pharisees, and synagogue rulers). With these lay folk, however, as Meier says, he kept the "lines of communication open" even if they were "often red hot." When it came to the Temple—its management, its liturgical praxis and personnel—the situation was far more neuralgic. Whatever the precise historical details may have been, a pattern of conflict emerges in the Synoptic Gospels. Jesus "engages in regular debate" and is even on friendly terms with many *lay* teachers. But with the priestly party in Jerusalem (which included lay Sadducean aristocrats)—the official "guardians of divine revelation and divine power"—Jesus' relations are rare and hostile.[69]

To return to the issue posed at the outset of this chapter, the Christian Scriptures do not portray Jesus as a "fallen-away Jew," a dropout who avoided the liturgies of Temple and synagogue. But these sources do suggest that his attitude toward these institutions and their rituals was complex. The Gospels reveal Jesus as a Galilean "lay theologian," a peasant-prophet working in a religiously and politically ideologized atmosphere dominated by priests and lay aristocrats whose power center was the Jerusalem Temple. The biblical narratives do not reduce Jesus to a one-dimensional figure; he was not a mere rabble-rouser resentful at being excluded from Jerusalem's power elites. Yet Jesus could be—and apparently was—highly critical of the very Temple whose rites he valued. Such reverence for Temple worship did not translate into compliance, complacency, or an uncritical attitude of mute acceptance. As Meier notes, a "pious laity, dedicated to the ideals of a holy priesthood conducting pure worship, can for that very reason be all the more critical of the flesh-and-blood priests before their eyes." Jesus' status as a marginalized lay prophet, preacher, and theologian was not, therefore, a neutral factor; it

---

68. Meier, *Marginal Jew*, 1:347.
69. Ibid., 346.

played a decisive role in the "development and denouement" of his life and ministry. Far from withdrawing, Jesus remained an active participant in the religious life of his people, joining other pilgrims at the Jerusalem Temple even as he "bewailed the failings of at least the upper-level priests who officiated there. The fact that his ministry made Jesus stand out from the run-of-the-mill laity made his criticism much more dangerous—for the priests and for himself."[70]

No doubt there was an edge to Jesus that could and did make others edgy. He was, John Dominic Crossan writes, "a Jewish peasant with an attitude, and he claimed that his attitude was that of the Jewish God,"[71] a God whom he preferred to address in the familiar Aramaic vernacular—*Abba*—rather than in the Hebrew *Ab* ("father") or *Abinu* ("our father") of formal Jewish prayer. When Jesus prayed "thy kingdom come" he embodied his hope that God would establish, once and for all, not a new religious doctrine or regime, but a renewed community of persons under *Abba*'s rulership. "The kingdom of God," writes Crossan,

> was never just about words and ideas. . . . It was about a way of life. And that means it was about a body of flesh and blood. Justice is always about bodies and lives, not just about words and ideas. Resurrection does not mean, simply, that the spirit or soul of Jesus lives on in the world. And neither does it mean, simply, that the companions or followers of Jesus live on in the world. It must be *the embodied life* that remains powerfully efficacious in this world. . . . There is . . . only one Jesus, the embodied Galilean who lived a life of divine justice in an unjust world. . . . There are not two Jesuses—one pre-Easter and another post-Easter, one earthly and another heavenly, one with a physical and another with a spiritual body. *There is only one Jesus, the historical Jesus who incarnated the Jewish God of justice for a believing community committed to continuing such incarnation ever afterward.*[72]

Bread is always about bodies, and bodies are always about justice. According to Luke, Jesus made that point clear at an early stage in his "journey toward Jerusalem." Returning to his hometown one Sabbath, he preached on a text from the prophet Isaiah, "The Spirit of the Lord is upon me . . . to bring glad tidings to the poor . . . liberty to captives . . . recovery of sight to the blind . . . to let the oppressed go free . . . to proclaim a year acceptable to the Lord" (Luke 4:18-19). Jesus opened his sermon with a one-liner: "Today this scrip-

---

70. Ibid., 347, 349.
71. Crossan, *Birth of Christianity*, xxx.
72. Ibid. (emphasis added).

ture passage is fulfilled in your hearing" (Luke 4:21). So far, so good. Quite probably his hearers already identified themselves with Isaiah's "poor." But Jesus moved quickly to make his meaning clearer: in Elijah's time, God overlooked the worthy widows of Israel and instead sent the prophet to a poor *gentile* widow (Luke 4:25-27). The implication was provocative: through prophets (like Elijah and, by inference, like Jesus) God's mercy is being universalized, reaching "non-chosen, needy people," women and men. God's compassion is not restricted to Israel; it is unconditional, and hence Jesus' hometown audience cannot identify themselves with Isaiah's "poor." They cannot "claim special treatment," nor can their opposition squelch the unfolding of God's work in Jesus himself.[73]

Here, then, is Jesus disrupting—deliberately, it would seem—a Sabbath-day synagogue liturgy. So much, he implies, for traditional Galilean reliance on family, clan, nation, and religion. Nor did Jesus' liturgical "mischief" stop there. As noted earlier, he seems to have enraged the religious authorities in Jerusalem both by "cleansing" the Temple and later (in the last week of his life), by staging a mock "triumphal parade" into the city, a parody of those solemn royal ceremonies used by the Herodian client-kings to impress the credulous citizenry each year at Passover (Mark 11:1-11; Matt 21:1-11; Luke 19:28-38; John 12:12-15). It is tempting to interpret Jesus' cleansing the Temple as a similarly staged demonstration, a potent piece of guerrilla theater. But the scene is not quite that simple. The Temple, after all, was the religious, liturgical, and commercial center of Jewish life; it was the very heart of how Jews understood their relationship with God. That is what made Jesus' defiance (if such it was) so dangerous. If the problem had been the Temple's *liturgies*, Jesus could simply have critiqued the music, the incense, the vestments, and the high priest's "presidential style."

But for Jesus, the problem wasn't liturgy or ritual; it was *relationship*—the bond between God and God's people. Jesus' demonstration against the Temple was bound to be perceived as a parable-in-action. It announced that God's relationship to the Temple (and thus to the people who worshiped there) was about to change—to change profoundly—and thus, that the traditional bonds connecting people, God, and Temple were about to be dislocated. Something new and radical was on the horizon. And that "something," according to John's Gospel, was *Jesus' own body*, a body destined to die and rise. Jesus' *body* is the "Temple" (see John 2:19), where the changing relationship between God and people will be seen, sealed, and savored as food and drink. From here on out, Jesus announced, the "Temple" is no longer a place

---

73. Robert Karris, "The Gospel According to Luke," in *The New Jerome Biblical Commentary*, ed. Raymond E. Brown et al., 43:61-62, p. 690.

but a person. From here on out, what is required to renew the relation between people and God is a *body*, a human body that can change and grow, shout and whisper, make promises and keep them, gurgle with happiness, taste the tart and the sweet, cry out in anger and pain—a body whose deeds are carved in bone, carried on breath and blood, given as bread and wine. Jesus didn't cleanse the Temple because it was "evil" (it was not), or because its liturgies were bad (they were not), but because the relationship between God and God's people was changing. The future of that relationship, Jesus believed, was bound up with the future of his own body.

CONCLUSION

As this chapter has shown, Jesus was a person who prayed—and a person who taught others to pray, to seek the "hallowing of God's name" and the coming of God's reign or kingdom. While Jesus worshiped in both Temple and synagogue, he was critical of both. This does not mean that Jesus was a fierce, first-century liturgical terrorist bent on subverting Jewish worship. On the contrary, like most Jews of his time, Jesus believed deeply in the bond between liturgy and life, worship and justice, ethics and ritual. As Paula Fredriksen comments, "For a Jew, both ethics and ritual stand on the same continuum, because both are equally the revealed will of God." The evangelist Mark subtly reminds readers of the role traditional piety played in the Lord's life when he mentions not only that Jesus frequented synagogues on the Sabbath, but that people seeking cures grabbed hold of "the fringes of his garment" (Mark 6:56). These fringes (still worn today by orthodox Jews) were not a decorative "fashion statement"; they were *ritual* in nature. Wearing ritual fringe underscored the idea that *all* Jewish life and liturgy (including the Temple's "mandated cult of sacrifices and offerings"[74]) are a holy sign of God's presence to a covenanted people.

It wasn't the Jewish liturgy that troubled Jesus; it was the *relationship* which that liturgy claimed to enact and embody. As I have noted frequently in this chapter, Jesus was a *Galilean;* he lived a life quite different from that of the "people in charge," the political and religious aristocrats in Jerusalem. Indeed, as Meier writes, most of Jesus' life was "insufferably *ordinary*, and his ordinariness included the ordinary status of a *layman*, without any special religious credentials or 'power base.'" Truth to tell, the bulk of Jesus' life seems to have been obscure, unmemorable, and uneventful. He had no PR network,

---

74. Fredriksen, *Jesus of Nazareth, King of the Jews*, 109, 107.

no handlers and spin doctors, and he seems to have had no inside connections to the religious and political "A-list" in Jerusalem. Jesus was a negligible nobody from nowhere, a woodworker—poor by our standards, but not necessarily by his. "Strange as it may seem," writes Meier, "Jesus grew up and conducted much of his ministry in an uncommonly peaceful oasis sheltered from the desert whirlwind that was most of Palestinian history." Thus, the Gospels tell us next to nothing about Jesus' career between the ages of twelve and thirty, and that "silence may have a simple explanation: *nothing much happened.*"[75]

During most of his life, then, Jesus was an "insufferably ordinary" person. He was and remained a devout Jew, though he died a *Roman* death. Yet even Jesus' execution was not unusual; crucifixion was the common Roman remedy for any perceived or threatened political insurrection. Even in death, Jesus remained "insufferably ordinary." He died hanging between two criminals, a convict condemned among other convicts. Yet this very ordinariness is what gave Jesus his astonishing power as prophet, healer, and proclaimer of God's realm or reign as it breaks into human lives, turning them inside out and upside down. This "nobody from nowhere," this marginal thirty-something Jewish peasant, this negligible Galilean prophet, somehow, amazingly, had found a way to empower others to continue doing what he had done. What made Jesus' preaching both powerful and accessible was its spontaneity, its plainness. *You* can do what I am doing, he argued. If you meet hunger, give it something to eat; if you meet thirst, give it something to drink; if you meet imprisonment, visit it; if you meet nakedness, clothe it.

Jesus did not reject Jewish liturgy, but he did redefine the relation between persons, world, and God. The place where much of this happened was the table. As the British scholar Norman Perrin wrote nearly forty years ago in his groundbreaking study *Rediscovering the Teaching of Jesus,*

> The central feature of the message of Jesus is ... the challenge of the forgiveness of sins and the offer of the possibility of a new kind of relationship with God and with one's fellow man. This was symbolized by a table-fellowship which celebrated the present joy and anticipated the future consummation; a table-fellowship of such joy and gladness that it survived the crucifixion and provided the focal point for the community life of the earliest Christians, and was the most direct link between that community life and the pre-Easter fellowship of Jesus and his disciples. ... [W]e are justified in seeing this table-fellowship as the central feature of

---

75. Meier, *Marginal Jew,* 1:351–52 (emphasis added).

the ministry of Jesus; an anticipatory sitting at table in the Kingdom of God and a very real celebration of present joy and challenge.[76]

Jesus empowered people by gathering them around the food and drink of a meal. At the end of the day, however, meals are never simply about food. A meal is a social *map* that defines (and may also defend or destroy) human relationships. *Who* eats *what* with *whom* is key. And precisely there, at table, Jesus' insufferable *ordinariness* begins to fade. The map Jesus proposed for meals was a radically inclusive one, at least if we are to believe Luke's Gospel. Scripture scholar R. Alan Culpepper reminds us how Luke presents Jesus as a prophet almost obsessed with a ministry to outcasts, sinners, Samaritans, tax collectors, women—the very people whom social and religious "big shots" often like to sideline and demonize. "Jesus refers to 'sinners,'" writes Culpepper, "more than does any other Gospel (17 times). . . . The term often emerges in the context of table fellowship and Jesus' practice of eating with those scorned by the religious authorities."[77]

Jesus thus appears to have believed that there is more to be learned from a self-confessed sinner than there is from a self-anointed saint. One of the most shocking things about Jesus' table ministry was thus his insistence on his—and *our*—fundamental *"right* to associate with *sinners*."[78] Recall the famous episode in Matthew's Gospel, when Jesus heals a paralytic (Matt 9:1-8). His action aroused fierce controversy because, besides healing the paralytic, he assured him of God's *forgiveness*. What angered the onlookers was Jesus' comment, "Courage, child, your sins are forgiven" (Matt 9:2), a comment that *preceded* any "confession of sin" by the paralytic on the stretcher. As Douglas Hare comments, "Jesus offers divine forgiveness *prior to* repentance, confession . . . [prior to a] request for forgiveness on the part of the paralytic. . . . To good religious people it was scandalous that Jesus kept such bad company. His enemies ridiculed him as a 'glutton and a drunkard, a friend of tax collectors and sinners.'"[79]

In short, Jesus chose not to wait until people "got religion" and became virtuous or saintly. He chose not to wait until human beings became ready to ask for forgiveness. Instead, Jesus seized the initiative, graciously creating the readiness in his hearers, and in this way he confirmed his right—and ours—to associate with sinners. Indeed, he claimed an inalienable right to call those sinners to table, to feast with the *un*righteous. Jesus insisted, outrageously,

76. Norman Perrin, *Rediscovering the Teaching of Jesus* (New York: Harper & Row, 1967), 107-8.
77. R. Alan Culpepper, "The Gospel of Luke: Introduction," in *The New Interpreter's Bible* (Nashville: Abingdon, 1995), 9:22-23.
78. Hare, *Matthew*, 101 (emphasis added).
79. Ibid., 101 (emphasis added).

that we not only have the right to hobnob with sinners, but that we have the right to sit at table with them, to eat and drink with them—humbly, joyfully, gratefully. Jesus' new "map for meals" meant that table is a place where sinners sit, a place where they feast in the presence of a "God with skin on." To *meet* this God, Jesus insists, what we need is not virtue but *hunger*—longing, yearning, desire. Hunger, as Marianne Sawicki has written, is "the baseline competence" we need for hearing God's word and for access to the Risen Lord. In Jesus' view, the table where sinners gather is nothing less than "the breast of God, where even little children may rest their heads"; it is his own feet, "where instruction flows sweet as kisses and clean as tears."[80] The Christian table is the place where the least, the littlest, and the lost can at last find a home.

So forgiveness was not only at the core of Jesus' preaching; it was at the heart of his table ministry as well. And this means that Jesus viewed ritual not as an opportunity to prove one's prowess (in virtue, in faith, in grasp of doctrine, in worship of God) but as an occasion to reveal one's need, one's hunger, one's yearning. What made Jesus' understanding of forgiveness, ritual, and their relationship innovative was his nonchronological view of time. As Thomas Sheehan says, Jesus did not think of past, present, and future as points on a diachronic time line; they were "eschatological categories that had to be read in terms of the only thing that mattered to Jesus," viz., the presence of God among human persons:

> The "past" was the reign of sin and Satan, the alienation of people from God, the weight of all that was impenetrable to the Father's gift of himself. And for Jesus all of that was gone or going. In its place came the "future," the presence of the Father himself among those who lived lives of justice and mercy. . . .
>
> The name Jesus used for this passing of the ages was "forgiveness"—but not in the usual religious sense of that term. The Father's forgiveness was not the canceling of an ontological debt . . . [n]or was it God's benign overlooking of one's personal transgressions. . . . Forgiveness, as Jesus preached it, referred not primarily to sin at all but to the crossing of the eschatological line. What was "given" in the Father's for-giveness was the eschatological future—that is, God himself. Thus, forgiveness meant the arrival of God in the present, his superabundant gift of himself to his people, his self-communicating incarnation.[81]

---

80. Marianne Sawicki, *Seeing the Lord: Resurrection and Early Christian Practices* (Minneapolis: Fortress, 1994), 291, 296.

81. Thomas Sheehan, *The First Coming: How the Kingdom of God Became Christianity* (New York: Random House, 1986), 66.

Of *abba's* for-giveness, Jesus' table ministry was map and icon. Taussig makes an excellent point in his study of Jesus' prayer life when he notes that the Lord's Prayer "demands engagement in the social situations of the ones . . . who are praying":

> One cannot pray about forgiveness without forgiving. On an even more intensely social level, people cannot pray about forgiveness without laughing at each other's resistance to being involved in the issue at hand.
>
> Similarly . . . one cannot pray about God's basileia/kingdom without . . . acting as if God's kingdom is already coming. One cannot pray about the holiness of God's name without challenging family idolatry. One cannot pray about one's need for bread without casting one's self on the care of others.
>
> . . . [T]he prayers of the historical Jesus almost require one to pray in a group that is ready to laugh, criticize, weep, argue, and resist. . . .
>
> This kind of praying does not involve projecting one's voice to heaven. It does not require escaping into an interior realm. It meets God in the situation itself.[82]

Without denying that God's presence is known and celebrated in the Temple liturgy, Jesus proclaimed that his *Abba* is also God of the ordinary. What made Jesus' vision distinctive—even dangerous—was not his revolutionary rhetoric but his conviction that God too is "insufferably ordinary." "The presence of God among men [and women] which Jesus preached," writes Sheehan, "was not something new, not a gift that God had saved up for the end of time. Jesus . . . proclaimed what had always been the case. He invited people to awaken to what God had already done from the very beginning of time."[83] We meet this presence, Jesus said, in the dull routines of daily life; we meet the divine in the daily, the sacred in the serendipitous, the lordly in the lowly, the holy in the homely and the human. This insufferably ordinary God is revealed in the fermenting leaven that a woman mixes into a batch of dough, in the lost coin a homemaker finds on her kitchen floor, in a dishonest but savvy servant's success in planning for his future. Like many of his contemporaries, Jesus was awaiting the "kingdom" or "reign" of God. But for Jesus, this "kingdom" is not so much "of" or "about" God; it *is* God—*Abba*, present, active, alive, on the loose, out of control. *Abba's* uncontrollable presence is not, however, a power that dominates, coerces or subjugates people (like most political or religious power does). For God's "reign" is revealed in

---

82. Taussig, *Jesus before God*, 129-30.
83. Sheehan, *First Coming*, 68.

and as the for-givenness that frees people; it is not about power but about *em*powerment.

This chapter has examined how Jesus—an "insufferably ordinary" Galilean, a marginal Jewish layman—reimagined both ritual prayer and the ways ritual rehearses and redefines the relationship between God, human persons, and world. The next chapter will explore how Jesus' reimagined world (his *Abba*'s "reign" or "kingdom") shaped a community whose "home" was the table and whose heart was service to the poor.

QUESTIONS FOR REFLECTION

1. In light of the matters discussed in chapter 3, can we still say that in their sacramental celebrations, Christians are "doing what Jesus did"?
2. The noted Scripture scholar John Meier describes Jesus as a "marginal Jew" from Galilee who carried out his ministry as a devout *layman*, not as member of a "priestly establishment." How did Jesus' identity as a lay preacher and prophet shape his views of ritual prayer and the way such prayer links us to God?
3. Given Jesus' teaching about prayer (in the Lord's Prayer), what does it mean to "hallow God's Name"?
4. "If the Lord's Prayer is a reliable guide to Jesus' own practice and thought about public prayer—and there are good reasons to believe it is—then we must say that Jesus understands the rituals of worship not as manipulative techniques for 'getting God to see things our way and giving us what we want,' or as opportunities to assert our triumphant hold on truth, but as acts of radical 'dispossession.' The basic ritual gestures that shaped the liturgy of Jesus' own people were acts of *receiving* rather than taking, of *divesting* rather than possessing" (p. 85 above). How does Jesus own Jewishness shape our Christian understanding of worship?
5. "Humankind has a future only because it has a memory; it lives from and for (i.e., *toward*) its memory. For memory has more to do with the future than with the past. Memory is the future, posing as the past and living in us without our knowing it" (p. 87 above). How does liturgy "remember"?

SUGGESTIONS FOR FURTHER READING

Fredriksen, Paula. *Jesus of Nazareth, King of the Jews: A Jewish Life and the Emergence of Christianity*. New York: Knopf, 1999. An important survey of Jesus' life and ministry that stresses his thoroughly Jewish identity.

LaVerdiere, Eugene. *Dining in the Kingdom of God: The Origins of the Eucharist According to Luke.* Chicago: Liturgy Training Publications, 1994. A study of Luke as a "eucharistic Gospel" that emphasizes the continued significance of Jesus' table ministry, then and now.

Meier, John P. *A Marginal Jew: Rethinking the Historical Jesus.* Vol. 1, *The Roots of the Problem and the Person.* Vol. 2, *Mentor, Message, and Miracles.* Vol. 3, *Companions and Competitlrs.* Anchor Bible Reference Library. New York: Doubleday, 1991, 1994, 2001. An ongoing study of the historical Jesus by one of the leading Roman Catholic Scripture scholars working today.

Stevenson, Kenneth. *Abba Father: Understanding and Using the Lord's Prayer.* Norwich: Canterbury Press, 2004. A scriptural and liturgical study of the Lord's Prayer by the renowned Anglican scholar and bishop of Portsmouth.

Taussig, Hal. *Jesus before God: The Prayer Life of the Historical Jesus.* Santa Rosa, Calif.: Polebridge Press, 1999. An accessible study of Jesus' prayer life that includes detailed, phrase-by-phrase comments on the Lord's Prayer.

4

Ritual's Realm

A World Reimagined

IN AN ESSAY WE WILL ENCOUNTER AGAIN in chapter 5, literary critic Luis León draws our attention to the creative ways Latina women transform and reinterpret traditional religious myths, symbols, and rites.[1] They do this not in formal seminars about theology, nor in official discussions with church leaders, but from within their unique experience of home and family, of *lo cotidiano*—the "birthing place" of "a Latino/a theology of grace."[2] Latina women are, writes Orlando Espín, the "living hermeneutic" of a popular Catholicism that serves as "symbolic home" for daily experiences of sin and grace. "Mature Latin women (our mothers, grandmothers, aunts, and older sisters)," he continues, "have been responsible for the survival and resilience of popular Catholicism. . . . [They are their] families wise interpreters of the biblical message and of the heart and mind of God, the teachers of ethics, and the leaders of our prayers, our family's living sacraments of God and the sacred."[3]

In their vital role as family prayer leaders and biblical interpreters, these women link faith to the daily experience of culture, class, and conflict in Latino/a communities. For as theologians like Espín point out, religion can exist "only where the experience of God has become truly incarnate in the culture, history, and life of the believing people," and hence, there can never be "*one single way of being Catholic or of experiencing grace and sin.*" How this experience is imagined (and *re*imagined), ritually and symbolically, thus makes an enormous difference to a community's experience of God. If, for example, Latinos/as in the United States are the objects of injustice, discrimination, racism, and bigotry, "then their Catholicism (and their experiences of

---

1. See Luis León, "The Poetic Uses of Religion in The Miraculous Day of Amalia Gomez," *Religion and American Culture* 9, no. 2 (1999): 205-31.
2. Orlando O. Espín, "An Exploration into the Theology of Sin and Grace," in *From the Heart of Our People: Latino/a Explorations in Catholic Systematic Theology,* ed. Orlando O. Espín and Miguel H. Díaz (Maryknoll, N.Y.: Orbis Books, 1999), 121-52, here 124.
3. Ibid., 127-32.

sin and grace) cannot possibly be understood without further prejudice unless the conflicts and suffering of those communities are admitted as truly *shaping their experiences* of God, of grace and sin, and their socialization of these."[4]

For as I pointed out in the prologue to this book, liturgical rituals are always about *connection*, about being connected and making connections—to God, people, and planet; to space, time, culture, and history, to difference and otherness, to memory and expectation. And because this is the case, the experience of God, sin, and grace can happen only at what I've called the "confluence of three essentially related liturgies," the liturgy of the world, the liturgy of the church, and the liturgy of the neighbor. To discern this confluence, to grasp how it impacts real life in real space and time requires not only the ability to imagine possibilities never before thought of, but to reimagine them.

Thus, while our first three chapters have examined ritual's roots, its roles and risks, and its rules (as related to the life and ministry of Jesus), we must now turn to the kind of world that ritual invites us to imagine, a world in which God's arriving kingdom reveals itself in those disturbing, offbeat stories the Christian Scriptures call "parables." A parable's strategy, as we shall see, is provocative; it aims to challenge hearers to *change*, to take up the work of conversion. Several examples of parabolic discourse—some recent and contemporary, some ancient and scriptural—will be discussed, and, on the basis of what we discover about these stories, we will explore liturgy and ritual as ongoing sources of revelation, a theme found in the documents of the Second Vatican Council, especially *Dei Verbum*, its Dogmatic Constitution on Divine Revelation. We begin by reflecting on "A Worn Path," a short story by the late American writer Eudora Welty.

PRELUDE

"The universe is made of stories, not of atoms."[5]

Phoenix Jackson . . . was very old and small and she walked slowly in the dark pine shadows, moving a little from side to side in her steps, with the balanced heaviness and lightness of a pendulum in a grandfather clock. She carried a thin, small cane made from an umbrella and with this she kept tapping the frozen earth in front of her. This made a grave and per-

---

4. Ibid., 135.

5. Muriel Rukyser, *The Speed of Darkness* (New York: Random House, 1968), 111. The quotation is from the title poem of the collection, "The Speed of Darkness," IX.

sistent noise in the still air, that seemed meditative like the chirping of a solitary little bird.[6]

As Eudora Welty's story "A Worn Path" opens, we learn that Phoenix Jackson is a grandmother making her way through Mississippi pinewoods toward a small town where she can buy medicine for her grandson, who is seriously ill. The way is long, the weather harsh, the people she meets bemused by her appearance. Asked her age by a stranger, Phoenix replies, "There is no telling, mister . . . no telling." She does not have to think about where she's headed; "she depended on her feet to know where to take her."[7] When she finally arrives at the doctor's office, Phoenix finds she's forgotten the reason for her trip until a nurse asks about her grandson and his sore throat: " 'Tell us quickly about your grandson,'" the nurse says, "he isn't dead, is he?" At that moment the reader suddenly realizes that no one—including Phoenix—seems to know whether the child is alive or not. And so the story ends, with ambiguity hanging in the air.

Decades later, Welty remarked that of all the questions students had asked her over the years, the "unrivaled favorite" was this: "Is Phoenix Jackson's grandson really *dead*?" "I had not meant to mystify readers by withholding any fact," Welty wrote; "it is not a writer's business to tease." She goes on to say that the story is told through the mind of Phoenix as she embarks on her errand, and from that perspective the boy still seems very much alive. Nevertheless, readers are free to think what they will; "the story invites you to believe that no matter what happens, Phoenix for as long as she is able to walk and can hold to her purpose will make her journey."[8]

At the end of the day, Welty reflects, the question that preoccupies students who read "A Worn Path" is probably the wrong one. It matters little to the story, whether the grandson is dead or alive. The overwhelming fact is that *Phoenix* is alive, and the story's only real certainty is *the worn path itself.* That path embodies what Welty calls "the deep-grained habit of love," the story's *real* subject. "The habit of love cuts through confusion and stumbles or contrives its way out of difficulty, it remembers the way even when it forgets, for a dumbfounded moment, its reason for being. The path is the thing that matters."[9] Phoenix and her path embody the urgency of love, and ulti-

---

6. Eudora Welty, "A Worn Path," in *The Collected Stories of Eudora Welty* (New York: Harcourt Brace Jovanovich, 1980), 142.

7. Ibid., 146.

8. Eudora Welty, "Is Phoenix Jackson's Grandson Really Dead?" in *The Eye of the Story: Selected Essays and Reviews* (New York: Randon House Vintage Books, 1979), 159-62, here 159.

9. Ibid., 161-62.

mately, whatever the grandson's actual fate may have been, the story is a hymn to life, not death. Welty summarizes her point succinctly:

> Like Phoenix, you work all your life to find your way, through all the obstructions and the false appearances and the upsets you may have brought on yourself, to reach a meaning. . . . And finally too, like Phoenix, you have to assume that what you are working in aid of is life, not death.
>
> But you would make the trip anyway—wouldn't you?—just on hope.[10]

I begin this chapter with the figure of Phoenix Jackson's journey because it embodies so much of what happens in the experience of ritual. Ritual is "done by heart"; it is a way of "thinking" with the body and of "remembering" with the skin. Our deepest motives and memories are buried in feet that remember the way, even when the mind "for a dumbfounded moment" forgets. Ritual is itself "a worn path" that puts flesh on the "deep-grained habit of love." The path itself is what counts. As I said in the second chapter, ritual is less a chain of religious or theological "meanings" and more a *meeting*, a *making*. In this, ritual shares common ground with art, because in art, as Eudora Welty says, the making is "the thing that has meaning, and . . . beauty is likely to be something that has for a time lain under good, patient hands. . . . [T]he making itself has shaped [the] work for good and all." And that is why the making—of art, of ritual—is itself "a bestowal of grace."[11]

But there is yet another reason for beginning with Phoenix. "The universe isn't made of atoms; it's made of stories." And whether she intended it or not, in writing her story "A Worn Path," Eudora Welty created a modern parable. Briefly defined, a parable is a story that raises troubling questions without providing comforting answers. A parable's strategy is quietly transgressive; it subtly subverts readers' expectations and provokes a crisis not merely at the level of "meaning" (semantics), but at the level of life itself (ethics). A parable's impact is thus like that of the ancient sculpture known as the *Belvedere Apollo,* whose head is missing, but whose torso concentrates such power and energy that, as poet Rainer Maria Rilke put it, its "curved breast" dazzles, and the very stone seems to "glisten like a wild beast's fur," to burst upon the viewer "like a star." We do not grasp the *Belvedere Apollo.* No; it seizes us, and demands "You must change your life."[12] Here too—like art—ritual summons change, conversion, new ways of seeing, hearing, sensing, knowing. Parable is provocation, whether the challenge comes from seeing sculpture or hearing a story.

10. Ibid., 162.
11. Eudora Welty, "Katherine Anne Porter: The Eye of the Story," in *Eye of the Story*, 40.
12. Rainer Maria Rilke, "Archaic Torso of Apollo," in *Ahead of All Parting: Poetry and Prose of Rainer Maria Rilke,* trans. Stephen Mitchell (New York: Modern Library, 1995), 67.

RITUAL

Stories Told by Hand

A bit later in this chapter we will return to this theme of parable as provocation, but we begin with the earliest kind of human stories. It is surely significant that the first human storytellers were not voices but *hands*. Perhaps that is because the hand is itself a story. The German architect Rudolf Schwarz (1897-1961), a pioneer in creating modern church buildings for modern cultures, once wrote that when it stretches "all its fingers outward from the palm," the hand is "an open star at the end of the arm." Hands tell *many* stories, Schwarz noted:

> The hand can radiate . . .
> The hand can hollow itself . . . fingers come together to form a bowl, empty and open in the movement of holding. . .
> The hand can touch . . . With the first gentle touch the reaching movement is reversed: surrender to the thing becomes submersion in it. Quietly the hand rests on the thing and fingers it. The hand can reassure, love and bless. Here being surrenders to being. Here is healing.

Above all, of course, the hand can *feel*. It thus "understands the world better than the eye," for "it 'sees' the world from all sides."[13]

Today we know that it took millions of years for those first tree-dwelling humanoid ancestors of ours to stand erect and walk upright, thereby freeing their hands from the basic function of locomotion and enabling them to design and manufacture tools, to gather and store food, to transport objects, to signal danger, to threaten aggression, to grasp, embrace, and hold another. *Hands*—free, feeling, fast, and flexible—became for us a *tool*, a *weapon*, and a *language*. We learned to speak with our hands, developing a grammar of gesture and communication long before we created those complex systems of vocal speech and thought we ordinarily call language. Hands were our first storytellers because they enabled us to "fiddle" with things, to pick them up, turn them over, inspect them by sight, smell, and touch. "The hand," wrote Schwarz, "makes an entire world."[14] It even notices the backs of things, their

---

13. Rudolf Schwarz, *The Church Incarnate*, trans. Cynthia Harris (Chicago: Henry Regnery, 1958), 18-19. On Schwarz, his connections with the liturgical movement, and the significance of his theories about modern church architecture, see Richard Kieckhefer, *Theology in Stone: Church Architecture from Byzantium to Berkeley* (New York: Oxford University Press, 2004), 229-64.

14. Schwarz, *Church Incarnate*, 18.

rough or smooth surfaces and porosity, their uneven bumps and dents. Hands made it possible to craft objects whose utility and significance could, literally, be *handed on* to other human beings.

Hence, the oldest human stories we possess are neither oral accounts passed on by word of mouth, nor written narratives, but *paintings* created by hand on cave walls at sites such as Altamira (in northern Spain) and Lascaux (about seventy-five miles from the French city of Bordeaux). These ancient scenes tell us about hunting and animals, beautiful red deer, wounded bears and lions, charging bison, and exotic cattle with spiraling horns. They were painted by unknown human artists, probably more than sixteen thousand years ago, and hence are far older than early written records such as the renowned *Epic of Gilgamesh*. The cave paintings at Lascaux show us human courage, ingenuity, inventiveness, and daring. They embody the reverence, awe, and love that anonymous hunters in prehistory felt for their prey. They open a window on the spiritual life of some of our earliest human ancestors— their intense love and gratitude for creation; their awareness of mystery; their abiding awe before the life-force flowing in the blood of bison, bears and humans; their hopes for the future; their concern for the generations that would follow them.

Those last two points are particularly telling. The paintings of Lascaux and Altamira trace an archaic eschatological expectation—human experience flowing forward, toward a future that already arrives in the very hope that prompted the artists to paint in the first place. Amazing, too, is what these early works of art tell us about the connection between hands and human identity. In an era before alphabets were invented, artists signed their work not with self-portraits or abstract marks but with *hands*. Hands seemed to be what was most human about themselves, the most decisive clue about who they were. To this day, do we not still speak about "handing on" a tradition, a message, a story, from one generation to the next?

Painted Prayers

It should thus come as no surprise that ritual prayer, in some cultures, is largely a matter of "praying by hand." About ten years ago, the Sackler Gallery in Washington, D.C., hosted an exhibit entitled "Painted Prayers: Women's Art in Village India." The exhibition drew attention, through photography and live demonstrations, to a devotional rite practiced each morning by many women in the South Indian state of Tamil Nadu. As Stephen Huyler describes it, the ritual embodies an ancient art in which chalky powder ground from parboiled rice is used to paint prayers on the "canvas" of damp dirt that forms a threshold before the doorway of their homes. These prayers are not words but *images*: intricate, luxuriant, painted by hand. They include lotus vines, for example, "serpentine and sensuous, bursting with budding and open flowers—the centrifugal symbol of the goddess that protects family and home, painted to encourage her beneficence and to keep evil from entering the house." Of their very nature, these painted prayers are evanescent. "The designs," writes Huyler, "are quickly smudged as the sun rises and people move in and out of the house. Within an hour or two no trace of them remains. *It is the moment of creation, the intent of the heart, that is important.* Art, like life, is considered transitory. Swept away each day, the paintings are newly created before the following dawn."[15]

The ritual prayers these South Indian women paint each morning to consecrate their homes and families remind one of a comment the late biblical scholar Carroll Stuhlmueller made about the Psalms. They are, he said, "a home lived in for many generations."[16] Its walls, once aglow with fresh plaster and paint, are soon nicked, smudged by the uproar of everyday life, the wear and tear of use. Over the years, as pets and people shuffle from room to room, the paint peels, a window sags, the sofa's color fades, a photo framed and forgotten leaves a bright patch on a grimy wall. Though the house creaks and crumbles, the laughter, tears, and music linger, echoing down the generations. In time, the psalter—Israel's house of prayer—was annexed by Jesus' disciples for purposes private and public. Christian apologists pushed the psalms well past the boundaries of poetry and prayer; in their hands these ancient poems were turned to other purposes—homiletic, hermeneutic, exegetical, catechetical, and even polemic. The psalms became a lens to focus the divine acting daily in the human. Soon they came to resemble painted prayers—swept away each day, to be newly created the next. Perhaps that is why ancient Christian monks felt obligated to pray the whole psalter—in effect, to paint the whole house—every single day. The psalms encircled time, encompassed it in an endless ring of daily praise and petition, complaint and lament.

These psalms, biblical poems, grew to resemble the rising and setting sun, shaping each day's light and shadow—a transitory work of art whose messages, like God's mercies, are new every morning. As Kathleen Norris com-

---

15. Stephen Huyler, "Transitory Art from Indian Villages," *The Chronicle of Higher Education,* August 18, 1995, B44.

16. Carroll Stuhlmueller, "An Introduction to the Book of Psalms," in *Psalms for Morning and Evening Prayer* (Chicago: Liturgy Training Publications, 1995), ix.

ments, concerning her experience of the psalms in monastic liturgy, "Bene-dictine worship is an immersion in words—primarily the poetry of the Psalms—and its daily rhythms make the liturgy itself a poem: oral, visceral, and much more than the sum of its parts." This liturgical experience led Nor-ris to new insight about both poetry and faith. "*Stop making sense*, I'd say to myself; sit in these words, this silence a while. Sing the psalm and see what happens." Slowly, Norris says, she acquired a new appreciation of "both faith and poetry as process. It was as a poet that I had learned to trust negative capability, to wait for the words that would take me past impasse into speech. Sweating out daily prayer in a monastery. . . I discovered that negative capa-bility is as necessary for prayer as for poetry. Perhaps it is indistinguishable from grace."[17]

READINESS FOR RITUAL: NEGATIVE CAPABILITY

The psalms, then, are painted prayer, daily as bread, nimble as grace. It is not surprising that they have always been in the background (and often in the foreground) of Jewish and Christian liturgy. Their "meanings"—as prayer, as poetry—emerge only when we *stop making sense*, only when we sit silently in the words awhile, waiting to see what happens. Here, Norris suggests, we meet *the* most basic requirement for participation in ritual prayer: *negative capability*. That phrase is borrowed from a famous letter written in Decem-ber 1817 by poet John Keats, who spoke about the specific quality most needed in art and literature, a quality Shakespeare embodied "enormously." "I mean Negative Capability," wrote Keats, "that is, *when a man is capable of being in uncertainties, mysteries, doubts, without any irritable reaching after fact and reason*."[18] Negative capability is a condition of receptivity, of tolerance for what Keats calls "half-knowledge," of resistance to the compulsion to have the whole shebang all at once.

Negative capability is thus at the heart of what we might call "readiness for worship." We have encountered the root of this readiness in an earlier chap-ter, where Louis-Marie Chauvet's notions of "assent to loss" and "consent to the presence of the absence" were discussed.[19] We meet it as well in the tra-

---

17. Kathleen Norris, "Stop Making Sense," in "Symposium on Writing and Spirituality," *Manoa* 7, no. 1 (Summer 1995): 115, 116 (emphasis added).

18. The text of Keats's letter is available online at http://www.mrbauld.com/negcap.html.

19. See chapter 1, "Ritual's Roots," above.

dition of Quaker worship, especially in what Friends call "silent waiting meeting." The quiet Keatsian condition of *"being in uncertainties, mysteries, doubts, without any irritable reaching after fact and reason"* is not passive inertia, but expectant receptivity. As French Quaker Pierre Lacout has written,

> In silence which is active, the Inner Light begins to glow. . . . For the flame to be kindled and to grow, subtle argument and the clamour of our emotions must be stilled. It is by an attention full of love that we enable the Inner Light to blaze and illuminate our dwelling and to make of our whole being a source from which this Light may shine out.
>
> Words must be purified in a redemptive silence if they are to bear the message of peace. The right to speak is a call to the duty of listening. Speech has no meaning unless there are attentive minds and silent hearts. Silence is the welcoming acceptance of the other. The word born of silence must be received in silence.[20]

"The right to speak is a call to the duty of listening. . . . Silence is the welcoming acceptance of the *other*." Such silence is similar to Norris's injunction, "*Stop making sense.*" Negative capability is neither "indolent, vacant musing" nor "sheer emptiness (absence of words, music, noise)"; rather it is "*an intensified pause.*"[21] Quakers in the United Kingdom describe the "sense" of their meetings in this way:

> In our meetings for worship we seek through the stillness to know God's will for ourselves and for the gathered group. Our meetings for church affairs, in which we conduct our business, are also meetings for worship based on silence, and they carry the same expectation that God's guidance can be discerned if we are truly listening together and to each other, and are not blinkered by preconceived opinions. It is this belief that God's will can be recognised through the discipline of silent waiting which distinguishes our decision-making process from the secular idea of consensus.[22]

Note that the "silent waiting worship" of Quaker meetings is not limited to formal occasions of praise and contemplation but embraces gatherings for practical "business" and "church affairs" as well. *All* are based on the "intensified pause" of active, expectant silence—whether the purpose is to listen for "what the Spirit says to the churches" (Rev 2:7) or to reach decisions affect-

---

20. Text available at http://www.quaker.org.uk/qfp/Chap.2.
21. Ibid. The quotations are from the London Yearly Meeting, 1884 and 1886, and author Rufus Jones (1937).
22. Text available at http://www.quaker.org.uk/qfp/Chap.3.

ing the entire community.[23] Note the continuity enshrined in this Quaker tradition. What other Christian communions call "liturgy" (and Friends call "meeting") is not ghettoized or sequestered from the rest of life in church and world. Hence,

> We meet together for common worship, for the pastoral care of our membership, for needful administration, for unhurried deliberation on matters of common concern, for testing personal concerns that are brought before us, and to get to know one another better in things that are eternal as in things that are temporal.[24]

Contemporary Quaker literature offers a set of principles about readiness for ritual (based on "negative capability") that Roman Catholics might do well to consider. Friends' meetings in the United Kingdom, for instance, can teach us the following:[25]

1. Liturgy learns by experiment even as it respects tradition.

We should be open to learning from the experiments undertaken by other meetings. Being set in an unsatisfactory routine "because we've always done it this way" may be as detrimental to seeking God's guidance as throwing our traditions to the wind. We are enjoined to live adventurously, but experiment must be grounded in the experience of generations of Friends, which offers us a method, a purpose and principles for the right conduct of our business meetings.

2. Liturgy doesn't lobby; it persuades.

We have learned to eschew lobbying and not to set great store by rhetoric or clever argument. The mere gaining of debating points is found to be unhelpful and alien to the spirit of worship. . . . Instead of rising hastily to reply to another, it is better to give time for what has been said to make its own appeal. We must always be ready to give serious, unhurried and truly sympathetic consideration to proposals brought forward from whatever part of the meeting. . . . The unity we seek depends on the willingness of us all to seek the truth in each other's utterances; on our being open to persuasion.

---

23. Note how Quaker tradition carefully distinguishes its own decision-making process from "the secular idea of consensus."

24. Text available at http://www.quaker.org.uk/qfp/Chap.3.

25. Quoted texts available at http://www.quaker.org.uk/qfp/Chap.3.

3. Liturgy prizes open minds and the ability to "listen without antagonism."

The right conduct of our meetings for church affairs depends upon all coming to them in an active, seeking spirit, not with minds already made up. ... But open minds are not empty minds, nor uncritically receptive: the service of the meeting calls for knowledge of facts, often painstakingly acquired, and the ability to estimate their relevance and importance. This demands that we shall be ready to listen to others carefully, without antagonism if they express opinions which are unpleasing to us, but trying always to discern the truth in what they have to offer.

4. Liturgy cherishes the contribution (the "ministry") of each member.

It is always to be recognised that, coming together with a variety of temperaments, of background, education and experience, we shall have differing contributions to make to any deliberation. It is no part of Friends' concern for truth that any should be expected to water down a strong conviction or be silent merely for the sake of easy agreement. Nevertheless we are called to honour our testimony that to every one is given a measure of the light, and that it is in the sharing of knowledge, experience and concern that the way towards unity will be found.

5. Liturgy's goal is always unity.[26]

The unity we seek depends on the willingness of us all to seek the truth in each other's utterances; on our being open to persuasion; ... We do not vote in our meetings because we believe that this would emphasise the divisions between differing views and inhibit the process of seeking to know the will of God. We must recognise, however, that a minority view may well continue to exist. When we unite ... we express, not a sudden agreement of everyone present with the prevailing view, but rather a confidence in our tried and tested way of seeking to recognise God's will. We act as a community whose members love and trust each other.

6. Liturgy seeks rather than decrees.

Our method of conducting our meetings for church affairs is an experience which has been tested over three hundred years. In days of hot

---

26. Recall that for Thomas Aquinas, the *res* ("ultimate purpose and intent") of the sacrament of the eucharist was nothing other than *unio ecclesiasticae corporis*, based on the common reception of Christ's body and blood. See *Summa Theologiae* IIIa Pars *Supplementum*, Q. 71, art. 9, corpus; ad 3um.

contest and bitter controversy the early Friends, knit together by the glorious experience of the Holy Spirit's guidance in all their affairs, came into the simple understanding of how their corporate decisions should be made.

7. Liturgy listens *even to those who are silent.*

Not all who attend a meeting for church affairs will necessarily speak: those who are silent can help to develop the sense of the meeting if they listen in a spirit of worship.

8. Liturgy opens new paths rather than shuts doors.

In a meeting rightly held a new way may be discovered which none present had alone perceived and which transcends the differences of the opinions expressed. . . . Those who have shared this experience will not doubt its reality and the certainty it brings of the immediate rightness of the way for the meeting to take.

9. Liturgy knows when and how to edit both itself and its participants.[27]

Friends . . . realise that a decision which is the only one for a particular meeting at a particular time may not be the one which is ultimately seen to be right. There have been many occasions in our Society when a Friend, though maintaining her or his personal convictions, has seen clearly that they were not in harmony with the sense of the meeting and has with loyal grace expressed deference to it. Out of just such a situation, after time for further reflection, an understanding of the Friend's insight has been reached at a later date and has been ultimately accepted by the Society.

10. Liturgy does not deliver communities from differences of opinion.

We must not expect to be delivered from differences of opinion—and indeed our life as a religious community would be dull and unprofitable if we were; but we do . . . hold firmly to our conviction that divine guidance is there to be found.

---

27. The idea of editing liturgy in order to adapt or accommodate traditional forms of worship to differing cultures and conditions was not invented at the Second Vatican Council (see, e.g., *Sacrosanctum Concilium* 37-40) or by "out-of-control" progressives after the council. Thus, for instance, in 1724, Pope Benedict XIII issued a rather drastically simplified version of the rites for Holy Week for use in small parishes where large numbers of singers and ministers were rarely (if ever) available. Benedict's *Memoriale Rituum*, the booklet containing these adapted Roman rites, continued to be reprinted, with papal approval, well into the twentieth century.

These ten principles, based on the experience of Friends' meetings, might well offer other Christian communions a way to embody the principles of negative capability and silent, active "expectant waiting" in their liturgical life. Such principles may not end the liturgy wars, but they could enhance "readiness for worship" among *all* participants and limit the collateral damage among combatants!

RITUAL AND PARABLE

Hearing the Parable

In the previous section, I argued that negative capability creates readiness for ritual and enhances the possibility of fruitful participation by all.[28] But earlier, in this chapter's opening paragraphs, I drew attention to the peculiar kind of story called "parable," and it is this "parabolic" aspect of ritual experience that will occupy us for the next several pages. Parables—whether ancient (like those of Jesus) or modern (like Eudora Welty's "Worn Path")—are deliberately provocative. Their purpose is not to illustrate, inform, inspire or entertain, but to startle—and perhaps to annoy.

At first this may seem incompatible with what was just said about liturgy in light of Quaker perspectives on peaceful, expectant waiting. Yet what could be more startling than a Sabbath-day meeting of Friends, its silence suddenly shattered by a young child leaping to its feet to chirp, "God is love!"?[29] My hope is to show that just as negative capability engenders readiness for ritual, so ritual opens us not merely (or mainly) to reassurance, but to the "dark side" of story.[30] We are meant to leave liturgy not somnolent and benumbed, but baffled, amazed, stirred up—and ready for action. Liturgy is not logic; it encourages us to

> see without looking, hear without listening, breathe without asking:
> The Inevitable is what will seem to happen to you purely by chance;

---

28. "Full, conscious, active participation" was, of course, the famous goal enunciated in *Sacrosanctum Concilium* 14: "Mother Church earnestly desires that all the faithful be led to that full, conscious, and active participation in liturgical celebrations which is demanded by the very nature of the liturgy. Such participation . . . is their right and duty by reason of their baptism."

29. Older readers may recall such a scene from the 1956 film *Friendly Persuasion,* directed by William Wyler. Based on a novel by Jessamyn West, the film tells the story of a Quaker family in Indiana in 1862.

30. See the classic short study of parable by John Dominic Crossan, *The Dark Interval: Towards a Theology of Story* (Niles, Ill.: Argus Communications, 1975).

> The Real is what will strike you as really absurd;
>
> Unless you are certain you are dreaming, it is certainly a
>   dream of your own;
>
> Unless you exclaim—"There must be some mistake"—you
>   must be mistaken.[31]

Liturgy, in sum, leads us to hear God's Word not only as paraenesis but as parable.

In unpacking the ritual impact of parable, Asian wisdom traditions may offer us insight— though, as always, one must be careful not to colonize other cultures with Western religious preoccupations. Consider, for example, the Zen Buddhist tradition of the *koan*, especially as it is used in monastic training.[32] A *koan* is a riddle without a solution, employed to show the inadequacy of logical reason and to provoke sudden enlightenment. One of the most trenchant descriptions of *koan* comes from a medieval sage, Chung-feng Mingpen (1263-1323 C.E.), who wrote: "It cannot be understood by logic; it cannot be transmitted in words; it cannot be explained in writing; it cannot be measured by reason. It is like ... a great fire that consumes all who come near it."[33]

It would be a mistake to assume that a *koan* aims its punch at the human intellect. The *koan* doesn't perplex the mind; it puzzles *life*. Thich Nhat Hanh, the popular Vietnamese Buddhist monk and writer, warns that "there is a big difference between a kung-an [*koan*] and a math problem—the solution of the math problem is included in the problem itself, while *the response to the kung-an lies in the life of the practitioner*."[34] A *koan* confronts its hearer with a "no-way-out situation" before which intelligence and reason are powerless. The crisis it provokes is existential rather than intellectual. As the Zen Master Hisamatsu put it: "*Nothing will do. What do you do?*"[35] That is the "fundamental *koan*," the common denominator that fuels their fire.

So a *koan* can be neither resolved nor explained. It challenges life, and experience alone will determine whether the *koan*'s question has ever been adequately "answered." (In this, the *koan* bears some resemblance to a point Louis-Marie Chauvet makes about Christian worship, which we noted in an earlier chapter: the liturgy of the *church* can be "verified" only *outside* itself, in

---

31. W. H. Auden, "For the Time Being: A Christmas Oratorio; Advent, IV," in *Collected Poems*, ed. Edward Mendelson (New York: Vintage Books, 1991), 354.

32. *Koan* is a Japanese word literally signifying a "public case"; it appears to be derived from the Chinese term for "official business."

33. Isshu Miura and Ruth Fuller Sasaki, *Zen Dust: The History of the Koan and Koan Study in Rinzai (Lin-chi) Zen* (New York: Harcourt, Brace & World, 1966), 5.

34. Thich Nhat Hanh, *Zen Keys* (New York: Doubleday, 1995), 57 (emphasis added).

35. Urs App, trans. and ed., *Master Yunmen: From the Record of the Chan Teacher "Gate of the Clouds"* (New York: Kodansha International, 1994), 53.

the liturgy of the *neighbor*.) Truth to tell, the *koan* has no correct answer; it leaves us in a condition of permanent undecidability, indeterminacy. That is due, in part, to the fact that while a *koan* "tempts the learner into logic, into the giving . . . of a rational response," he or she "must be taught to resist the temptation."[36] The only real answer to a *koan* is another *koan*, signaled (but never captured) by a physical gesture that hints that the person wrestling with the riddle has reached a truth beyond human inspection, criteria, or claims of veracity. Two examples will illustrate this point. The first is a story from *The Iron Flute*, a collection of *koans* compiled by the eighteenth-century Japanese master Genro:

> Three monks, Hsüeh-feng, Ch'in-shan, and Yen-t'ou, met in the temple garden. Hsüeh-feng saw a water pail and pointed to it. Ch'in-shan said, "The water is clear, and the moon reflects its image." "No, no," said Hsüeh-feng, "it is not water, it is not moon." Yen-t'ou turned over the pail.[37]

If one were forced to say which of the three monks was "right," it would be Yen-t'ou. Moving beyond human intelligence's comforting constructs of affirmation/denial (yes/no, *sic et non*), he simply turned over the pail. In contrast, Ch'in-shan was caught in the world of (self-imposed) meanings and representations ("water . . . reflects"), while Hsüeh-feng couldn't get past that world's either/or system of affirmation and denial ("not water, not the moon"). Yen-t'ou would get the A for the class, though of course Zen doesn't offer classes, report cards, or promotions. Instead, it challenges us to move toward "enlightenment," an immediate, intuitive grasp of truth and reality that may, for all the world, look like madness or folly. When Yen-t'ou turned over the pail, he not only erased even Hsüeh-feng's denial, but showed that Zen itself is neither philosophy nor religion.[38]

Another famous *koan* is popularly known as "the sound of one hand." It goes something like this: "Master: In clapping both hands a sound is heard. What is the sound of the one hand?" Once more, the "answer" is a wordless bodily gesture: "The pupil faces his master, takes a correct posture, and, without a word, thrusts one hand forward." As Yoel Hoffmann notes, such a "demonstrative, wordless form of argument is not totally foreign to Western

---

36. Yoel Hoffmann, trans., *The Sound of the One Hand: 281 Zen Koans with Answers* (New York: Basic Books, 1975), 28. There is a (deliberate?) irony in the subtitle of Hoffmann's book, because, as noted above, a *koan* does not have an "answer" in any traditional Western sense.

37. Nyogen Sensaki and Ruth Strout McCandless, *The Iron Flute: 100 Zen Koans* (1964; Boston: Tuttle Publishing, 2000), 35.

38. Ibid., 36. By removing Zen from the categories of philosophy or religion, the great masters gave it complete independence from human systems of calcuation and hermeneutics, such as theology.

thought."[39] A famous example is Samuel Johnson's "refutation" of the philosopher George Berkeley's denial that matter really exists. Coming out of church one Sunday morning, Johnson was told, according to his biographer Boswell, that while Berkeley's teaching was not true, it could not be logically refuted. Hearing that, Johnson kicked a large stone so hard he "rebounded from it," saying "I refute it *thus!*"[40] As Hoffmann comments, Johnson's "answer" to Berkeley was, "by Zen standards," the right one. "To answer Berkeley's reasoning with reasoning would be a mistake, a trap," even though most Western philosophers would consider Johnson's reaction irrelevant (it doesn't "prove anything"). Still, while you can't really kick an argument, Johnson's Zen-like foot-against-stone works. Berkeley's view was designed to cause a change in the way people perceive and interact with the world. Johnson, kicking the stone, denies Berkeley's right to "tamper with his natural reaction to objects or, for that matter, with his religious views."[41]

Parables challenge hearers in a similar manner. Most of our reactions to God, world, and others are shaped by stories that biblical scholars and historians of religion call "myths." Myths are not falsehoods, nor are they "synonymous with sophisticated lying"; but they *do* seek to massage our experience into patterns of "meaningful" experience.[42] In this sense, myth has a "reconciling" function; it seeks to overcome contradictions, to resolve rational or moral dilemmas, to answer tough questions such as, How could a good God create a world where so much evil happens? A Zen-like answer to that last conundrum might be laughter, or a countercomment such as, "To thicken the plot." Myth, in contrast, would seek to *enlighten, explain,* and *reconcile* hearers to life in an imperfect universe. It might tell, for instance, how an early act of human disobedience to God's decree brought moral ruin to the whole world (see Gen 3).

Parable's purpose is far more provocative. Instead of offering explanations that reconcile, it proposes challenges that provoke. A parable seeks solutions through life and action—turning over a pail of water, kicking a stone, thrusting a hand out of a wide sleeve—rather than through analysis and thought. Thus, even though the Bible's mythic material forms a major part of what we read and preach about in Christian worship, liturgy's primary intent is parabolic. When the U.S. bishops' 1982 document *Fulfilled in Your Hearing* says that a homily is "not a talk given on the occasion of a liturgical celebration," but an intrinsic part of the liturgy itself whose aim is to "lead a congregation

---

39. Hoffmann, *Sound of the One Hand,* 28-29.
40. Ibid., 29.
41. Ibid.
42. See Crossan, *Dark Interval,* 48.

into the Eucharist," it is hinting that the basic structure of liturgical prayer is parabolic rather than mythic.[43] Even when they speak the reassuring, reconciling language of familiar story, both the Liturgy of the Word and preaching aim to be "the sound of the one hand."

In other words, liturgy reads even myths *parabolically*, just as it reads the world and our experience of it in the same way. It thus nudges us not toward reason but toward *action* prompted by a faith that frees but doesn't always say how or why. Our communal response to the Word proclaimed and preached in the assembly is not a seminar but activity in which we discover (parabolically!) that the gifts *we* bring to the table never belonged to us in the first place. Moreover, in receiving these gifts (redefined on *God's* terms as holy food and drink), we acknowledge that *they* do not get changed into *us*; rather *we* get changed into *them*. The body of Christ *on* the table makes us the body of Christ *at* the table. Only this makes it possible for us to "do as he did," to become bodies broken in mercy and justice for the life of the world.

If myths are "agents of stability," parables are agents of change that aim to question, not reassure, us.[44] Crossan summarizes this point succinctly: "You have built a lovely home, myth assures us; but, whispers parable, you are right above an earthquake fault."[45] Ritual's strategy—in the Christian liturgy, at any rate—is to urge us beyond our comfort zone, to let ourselves be "parabled" or "*koan*-ed" in the direction of a wisdom that exceeds human reason and challenges us, like the *Belvedere Apollo*, to change our lives. Liturgy may speak "myth," but its native language is parable, the "sound of the one hand." Two examples of Christian parable—one ancient and biblical, the other modern and fictional—will help illustrate this dimension of ritual experience.

Jesus, "Parabler of the Kingdom"

Jesus' parables constitute a coherent, distinctive body of stories that, in the view of modern scholars, are almost certainly authentic—even if their final shape cannot be traced back to Jesus directly. Bernard Brandon Scott notes that two points support the authenticity of the parable tradition as traceable to the historical Jesus: (1) The stories are relatively few in number, and (2) their themes are astonishingly similar.[46] Those themes are typically provoca-

---

43. See U.S. Catholic Bishops, *Fulfilled in Your Hearing*, no. 60; text in *The Liturgy Documents* (3rd ed.; Chicago: Liturgy Training Publications, 1991), 1:361.

44. Crossan, *Dark Interval*, 56.

45. Ibid., 57.

46. Bernard Brandon Scott, *Re-Imagine the World: An Introduction to the Parrables of Jesus* (Santa Rosa, Calif.: Polebridge Press, 2001), 4. As Scott observes, parables occur only in the Synoptics and

tive and often quite humorous. One of the misfortunes of modernity is our loss of contact with the *humorous* side of Jesus' teaching. We think of him as a young Clint Eastwood, soberly skulking around Palestine with thin, pursed lips, a rock-like chin, and a hard glint in his eye. The parables, however, reveal Jesus' considerable talent as a stand-up comic. Take Jesus' parable of the mustard seed, for example. Crossan shows how Jesus' brief description of God's reign or kingdom as a mustard seed (Mark 4:30-32) is an intentionally humorous satire on traditional biblical images.[47] Any farmer can tell you that the mustard plant is a nuisance, a pain in the posterior. Left to grow unchecked, mustard takes over a field, growing wildly and rapidly, choking out cultivated crops. And while it is surely true that it "springs up and becomes the largest of plants and puts forth large branches, so that the birds of the sky can dwell in its shade" (Mark 4:32), that's a *problem*, not a solution. No farmer wants birds munching either the seed he sows or the grain he intends to harvest!

Moreover, Jesus' mustard-seed parable also makes, in Scott's words, "light-hearted burlesque." Biblical tradition, after all, liked to boast of God's power and action as similar to the towering "cedar of Lebanon." That is the image used by the prophet Ezekiel, for instance, to describe the mighty people of the coming messianic era (Ezek 17:22-23). In a few choice words, Jesus manages not only to praise a plant that *contaminates* fertile fields; he also stirs up antagonism among devout hearers who think Ezekiel's "mighty cedar of Lebanon" (as metaphor for God's rule) is anything but a joke. Worse still, as Scott points out, the farmer of this tiny story is guilty of violating the biblical law governing purity (clean vs. unclean). That law prohibited the mingling of "different classes of plants, animals, and fibers."[48] The "code of legal holiness" in Leviticus 19:19 says: "Do not sow a field of yours with two different kinds of seed."

Hearers of Jesus' parable were apt to have been scandalized. After all, he not only seems to poke fun at the Bible; he also neglects or ignores the laws governing ritual purity. Hearers are left wondering, "Is God's reign really a nuisance? Is it a puny runt like a mustard seed? Is it a worrisome weed that chokes out good crops? Is God's action in the world like *that*? Is God's "kingdom" like Charlie Brown's pathetic Christmas tree—a scrawny trunk with two shreds of tinsel drooping from its bare branches? And as if these innu-

in the noncanonical (though important) *Gospel of Thomas*. None is found on the lips of Jesus' opponents, in John's Gospel, or in Paul's letters. "The narrowness of the tradition," he writes, "impresses me and appears to point to one source"; moreover, if "we examine all the parables as a corpus they cohere, they makes sense as a group."

47. See Crossan, *Dark Interval*, 93-96.
48. Bernard Brandon Scott, *Hear Then the Parable* (Minneapolis: Fortress, 1989), 386, 381.

endoes were not troublesome enough, what about that matter of ritual purity and cleanness? These, after all, were matters of *God-given* law. Surely God could not intend to manifest the "kingdom" among the unclean, the insignificant, the "irregular!"

Jesus' parable provokes; it urges hearers not only to reimagine the relationship between God, world, and people; it also invites them to think the unthinkable. Nowhere is this challenge more evident than in another of Jesus' bombshells, the tiny parable of the woman who mixes leaven in dough to bake bread (Matt 13:33; Luke 13:20-21). "The kingdom of heaven is like yeast that a woman took and mixed with three measures of wheat flour until the whole batch was leavened." On the surface, this one-sentence story is as innocent as a country kitchen. It evokes images of rising dough and the aroma of baking loaves in warm ovens. But consider. Leaven is made "by taking a piece of bread and storing it in a damp, dark place until mold forms. The bread rots and decays, unlike modern yeast, which is domesticated."[49] It is this rotting substance that the woman mixes into her dough. Decaying matter is, of course, unclean and, worse, it *spreads* uncleanness like a contagion ("one rotten apple spoils the whole bunch"). Surely the "kingdom of heaven" couldn't be a rotting contagion, could it? And if it is—what then? One is left with unanswerable riddles that are almost too scary to contemplate.

Yet raising such uncomfortable questions seems to have been Jesus' intention. Most hearers of the parable would have likened God's work not to leaven but to *un*leavened (that is, uncorrupted and uncorruptable) bread. But Jesus' story ends with all the bread *leavened*—in effect, contaminated, unclean. The implications are enormous. "This one sentence parable," writes Scott, "redefines the divine." Moreover, it isn't the divine that transforms the unclean (leaven) into the clean (unleavened); no, the opposite happens—"the divine becomes unclean, or to restate the insight even more provocatively: God becomes unclean."[50] God too claims a "right to associate with sinners," to make their cause God's own. Jesus' shocking story gives raw, outrageous meaning to the old biblical adage, "My ways are *not* your ways!" Hearers are compelled to rethink religion from both the top down and the bottom up.

Liturgy provokes us to hear *all* God's words parabolically, of course, and not only Jesus' stories of mustard seed and leavened dough. This is a particularly difficult task in an age that wants to separate faith from politics (except on "right to life" issues) and to purge worship of anything that might "upset the faithful." It is assumed that liturgy's purpose is to convert parable to myth,

---

49. Ibid., 324.
50. Scott, *Re-Imagine the World*, 121.

so that people can leave church feeling "reconciled" and "good about them-selves." There is danger in this position. In his gutsy commentary on the prophet Isaiah, Daniel Berrigan lampoons those who think this way:

> Perhaps this God of ours can be cajoled, persuaded to stand with us, with our armies, our gross national product, our pentagon, our world markets, our NAFTA stretching ever farther, continental and worldwide, insatiable, predatory. Perhaps this God is amenable to fine words, songs, gestures, coins raining down, grandiloquent art and architecture. Perhaps Yahweh is like us, a godfather tut-tutting our little weaknesses. Perhaps our God can be hoodwinked.[51]

We should recognize that much of what we acknowledge as God's inspired biblical Word was itself shaped by political pressure. Our modern impulse to avoid dealing with anything that seems to "take sides" results not only in desultory liturgy (what pleases everyone is bound to please no one), but in "consciences that have been deformed."[52] The fact of the matter is that if God's Word is heard parabolically—as liturgy intends it to be—it *will* roil hearts and rile emotions. To those who believe they're in charge, God's Word will always be unacceptable, and, as Daniel Berrigan wisely warns,

> The unacceptable character of God's word inevitably revolves around mat-ters of justice. . . . When justice is neglected . . . consciences have been deformed. . . .
>
>   The deformation continues, indeed flourishes, in our day. Things as they are, which is to say politics as they are, war, preparation for war, maltreat-ment of the innocent—these have hardened into a dogma. . . .
>
>   The word of God is itself judged as purely apolitical. The god thus pre-sented is of course acceptable—to the unjust above all. For such a god offers no objection, no contrary word, no rage in the face of manifest injus-tice.[53]

As Berrigan goes on to point out, the military elite in San Salvador who were responsible for slaughtering the Jesuit missionaries there in November of 1989 ended their planning meeting (just prior to the massacre) with a prayer "to the effect that God might bless their deed. It was after all, entered on 'for God and country.'" Isaiah's Suffering Servant (whom Christians later linked to the figure of Jesus) saw through such shams, the "suppurating crime, bleeding away behind the god-talk, the god-worship, the god-prayer, the

---

51. Daniel Berrigan, *Isaiah: Spirit of Courage, Gift of Tears* (Minneapolis: Fortress, 1996), 33-34.
52. Ibid., 131.
53. Ibid.

blessing from the corrupt sanctuary."[54] It is sobering to reflect that some of the harshest words in Scripture are hurled against worship and worshipers: "I hate, I spurn your fests, I take no pleasure in your solemnities. . . . Away with your noisy songs! . . . If you would offer me holocausts, then let justice surge like water and goodness like an unfailing stream. . . . Hear this, you who trample upon the needy and destroy the poor of the land" (Amos 5:21, 23-34; 8:4).

Modern Parables

Like Zen *koans*, Jesus' parables and liturgy's rituals elicit a crisis that has to *be lived* through and not merely thought through. The crisis is ethical, to be sure, but it is also a crisis of *recognition*. The Christian biblical language of conversion, epitomized by the Greek verb *metanoein*, means not only "to change one's mind" (and hence, repent), but to recognize and respond. This means, as Jesus' parables suggest, that one must take off the blinders and learn to see God at work in unlikely places, among unexpected people—the unclean, the unworthy, the unwanted, the ungrateful, the ungodly. A memorable example of this need to "recognize and respond" appears in Flannery O'Connor's chilling short story "A Good Man Is Hard to Find," a darkly comic tale that centers on a vacation trip taken by a woefully dysfunctional family from suburban Atlanta. The chief co-dependent in this family is a matriarch whom O'Connor calls "the Grandmother," a cunning woman with an iron will and a voice as smooth as chiffon. She is a church-going, Bible-reading Christian whose deeply religious persona masks her passive-aggressive, xenophobic side. She is also the family's professional "martyr," forever suffering from and "for" others.

The plot line of "A Good Man Is Hard to Find" is fairly simple. As the story opens, Granny's son, a wimp named Bailey, tells his mother that the family is going to vacation in Florida, and that the family cat (Pitty Sing) will definitely *not* be going along with them. Granny, of course, has no intention either of going to Florida (*she* wants to go to Tennessee) or of leaving her beloved pet at home. With the cat safely concealed in her handbag, Granny settles into the backseat of the car, poised to preside over the entire vacation. From the get-go, she complains, scolds, and schemes until Bailey finally agrees to turn off the highway to Florida and onto a country road that will lead (so she insists) to a beautiful old antebellum plantation. Unfortunately, Bailey's sharp turn onto the bumpy dirt road jolts the sleeping cat awake. The

54. Ibid., 132.

animal leaps, terrified, into the front seat, clawing Bailey and causing him to skid off the road into a steep ravine. When the car finally rolls to a halt at the edge of a wood and the family disembarks, they find themselves surrounded by three armed men, escapees from a local prison. Their leader is a psychotic serial killer whom O'Connor calls "the Misfit." The meeting between Granny and the Misfit is, quite literally, the beginning of the end for this family. One by one, in cold blood, the escapees escort each member into the woods. Bang! Bang! At last, only the Grandmother remains. In an effort to save her own life, the old woman summons up every bit of religious virtue she possesses. "Pray. . . *pray!*" she urges the Misfit. "Turn to *Jesus*. Jesus will help you." But the Misfit replies with his crazed, criminal logic "I don't want no hep . . . I'm doing all right by myself."[55]

O'Connor uses the confrontation between the devout Grandmother and the diabolical Misfit to explore what is really at stake in the process of Christian conversion. And as often happens in O'Connor's stories, the reader meets some sharp, parabolic reversals of role and expectation. In spite of her religious rhetoric, the Grandmother's moral universe, we discover, is breathtakingly narrow and naive. Her character is accurately summarized by the Misfit when he remarks, "She would of been a good woman if it had been somebody there to shoot her every minute of her life"[56] In spite of her incessant calling upon Jesus, the Grandmother fails to understand the real (if twisted) religious crisis that haunts the Misfit. At one point near the end of the story, the only words Granny can say are "Jesus, Jesus," to which the Misfit replies:

> "Yes'm," the Misfit said as if he agreed. "Jesus thrown everything off balance. It was the same case with Him as with me except He hadn't committed any crime and they could prove I had committed one because they had the papers on me. . . . Of course . . . they never shown me my papers. That's why . . . I call myself The Misfit . . . because I can't make what all I done wrong fit what all I gone through in punishment." . . .
>
> "Does it seem right to you, lady, [the Misfit continued] that one is punished a heap and another ain't punished at all?"[57]

Hidden deep within the Misfit's psychopathic "logic" is a genuine, if parabolic, insight: "Jesus thrown everything off balance!" Like most of O'Connor's characters who symbolize evil, the Misfit has an unerring sense of the truth, of what's *real*. He is not, of course, a *good* man (recall the story's title);

55. Flannery O'Connor, *The Complete Short Stories* (New York: Farrar, Straus & Giroux, 1971), 130-31.

56. Ibid., 133.

57. Ibid., 130-31.

he's a psychotic killer who presides over the cold-blooded execution of an entire family. But none of the other characters in O'Connor's story is very virtuous either. In spite of his malevolence, it is the *Misfit*—with his cold, unyielding eye for truth and death—who enables us to see just how shallow, hypocritical, and silly the old Grandmother is, in spite of all her palaver about prayer and Jesus. When the Misfit says there "ain't no pleasure but meanness," we can hear O'Connor's implicit critique of contemporary Christianity, which she viewed as too soft and comfortable to have any real impact on a world as harsh and dreadful as ours. In O'Connor's story, it isn't the Grandmother's religion and virtue that convert the coldhearted Misfit; rather, it's the Misfit who becomes the source of revelation and grace, the channel of mercy, for an old woman whom religion had actually blinded to the truth about herself and her world.

Like many of O'Connor's finest fictions, "A Good Man Is Hard to Find" thus defies conventional interpretation. Clearly, there are conversions in the story. Clearly, mystery and grace are at work. But who gets saved—and at what cost? O'Connor's story answers these questions—but not in the way we expect. At story's end, when the Grandmother realizes she has but moments left to live, all her phony religious scaffolding falls and the old woman's faith hits bottom. She mumbles to the Misfit that maybe he's right, maybe God doesn't raise the dead after all. At that moment, everything in the story changes. Grace lights the scene like a blazing comet, burning everything in its path. The Misfit suddenly becomes aware of his human bankruptcy and moral destitution, and the Grandmother's vision clears. This is how O'Connor describes the scene:

> "Maybe He didn't raise the dead," the old lady mumbled, not knowing what she was saying and feeling so dizzy that she sank down in the ditch with her legs twisted under her.
> "I wasn't there so I can say He didn't," The Misfit said. "I wisht I had of been there," he said, hitting the ground with his fist. "It ain't right I wasn't there because if I had of been there I would of known. Listen lady, ... if I had of been there I would of known and I wouldn't be like I am now." His voice seemed about to crack and the grandmother's head cleared for an instant. She saw the man's face twisted close to her own as if he were going to cry and she murmured, "Why you're one of my babies. You're one of my own children!" She reached out and touched him on the shoulder. The Misfit sprang back as if a snake had bitten him and shot her three times through the chest. Then he put his gun down on the ground and took off his glasses and began to clean them.[78]

---

[78] Ibid., 132.

The horror and cruelty of this scene are almost unimaginable. Yet in O'Connor's understanding of conversion, grace, and mystery, it is a scene of salvation. Who experiences conversion in this story? Who gets saved, and at what cost? Most readers would assume that the only candidate for conversion is the Misfit; but he is too psychotic and evil to change. However, in a letter written to Andrew Lytle in 1960, Flannery expressed the view that grace touched the *Grandmother*, in spite of her superficiality and selfishness:

> There is a moment of grace in most of the stories, or a moment where it is offered, and is usually rejected. *Like when the Grandmother recognizes the Misfit as one of her own children and reaches out to touch him.* It's a moment of grace for her anyway—a silly old woman—but it leads him to shoot her. This moment of grace excites the devil to frenzy.[59]

Elsewhere in O'Connor's letters, a darker, more difficult, and decidedly parabolic interpretation of the story emerges. Only a couple of months after her letter to Andrew Lytle, Flannery wrote to novelist John Hawkes and suggested that grace embraces *both* the Grandmother and the Misfit—in different ways, for different reasons. This is how Flannery explained it:

> Grace, to the Catholic way of thinking, can and does use as its medium the imperfect, purely human, and even hypocritical. Cutting yourself off from Grace is a very decided matter, requiring a real choice, act of will, and affecting the very ground of the soul. The Misfit is touched by the Grace that comes through the old lady when she recognizes him as her child, as she has been touched by the Grace that comes through him in his particular suffering. His shooting her is a recoil, a horror at her humanness, but after he has done it and cleaned his glasses, the Grace has worked in him and he pronounces his judgment: she would have been a good woman if he had been there every moment of her life. True enough. . . .[60]

The Catholic view of grace, O'Connor held, stretches our understanding to the breaking point—and beyond. For the grace of conversion demolishes all our categories of right and wrong, good and bad, virtue and vice, saint and sinner. Until we have let go—and let go absolutely—of *all* our familiar categories, including all our so-called *moral* categories, we can never know the grace of conversion or experience the unutterable mystery of God's mercy, compassion, and presence. What gets in the way of conversion for most people, O'Connor believed, is not their viciousness but their virtue. In this sense,

---

59. Flannery O'Connor, *The Habit of Being: Letters,* edited and introduced by Sally Fitzgerald (New York: Farrar, Straus & Giroux, 1979), 373.
60. Ibid., 389.

the Misfit is seen by O'Connor as a better candidate for God's mercy than the mindlessly "virtuous" Grandmother. And indeed, it is not until the Grandmother faces complete hopelessness and extinction that she is given the saving gift of sight. Her head clears for one awful moment, and she recognizes the bloody, tattered humanity of her killer. By accepting this God-forsaken, God-rejecting sinner as "one of my [own] babies," this once proud woman sees for the first time *her own sinful nature*—and in that epiphany, she finds salvation. Catholic theology sees grace as ultimately social, and hence O'Connor's intuition was right: each of these characters becomes, improbably, the source of grace for the other. True, the human cost is horrible. The Misfit's actions remain unconscionable, but at the end, both he and the Grandmother are struck by the "blasting, annihilating light" required for conversion and redemption. As O'Connor wrote in 1961, in a letter to her close, mysterious friend (known to us only as the letter A): "I don't know if anybody can be converted without seeing themselves in a kind of blasting annihilating light, a blast that will last a lifetime."[61]

RITUAL AS REVELATION

From both the parables of Jesus and the short fiction of Flannery O'Connor, the same pattern emerges. Ritual leads to revelation—the unexpected disclosure of grace in unexpected places among unlikely people. The ritual may be as homely as kneading leaven into dough or as horrific as a serial killing, but in each case—to paraphrase the ending of another O'Connor parable—the Holy Spirit, emblazoned as fire or ice, "continues, implacable, to descend" upon our tattered humanity.[62] Or, as the story of Jesus' return to his hometown to preach at Sabbath synagogue service tells us, God's Word, ritually rehearsed among a people, will inevitably lead to the same, potentially parabolic conclusion: "Today this scripture passage is fulfilled in your hearing" (Luke 4:21). God's Word never merely speaks; it also *does*, acts, confronts worshipers with the troubling prospect of a revelation they may not wish to hear or see, a "blasting, annihilating light."

To many, the claim that ritual is a "source of revelation" may seem extravagant. Theologians working in the period prior to the Second Vatican Council commonly argued that divine revelation—in the more limited, technical sense—has only two sources: Scripture (the inspired literature of the Bible)

61. Ibid., 427.
62. See Flannery O'Connor, "The Enduring Chill," in *The Complete Stories of Flannery O'Connor* (New York: Farrar, Straus & Giroux, 1971), 357-82, here 382.

and "tradition" (authoritative teaching interpreted, defined, or defended by the church's magisterium). At and after Vatican II, however, theological understanding about when and how God reveals—that is, discloses and bestows the Word on humanity's behalf—began to expand. That such an expansion was happening became clear during the debates that surrounded the council's 1965 Dogmatic Constitution on Divine Revelation, known by its first two Latin words, *Dei Verbum* (hereafter DV). The new approach to revelation was driven, in part, by advances in Scripture study and, in part, by the increasing importance of the interreligious dialogue, which the council also discussed.[63]

During the contentious conciliar debate over the first draft of *Dei Verbum*, Albert Cardinal Meyer of Chicago delivered a brief but potent speech that helped determine the document's final shape.[64] Revelation, Meyer argued, is essentially "living, dynamic, and comprehensive," and hence *Dei Verbum* affirms that it consists "not only in doctrinal propositions but also in the *worship* and *practice* of the whole church." For "tradition develops not only through definitions of the magisterium, but also 'through the contemplation of believers . . . and from the intimate sense of spiritual realities which they experience.'"[65] Cardinal Meyer agreed with this more expansive notion of Christian tradition, but he noted that perhaps something was missing. Precisely because it *does* extend "beyond the limits of the infallible magisterium, tradition itself is exposed to the real limits and defects found in a pilgrim church, a church of sinners which recognizes divine realities only 'indistinctly, as in a mirror.'"[66] In other words, tradition has to make room for the parabolic revelations of grace that may visit a pious grandmother through a psychotic misfit. Moreover, Meyer noted, a glance at the church's long history abundantly demonstrates that in some periods, important matters have been neglected (e.g., the Bible) and vital doctrines (e.g., Christ's resurrection) obscured. Meanwhile, distortions have flourished, for example, "a moralism marked by exaggerated casuistry, a non-liturgical piety." It might be advisable, Meyer concluded, to admit the limitations of a "church of sinners" in the final text of *Dei Verbum*—perhaps in words like these:

---

63. Portions of what follows in the next several paragraphs appeared in different form in my "Amen Corner" column in *Worship* 79, no. 4 (July 2005): 357-69.

64. The debates over *Dei Verbum* took place during the council's third session in 1964, though the document was not approved and promulgated until the fourth session (1965). Cardinal Meyer's speech was given on September 30, 1964. Its Latin text may be found in *Acta Synodalia Sacrosancti Concilii Oecumenici Vaticani II*, Vol. III, Pars III (Vatican City: Typis Polygottis Vaticanis, 1974), 150-51. *Dei Verbum* was approved and promulgated on November 18, 1965, during the council's final session. An English synopsis of Meyer's speech may be found in *Council Daybook: Vatican II, Session 3*, ed. Floyd Anderson (Washington, D.C.: National Catholic Welfare Conference, 1966), 83.

65. *Acta Synodalia*, III/III, 150.

66. *Acta Synodalia*, III/III, 150; the scriptural allusion is to 1 Cor 13:12.

Nevertheless, neither always nor in all things does this living tradition grow and progress. For when a church of pilgrims contemplates divine realities, it may fail in some matters and in fact does fail. Therefore [the church] carries within itself the constant norm of holy Scripture, and by comparing its life to that norm, it ceaselessly corrects and improves itself.[67]

Cardinal Meyer's comment about the real limits of living tradition in a church of sinners did not make it into the final text of *Dei Verbum*, and that caused at least one prominent postconciliar commentator, Joseph Ratzinger (now Pope Benedict XVI), to complain about the document's "over-optimistic view of revelation." Explicitly citing Meyer's speech, Ratzinger wrote in a commentary on *Dei Verbum*, "[N]ot everything that exists in the Church must for that reason be also a legitimate tradition; . . . not every tradition that arises in the Church is a true celebration and keeping present of the mystery of Christ." For *that*, Ratzinger argued, is what tradition ultimately is: "the many-layered yet one presence of the mystery of Christ throughout all the ages . . . the totality of the presence of Christ in this world."[68]

It was, in fact, the desire for a clearer and more comprehensive account of revelation—a desire explicitly expressed by bishops like Cardinal Meyer—that caused what is now *Dei Verbum*'s paragraph 8 to be inserted into the document's final draft.[69] Almost certainly, this important paragraph, which both broadened and deepened our understanding of revelation, was the work of the great Dominican theologian Yves Congar.[70] In his postconciliar work *I Believe in the Holy Spirit*—often described as his "*Summa pneumatologica*"—Congar characterized the life of the church as "one long epiclesis" rising from the sacraments of initiation and embodying its identity. (The word "epiclesis" refers, of course, to that portion of the eucharistic prayer that asks the Spirit to transform *both* the gifts of bread and wine, making them Christ's body and blood, *and* the people who receive them, making them "one body, one Spirit

---

67. See *Acta Synodalia*, III/III, 150-51.

68. See Joseph Ratzinger, commentary on chapter 1 of *Dei Verbum*, in *Commentary on the Documents of Vatican II*, ed. H. Vorgrimler, trans. L. Adolphus, K. Smyth, and R. Strachan (5 vols.; New York: Herder & Herder, 1967-69), 3:173.

69. See ibid., 184; see also 155-66, for a brief history of the origins and background of *Dei Verbum*, as well as its relation to earlier conciliar teachings of Trent and Vatican Council I.

70. Ibid., 184. Ratzinger writes: "It is not difficult (as in the additions in which Article 7 goes beyond Trent) to recognize the pen of Y. Congar in the text and to see behind it the influence of the Catholic Tübingen school of the nineteenth century with . . . its dynamic and organic idea of tradition, which in turn was strongly impregnated by the spirit of German Romanticism." One senses here that Ratzinger believes the Tübingen school was tainted by German Romanticism, and that this flaw contributed to *Dei Verbum*'s failure to take the negative aspects of church history into account—aspects that Cardinal Meyer alluded to in his speech of September 30, 1964. However, to say that Congar embraced German Romanticism—an accusation insinuated on p. 184 (and footnote 9) of Ratzinger's text—seems unfair and unproved.

in Christ.") "The whole Church—," wrote Congar, "its people, its ministers, its treasure of the means of grace and its institution—is [the] sacrament of salvation. . . . 'I believe the holy Church' is conditioned by the absolute 'I believe in the Holy Spirit.' This dogma means that the life and activity of the Church can be seen totally as an epiclesis."[71]

Congar's insights certainly seem to have been incorporated into the final text of *Dei Verbum* 8. For example:

> What was handed on by the apostles includes everything which con-
> tributes to the holiness of life, and the increase of faith of the People of
> God; and so the Church, in her *teaching, life, and worship* . . . hands on to
> all generations all that she herself is, all that she believes. This tradition . . .
> *develops* in the Church with the help of the Holy Spirit. For there is a
> growth in the understanding of the realities and the words which have
> been handed down. (DV 8)[72]

Not only does *Dei Verbum* insist that revelation is transmitted (as tradition) through three principal processes (teaching, life, and worship); it also
affirms that development and growth in understanding happen through three
similar processes: "the *contemplation and study of believers* who ponder these
things in their hearts," the "intimate sense of spiritual realities which they
experience," and authoritative "*preaching*" (DV 8). Teaching, life, and worship;
prayerful study, experience, and preaching: all these are vital ways God's revelation unfolds in the lives of a pilgrim people. And here too one sees the
hand of Yves Congar at work:

> Revelation consists of what God . . . has communicated to us through the
> history of his people as interpreted by the inspired prophets and wise men
> of Israel and later, in regard to the decisive event of Jesus Christ, the evan-
> gelists, the apostles and their spokesmen. . . . We should not interpret sim-
> plistically the idea that revelation closed with the death of the last apostle.
> . . . Our experience of the Spirit has continued since then. It is as intense
> and urgent as it ever was in the past. . . . By "experience," I mean our per-
> ception of the reality of God as he comes to us, is active in us and oper-
> ates through us, drawing us to him in communion and friendship, as one
> being exists for the other.[73]

---

71. Yves Congar, *I Believe in the Holy Spirit*, trans. David Smith (3 vols. in 1; New York: Cross-road, 1983), 3:267, 271.
72. The English translation is the one found in Walter Abbott and Joseph Gallagher, eds., *The Documents of Vatican II* (New York: Guild Press, America Press, Association Press, 1966), 116.
73. Congar, *I Believe in the Holy Spirit*, xvii.

Dei Verbum 8 thus calls our attention not only to the complexity of revelation as transmitted through a *variety of processes* that, taken together, constitute "tradition"; it also points to *the distinctive relation between ritual and revelation*. A single paragraph does not a whole document make; still, *Dei Verbum's* emphasis on worship as "revelatory source" is noteworthy. The bishops at Vatican II expanded not only our comprehension of what revelation is and how it is transmitted, but also our grasp of how closely revelation's symbolic structure is related to the worship and ritual experience of a pilgrim church, a "church of sinners." In sum, the bishops recognized revelation not only "in the explicitly traditional statements of Church doctrine, *but in the unstated—and often unstatable—elements of the whole service of the Christian worship of God and the life of the Church.*"[74]

REVELATION AND THE MYSTERY OF GOD

A theology of revelation obviously cannot avoid the question of God. For postmodern thinkers, especially, this is a highly neuralgic question, because it asks whether we can "name" God at all—and whether, if we do, we have really encountered *God* or merely heard ourselves talking.[75] Nor is this an issue for theology alone; it concerns worship as well. Liturgy constantly calls God names, or at least *tries* to name God in prayer. Yet here a problem arises. To *name*, in our experience, usually means to *claim*, to mark, to lay hold of. Yet when the liturgical assembly utters God's name, it acknowledges that its effort stumbles. In the Roman rite, we begin the liturgy with rituals of purification and penitence that remind us we are not well prepared to do what we are about to do. Liturgical language is public speech from a church of sinners. It is speech that stutters. The language of Christian worship is speech that suffers defeat every time it tries to detain or define the divine. Ours are wounded words that want to go where they know they cannot go—into the heart of God's mystery. Worship's words thus drive us toward the brink of trespass, of transgression. We dare to "name" the Name, knowing all the while

---

74. Ratzinger, commentary on DV 8, in *Commentary on the Documents of Vatican II*, ed. Vorgrimler, 184.

75. See John D. Caputo, *The Prayers and Tears of Jacques Derrida* (Bloomington: Indiana University Press, 1997), 1-68. Caputo discusses Derridean "deconstruction," noting that Derrida seeks not to deny or destroy the Name of God, but precisely to guard its irreducible otherness. "Deconstruction does not set itself 'over' the name of God but below God, so that God is always *tout autre*, ahead of it, before it, more than it" (p. 66). Thus, Caputo continues, "[d]econstruction affirms, says yes to, gives its assent and consent, has a faith in what is to come, prays and weeps for what is coming, for 'my God'" (p. 67).

that worship isn't a matter of *our* naming God, but of *God* naming and claiming *us*. As Jean-Luc Marion writes,

> The Name . . . has to be dwelt in without saying it, . . . by letting it say,
> name, and call us. The Name is not said by us; it is the Name that calls us.
>   And nothing terrifies us more than this call, "because it [is] . . . a fear-
> ful task to name with our proper names the One to whom God has
> bestowed the gift of the name above all names.[76]

The liturgical attempt to name God is thus an impossible task. God is
always more elusive than our eloquence. That is one reason why Christian rituals are endlessly repeated. God's pilgrim people, a church of sinners, keeps
"trying to get it right," knowing all the while that it never will. For "it is only
when you give yourself to, surrender to, and set out for the wholly other, for
the impossible, only when you go where you cannot go, that you are really on
the move."[77] The nearer we get to the incipit of any prayer, the more radiantly
and blissfully "out of control" God seems to become.

So when we speak about "naming God" in the liturgy, we are not claiming
to take possession of God; we are asking God to take possession of us. We
are hoping that the Name will "say, name, and call us." The theological basis
for all this may be found in the work of the astute and saintly Jesuit Karl
Rahner. It was Rahner who helped us understand that the proper coefficient
of revelation is not *ratio* (the human power of reason and intelligence) but
Mystery.[78] Thus, revelation is not primarily the disclosure of "secrets" (hidden
things, objects, persons, truths, or teachings), but God's self-communication
in history, in symbolic words and deeds, *verba et gesta*. In this self-communication, God does not cease to be Mystery, and hence our "knowing" God piv-
ots upon an *unknowing*. Thus, too, the "vision of God" (which we hope to see)

76. Jean-Luc Marion, *In Excess: Studies of Saturated Phenomena*, trans. Robyn Horner and Vincent Berraud (New York: Fordham University Press, 2002), 162. In the second paragraph, Marion is cit-ing Basil of Caesarea (*Against Eunomius*), who in turn cites Phil 2:9. An earlier version of this essay, with important reactions from and dialogue with Jacques Derrida, appears in *God, the Gift, and Post-modernism*, ed. John D. Caputo and Micahel J. Scanlon (Bloomington: Indiana University Press, 1999), 20-53.
77. Caputo, *Prayers and Tears of Jacques Derrida*, 50.
78. See Karl Rahner, "The Concept of Mystery in Catholic Theology," in *Theological Investiga-tions*, vol. 4, trans. Kevin Smyth (New York: Seabury Press, 1974), 36-73. As Rahner noted in these three seminal essays, scholastic theology, largely adopted by the bishops at Trent and at Vatican I, related Mystery and its revelation primarily to *reason*, but "if we take our concepts from the history of revelation and biblical theology, we shall have to add that it is by his *action* upon us that God imparts truths to us. The wider concept is that of a revelation which is action and event" (ibid., 39). Moreover, if reason is revelation's proper coefficient, then Mystery is "provisional"; that is, we humans will eventually "figure it out." This cannot be said, however, of the Mystery of God, for even in heaven, that Mystery will remain infinite and incomprehensible, ever deeper and more aluring, yet still irre-ducible (ibid., 41-48).

does not involve "taking off the wraps," but dwelling in "the permanent presence of the inexpressible and nameless," where "it is impossible to distinguish between what one comprehends . . . and what one does not comprehend," for "vision must mean grasping and being grasped by the mystery." And therefore, "the supreme act of knowledge is not the abolition or diminution of the mystery but its final assertion, its eternal and total immediacy."[79]

Rahner's insistence on the absolute Mystery of God does not mean that human persons can have no *experience* of God. The One who is "incomprehensible and nameless" draws incomprehensibly *near* to us, not only naming us (i.e., giving us our identity) but letting us share the divine nature[80] at the very heart of our human lives and history. Thus, in Rahner's perspective, revelation is fundamentally the real and direct communication of God to the world, its history and its peoples.[81] Several consequences follow:

First, revelation is primarily an *activity*; it is "the ongoing outpouring of God's creative formative love into the entire world," and this divine self-communication "influences the world at every phase of its coming-to-be, and not just within the confines of the biblical world alone."[82]

Second, revelation is *promissory*, *participatory*, and *historical*. While we humans dwell in an unfinished, evolving universe, we "followers of the biblical tradition" do not believe that this universe is utterly indifferent to our presence. On the contrary, we believe we

> have heard a "word" speaking out to us in our apparent lostness, a light shining in the darkness, a divine voice telling us we are not alone and that the cosmos has from the beginning been delivered from its apparent companionlessness. The breaking through of this word into the silence of the universe may be called "revelation."
>
> This word is communicated essentially in the form of *promise*.[83]

Concretely, this promise takes the form of *hope*, of trust in a great future initiated by a self-giving God who calls people daily (thus *historically*) to

---

79. Ibid., 41.

80. Thus, the title of Paul VI's apostolic constitution on the sacrament of confirmation, *Divinae consortium naturae*. The biblical basis is to be found in 2 Pet 1:4 and Eph 2:18.

81. Rahner explains in greater detail what he means by the "self-communication of God" in *Encyclopedia of Theology: The Concise Sacramentum Mundi*, trans. J. Griffiths, F. McDonagh, and D. Smith (New York: Seabury Press/A Crossroad Book, 1975), 1466-68 (s.v. "Revelation, II"). See also Gerald O'Collins, "Revelation," in *The HarperCollins Encyclopedia of Catholicism*, ed. Richard P. McBrien (San Francisco: Harper, 1995), 1112: "Revelation is essentially God's self-communication, a loving and utterly gratuitous invitation to enter a dialogue of friendship."

82. John F. Haught, "Revelation," in *The New Dictionary of Theology*, ed. Joseph A. Komonchak, Mary Collins, and Dermot A. Lane (Wilmington, Del.: Michael Glazier, 1987), 884.

83. Ibid., 887. On the promissory character of revelation, see further Norbert Schiffers, "Revelation, I," in Rahner, *Encyclopedia of Theology*, 1454-55.

communion with the divine and with one another. Such was the call that summoned Abraham "to leave his ancestral home and venture forth into the unknown"; that aroused and sustained belief in the future among the children of Israel; that provoked faith in a "word of promise" that can and will break through "the apparent silence of the universe," that erupts into the world in such a way that the history of God becomes the history of God-with-us.[84] For "we belong to a history whose meaning is promise," and our participation in the "shared memory of a people" binds us to a self-revealing God who acts in human history so decisively that the Word itself takes flesh in Jesus Christ.[85]

Third, revelation is ultimately *one* mystery, not many, and for that reason *Dei Verbum* 2 adopts the language of Ephesians 1:9, which speaks of "the *mystery* [singular; Greek *mystērion*] of God's will" made visible "as a *plan* [singular; Greek *oikonomia*, 'economy'] for the fullness of times." This turn to biblical language (*one* mystery of salvation, not many mysteries) is significant, for as Gerald O'Collins notes, the notion of one, historic revelation "contrasts with Vatican I's revealed 'mysteries' (plural)."[86] Moreover, this shift in language has been maintained in the postconciliar period, especially "in the encyclicals and other major documents of Pope John Paul II, who consistently spoke of "the one mystery of redemption or revelation in Christ."[87] As the late Jacques Dupuis argued, this notion of *one* divine revelation, *one* plan of salvation, not only has enormous significance for interreligious dialogue but also forms the basis for John Paul II's insistence on the "presence and universal action of the Spirit of God" among all peoples, especially "in their religious traditions."[88] As he said in a speech to members of the Roman curia in 1986, "We may think that any authentic prayer is aroused by the Holy Spirit, who is mysteriously present in the heart of every human being."[89] The Spirit's

---

84. Ibid. Cf. Schiffers, "Revelation, I," 1454. In effect, the Word of God "becomes history and history becomes a demonstrative word pointing to God's revelation being fulfilled.... God's revelation, still unimaginable to purely human thought, is experienced in the human action which is called history" (p. 1455).

85. Haught, "Revelation," 890. Note, however, that the incarnation of the Word and the ministry of Jesus do not, taken alone, constitute revelation, a point emphasized in *Dei Verbum* 4: "For this reason Jesus perfected revelation by fulfilling it through his whole work of making himself present and manifesting himself; through his words and deeds [*verba et gesta*, a phrase also used in DV 2, "This plan of revelation realized by *deeds and words* having an inner unity"], his signs and wonders, but especially through his death and glorious resurrection from the dead and final sending of the Spirit of truth" (4).

86. O'Collins, "Revelation," 1112.

87. Ibid.

88. Jacques Dupuis, *Toward a Christian Theology of Religious Pluralism* (Maryknoll, N.Y.: Orbis Books, 1997; rev. ed., 2001). For the specific quotations in this sentence, see Jacques Dupuis, "The Church's Evangelizing Mission in the Context of Religious Pluralism," *The Pastoral Review* online (March 2005): 8.

89. Dupuis, "Church's Evangelizing Mission," 8.

presence and action permeate, in fact, not only the lives of individual persons but the religious life of entire populations: "The Spirit's presence and activity affect not only individuals but also society and history, peoples, cultures, and religions."[90]

Fourth, revelation's structure is *sacramental.* The model of revelation embraced by *Dei Verbum* (and rooted in the work of theologians such as Yves Congar and Karl Rahner) assumes that when God *speaks*, God *shows*; and when God shows, God *gives*. If God's Word is unfailing, then it does what it says and gives what it does. That is why Karl Rahner emphasized revelation as God's symbolic self-disclosure and self-bestowal; it is also why theologians after him have further developed his model of "symbolic mediation."[91] For revelation *transforms* in much the same way that the symbols of sacramental worship do. And by transforming, revelation leads us not to propositional or "speculative" knowledge, but to "participatory knowledge."[92] The reason lies in the nature of symbols themselves, for they too are *actions*—worlds we are invited to inhabit, not objects "to be manipulated through mime and memory."[93]

Fifth, revelation is *response. Dei Verbum* 5 insists that revelation calls human persons to the "obedience of faith" (Rom 16:26), but this obedience is "total," a free commitment of one's whole self to God. Such obedience is not merely "intellectual submission"; it opens a dialogue between God and people, a "dialogue of faith" that expresses itself in biblically based prayer, especially in the liturgy (DV 25).

WHAT RITUAL REVEALS

Dei Verbum concludes, therefore, by commenting explicitly on the common ground linking liturgy and revelation. Both are interactive and participatory; both flow from a "dialogue of faith"; both are structurally symbolic, sacramental. Moreover, while both ritual and revelation are *intelligible* (and indeed, *must* be), the Mystery whose arrival they disclose and bestow shatters the human horizons of intelligibility.[94] As Louis-Marie Chauvet has warned,

---

90. Pope John Paul II, *Redemptoris Missio* 28; English translation: *On the Permanent Validity of the Church's Missionary Mandate* (Washington, D.C.: USCC, 1991), 47.

91. See, e.g., Avery Dulles, *Models of Revelation* (Garden City, N.Y.: Doubleday, 1983), 131-54.

92. Ibid., 136.

93. Nathan Mitchell, "Symbols Are Actions, Not Objects," *Living Worship* 13, no. 2 (February 1977): 1-2, cited in Dulles, *Models of Revelation*, 136.

94. This is the reason why postmodern theologians such as Jean-Luc Marion propose a "third way" (called "de-nomination") for speaking about God—a way that exceeds the traditional predications of "affirmation" (presence) and "negation" (absence). Sometimes they refer to this as a "pragmatic theology of absence," which signifies not a theology of the "non-presence of God," but rather, that the

we must not attempt—in either theology or sacramental worship—to make God a "principle of validation *of* humans *by* humans," for this constitutes a refusal to let God be God.[95] We need, instead, to take on the far more daunting challenge of grappling with a God whose *glory* is revealed "in the disfigured humanity of the Crucified," a God who "has identified God's self with the abandonment of Jesus by God," a God who "withdraws precisely within proximity," and hence, in Christ, became a "void, a form hollowed out to receive the fullness of God."[96] Neither theology nor liturgy can afford to forget that Jesus died "abandoned by God," that "God identified God's self with the human being Jesus doomed to death—and *this* is precisely what the Easter faith affirms."[97] Worship can never be "high Mass," a self-congratulatory exercise in the smugness that thinks it is in serene possession of all the truth, all the time. If the church must be (or become) a "little church" *of* the poor and the powerlessness, then its liturgy must likewise make room for Jesus' loud cry on the cross, for lamentation, for the prayers and tears of suffering humanity.

What, then, does ritual "reveal," and why is that revelation vital for Christians? My answer is that ritual reveals through *reversal;* it offers presence through absence and proximity through distance; it delivers promise through paradox and possession through dispossession. Commenting on Israel's ritual of offering firstfruits (e.g., at Passover), Chauvet notes, as we have seen, how those offerings form a foundation for *all* liturgical remembering, for all cultic "memorial." "The offering of first-fruits," writes Chauvet, "is the figure where object and sign, non-possession and possession, attainment and expectation, heaven and earth, God's grace and the human work intersect each other." Just as Israel could receive and "possess" the land and its bounty through dispossession (i.e., by giving its produce away through a ritual offering of firstfruits), so every cultic action that "remembers" must be verified "in the ethical action of sharing with those who have nothing."[98]

This paradigm holds true for Christian worship as well. Chauvet comments that our liturgical life is rooted in a "memory" whose essential nature

---

"name(s)" we give God must serve "to shield God from presence" (i.e., from confinement to or containment within our human horizons of predication). Thus, Marion can write: "The Name [of God] does not name God as an essence; it designates what passes beyond every name. The Name designates what one does not name and says that one does not name it." See *In Excess*, 156-57.

95. Louis-Marie Chauvet, *Symbol and Sacrament: A Sacramental Reinterpretation of Christian Existence*, trans. Patrick Madigan and Madeleine Beaumont (Collegeville, Minn.: Liturgical Press/A Pueblo Book, 1995), 499.

96. Ibid., 494, 498. Chauvet is here citing the work of both Eberhard Jüngel ("has identified God's self with the abandonment . . .") and Walter Kasper ("withdraws precisely within proximity").

97. Ibid., 498.

98. Ibid., 237, 236.

is *eschatological*; "it is a *memory* of the *future*." As Christians understand it, the *eschaton* is not a deferral that renders the world's history an insignificant "waste of time." Our salvation, after all, happened *within* history, within our world. The "eschaton" is our name for that ongoing process by which Christ's glorified humanity continues to raise the world, just as his own body was raised. The Spirit, released and poured out from Jesus' broken body "inaugurates the participation of humanity and the universe in the Pasch of the Lord." Eschatology thus needs our "present history" as its very condition of possibility, and the eschatologcial character of Christian cult "implies a return to the historic-prophetic dimension of the Jewish cult whose heir it is."[99] In short, the paradigm of ritual dispossession—of a "liturgy of the church" that becomes a "liturgy of the neighbor"—is revealed as central to the definition of Christian worship.

Thus, only when we hear the liturgy of reconciliation's "eschatological" proclamation and assurance of God's forgiving love can we come to recognize ourselves as sinners. Only when the eucharist proclaims "the death of the Lord until he comes" (the memorial of his conclusive sacrifice) can we see God's glory shining on the face of Christ Jesus. Only when we ingest a scrap of bread and a swallow of wine so meager they leave us *more* hungry, rather than less so, can we come to understand not our desire for God, but God's infinite longing for us. Ritual is revelation's way of coming home to history.

CONCLUSION

If stories are something human, it should not surprise us to find that in the New Testament Jesus is portrayed as a master storyteller. Jesus not only told stories in his ministry of preaching the kingdom or reign of God; he himself became the central story of Christian faith—the *storyteller* became the *story*, just as the *bread-breaker* became the *bread broken*. The British fantasy writer J. R. R. Tolkien, author of *The Lord of the Rings*, once remarked that the Gospels are the supreme example of the "eucatastrophe"—the story with a sudden, joyous turn, the tale that begins and ends in happiness. Jesus' parables do not reject the human imagination; they redeem it. As Tolkien put it,

> [I]n God's kingdom the presence of the greatest does not depress the small. Redeemed [humanity] is still [human]. Story, fantasy, still go on, and should go on. The gospel has not abrogated legends; it has hallowed

---

99. Ibid., 239 (emphasis added), 240.

them, especially the "happy ending." The Christian has still to work, with mind as well as body, to suffer, hope, and die; but he [or she] may now perceive that all . . . bents and faculties have a purpose, which can be redeemed. . . . All tales may come true.[100]

The capacity to reimagine the world is an essential part of our "readiness for ritual." Ritual is revelatory not because it discloses new doctrines or presents ideas that are novel and innovative, but because it empowers us to perceive and experience the world itself as the space where God's unfailing Word does what it says and gives what it does. The Emmaus story in Luke 24:13-35 offers a fine parable about the revelatory nature of Christian liturgy. It is parabolic because the story's "moment of recognition"—Jesus is "made known" to the disciples "in the breaking of the bread" (v. 35)—is accompanied by an utterly disconcerting and unexpected result: "Their eyes were opened and they recognized him, but *he vanished from their sight*" (v. 31). As counter-intuitive as it may seem, Jesus' *disappearance* (as we have noted earlier in this book) is actually revelatory. And what it reveals is essential for grasping the connection between liturgy and faith. As Shane Mackinlay notes, the action of breaking bread "manifests the presence of the risen Jesus" to the disciples "because of its connection with the Last Supper. There, Jesus' actions of self-giving love (in washing the disciples' feet and giving himself with the bread and wine) both anticipate his self-giving on the cross, and demand that his disciples give of themselves in the same way."[101]

In other words, the first thing Jesus' disappearance discloses is the need for the disciples to "cross the frontier" from familiar "liturgy of the church" to the "liturgy of the neighbor." But this crossing can happen only through faith. According to Mackinlay, the disciples' faith "is not constituted by a *conceptual understanding* of Jesus' claims, but rather by the *acceptance* of those claims—both the ones that he makes about himself, and also the ones that he makes on them." Their existential acceptance of the risen Jesus in faith opens for the disciples a "space . . . in which his revelation can be manifested to them, and so their eyes are opened to recognise him in his glory." The key here is "openness." Faith is precisely "openness to receiving revelation, . . . acceptance of the claims made in revelation, . . . trust in what is given, . . . preparedness to make a personal commitment in response." What had prevented the disciples from recognizing the stranger on the road to Emmaus was not a lack of proper doctrines, ideas, or concepts, but their failure to accept the ethical, existential

---

100. *The Tolkien Reader* (New York: Ballantine Books, 1966), 71-73.
101. Shane Mackinlay, "Eyes Wide Shut: A Response to Jean-Luc Marion's Account of the Journey to Emmaus," *Modern Theology* 20, no. 3 (July 2004): 447-56, here 452-53.

responsibilities Jesus' own actions implied (complete self-surrender, unconditional service to others). The trigger that finally opens them to faith is Jesus'
ritual action of breaking bread. This liturgy provided, at last, the "hermeneutic space in which Jesus' revelation" could be "manifested to them—a revelation so dazzling that he disappears from ordinary visibility" and must
thereafter be sought in the practice of justice and mercy, in the "liturgy of the
neighbor."[102]

Such, finally, is the "revelation" every Christian ritual discloses and invites
us to embrace in faith. It cannot be understood by logic; it cannot be transmitted in words; it cannot be explained in writing; it cannot be measured by
reason. It is, as the great Chinese master Chung-feng Ming-pen (1263-1323
C.E.) wrote of the *koan*, "like . . . a great fire that consumes all who come near
it."[103]

QUESTIONS FOR REFLECTION

1. In what senses is it true that "the universe is made of stories, not of atoms"?
2. "The psalms . . . are painted prayer, daily as bread, nimble as grace. It is not surprising that they have always been in the background (and often in the foreground) of Jewish and Christian liturgy. Their 'meanings'—as prayer, as
   poetry—emerge only when we *stop making sense*, only when we sit silently in
   the words awhile, waiting to see what happens" (p. 116 above). Why, as writers
   like Kathleen Norris suggest, is "negative capability" the "most basic requirement for participation" in liturgical prayer?
3. Chapter 4 proposes ten qualities (pp. 118-20 above) that are central to the way
   liturgy "works" and to what it teaches us about relations between God and
   community. What items would you put on (or remove from) this list?
4. "If myths are 'agents of stability,' parables are agents of change that aim to question, not reassure, us" (p. 125 above). How does liturgy's parabolic structure
   help to lead us toward an experience of ritual as "revelation"?
5. Liturgy and revelation are "interactive and participatory; both flow from a 'dialogue of faith'; both are structurally symbolic, sacramental. Moreover, while
   both ritual and revelation are *intelligible* (and indeed, *must* be), the Mystery
   whose arrival they disclose and bestow shatters the human horizons of intelli-
   gibilitiy" (p. 141 above). What does it mean to say that liturgy "reveals" by
   means of "reversals" (presence through absence, proximity through distance,
   promise through paradox, possession through dispossession)?

102. Ibid., 452, 453.
103. Miura and Sasaki, *History of the Koan*, 5.

SUGGESTIONS FOR FURTHER READING

Catholic Bishops of the United States. *Fulfilled in Your Hearing.* In *The Liturgy Documents,* 1:342-76. 3rd ed. Chicago: Liturgy Training Publications, 1991. This document from the U.S. Catholic bishops is an important statement not only about preaching but about the deeper relation between Word and sacrament in the church's ritual celebrations.

Crossan, John Dominic. *The Dark Interval: Towards a Theology of Story.* Niles, Ill.: Argus Communications, 1975. A lucid account of myth and parable as these shaped the preaching of Jesus and continue to influence our understanding of Christian conversion.

Dupuis, Jacques. *Toward a Christian Theology of Religious Pluralism.* Maryknoll, N.Y.: Orbis Books, 1997. Rev. ed., 2001. A seminal work on the meaning of Christian revelation in light of today's interreligious dialogue.

Rahner, Karl. "The Concept of Mystery in Catholic Theology." In *Theological Investigations,* 4: 36-73. Translated by Kevin Smyth. New York: Seabury Press, 1974. These three essays, though quite difficult, are vital for a proper understanding of what Christian theology means when it refers to the "mystery of God" or to the "mysteries of salvation."

Scott, Bernard Brandon. *Re-Imagine the World: An Introduction to the Parables of Jesus.* Santa Rosa, Calif.: Polebridge Press, 2001. Written for nonspecialists, Scott's work is a helpful study of Jesus' use of parables in his preaching ministry.

Part 2

Polyphony

The Languages of Liturgy

5

The Book of the Body

IN PART 2 OF *MEETING MYSTERY*, we turn to the multiple "languages" that liturgy speaks. By "language," here, I mean not only—or even primarily—the verbal speech by which we say something to someone about something, but the more basic patterns of communication by which we humans share emotions, thoughts, ideas, plans, and dreams. The rituals of Christian liturgy are, by definition, polyphonic, polyglot. They weave together, simultaneously, several languages (verbal and nonverbal) through which we interact and communicate with one another and with God. The most basic language liturgy speaks is *the body itself*, and hence, it will form the focus of chapter 5.

"God's Word at the mercy of the body," is how French theologian Louis-Marie Chauvet defines Christian sacrament—and for good reason. The most obvious aspect of ritual is *action*, and the most obvious aspect of action is *the body's movement through space and time*. Liturgy is embodied action. We belong to the liturgy by belonging to our bodies (in this world and the next). The body is thus the inescapable "site" of liturgical celebration, more primary and more essential than churches, sanctuaries, books, and furniture. "Body" is liturgy's native language, its first speech—much as poetry means in the mouth before it ever means in the mind. Poetry begins as a deliciousness of the senses, as the *body's* joy in experiencing the world; only later does the mind begin to resist what claims to "be" and to "be real." Thus too, ritual's parabolic hearing of the Word, discussed in the previous chapter, is not a retreat from the world but a reading of that world, an embodied interpretation of how God, things, events, and human persons are related to one another under grace.

Nowhere are these facts more evident than in the religious experience of Latino/a communities. As Orlando Espín points out, what social scientists sometimes call "folk" or "popular" religion is not a mere "adjunct" grafted onto the "official Catholicism" practiced by Latinos/as. "Popular Catholicism," he writes,

> embodies and . . . organizes daily relationships and symbolically expresses their connections to/with the broader social networks—including the

"sacred" networks—through the rites, beliefs, objects, and experiences of the people's religion. Latinos/as are convinced, because of experiences mediated by their popular religion, that God is on their side, fighting their battles with them, suffering their pains and humiliations with them, in solidarity with them in their struggles for dignity and justice, and empowering them to overcome the sin that seeks to overwhelm them in society and family.[1]

Just as the human body is the basic site of liturgy, so too the body belongs at the heart of popular Catholicism. For within the Latino/a perspective, our meeting with God always exists "within the context of *lo cotidiano*. Its various elements intertwine in and are shaped by the public and private spheres that in turn exist (equally intertwined) in *lo cotidiano*. Popular Catholicism is not a parenthesis to real life. It is part, mirror, and hermeneut (interpreter) of daily life."[2]

A stunning illustration of this point appears in *The Miraculous Day of Amalia Gómez*, by the Chicano novelist and playwright John Rechy. Rechy's novel portrays very powerfully the way "the Chicano working poor . . . use and remake religious narratives with poetic license—connecting *cognition* and *practice*—by means of which hope and power are contextually created."[3] This vital connection between thought (cognition) and embodied ritual (practice) is what literary critic Luis León calls "religious poetics." "Religious poetics," writes León, "names the . . . religious practices that Chicanos (and others) employ in their attempts to manage the harsh realities that characterize significant dimensions of everyday life in barrios throughout the Mexican Americas and beyond. . . . Rechy's Amalia Gómez portrays in intimate detail the movements that lead to poetic religious (re)creation."[4] This poetics of religious (re)creation is not merely—or primarily—cognitive; it is born of the body, inscribed on the body. It constitutes a veritable *poetics of the body*.

In Rechy's novel, we meet a Chicana woman whose consciousness, heart, and body have been shaped by her family's *religiosidad*, even though she later abandons official church teachings on divorce, abortion, and sex outside marriage. Born in El Paso, Amalia came from a family whose principal religious icon was "La Dolorosa," the Mother of Sorrows. Yet Amalia cannot accept the idea that life was made simply for struggle and suffering. She refuses to

1. Orlando Espín, "An Exploration into the Theology of Grace and Sin," in *From the Heart of Our People: Latino/a Explorations in Catholic Systematic Theology,* ed. Orlando O. Espín and Miguel H. Díaz (Maryknoll, N.Y.: Orbis Books, 1999), 121-52; quotation from 127.
2. Ibid.
3. Luis León, "The Poetic Uses of Religion in The Miraculous Day of Amalia Gómez," *Religion and American Culture* 9, no. 2 (1999): 205-31, here 206.
4. Ibid.

become a "woman of sorrows" and seeks instead to create a life of "joy and religious hope for herself." She sees in the Virgin of Guadalupe not an icon of "submission and passive endurance of suffering," but a woman exquisitely "sensitive to the peculiar trials of women."[5]

Amalia's story reaches its climax when, on her "miraculous day," she finds herself wandering, dazed and dirty, in an upscale Los Angeles shopping mall, a temple of American consumerism whose "sacred space" houses those rituals of commerce and exchange that energize the American economy.[6] Surrounded by secular shopping rites and exhausted by the sheer bleakness of her life, Amalia is about to leave the mall when she unexpectedly becomes the center of a drama. A gun-toting psychopath seizes her, using her body as a human shield to cover himself from deadly assault by the police: "Hands grabbed her. A man was pulling her against him. His arms locked under her neck. He pressed a gun against her temple."[7]

In a split second, Amalia's body had become the site of a life-and-death struggle whose stakes couldn't be higher. Overcome by terror, she suddenly falls to the ground, uttering the cry of Mexican liberation: "*No more!* she screamed. And she thrust the man away from her with ferocious strength and she flung her body on the concrete."[8] Exposed, her assailant is immediately gunned down by the police, and as he drops into her lap, he seems to whisper, "Bless . . . me!"[9] Without a moment's hesitation, Amalia complies, forgiving her aggressor: "She knew with startling clarity that by blessing this dying man she would be blessing away something in her whose death she welcomed." And at that very moment, borne by the beam of a TV camera, "she saw dazzling white radiance enclosed in a gleam of blue and within it on a gathering of red roses stood . . . *The Blessed Mother, with her arms outstretched to her.*"[10] "Suddenly with all her heart Amalia knew" that the Virgin was not simply "La Dolorosa," but the Mother of Life; she *knew in her body* "and would never doubt it, because a surge of life was sweeping away all her fear and she felt resurrected with new life. Triumphant, she stood up. 'Yes!' she said exultantly, 'I am sure'!"[11]

Despite her distance from many official Catholic doctrines, Amalia Gómez is, to use Orlando Espín's evocative phrase, a "living hermeneutic" of the grace that overcomes sin. The embodied "dynamics of conflict, which so

---

5. Ibid., 213, 214.

6. See the analysis in León, "Poetic Uses," 220-21.

7. John Rechy, *The Miraculous Day of Amalia Gómez* (New York: Arcade, 1991), 204.

8. Ibid., 205. See Rechy's own intepretation of this scene, "Outlaw Aesthetics: Interview with John Rechy," *Diacritics* 25, no. 1 (Spring 1995): 120.

9. Rechy, *Miraculous Day of Amalia Gómez*, 205 (ellipsis in original).

10. Ibid., 205, 206 (italics in original).

11. See ibid., 206.

deeply wound and shape our society," writes Espín, "also affect Latino/a daily relationships. Indeed, the latter are the 'social sacrament' of the former." For popular religion "does not refer solely to those relationships or contents that might be typically labeled religious in European-American culture—it refers to *all* human relationships, including the religious ones. Popular Catholicism is like an epistemological womb within which all of daily reality is produced and reproduced. Therefore, any attempt at retrieving and/or authentically constructing a Latino/a (Catholic) theology of grace and sin *must* go to and through popular Catholicism."[12] The speech of sin and grace is itself, inevitably, the *body's* speech.

In sum, Amalia's pilgrimage from suffering and sacrifice to redemption requires her to visit numerous sites within the world of Chicano/a religious symbols, and at each site she both takes and leaves something.[13] Ultimately, at novel's end, she finds her own redemptive ritual (mediated, somewhat comically, through the ubiquitous medium of television), receives her redemptive vision of the Virgin of Guadalupe, and "as a result, takes possession of her body/spirit/mind." Amalia is in many respects a "postmodern pilgrim," pragmatically inventing "new sources, places, and modes of religious authority that make the 'sacred' or religion 'click.'"[14] And through it all, she knows—in her flesh more than in her mind—that she bears in her body "the dying of Jesus, so that the life of Jesus may also be manifested" (2 Cor 4:10).

This chapter, then, will highlight liturgy's first and most obvious language—the body. It begins with a brief discussion of attitudes toward the body in Christianity's crucial formative period, then moves to the postmodern retrieval of human bodiliness as a theological site essential for understanding how the body is related to faith and to faith's celebration in worship.

REFLECTIONS ON THE BODY IN EARLY CHRISTIANITY

As Amalia Gómez recognized, the body is at the center not only of religious ritual but of one's entire experience of the Source of Life. In this, she reflects the common consensus of Christians through countless generations. Still today, most of the major issues agitating Christians seem to revolve around the meaning of our *bodiliness*. Human self and human body, we've come to understand, form a bond, an indissoluble unity. We not only have bodies; we *are* bodies. Even in death, the body "commands the respect of identity. No

---

12. Espín, "Exploration into the Theology of Grace and Sin," 127.
13. León, "Poetic Uses of Religion," 222-23.
14. Ibid., 223.

longer a human presence, it still reminds us of the presence that once was utterly inseparable from it."[15] Christian theology has a long tradition of affirming the unity of soul and body, in part because, in Aristotelian philosophy, the soul is considered the body's *substantial form* (its activiating principle, the principle that animates our flesh).[16] But another Christian tradition also exists, one that is more difficult to reconcile with the Bible. This is the tradition based on a species of Greek philosophical dualism that considers the body a tomb or prison (*sōma* [body] = *sēma* [tomb]), and hence treats body and soul as irreconcilable forces at war within the human person.

Unfortunately, this second, distorted tradition has shaped a great deal of Christian history and has led to the notion that the body should be feared, mistrusted, despised, punished, discounted, or ignored. "Christian asceticism has never felt entirely at home with the body, to which it has reacted with, at best, ambivalence and, at worst, a positively destructive dualism."[17] Still, from the beginning, Christians have affirmed that they will share the destiny of Jesus' own body, a body that is risen and glorified. So while Christian asceticism has exhibited anxiety and discomfort about the body, Christian creeds have emphasized its salvific future: "We look for the resurrection of the dead, and the life of the world to come." As the early Christian writer Tertullian put it in a classic formula, *caro cardo salutis*, "flesh is the hinge of salvation":

> The flesh is the hinge on which salvation depends. As a result, when the soul is dedicated to God, it is the flesh which actually makes it capable of such dedication. For surely the flesh is washed, that the soul may be cleansed; the flesh is anointed, that the soul may be consecrated; the flesh is sealed, that the soul too may be fortified; the flesh is shadowed by the imposition of hands, that the soul too may be illumined by the Spirit; the flesh feeds on the body and blood of Christ, that the soul as well may fatten on God. (*On the Resurrection of the Flesh* 8)[18]

Sacramental liturgy, Tertullian emphasizes, is inescapably a prayer of the body. But this positive view has not always prevailed during the past two millennia of Christian history. Research published over the past two decades has focused on the new attitude toward the human body that began to emerge in

---

15. Cited in James F. Keenan, "Current Theology Note: Christian Perspectives on the Human Body," *Theological Studies* 55 (1994): 330-46, here 330 n. 3.

16. Ibid., 330. It should be noted that in Aristotle's philosophy "form" and "matter" are related to each other as "act (or actuation)" to "potency."

17. Keenan, "Perspectives," 331 n. 10.

18. Latin text in A. Kroymann, ed., *Quinti Septimi Florentis Tertulliani Opera*, Part 3 (Corpus Scriptorum Ecclesiasticorum Latinorum 47; Vienna: F. Tempsky, 1906), 36-37; English translation in Paul F. Palmer, *Sacraments and Worship* (London: Darton, Longman and Todd, 1955), 108.

the Mediterranean region between the second and fifth centuries of the Common Era. During this period the body was undergoing a radical reevaluation. A new conception of bodiliness and personhood was being shaped by Christian thinkers like St. Augustine, who, in his *Confessions*, paid close attention to the self's interior monologue, its self-reflexive conversation. Such attention was crucial to the evolution of that literary form we now recognize as autobiography, the "self's story of the self." As Gedaliahu Stroumsa has written,

> the maturing corpus of Christian thought from the second to the fourth centuries, culminated with the notion of a radical reflexivity of the self, a notion introduced in its clearest form by Augustine and . . . bequeathed by him to the Western tradition of thought. It should be argued forcefully that this new notion was not only a product of the times but was developed in Christianity. The lack of a similar reflexivity of the self in the classical world is evident in the teachings of the different philosophical schools, which, in various ways, all show a basic lack of interest or respect for the self, the individual, and the particular.[19]

This means, of course, that the historical period *prior* to the second-to-fifth centuries C.E. was characterized by an *"absence of the subject,"* an absence of the "reflexive self" as we have come to know and understand it in the West. "No ancient, not even the poets, is capable of talking about oneself. Nothing is more misleading than the use of 'I' in Graeco-Roman poetry."[20]

But with the coming of Christianity, and especially with its revitalization after the "peace of Constantine" in the early fourth century C.E., the human person as "self" or "subject" began to emerge, largely as the result of a new anthropology. As I noted above, we hear that "self" speaking in the *Confessions* of St. Augustine, and before him, we hear this "new human subject" expressing itself in the philosophical and scientific circles of the Roman Empire that were studied by the late French philosopher Michel Foucault in the third volume of his *History of Sexuality*.[21] Foucault studied the way this "new sense of self" was developing through an emphasis on "care of the self" (in Greek, *epimeleia heautou*). There was an enormous difference, however, between the pagan notion of *epimeleia heatou* and the "care of the self" later developed by Christian intellectuals and ascetics, who stressed renunciation

---

19. Gedaliahu G. Stroumsa, "*Caro Salutis Cardo:* Shaping the Person in Early Christian Thought," *History of Religions* 30, no. 1 (1990): 25–50, here 27.

20. Ibid., citing Paul Veyne.

21. Michel Foucault, *The History of Sexuality*, vol. 3, *The Care of the Self*, trans. Robert Hurley (New York: Vintage Books, 1990).

and the "deciphering" (or erasure) of the self in service of God. The pagan notion seems to have relied on the idea that the real or true self lies deeply hidden, buried, and that it must be *retrieved* and so *released*. (Recall the ancient Greek notion, mentioned above, that the body is a tomb or prison, *sōma* = *sēma*.) Self-knowledge would thus amount to an act of retrieval, a finding of something formerly lost.

By contrast, "Christian thinkers were striving, to a great measure success-fully, to establish a new conception of the human person, a person to be first retrieved *but then developed and cherished*."[22] What was needed (so Christians thought) was not the retrieval of a self buried under layers of denial or decep-tion but a self recovered and then developed through a regimen of renuncia-tion, moral progress, personal reform, and conversion. This emergent Christian self was dynamic, processive, a person in progress toward ethical and moral redefinition. For Christians, "turning upon oneself and reforming oneself was perceived as part of an ongoing and indivisible process of con-version (*metanoia*), that is, making constant efforts to turn away from former habits of thought, feeling, and behavior."[23]

This emerging, reflexive, converting Christian self or subject depended, for its development, on two theological notions that were unknown and hence unavailable to the world of classical antiquity. First, there was the biblical notion that human beings are created "in the image of God" (see Gen 1:26-27). Such a notion—human beings as the very likeness of God—permitted one to understand that each person is an indivisible and irreducible unity. In short, a human being is not a loosely federated collection of optional "parts"—body, soul, spirit, mind, and so on—but a *single unified reality*. No longer could one pit soul (spiritual, lofty, heavenly) against body (base, crass material), for even sexuality, sexual identity, sexual differentiation, is rooted in the work of a creating God whose image humans are.

A second factor also helped shape the emerging Christian self. Besides the well-known duality between soul and body, there was a division that seemed to make the self a stranger, even to *itself*. This estrangement was known in biblical and theological language as sin, a rift *within* the human self so pri-mal, so pronounced, that it makes possible the very reflexivity that constitutes "personhood" in the first place. Thinkers like Augustine came to believe that this rift not only estranges us from self, others, and God, but inevitably makes our self-awareness a *sinful* self-awareness. To be conscious at all is to be aware of oneself as sinner. So the emerging Christian self was simultaneously *justus et peccator* (righteous, yet sinful)—created as a *unity* in God's image and, at the

---

22. Stroumsa, "*Caro Cardo Salutis*," 29 (emphasis added).
23. Ibid., 29-30.

same time, split, riven, estranged, an alien in enemy territory. The human person is both a dynamic subject "in the likeness of God" and a stranger exiled from its own deepest roots, a sinner.

Still another factor influenced the emerging "self" of Christian thought, and that was the astonishing power of Paul's metaphor of the body: Christians are not loosely connected individuals; they constitute a new *social* reality, the body of Christ, flesh of his flesh and bone of his bone (as some early manuscripts of Eph 5:30 put it), members of one another (1 Cor 12:5). The Pauline metaphor had a decisive impact on emerging Christian anthropology. If Genesis clarified the radical source of human personhood (a unity of body and spirit created in God's own image), Paul clarified the common destiny of those persons. If Christians are Christ's body, they must also share his resurrection. "We look for the resurrection of the dead and the life of the world to come," as we say every Sunday in the Creed at Mass.

Taken together, these three notions—the human person as image of God, the self as split by sin, Christian identity as social—began to coalesce as early as the second century in the work of theologians and pastors such as Bishop Irenaeus of Lyons, who wrote that if God did not intend to *save* our flesh, God would not have *become* our flesh.[24] Christians had begun to redefine anthropology, to reinterpret what constitutes the essence or "essential character" of human personhood. The essence of a human person is not *soul* but an indivisible *unity* of body and soul *in which neither can be understood except in terms of the other*. Body defines soul as much as soul defines body. In itself, this notion may have had Aristotelian antecedents, but Christians took the idea a crucial step further. They argued that flesh shares the same destiny as soul, and that this destiny is divine. As Irenaeus insisted, when commenting on the Christian eucharist,

> We offer to God that which is His own, and in so doing we proclaim the union of flesh and spirit, and confess our belief in the resurrection of both flesh and spirit. For, just as bread from the earth, receiving the invocation of God, is no longer common bread but a Eucharist consisting of two elements, an earthly and a heavenly, even so, our bodies, partaking of the Eucharist, are no longer corruptible, possessing as they do the hope of resurrection unto life eternal. (*Against Heresies* 4.18.5)[25]

---

24. See Stroumsa, "*Caro Cardo Salutis*," 42 and n. 64.
25. Latin and Greek texts in A. Rousseau et al., eds., Irénée de Lyon, *Contre les heresies* (Sources chrétiennes 100/2; Paris: Cerf, 1965), 610-12; English translation in Palmer, *Sacraments and Worship*, 108.

Body and soul and are destined for *the same salvation*. Thus, Tertullian could insist that whatever God has planned for humankind is given not to the soul alone but also to the flesh. *Caro cardo salutis*. As G. Stroumsa writes,

> Through his insistence on the resurrection of the whole human composite, Tertullian is brought to some quite interesting reflections on the preservation of human identity: the notion of change must be clearly distinguished from that of destruction. "To be transformed is to be in a different way. Thus, when one is differently, one can still be oneself." . . .
>
> The implications . . . [are] momentous. No pagan philosopher could have wished or dared express such love for the human body, a love that God was the first to show. *Caro salutis cardo*: the discovery of the person as a unified composite of soul and body in late antiquity was indeed a Christian discovery.[26]

Tertullian's insight is glossed in a poem by the twentieth-century American poet Anne Sexton, who suggested that God craves not the human soul but the physical realities of earth. God, she says,

> envies the bodies,
> He who has no body.
> The eyes, opening and shutting like keyholes . . .
> the skull with its brains like eels . . .
> the bones and their joints
> that build and break for any trick . . .
> He does not envy the soul so much . . .
> but He would like to house it in a body
> and come down
> and give it a bath
> now and then.[27]

Sexton was implicitly affirming a key point of Christian anthropology: that God cherishes bodies and calls them to share Christ's own risen destiny. Speaking of that destiny, St. Augustine wrote: "There will be one Christ loving himself. For when the members love one another, the body loves itself."[28]

The theological anthropology that was taking shape in the early, critical centuries of the Common Era was less a conclusion reached through philo-

---

26. Stroumsa, "*Caro Cardo Salutis*," 44.

27. Anne Sexton, *The Awful Rowing Toward God* (Boston: Houghton Mifflin, 1975), 24-25.

28. *Et erit unus Christus amans seipsum. Cum enim se invicem amant membra, corpus se amat* (Augustine, Commentary on the First Letter of John 10.3). Latin text in P. Agaësse, ed., *Saint Augustin, Commentaire de la première épitre de s. Jean* (Sources chrétiennes 75; Paris: Cerf, 1961), 298, 300.

sophical argument than a conviction arrived at through ritual practice. It was an anthropology enacted, ritually embodied, in baptism, where, through a physical act of washing, the Christian was received into the deepest—and most bodily—fact of existence, union with Christ through union with the body of Christ (the church, the celebrating assembly). Each conditions the other—one cannot be joined to Christ without being joined to the church, nor joined to the church without being joined to Christ. Individual and corporate existence, like individual and corporate destiny, define each other. Salvation consists not in self-knowledge, but in love. Moreover, it is God's love for us that makes our love for God (*and* for others, *and* for self) possible.

In sum, the new Christian anthropology that emerged in the second-to-fifth centuries C.E. emphasized two critical points. First, human identity is corporate and social in both its source (God) and its destiny (union with the body of Christ and hence with that body's resurrection). Second, since identity is radically embodied and social, the human subject—beset by a paradoxical tension between freedom and sin—is also embodied and social. Human subjectivity is thus *inter*subjectivity; reflexive selfhood leads not to "splendid isolation," but to communion-of-life-with-others. As Stroumsa observes,

> the wounded and contrite self develops ... humility toward itself and compassion toward others. This compassion becomes the new basis of ethics: the recognition of one's duties toward others as the only possible way of retrieving the imago dei [*sic*] and achieving a total reunification of the self. If this new ethics supposes religious foundations, it also has political implications. . . . In its very brokenness and incompleteness the created cosmos reflects, just like the human person, the hidden presence of its Creator. Christian ethics and politics are hence possessed of a double and ambiguous character: together with their orientation toward the salvation of mankind, between mystical past and eschatological future, they are, fundamentally, ethics and politics of imperfection. . . . Only through compassion for one's neighbor can one hope to reach oneself.[29]

THE MODERN RETRIEVAL OF THE BODY
AS A THEOLOGICAL SITE

At a fairly early stage of its development, therefore, Christian anthropology sought to connect not only soul/self/subject and body, but to see in this con-

---

29. Stroumsa, "*Caro Cardo Salutis*," 49-50.

nection a new foundation for ethics and politics. The Second Vatican Council revisited this ancient insight in its final (and arguably most radical) document, *Gaudium et Spes* (GS), the Pastoral Constitution on the Church in the
Modern World, approved on December 7, 1965. *Gaudium et Spes* 22 is a particularly important statement about how Christians understand not merely
the origin and destiny of believers in Christ but the vocation of the whole
human family. Christians, that paragraph notes, are a unity of spirit and flesh
that awaits "the redemption of the body (Rom 8.23), even though they must
"battle against evil and . . . suffer death." Still, "linked with the paschal mystery and patterned on the dying Christ," they will "hasten forward to resurrection in the strength which comes from hope." Then *Gaudium et Spes*
makes an extraordinary claim, the ramifications of which we are still trying
to understand:

> All this holds true not only for Christians, but for all men [and women]
> of good will in whose hearts grace works in an unseen way. For since
> Christ died for all . . . and since the ultimate [human] vocation . . . is in fact
> one, and divine, we ought to believe that the Holy Spirit in a manner
> known only to God offers to every [person] the possibility of being asso-
> ciated with this paschal mystery. (GS 22)

Here the council not only recapitulated ancient teaching about the vocation of Christians but broke new ground in our relations with other faiths and
cultures, moving us, in the words of the late Jacques Dupuis, "from confrontation to dialogue."[30] We must avoid, of course, finding *our own* beliefs
in other cultures while ignoring their own. But the intent of *Gaudium et Spes*
is clear: it sought, as Dupuis insisted, to emphasize that there is only one plan
of salvation for humanity, a plan to which all are invited. There is no "two-
track" system for calling human beings into communion with the Holy. For
earlier in that same paragraph (GS 22), the council had affirmed that "by his
incarnation, the Son of God *has united himself in some fashion with every
human being*: He worked with human hands, he thought with a human mind,
acted by human choice, and loved with a human heart." Dupuis's comments
on this passage are well worth quoting:

> The incarnation represents the most profound and immanent way in
> which God personally committed himself to humanity in history. It fol-
> lows from this that the Jesus Christ event in its entirety, from the incar-
> nation to the resurrection and glorification, seals the decisive pact which

---

30. See Jacques Dupuis, *Christianity and the Religions: From Confrontation to Dialogue*, trans.
Philip Berryman (Maryknoll, N.Y.: Orbis Books, 2003).

God institutes with humanity. It is, and remains, throughout history the sacrament and seal of that pact.[31]

At the same time, the saving significance of Christ's incarnation and paschal mystery leaves open, as Dupuis notes, a "space for an illuminating and salvific action of the Word as such, both before the incarnation and after the resurrection of Jesus Christ."[32] This "universal action of the Word" is not in competition with the Christ-event, but is "organically combined" with it in a "unique divine plan" for all humanity, a plan that *Gaudium et Spes* 22 explicitly affirms.

Other twentieth-century theologians also worked to expand and develop early Christian anthropology. Karl Rahner, for instance, used a basically transcendental Thomist framework to insist that all Christian theology is actually "theological anthropology." Rahner argued that in the anthropology of Thomas Aquinas (which used the Aristotelian categories of matter and form to describe the relation between flesh and spirit), the body is "the substantial 'expression' of the soul in which the soul first achieves its concrete reality"; hence,

> the soul cannot fulfill itself without making use of matter, [and] the greater its self-fulfillment, that is to say, the more [a person] becomes spirit, the more the soul [i.e., the person] becomes the body. This means that the body is the medium of all communication and that conversely the soul fulfils itself in proportion as [humans] live with bodily [human beings] in a bodily world.[33]

If "spirit," Rahner argued, is "characterized by an openness toward being and at the same time by an awareness of what itself is and is not"; if spirit is fundamentally constituted by "two opennesses"—to universal being *and* to itself—then we may say that "spirit" equals, simultaneously, *transcendence* (an essential and inexhaustible "reaching beyond" the self toward absolute Otherness) and *reflexivity* (i.e., self-possession in self-consciousness and freedom).[34]

Rahner recognized, however, that in our *human* experience, "spirit" can never be severed from body. "The finiteness of the human spirit," he wrote,

> is primarily shown by the fact that it is capable of only partial and incalculable encounter with the "other" and the "alien" which happens to cross

---

31. Ibid., 158.
32. Ibid., 159.
33. Karl Rahner and Herbert Vorgrimler, *Theological Dictionary*, trans. Cornelius Ernst (New York: Herder & Herder, 1965), 60.
34. Ibid., 444, s.v. "Spirit."

its path, and therefore cannot dispense with a body of its own to form a bridge between subject and object. Thus the human spirit is not "pure spirit" but essentially a "spiritual soul," whose ties with the body—and thereby with space and time—make it the specifically "human spirit." In its thinking, knowing and willing this human spirit is referred to the sensuality of the whole man, composed of spirit and body.[35]

Rahner's thought is not easy to grasp, but his final conclusion may be repeated here with some concision. Flesh and spirit, soul and body, are not competitors; we cannot enhance one by forfeiting (or neglecting) the other. Human personhood is a *unity*; hence, the more I become "body" the more I become "spirit"; while the more I become "spirit" the more I become "body." The two are directly (not inversely) proportional.

Nor is all this merely a matter of philosophical speculation. It is firmly rooted in Christian revelation. There are not two Jesuses, one human and the other divine; one earthly, the other heavenly. Jesus Christ is one person, who accomplished salvation for us in his historical, human body person, a body surrendered, "given up for you." At the supper he shared with his friends the night before he died, Jesus showed his body and blood not only as food and drink, but as *signs* for us, realities that come to light only in the *body*—his body and ours. "The fact," wrote Rahner,

> that with her constitution as People of God the Church realizes herself essentially in the sacraments and the announcement of the basileia [reign or kingdom of God] shows that *an essential feature of bodily life—communication by sensible signs—is also an integral element of human salvation.* . . . [T]he salvation Christ has wrought must also necessarily *come to light in the body.* . . [I]t will be seen that it was an error ill beseeming Christians to banish grace to the realm of the "soul alone," for in that Body [of Christ, the church], possessed by grace and become the expression of grace, is the one entire [hu]man and the whole of humanity, blessed bodily in the bodily presence of Christ.[36]

Grace and salvation are bodily matters, and since Christ has "united himself in some fashion with every human being" (GS 22), they are matters affecting all persons. Liturgy, ritual, and sacrament might be defined not only as "the Word of God at the mercy of the body," but as "grace and salvation coming to light in the body." Grace has as much to do with the welfare of our flesh as it does with the welfare of our "souls." That is why Christian liturgy

---

35. Ibid., 445.
36. Rahner and Vorgrimler, *Theological Dictionary*, 61.

has traditionally spoken of the eucharistic food and drink as a "medicine for healing soul and body." For grace (God's free and gracious self-bestowal) always points toward the *eschatological* (i.e., the full, final, definitive) consummation of human beings and their history. In this, the church, as Vatican II insisted, is a sacrament of the world itself, the *embodied* world of humanity: "the whole of humanity, blessed bodily in the bodily presence of Christ," to use Rahner's language. For Christians, even eschatology (*especially* eschatology) is anthropological and requires the presence of the body. As Karl Rahner liked to say, we Christians are "the most sublime of materialists."[37] This is so because Christian theology embraces an ecology of both the human body and the human world—*both* are destined for transfiguration.

> [Our] flesh is redeemed and glorified, for the Lord has risen for ever. . . . [and so] we have to love our own [bodiliness] and the worldly environment [in which it lives]. . . . As materialists we are more crassly materialist than those who call themselves so. . . . We recognize and believe that this matter [this body, this world] will last for ever, and be glorified for ever. It must be glorified. It must undergo a transformation the depths of which we can only sense with fear and trembling in that process which we experience as our death. . . . [Our body, our flesh] remain. . . . [They celebrate] a festival that lasts for ever.[38]

Rahner's point about the spiritual power and transfigured destiny of matter is both ancient and new. For Christians, the mystery of matter reveals the mysteries of the spirit. That is the fundamental law of the Christian economy, and it helps us see why Rahner thought that all Christian theology is theological anthropology, and why "Christology, whether regarded from the divine point of view or the human, appears as the most radical and perfect recapitulation of theological anthropology."[39] In a Christian anthropology, bodiliness (whether Christ's or ours) is not a mere utilitarian instrument, useful for a time, then easily discarded. Rather, Jesus' embodied humanity signifies that our flesh belongs forever to the very definition of the Divine.

CHRISTIAN ANTHROPOLOGY AND ITS LINKS TO LITURGY

We are now in a position to examine how Christian anthropology—with its distinctive focus on that "*embodied* intersubjectivity" we call the human per-

---

37. Karl Rahner, "The Festival of the Future of the World," in *Theological Investigations*, vol. 7 (New York: Seabury Press, 1977), 183.
38. Ibid., 183-84. Material in brackets added for clarification.
39. Rahner and Vorgrimler, *Theological Dictionary*, 27.

son—both shaped and was shaped by the rituals of liturgy and sacrament. Several points will help establish what it means to say that Christian worship is "the prayer of the body," that liturgy speaks "body" as its native tongue.

An Embodied Existence

Our brief review of early Christian innovations in anthropology confirms a point that the great Protestant exegete Rudolf Bultmann made in the last century: viz., that for thinkers like Paul, "*sōma* [body] belongs inseparably, constitutively, to human existence. . . . The only human existence there is— even in the sphere of the Spirit—is somatic existence."[40] One might say that for Paul, as twenty centuries later for Karl Rahner, theology is anthropology. Body is "the basis for the metaphysical unity of the [human] person," and it also creates "the possibility of relationship between persons."[41]

The Body's Destiny

The resurrection (of Jesus and of us)

> does not imply the thesis of an immortal soul; on the contrary, it suggests the idea that the body is the whole man [or woman]. In short, the aim of resurrection is a human body which is able to explain human existence, personality, and relatedness. Through their corporeality, believers are related, and thus can be caught up in Christ, who transforms that corpo- reality. So Scriptures reveal not simply who we are in Christ, but who we will be. If our corporeality encompasses our existence and is the basis for our relationality, then the resurrection of our bodies means that we will never be at war within our bodies again.[42]

Our belief in the shared resurrection destiny of all humanity (GS 22) signi- fies that the Easter mystery is not simply an "object of Christian faith" but an ethical imperative. If flesh is as precious as spirit, then the body's ultimate fate is as significant as the soul's (recall the judgment scene in Matt 25:31-46). In short, Christians understand bodily resurrection as creedal datum, eschato- logical promise, and moral task.

---

40. Rudolf Bultmann, *Theology of the New Testament*, trans. Kendrick Grobel (2 vols.; London: SCM, 1952), 1:192.

41. Keenan, "Perspectives," 332.

42. Ibid., 333.

In contrast to philosophies that exclude the body from genuine "self-knowledge," Christians have insisted that human destiny—as defined in and by the risen Christ—is "the opportunity and the demand for all people to find in their own bodies the fullness of the Spirit of Christ. . . . Thus when Christianity, on the belief that the human is in God's image, made integrating the body and soul both a theological expression of humanity's integrity and a normative task, it proposed to the Western world a new claim on the human body."[43]

Who Owns the Body?

Christianity's "new claim on the human body" represented a significant shift in understanding who or what controlled (i.e., held final power over) the body. As Peter Brown's studies have shown, the late antique world assumed, rather uncritically, that the *polis* (the city, the state, the "government") had control over bodies. The body *belongs* to the state, is the property of the state. Such control was deployed primarily in two ways: (a) through the inculcation of self-discipline (since control of one's body mapped the "good order" of society as a whole), and (b) through the disciplined control of reproduction (sexuality, the generative lever of life). Such dual control assured the Roman state both "its pride and . . . the children it needed, and, in return, [the state] gave . . . citizens the freedom to do whatever they would with their bodies so long as they did it with proper discipline."[44]

In such a system, the state invests the human body with a dignity that is derived from the state's own interests, and not from the body's inherent dignity and integrity. Christians, in contrast, had a very different idea. As Peter Brown summarizes it,

> Christian attitudes to sexuality delivered the death-blow to the ancient notion of the city as the arbiter of the body. Christian preachers endowed the body with intrinsic, inalienable qualities. It was no longer a neutral indeterminate outcrop of the natural world, whose use and very right to exist was subject to predominantly civic considerations of status and utility.[45]

Christianity took the body back from the *polis* (the government) and gave it

---

43. Ibid., 335.
44. Ibid., 336.
45. Peter Brown, *The Body and Society: Men, Women, and Sexual Renunciation in Early Christianity* (New York: Columbia University Press, 1988), 437.

back to the person who has it, who *is* it. This return of the body to its rightful owner had special significance for women. In the state-ownership schema, a woman's body was above all utilitarian: she was a boon to the state by bearing children. But Christianity proposed models quite at odds with this view. Women who were widows or virgins managed to free themselves from bondage to reproduction in order to live lives of generosity well beyond the state's utilitarian goals. As Brown observes, in the Latin West, it was Ambrose, particularly, who crafted a paradoxical rationale for this new understanding of women. He writes:

> Ambrose's . . . notion of virginity made concrete the integrity of the Catholic church in a hostile society while it endowed the Church with a sense of momentum over against the outside world. . . . Precisely because the normal [i.e., state-sponsored], sexual associations of a woman's fecundity had been renounced, the bodies of virgins were calculated to conjure up, in the mind of believers, all that was most "untainted," and so most unambiguously exuberant, in the notions of fertility, of continuity, and of creativity. The closed womb was not only a barred gate. Precisely because it was so closed, it could be most open: it was also a bubbling cauldron; it was a source from which light streamed; it was a cloud showering gentle rain [images used by Ambrose]. By reason of the very closedness of her body, the mind, the heart, and the hands of the virgin woman had come to open wide—to the Scriptures, to Christ, and to the poor.[46]

Of course Brown's enthusiasm for Ambrose's innovative view of virginity is not shared by everyone. One may well wonder whether the passing of a woman's body from *state* control to *church* control constitutes any advance at all in personal freedom for women. History shows that the church has a habit of expecting *all* women to be submissive, compliant, obedient—hardly a model that matches Jesus' own view. In the parabolic story of the gentile Syrophoenician woman (Mark 7:25-30; Matt 15:21-28), Jesus' Jewishness is stressed ("it is not right to take the food of the children and throw it to the dogs" [Mark 7:27]), and he seems to regard her as unclean. Yet by the time the story ends, Jesus has let his own view of matters (gentiles have no right to the blessings of God's reign) be changed by the woman's wisdom and determination: "Great is your faith! Let it be done for you as you wish" (Matt 15:28). In sum, the church has had (and continues to have) trouble living up to its own insight about "who owns the body."

---

46. Ibid., 363.

Bringing the Body's Vernacular to Worship

How we answer the question, Who owns the body? has a direct bearing on our understanding of liturgy's sacramental rituals. Readers old enough to remember the preconciliar Mass will recall that the rubrics of the Roman Missal of 1570 (the so-called Tridentine missal) regulated the priest's gestures in minute detail. Rigorous bodily discipline and control were enlisted to signal solemnity and decorum. The priest's hands were held close to the body and lifted ever so slightly; the voice was kept low (except when singing); the eyes were lowered, even when greeting the people with the words *Dominus vobiscum* ("The Lord be with you"). To some degree, the ritual economy priests practiced while celebrating the eucharist was typical of ritual gestures still found in other cultures (for instance, the stylized motions employed in *chanoyu*, the traditional Japanese tea ceremony). At the same time, the priest's bodily movements mapped the church's self-understanding: a body whose members are subject to minute regulation by authoritative leaders (e.g., bishops, the pope).

Ironically (or perhaps intentionally), the cramped, highly controlled gestures of the Tridentine liturgy were put in place at precisely a period when Western art seemed headed in a different direction, one that vigorously affirmed the humanity of Christ (and of Christians). Leo Steinberg's controversial study *The Sexuality of Christ in Renaissance Art and in Modern Oblivion*, inspired by his work on Ghirlandaio's late-fifteenth-century painting, the *Adoration of the Magi* (now in the Uffizi Gallery, Florence), shows just how far Renaissance and early modern interest in Christ's bodiliness went.[47] What initially drew Steinberg's attention was the object of the wise men's gaze: the genitals of the infant Jesus. Further investigation revealed that the open display of Christ's genitalia was something of a commonplace in Renaissance art. These bodily organs are depicted again and again, and Steinberg came to the conclusion that artists were acting not from prurient curiosity but from a desire to depict Christ in his full, integral humanity.

Based on his own research, the distinguished American Jesuit historian John O'Malley concurred with Steinberg's conclusions. In spite of perceptions to the contrary, writes O'Malley, "it was in *Rome* in the seventy-five years before the outbreak of the Reformation that *the most original and creative theological work was being done in all of Europe*," and one of the "most striking characteristics" of that theology was "its treatment of the mystery of

---

47. Leo Steinberg, *The Sexuality of Christ in Renaissance Art and in Modern Oblivion* (2nd ed., revised and expanded; Chicago: University of Chicago Press, 1996). Steinberg's study was originally published in 1983 (New York: A Pantheon/October Book).

the Incarnation."[48] In their reflection on Christ's humanity, Renaissance theologians revived what O"Malley calls "epideictic rhetoric," the "rhetoric of
panegyric that ... rehearsed the life and deeds of its heroes" by meditating on
the details of their biographies.[49] In spite of its rubrical conservatism, the
liturgy of the Roman rite in the late medieval and early modern periods had
adopted some features of this epideictic rhetoric. For instance, the rubrics for
Mass prescribed that the celebrant and congregation "fall to its knees at only
one point during the recitation of the ... Creed," at the words, "by the power
of the Holy Spirit he was born of the Virgin Mary, and became man" (*et
incarnatus est de Spiritu Sancto ex Maria Virgine, et homo factus est*).[50] But even
more telling, perhaps, is the detailed attention Christ's humanity received
during the liturgical year and in preaching. Historically, the incarnation
began with the angel Gabriel's message to Mary and her acceptance of it
(Luke 1:26-38), but Renaissance thinkers understood that the actual manifestation of this mystery to the world happened in stages: in Christ's birth at
Bethlehem, in the Magi's visit to the crib, and "most unmistakably of all when
he was subjected to the rite of circumcision."[51] All these events were celebrated as major festivals in late-medieval and early modern Catholicism. In
its ritual practice, the liturgy borrowed a page from God's own "epideictic
rhetoric," whose drama reached climax in the ritual of Christ's blood, shed for
the first time at his circumcision.

Sermons on Christ's circumcision are understandably rare today, but one
given to the papal court by Francesco Cardulo, ca. 1495, argues, as O'Malley
observes, that the humanity of Christ is most intensely visible in the "palpable reality of the male member that 'is fondled, taken in the hand, receives a
wound, feels pain'—*quod attrectatur, quod sumitur in manus, quod plagam
recipit, quod sentit dolorem.*" The word *attrectare*, O'Malley writes, "is not a
particularly respectable word and sometimes has the erotic connotations of
our equivalent, 'fondle.'" Even without the possibly scurrilous connotations,
hearers today would probably find such homiletic remarks in questionable
taste, but in a less squeamish era, artists and preachers proudly celebrated the
undeniably sexual character of Christ's humanity. As for the full-frontal
nudity of sacred figures in Renaissance art, O'Malley suggests that the fif-

---

48. John O'Malley, "Postscript," in Steinberg, *Sexuality of Christ* (1983 edition), 199-203, here 200
(emphasis added).
49. Ibid. O'Malley notes that epideictic rhetoric was related to an "older ... independent tradition that [had] developed with Bernard [of Clairvaux] in the 12th century and with the Franciscans
in the 13th and 14th that loved to meditate on the humanity of Christ."
50. Ibid., 201. To this day, these two lines in the Creed, when recited at Sunday Mass, are the
ones that are accompanied by a gesture of reverence: "All bow during these two lines."
51. Ibid.

teenth and sixteenth century debates about Christ's poverty (especially as a reformist model for clerical life) may have led to artistic representations of the medieval slogan, *Nudum sequi nudum Christi* ("to follow in nakedness the naked Christ").[52]

Rubrics embody ritual's rhetoric, so the dramatic epideictic emphasis on Christ's physical humanity during the recitation of the Creed would have made an impression on "any artist sensitive to the religious subjects he was called upon to paint." There can be little doubt, then, that Renaissance painters (mostly men) saw the *ostentatio genitalium* as indisputable proof of Jesus' humanity and as affirmation of the theme of "human dignity" popular in that period.[53] What is not so clear is how Christ's humanity was understood. There is a temptation to assert that these artists meant to emphasize *gendered* humanity. But in a reply to Steinberg's work, Caroline Walker Bynum notes that in late medieval painting (during the period just prior to the Renaissance), artists also depicted a *lactating* body of Christ, a nourishing, maternal body. Bynum argues, however, that these paintings of a lactating Christ do *not* emphasize a *gendered* body. The lactation affirms, rather, Christ's *fully human* character—not his "feminized" body. "Humanity," Bynum writes, "is genderless. To medieval women humanity was, most basically, not femaleness, but physicality, the flesh of the 'Word made flesh.'"[54] In Bynum's view, the pictures of Jesus lactating do not show us Christ's "feminine dimension," but simply record the *complete humanity* of Christ. For medieval women (some of whom were surely painters), Jesus did not represent "part of" humanity (mere maleness or femaleness) but rather humanity in its exuberant fullness. For them, if the Word-made-flesh doesn't lactate, *no one* lactates (because the nurture lactation provides would no longer belong to the fullness of humanity).

Bynum claims, then, that just as Christian anthropology came to view the human person as "embodied intersubjectivity," so medieval women reclaimed their bodies as *subjects* and not as objects to be controlled (by prayer, fasting, ascetical discipline, church authority). Medieval women began to understand *themselves* as bodies, as embodied intersubjectivity. In an age in which male priests had access to the Lord's body in the eucharist in ways no layperson did, these women managed to retrieve, through their own communion with the body of Christ, "the prototype for full personal integration and the grounds for the full inclusion of all humanity. In their bodies, through . . .

---

52. Ibid., 202.
53. Ibid., 201.
54. Caroline Walker Bynum, "'. . . And Woman His Humanity': Female Imagery in the Religious Writings of the Later Middle Ages," in *Fragmentation and Redemption: Essays on Gender and the Human Body in Medieval Religion* (New York: Zone Books, 1991), 151-79, here 179.

mystical visions and even mystical unions, women experienced the suffering and redeeming body of Christ. Full integration was found precisely in and through the body."[55] These women had discovered that selfhood and subjectivity are themselves incarnate, and that bodiliness is our primary mode of access to the sacred.

The Body's Vernacular and the Space of Worship

This theme continued, especially during the so-called Counter- (better, Catholic-) Reformation that was picking up steam at the end of the sixteenth century and the beginning of the seventeenth. Here too, though it may seem counterintuitive, the conservative rigidity of the ritual reforms that followed the Council of Trent, do not necessarily give us an accurate picture of how Catholics understood the relation between their bodies, Christ's body, and the liturgy. Art may be a better guide. Take, for instance, the work of the painter known as Caravaggio (Michelangelo Merisi [1571-1610]). Caravaggio's relatively short and violent life is itself fascinating, but his importance here lies in the extraordinarily innovative character of his painting, much of which was done for ecclesiastical patrons (cardinals, religious orders) and for liturgical purposes (as altarpieces).[56] Art historian and biographer Helen Langdon observes that Caravaggio's work has a formal ritual quality but at the same time a breathtaking *naturalism* that was the envy of his contemporaries.[57] Not only did Caravaggio paint directly from life (without preliminary sketching), but he painted life in all its ambiguous immediacy. His sole surviving "still life" painting of fruit and flowers is notorious for its wilting vines, fruit well past ripe, insect-bitten leaves, and battered baskets pushed so far forward they seem about to break the picture's plane and topple off the table.[58] Still, in spite of this painting's "windfall apples and bruised pears," it embodies a deeply spiritual sense that stresses—as had early Christian bishops like John Chrysostom and modern ones like Caravaggio's contemporary, Charles Borromeo—the "beauty of the small and humble products of nature," the supreme value of the "utterly ordinary and everyday," the lowly.[59]

Our attention here, however, is on Caravaggio's religious subjects and on

---

55. Keenan, "Perspectives," 339-40.
56. An audacious study of Caravaggio's life and work, especially his relations with the church of his day in Rome and southern Italy, may be found in Peter Robb, *M: The Man Who Became Caravaggio* (New York: Henry Holt and Company/A John Macrae Book, 1999).
57. Helen Langdon, *Caravaggio: A Life* (New York: Farrar, Straus & Giroux, 1999), 5, 167-68.
58. See examples in Langdon, *Caravaggio*, plate 12, between pp. 116 and 117.
59. Ibid., 116-18.

his liturgy-related work (those paintings destined to form an integral part of the ritual setting for the eucharistic celebration, such as his canvases depicting the call and martyrdom of the evangelist Matthew, still on view in the Church of San Luigi dei Francesi, Rome).[60] In their own way, the naturalism of Caravaggio's religious paintings are as startling as Renaissance depictions of Christ's genitalia. He refused to sanitize either his subjects or their situations. Take Caravaggio's *Madonna of the Pilgrims*, painted as an altarpiece for the Roman Church of Sant' Agostino, ca. 1604.[61] The painting caused an immediate brouhaha, in part because its Mary was not a distant ethereal ascetic but a warmly human, "sexy young housewife coming to the front door of what looked like a very ordinary Roman home—a handsome doorway, the frame a bit chipped and a patch of stucco missing from the wall, exposing the bricks beneath."[62] The pilgrims who gaze up at the woman and "the overgrown naked boy child in her arms" are a shabby couple who look like they've "just knocked," the one "a bearded barefoot man in his thirties with patched britches," the other "a considerably older and worn looking woman, old enough to be the man's mother, who'd already lost her teeth and had her hair scarfed against roadside dust."[63] Both Mary and the pilgrims are poor, and both have filthy feet—a provocation, surely, in a painting destined to hang over a major altar, during celebrations of the eucharist, in a city that increasingly feared and loathed the presence of the poor.[64]

The scandal was not only that Caravaggio had rewritten an icon, but that he had brought the human condition, unwashed, smack into the middle of the space for celebrating liturgy. "It was," writes Helen Langdon, "entirely new for the humble poor to appear centre stage in a public altarpiece," and while the *Madonna of the Pilgrims* does not show the "real squalor in which the Roman poor truly lived," it certainly appeals to a spirituality (associated with figures like St. Philip Neri) that stressed compassion and solidarity with homeless vagrants.[65] In Caravaggio's canvas the rhetoric of Counter-Reformation triumphalism had not yet drowned out the epideictic rhetoric (stretching back to the High Renaissance) that cherished the human in all its dimensions, from genitalia to dirty feet. At a profound level, the *Madonna of*

---

60. For the Matthew paintings, see Langdon, *Caravaggio*, plates 18-29, between pp. 212 and 213.
61. See a color plate of this painting in Langdon, *Caravaggio*, plate 31, between pp. 308 and 309.
62. Robb, *M: The Man Who Became Caravaggio*, 265.
63. Ibid.
64. Ibid., 268. In the very year that Caravaggio painted the *Madonna of the Pilgrims*, the city of Rome had cracked down on vagrants, in part because the poor were perceived to be a menace and an embarrassment in a newly refurbished, "showcase" Rome that wanted to model Counter-Reformation piety; see ibid., 266-67 for details.
65. Langdon, *Caravaggio*, 287.

the Pilgrims was an "in your face" manifesto, both theological and liturgical. For the first time in post-Reformation Rome, Mary is painted as "a deeply ambiguous figure, warm, fleshly (we felt the imprint of her fingers against the child's body) . . . welcoming," while the poor are thrust directly before the eyes of a "courtly élite."[66] Unlike the kitsch produced by many of his contemporaries, Caravaggio's *Madonna of the Pilgrims* shows a "scene from ordinary life" purged of ordinary religious rhetoric and "transcendental messages."[67]

Thus, while vernacularism did not make its way into the language of the post-Tridentine Mass, it certainly did refashion the ritual spaces that shaped liturgical celebration. Langdon observes that theoretically, according to Counter-Reformation treatises on church art and architecture, sacred images—especially those linked to the liturgy—were to observe strict criteria of decorum and theological propriety. But in Caravaggio's "harsh vernacular" we not only meet saints whose real-life models were prostitutes; we also encounter the humble, the dirty, and the poor "in a way strikingly new in art." Caravaggio was creating "a shock of humility, pushing the world of the poor before an élite audience, and using a language that seems rough and vernacular, and available to everyone." A vernacularism of this kind was subversive, parabolic, yet "profoundly Catholic."[68] After all, Peter Robb points out, one of Caravaggio's major altarpieces, the *Martyrdom of St. Matthew*, shows a Mass *interrupted* by a murder! Desecration in the sanctuary! Another, his notorious *Seven Works of Mercy*, paints pious actions "as street life and as theater." Instead of showing idealized virtue, it depicts "mercy in everyday life, a mercy without pity, pathos, gratitude. Mercy as the satisfaction of basic needs. Mercy, indeed, as business." We see a "starving old bearded prisoner" sucking milk from his daughter's breast, the young woman hitching up "her bodice as best she could" and looking around as if to dare anyone who "might feel like making a comment." A few drops of the daughter's milk trickle down the old man's beard, *"just as happens in everyday life."*[69] All this, again, in an altarpiece intended to frame and interpret liturgical celebration!

In Langdon's analysis, the "harsh vernacular" of Caravaggio's *Seven Works of Mercy* seems deliberately to exclude "the world of the wealthy" and to return directly to the judgment scene of Matt 25:31-46. It shows the dark conditions under which much of humanity (then as now) works out its salvation. In his altarpiece, Caravaggio paints a web of allusions not only to biblical precedents and lives of the saints, but to the turbulent life of center-city

66. Ibid., 287, 289.
67. Robb, *M: The Man Who Became Caravaggio*, 124.
68. See Langdon, Caravaggio, 250-51, 224-25, 226.
69. Robb, *M: The Man Who Became Carravagio*, 371, 372 (emphasis in original).

Naples (where the church that commissioned his work was located). He shows the "frenetic whirl of activity," the "brutal contrasts between extreme poverty and luxury," giving a "contemporary scene a universal meaning." Caravaggio's vision of liturgy—his understanding of what belongs in the space Mass is celebrated—is provocative, parabolic. The divine and human meet "on the streets of Naples," just as in Caravaggio's painting of the *Supper at Emmaus*, Christ is present as "a contemporary figure, from the ordinary, working world." If the Council of Trent prohibited vernaculars in liturgical *speech*, artists like Caravaggio found ways to bring the language of ordinary people into liturgical *space*. By reimagining God's Word and retrieving its parabolic punch, he created a space for worship that would challenge "a polished elite . . . push the religion of the poor before them . . . and value rough and vernacular modes of expression."[70]

In sum, the modern process of "vernacularizing" the liturgy did not begin at and after the Second Vatican Council, when rites were reformed and the world's vernacular languages began to be used in the Roman liturgy. The process was already well under way in the visual arts long before it manifested itself in liturgical texts and rites—in Renaissance painters' focus on the full humanity of Christ and in Caravaggio's "harsh vernacular" of dirty feet and Neapolitan street life.

Body and History

Caravaggio's vernacularism anchored both Christ's body and ours in history, linking them to the "mean streets" of Naples and to liturgical spaces where divine and human *meet*, without detriment to either. His vernacularism resisted any attempt to etherealize or "spiritualize" Christ's body—or ours— and hence his painting of Christ at the supper of Emmaus is "a contemporary figure from the ordinary, working world."[71] In this, Caravaggio was adhering to an important theological principle: viz., that neither our bodies nor Christ's can lose their links to history. Jesus' risen body keeps the prints of the nails—a sign, surely, that Christ's glorified humanity cannot be separated from the body that suffered death on the cross and poured out its blood "for you and for many." As Xavier John Seubert has written, the mystery of the incarnation signifies that history and humanity forever belong to God's divinity: "Jesus is God through relationship that is the substance of God—

---

70. See Langdon, *Caravaggio*, 329-30, 231, 239.
71. See ibid., color plate 30, between pages 308 and 309.

and this now takes place forever within his bodiliness that is irrevocably one with human history. We are saved by relating our lives in all our bodiliness to that relationship *within* our history, not by securing our escape or release from it."[72]

Despite this, Christianity is heir to a tradition (in theology, liturgy, and spirituality) that has often minimized the significance of human bodiliness and its salvific destiny. It has been said, for example, that Aquinas's "conception of what being human means must be understood in terms of the body existing in the world of the soul rather than the opposite."[73] Indeed, in line with other medieval thinkers, Thomas sees the human body—in its present condition, at any rate—as essentially "flawed," for our future is not weak flesh that decays but "an incorruptible resurrected body."[74]

Patrick Quinn has suggested that Aquinas's view of the body was shaped by two concerns: first, that the ultimate "model" for the human is a person so "spiritually integrated that the body itself can transcend the limitations of matter"; and second, that true human bodiliness is to be sought in the incorruptible. These concerns matched the two principal goals of Aquinas's anthropology. He wanted to guarantee that in the risen state, our intellect can function freely (just as he wanted it to function freely in our earthly state). Aquinas thus tended to privilege mind over matter because he was eager to maintain the untrammeled freedom of the human intellect, its limitless potential for unrestricted inquiry. Aquinas's second goal was to base the ultimate *identity* of the human body on a spiritual rather than a material principle. This is clear from his discussion of the body's role after the resurrection (both Christ's and ours). According to Quinn, on one hand, Aquinas affirms that risen persons are not disembodied, and that "separation from the body" would prevent "the soul from tending with all its might to the vision of God's essence"; in short, only when the body is present can our knowledge of God's nature be "perfect [i.e., complete] in every way." But on the other hand, Aquinas seems puzzled about what role the body might conceivably play once "human desire is satisfied with the vision of God's essence."[75] If God's true essence is known by the soul, how can the body add anything to human happiness once we reach our resurrection destiny?

Aquinas's difficulty in "making room for the human body in glory" is one reason why modern theologians like Karl Rahner concluded that the lan-

---

72. Xavier John Seubert, "'But Do Not Use the Rotted Names': Theological Adequacy and Homosexuality," *Heythrop Journal* 40, no. 1 (January 1999): 75.

73. Patrick Quinn, "Aquinas's Concept of the Body and Out of Body Situations," *Heythrop Journal* 34 (1993): 387-400, here 396.

74. Ibid.

75. Ibid., 396, 398.

guage of "separation of soul from body" is an inadequate way to describe our condition after death.[76] As Quinn notes, Aquinas's anthropology had its philosophical roots

> in the twin influences of Platonism and Aristotelianism which are discernible in the blend of Neoplatonism that appears at times in his writings. When we take this into account together with his Christian belief in ultimate bodily resurrection and his conviction that human happiness is attainable through a direct vision of God's essence, it is not difficult to appreciate how the ambiguities and incompatibilities in his theory of human bodiliness might have arisen.[77]

Because of such limitations, thinkers like Rahner preferred to view death as entering into a new relationship with the world (rather than as vanishing into an "otherworldly" state). "Death," he writes, "is something that happens to man as a whole being and as a spiritual person: the conclusive finality of his free personal growth. . . . While plants and animals 'perish,' only man really 'dies.'"[78] Death does not release the soul to wander about aimlessly in the cosmos, unconnected to anything else. We remain essentially connected to the material even in our death:

> [T]he spiritual soul has opened itself to the world through its bodiliness even before death. . . . It is never a closed, windowless monad but is always in communion with the whole world. This . . . relationship means that the soul, by giving up its limited bodily shape in death and opening itself to the All, becomes a contributory cause of the whole world, even of the world as the basis of the personal life of other psychosomatic beings. . . . The whole of created being, the world, gradually grows towards its definitive state in and through the incarnate spiritual persons whose "body," in a sense, is the world.[79]

In other words, even in ordinary life, our bodies are never merely the sum total of our organs, physical functions, fluids, and failures. Our body is also the history of our enfleshed relationships with others, with space, time, and events, with the world's evolving material structures. That relation changes but continues after death and will climax, according to Christian faith, when we share "the resurrection of the dead and the life of the world to come." That is one reason why Christians react to death ritually, liturgically, surrounding

---

76. See Rahner and Vorgrimler, *Theological Dictionary*, s.v. "death," 115-20; see also s.v. "body," 59-61.

77. Quinn, "Aquinas's Concept," 399.

78. Rahner and Vorgrimler, *Theological Dictionary*, s.v. "death," 116.

79. Ibid., 116-17.

the body of the deceased with the symbols of its baptism (water, a white pall or garment), as pledge of its own personal Easter. It is also why, at funerals, the eucharistic prayer may begin with a preface that affirms, "for your faithful people life is changed, not ended." In glory, even the body's relation to the world is renewed, for grace, as Rahner writes, can never be banished "to the realm of the soul alone." In Christ salvation itself comes to light in a body, and hence our personal destiny is a body that is "possessed by grace" and expresses our union with "the whole of humanity, blessed bodily in the bodily presence of Christ."[80]

TRANSFIGURED BODY, TRANSFIGURED WORLD

Our review of Christian anthropology has explored some of the reasons why the human body—its origins and destiny; its control and reproduction; its sexual and political significance—is such a lightning rod for Christians today. Still, as we've seen, contemporary scholarship has reached consensus on a surprising number of points about the body's meanings in Christian tradition. They agree, for instance, that the human person is not someone who *has* a body but someone who *is* a body, and that the body is not an *object* (a machine, a tool, a "husk" or prison) but a *subject*. In a profound sense, as Caroline Walker Bynum's work shows, the body *is* the self, and hence, the Western discovery of "subjectivity" is a discovery made in and of the body. In a word, the body is the *whole human person* in relation to God, world, and others. It is the supreme and privileged meeting place between God and humanity. Even the attitudes of the hard sciences (biology, chemistry, biochemistry, medicine) toward human bodiliness have changed. Today, as philosopher Mark Johnson notes, most researchers recognize that "any adequate account of meaning and rationality must give a central place to embodied and imaginative structures of understanding by which we grasp our world."[81] Reason is not purely abstract and transcendent after all. Human understanding is *incarnate*; hence the task of modern science is to "put the *body* back into the *mind*."

Theology takes such speculation a crucial step further by asserting that history's meanings and goals will be achieved *only in a transfigured world of glorified bodies*. In a word, the world's future is a body, as Karl Rahner once suggested in a homily on the ascension, "The Ascension is a festival of the

---

80. Ibid., 61.
81. Mark Johnson, *The Body in the Mind: The Bodily Basis of Meaning, Imagination, and Reason* (Chicago: University of Chicago Press, 1987), xiii.

future of the world . . . for the Lord has risen for ever. We Christians . . . recognize and believe that this matter will last for ever, and be glorified for ever. . . . God has assumed it as his own body. *Non horruisti virginis uterum. Non horruisti materiae beatam aeternitatem*" ("You did not disdain the Virgin's womb; you did not disdain the blessed eternity of matter").[82]

As we have seen, therefore, Christian teaching about resurrection focuses not on an "immortal soul," but on a human body that forever enacts human existence, personality, and relatedness. Nor is resurrection the exclusive province of Christology; it also affirms that "through their corporeality, believers are related, and thus can be caught up in Christ, who transforms that corporeality."[83] Christians insist not only on conversion of heart, soul, and mind but also on the body's final transformability. That is why Christian preaching "endowed the body with intrinsic, inalienable qualities. It was no longer a neutral indeterminate outcrop of the natural world, whose use and very right to exist was subject to predominately civic considerations of status and utility."[84]

All this has a direct bearing on liturgical theology. Take the celebration of the eucharist as an example. The body of Christ offered to Christians in consecrated bread and wine is not some*thing* but some*one*. In the eucharist Christ is present not as an object to be admired but as a real person (an embodied subject) to be met. Thomas Aquinas understood this well, and so insisted that the ultimate intent of celebrating eucharist is not to produce an object for veneration but *to create that united body of Christ which is the church*.[85] Roman Catholic eucharistic tradition thus insists that the christological cannot be separated from the ecclesiological. The body of Christ is not only *on* the table but *at* the table. We become one with *Christ's* body when we join ourselves to the Spirit-filled body of believers through grace, faith, and the paschal sacraments of initiation. Indeed, as the New Testament shows, it was precisely the early church's empirical experience of Christ's continued presence and activity in the Spirit that made Easter faith possible and plausible. The post-Easter narratives are not descriptions of what happened to Jesus' body, but stories about what happened to the *disciples*, how they "came to believe." Easter says not only that "Jesus is risen," but that through the Spirit's power *the body of Christ has become a people*. The implications of

---

82. Rahner, "Festival of the Future of the World," in *Theological Investigations*, 7:183-84.
83. Keenan, "Perspectives," 333.
84. Brown, *Body and Society*, 437.
85. See Thomas Aquinas, *Summa Theologiae*, Supplementum, Q. 71, art. 9, corpus, ad 3.

this point are vast. As Mary Collins has noted, it means that "we must rethink the familiar grammar for the symbol Body of Christ as it relates to resurrection belief, to the Spirit-filled church, and to the sacrament of the eucharist."[86]

When we think of Easter, we usually think of it in christological terms (what happened to Jesus Christ, and how does what happened affect us?). Yet the *ecclesiology* of Easter is equally essential to Christian faith. That is why the Bible's postresurrection narratives speak not only of an empty tomb and the disciples' conversions, but of "church foundations," *how those who believed the Easter message began to unite as communities*. (That is the "plot line," if you will, of the entire book of Acts.) The mysteries of Easter, eschatology, and eucharist are understood as *ecclesiological* ones. Through them, the body of Christ becomes not a symbol of particularity but of inclusivity: all humanity is called to share the eschatological feast of God-with-us. Hence, Easter, eschatology, and eucharist deal with the destiny of our species and our planet, not only with the person and destiny of Christ. For this reason, Christians from earliest times have seen in Christ's body (understood in its ecclesiological and eucharistic fullness) "the prototype for full personal integration and the grounds for the full inclusion of all humanity."[87]

In sum, we must see "the salvific action of the Word incarnate in Jesus Christ"—an action that includes the paschal mystery—in global perspective. God's action embodied in Christ is not only vital for Christians but can be seen as "the sacrament of a broader action, that of the eternal Word of God which embraces the whole religious history of humanity."[88] As Claude Geffré observes,

> The very law of God's incarnation through the mediation of history leads [us] to think that Jesus does not put an end to the history of God's manifestations. . . . In conformity with the traditional view of the fathers of the church it is . . . possible to see the economy of the Son incarnate as the sacrament of a broader economy, that, namely, of the eternal Word of God which coincides with the religious history of humankind.[89]

This means, paradoxically, that we can discover the ultimate significance of what *we* believe as *Christians* only through ongoing dialogue and communion

---

86. Mary Collins, "Eucharist and Christology Revisited: The Body of Christ," *Theology Digest* 39, no. 4 (1992): 321-32, here 329.

87. See Keenan, "Perspectives," 339, 344.

88. See Dupuis, *Christianity and the Religions*, 145.

89. Cited in Dupuis, *Christianity and the Religions*, 145.

with other faith traditions. As Thomas Aquinas knew, the category of sacraments and sacramentality cannot be confined to Christianity; it belongs to the very nature of God's interactions with the world.[90] Today, as a result, we must see sacrament as a category whose dimensions continue to expand, as they have throughout human history. Not only does God communicate with the world sacramentally in the religion of Israel and in Christ, God also continues to communicate sacramentally with the world among "members of other religious traditions," to disclose (to them and to us) "the salvific value" of those traditions.[91]

This inclusive character of sacrament should not surprise Roman Catholics. In its 1999 document "Toward a Pastoral Approach to Culture," the Pontifical Council for Culture argued (quoting John Paul II):

> All culture "is an effort to ponder the mystery of the world and in particular of the human person: It is a way of giving expression to the transcendent dimension of human life. The heart of every culture is its approach to the greatest mystery: the mystery of God." Hence the decisive challenge of a pastoral approach to culture, [for] "A faith that does not become culture is a faith not fully accepted, not entirely thought out, not faithfully lived."[92]

As we have seen earlier in this chapter, culture is a condition of human societies; it is *the* primary condition of our bodiliness. Our bodies are not merely meat, eggs, and seeds, but connections to culture. Vatican II reminded us that in our "very bodily condition" we summarize

> the elements of the material world. Through human persons, those elements are brought to their highest perfection and can raise their voice in praise freely given to the Creator. For this reason, humans may not despair of their bodily lives. Rather, they are obliged to regard their bodies as good and to hold them in honor, since God has created them and will raise them up on the last day. Nevertheless, human beings have been wounded by sin. They find by experience that their bodies are in revolt. Human dignity therefore requires that persons should glorify God in their bodies and not allow them to serve the evil inclinations of their hearts. (GS 14)

---

90. See, e.g., Aquinas's discussion of the "sacraments of the old Law" in *Summa Theologiae* IIIa Pars, Q. 61, articles 3 and 4.

91. Ibid. It should be noted that this point of view was also found in the encyclicals of the late Pope John Paul II.

92. Pontifical Council for Culture, "Toward a Pastoral Approach to Culture"; English translation in *Origins* 29, no. 5 (June 17, 1999): 67. The second quotation is from John Paul II's 1982 letter establishing the Pontifical Council for Culture.

BODY AS A CONTESTED SITE

Despite this optimistic assessment, "hot button" issues about the body continue to make headlines—from abortion, to homosexuality and gay marriage, to debates about euthanasia, capital punishment, and stem-cell research. The body today has become a contested, politicized site. Christian history suggests that such debates aren't new. As Wayne Meeks writes in his magisterial study *The Origins of Christian Morality*, Christians from the get-go have seen the body as both "sign and problem."[93] Conflicts about bodies at worship were already roiling the Corinthian community in Paul's day, so the liturgy wars of the twenty-first century certainly have notable precedent. The logic of ritual is, as I've been arguing throughout this chapter, a logic of the body. It is enacted "in the physical movements of the body, and thereby lodged beyond the grasp of consciousness and articulation."[94] That is why quarrels about ritual action (liturgy, worship) cannot be resolved through the application of reason and cognition or by appeals to authority. When the bishops at Vatican II called for "full, conscious, active participation" (*Sacrosanctum Concilium* 14), they acknowledged that by its very definition liturgy is "lodged beyond the grasp of consciousness and articulation." They deliberately turned *away* from reductive modes of participation based solely on "interiority" and the isolating autonomy of the self. Instead, they proposed a kind of participation based on the body's engagement in liturgy's *verba et gesta* through speech and song, deeds and dialogue, acclamation and response, posture and movement.

By calling *twice* within its first two sentences for "full and active participation by all the people" (*totius populi plena et actuosa participatio*), *Sacrosanctum Concilium* 14 deliberately directed our attention to the role of the body—personal and corporate—in the liturgical act. The council thus made, as the centerpiece of its reform, the retrieval of worship as an *embodied action by the entire assembly*. Moreover, by insisting on the unity of the liturgy's twin tables,[95] the council strengthened its case for a participation that invites not only intellect and interiority but *the prayer of the body itself*. Because word and sacrament are inseparably united in the act of worship, all public prayer is

---

93. Wayne A. Meeks, *The Origins of Christian Morality: The First Two Centuries* (New Haven: Yale University Press, 1993), 130-49.

94. Catherine Bell, *Ritual Theory, Ritual Practice* (New York: Oxford University Press, 1992), 99.

95. "The liturgy of the word and the eucharistic liturgy are so closely connected . . . that they form but one single act of worship" in which the "faithful should be seduously taught to participate" (SC 56).

necessarily "worded" and trinitarian, which means that our very bodies are "inscribed into the Word of prayer, which through the Spirit returns to the Father."[96] Insofar as we worshipers are members of Christ, our prayer "is of the body, and so takes for granted the assembly, the *ecclesia*, the body of Christ."[97]

The Body's Polyphony

The human body, as this chapter has argued, is intrinsically polyphonic; it speaks several languages simultaneously, just as liturgy and ritual do. Moreover, Vatican II's preference for dynamic, corporate images to describe "active participation" resonates well with many of the conclusions reached by modern biblical research and anthropology. Not only is the body our richest source of metaphors; it is also a complex ensemble of signs that points, as we have seen, to the final, corporate destiny of humanity itself.[98] Such a destiny is already implicit in the Semitic notion of the human person as "not an individualized entity but an ensemble of diversely qualified relations."[99] For that reason, too, the resurrection-destiny shared by Christ and Christians does not, as we have seen, focus on an "immortal soul," but presupposes that the body is in fact *the whole person* as simultaneously individual and social. Thus, Easter's goal is not disembodied immateriality, but a glorified bodiliness that embraces "existence, personality, and relatedness."[100] Indeed, as a recent study by N. T. Wright shows, the "continuity between the present body and the future resurrection body" not only "gives weight to the present ethical imperative[s]" of teachers like Paul, but also affirms that "what Christians presently do with their bodies matters, matters eschatologically."[101]

As our discussion earlier in this chapter on the origins and evolution of a distinctively Christian anthropology has shown, believers came to understand the body as the privileged interpreter of human life in the world and the key to both social structures and interpersonal relations. But teachers like Paul went even further by reinterpreting our bodiliness in relation to Jesus' cruci-

---

96. Laurence Paul Hemming, "The Subject of Prayer: Unwilling Words in the Postmodern Access to God," in *The Blackwell Companion to Postmodern Theology*, ed. Graham Ward (Oxford: Blackwell, 2001), 445.

97. Ibid.

98. On this point, see again Vatican II's *Gaudium et Spes* 22.

99. Antoine Vergote, "The Body as Understood in Contemporary Thought and Biblical Categories," *Philosophy Today* 35 (1991): 93-105, here 96.

100. See Keenan, "Perspectives," 333.

101. N. T. Wright, *The Resurrection of the Son of God*, vol. 3 of *Christian Origins and the Question of God* (Minneapolis: Fortress, 2003), 289-90.

fied and risen body. Thus Paul freely made use of familiar social metaphors—the common weal as "body"—while tweaking them in distinctive ways. Meeks notes that the moral philosophy fashionable in Paul's day would have used the sociopolitical metaphor of body (the "body politic") for *conservative* purposes—to preserve intact the status and authority of Rome's imperial regime. But while Paul uses "the body" in a manner that is "still a metaphor . . . still political . . . still conservative," he relates it not to a coercive regime but to "the internal order of a cult community, in which leadership roles are thought to be 'gifts' by the Spirit and consequently may come to people who do not belong to the levels of society that ordinarily are thought to be the heads and eyes." In short, Paul sees the body as a fertile sign of new, God-initiated social arrangements that may (and often *do*) subvert the customary expectations of citizens and even of church members. Thus, Paul recognizes the Spirit's work in the Christian assembly, creating an "order" substantially at variance with that of the empire, an order that may elevate unlikely people (e.g., Paul himself!) to unexpected positions of leadership. For the most part, Paul approves this "charismatic governance" of the liturgical community, though he objects to "the competition for new status within it made possible by the new talents raised up by the Spirit."[102]

Paul's pastoral theology thus perceives the "crucifixion and resurrection of Jesus' body" as a kind of contagion, a reinterpreted "master metaphor infecting the commonplace political one."[103] The effects of this master metaphor, writes Wayne Meeks,

> are *implicit* in 1 Corinthians 12, in the form of the care for each other that is the duty of the individual "limbs" of the body. They become explicit elsewhere, for example in Paul's use of the Christ-hymn in . . . Philippians 2 and in his discussion of the obligation of the more powerful and knowledgeable members of the community for those whom they regard as "weak" (1 Cor 8-10; Rom 14-15).[104]

Note, then, that in Paul's hands, the sociopolitical commonplaces (body as conservative metaphor of the common weal) have been turned toward new and challenging purposes. To the power elite within the Roman empire, the metaphor of the body bespoke coercion, the power to subjugate others and to enforce the will of an absolutist state. The body was a site of subjugation or (for the privileged few) of sovereignty. In contrast, Paul's master metaphor of "body" became the icon of power *emptied*, erased—of powerlessness, *kenōsis*,

---

102. Meeks, *Origins of Christian Morality*, 134.
103. Ibid.
104. Ibid., 134-35 (emphasis added).

self-surrendering love that lets go to give others life. In Paul's eyes, Jesus' body—dead, raised by the Spirit, and returned to the Father's right—redefines all other bodily metaphors, "overpowers" them through kenotic powerlessness, and reinterprets life itself as a "magnifying of Christ *in my body*, either by life or by death" (Phil 1:20).

From the beginning, then, the body, a complex ensemble of signs, has been at the center of the church's self-understanding and thus at the center of its worship. The human body, reinterpreted through the mystery of Christ, "emerges as central not only for the self-understanding of the individual Christian but also for the entire believing community."[105] Body thus became the basis for personal integration and social cohesion, precisely because its final destiny is revealed in Christ dead and risen—a point Paul was already making in his debates with the community at Corinth. Moreover, as Jerome Neyrey's studies have shown, Paul's use of body metaphors reconstructs the theology of membership among the people of God.[106] Israel's purity laws, like those of other ancient cultures, had served to establish social *boundaries* (who belongs, who doesn't) and to regulate *behaviors* through moral norms designed to protect and govern both the personal and the social body. By challenging these purity laws in his own ministry—touching ritually impure persons (e.g., lepers), eating and drinking with "sinners"—Jesus proposed a "new hermeneutics for determining membership in the community" of God's holy people.[107]

Thus, in its very origins, the Christian liturgical assembly was not a community of the pure and powerful, but a congregation overwhelmed by newness. It was a body of bodies convinced that "Easter innovates, and does so radically"; convinced, too, that this innovation "has a name," Jesus Christ—a person whose own body, breaking through death to a life no one had ever lived before, has become a *people*, a new creation, a community thrown forward into a world so freshly minted that its citizens must "relearn everything, like children (or rather, like an old person, overcome by newness)."[108]

Body as Narrative

Jesus' reforming approach to ritual purity, Easter's radical newness, and Paul's "new hermeneutics of belonging" all point to the *body* as the privileged site

---

105. Keenan, "Perspectives," 334.
106. See especially Jerome Neyrey, "The Idea of Purity in Mark's Gospel," *Semeia* 35 (1986): 91-128; idem, "Body Language in 1 Corinthians," *Semeia* 35 (1986): 129-70.
107. Keenan, "Perspectives," 334.
108. See Jean-Luc Marion, "The Gift of a Presence," in *Prolegomena to Charity*, trans. Stephen Lewis (New York: Fordham University Press, 2002), 124.

for God's self-disclosure and self-bestowal. The body is not simply a symbol of the new situation created for humanity at Easter; it is also a *narrative* that tells us who we are (body of Christ, church) and who we are to become (sharers in the eschatological victory embodied by the risen Jesus). Christ's glorified body—broken at table, broken in death, raised in the Spirit—has itself become the "story line" of a new humanity.

For Christians, moreover, the body (Christ's and ours) not only *shows;* it *tells*—it is simultaneously *symbol* and *story*. If this sounds suspiciously like a short definition of sacrament, it should. Like the body itself, sacrament is a site of *exchange*; it is "commerce," transaction, something human between us and God. These exchanges inevitably have a story line, a narrative structure, for the simple reason that sacraments—like the Lord's Prayer, as we discussed it in chapter 3—are themselves a brief synopsis of the Gospel.[109] Sacraments derive their narrativity from bodily life (ours and Christ's); for the body's complex stories are condensed as symbols, and symbols are "(trans)actions that disclose relationships."[110] In sum, every sacrament tells the embodied history of a relationship between us and God—a relationship seen through the prism of Easter.

The human body is thus more elemental than consciousness itself, for one may have/be a body without consciousness, while, in this life at least, one is never conscious without the body. Our experience of the self is rooted in our experience of the flesh, as postmodern theologians like Jean-Luc Marion point out.[111] The radical, this-worldly source of Christian ritual symbols and sacraments is the body—the *human* body *in relation to other bodies*.

This point connects with what I said earlier about the body as a site of commerce or exchange. It is no accident that sacraments signify through physical gestures of touch, for skin is the fundamental speech of our interac-

---

109. This is also the fundamental reason why Word and sacrament cannot be separated from one another, and why the Second Vatican Council insisted on the essential unity of the two tables (Word and Bread) in the liturgy.

110. Nathan D. Mitchell, "Symbols Are Actions, Not Objects—New Directions for an Old Problem"; entire issue of *Living Worship* 31 (February 1977).

111. "Ego receives itself from the very thing (flesh) it receives," writes Marion. "The ordinary definition of a phenomenon is adequation between 'the appearing' and 'what appears.' But in flesh, this distinction cannot precisely be found. In the case of flesh, uniquely, the perceived is one with the perceiver. It is therefore necessary to think the taking of flesh starting from givenness, as the basic determination of every phenomenon." Marion goes on to argue that flesh is primordial; it "only ever refers back to itself, in the indissoluble unity of the felt and of the feeling." It is thus the task of flesh to "render me to myself, to assign me to myself." In short, "flesh takes me before I take it." Thus, I do not "choose" my flesh. "Flesh always already takes me; I do not give myself my flesh; it is flesh that gives me myself. In receiving my flesh, I receive me myself. In this way I am 'gifted'—i.e., given over to—myself." See Jean-Luc Marion, *In Excess: Studies in Saturated Phenomena,* trans. Robyn Horner and Vincent Berraud (New York: Fordham University Press, 2002), 97-103. Note, however, that for Marion "flesh" is a more fundamental and comprehensive category than "body."

tions with world, others, and God. It is the human organ through which we are in the world, and the world is in us. Skin is permeable, a porous membrane that lets in and lets out. "The skin," writes Michael Sims, "is the line at which we become individual animals moving self-contained through the world."[112] It is our *largest* human organ, indispensable for our interactions with the world and one another. "No other part of us makes contact with something not us but the skin. . . . It's waterproof, washable, and elastic."[113] So skin organizes and extends our bodily life. It is "an ideal canvas to decorate with paints, tattoos, and jewelry," and even its holes are crucial. Both mouth and ears are holes in the skin: the mouth, a "fuel processor, poison tester, and microphone"; the ear, "a hole with a satellite dish built around it."[114] Skin thus makes the body's story visible and audible, and, just as importantly, it connects bodies to cultures, since each of us comes from a culture that tells us—in often agonizing detail—just what to do with our bodies.[115]

The body thus *belongs* to liturgy and sacrament because on it is written the whole history of our connection to culture and so of our relations to God, world, self, and others. That is why Christian eucharistic prayers often rehearse the story of salvation as a narrative that embraces natural history (cosmology and creation) and/or cultural history. Here, for instance, is part of a Gallican *contestatio* (preface) that praises God's salvific action by rehearsing, vividly, how earth and humans came to be:

> When you had overcome chaos and the confusion of the beginning and the darkness in which things swam, you gave wonderful forms to the amazed elements: the tender world blushed at the fires of the sun, and the rude earth wondered at the dealings of the moon. And lest . . . the sun's orb shine on emptiness, your hands made from clay a more excellent likeness, which a holy fire quickened within. . . . We may not look, Father, into the inner mysteries. To you alone is known the majesty of your work: what there is in man, that the blood held in the veins washes the fearful limbs

---

112. Michael Sims, *Adam's Navel* (New York: Viking, 2003), 11.

113. Diane Ackerman, *A Natural History of the Senses* (New York: Vintage Books, 1991), 68. Our skin, Ackerman points out, "is alive, breathing and excreting, shielding us from harmful rays and microbial attack, metabolizing vitamin D, insulating us from heat and cold, repairing itself when necessary, regulating blood flow, acting as a frame for our sense of touch, aiding us in sexual attraction, defining our individuality, holding all the thick red jams and jellies inside us where they belong" (p. 67).

114. Sims, *Adam's Navel*, 15.

115. See ibid., 2: "Each of us has one body, and each of us comes from a culture that tells us what to do with it. In the same crowd there may be Orthodox peyot and skinhead pates, straightened hair of African origin and curled hair of European origin, artificial fingernails and painted toenails . . . false teeth and tucked necks, shaven legs and unshaven underarms, plucked eyebrows and rouged cheeks, enlarged breasts and reduced noses, calves taut in high heels and earlobes stretched by jewelry."

and the living earth; that the loose appearances of bodies are held together by tightening nerves, and the individual bones gain strength from the organs within them.[116]

Similarly, the anaphora of St. Basil narrates, in brief, the history of God's transactions with culture, leading to the sending of prophets and, finally, "of the Son himself, through whom also you made the ages."[117]

The body's narrative is thus a cultural one, as inculturated as the stories embodied in sacrament and liturgy. It is the cultural site on which the world writes its history. Every day, writes Michael Sims,

> we wallow in the luxurious physicality for which the angel yearns. The human body perceives the world through its senses, and there is no sense but touch. Through your body the world touches you. You taste chocolate and champagne when their molecules caress your tongue. You hear music when sound waves play the tympani in your ears. You smell coffee because tiny particles of it float through the air and touch the receptors in your nose. Photons enter your eyes and enable you to see the color of sunlit leaves.[118]

Perhaps even angels finally "tire of their eternal voyeurism" and "hunger to grasp a pencil, caress an ear, stretch their toes, feed a cat, . . . acquire blackened fingers from reading a newspaper."[119]

CONCLUSION

Chapter 5 has focused on the liturgy's first and most obvious language—the body. We examined attitudes toward the body in early Christianity, the gradual evolution of a distinctively Christian anthropology, the modern retrieval of the body as a "theological site," and the indissoluble links between our bodiliness and liturgical celebration. Human beings, as far as we can tell, were the first animals to write the history of their relation with God on their bod-

---

116. This text is taken from the *Missale Gallicanum Vetus* (the "Mone Masses"), ed. Leo Eizenhöfer (Rerum Ecclesiasticarum Documenta, Series major; Fontes III; Rome: Herder, 1958), no. 282 (p. 78). The English translation may be found in *Prayers of the Eucharist, Early and Reformed*, ed. R. C. D. Jasper and G.J. Cuming (2nd ed.; New York: Oxford University Press, 1980), 106.

117. English translation in Jasper and Cuming, *Prayers of the Eucharist*, 98-104; Greek text (according to Codex Barberini gr. 336 and Codex Grottaferrata) in *Prex Eucharistica*, ed. Anton Hänggi and Irmgard Pahl (Spicilegium Friburgense 12; Fribourg [Suisse]: Éditions Universitaires, 1968), 230-42.

118. Sims, *Adam's Navel*, 2-3.

119. Ibid., 2.

ies. We Christians do this still—in the liturgy of initiation, for instance, when we wash the candidate's body, plunging it into the story of Christ's dying and rising, and then paint it with fragrant chrism, marking the body as the Spirit's new home. "Body" is the first story we hear in the crib and our "farewell address" when we leave the world. That is surely why theologians such as Thomas Aquinas acknowledged that sacramental signification arises from bodily language that is simultaneously verbal and gestural.[120] That is also why Aquinas had no difficulty accepting what scholastic theology before and after him affirmed: "From the side of Christ asleep on the cross the sacraments flowed, i.e., the blood and water from which the church itself came to be."[121] Yet Christ's body is not only the source of sacrament(s); it is also our *future.* For our future, Karl Rahner once said, is heaven, and heaven is nothing less than Christ's body, the "abiding of personal creatures in the presence of God, . . . the gathering of [hu]mankind . . . into the definitive Body of Christ, . . . to commune with God who is made (and remains) *man*; hence it is that we shall 'see one another again,' that the human relationships of this world continue in heaven."[122] Thus, Christ's humanity is a permanent part of that one world whose transformation began at Easter.[123]

From the beginning, therefore, Christians have recognized that God's own kenotic life can—indeed, *must*—be written on human bodies, since, in the body of the crucified and risen Jesus, the fullness of God's life lays hold of all the processes of history and creation, to begin their transformation into glory. It was this conviction, perhaps, that led to those revolutions in painting embodied not only in Caravaggio (whose work we discussed earlier in this chapter), but even earlier in the work of Giotto (ca. 1264-1337). Painters prior to Giotto had avoided (or failed at) realistic representation, especially when it came to the human figure. But Giotto began giving his figures real *bodies*, emotions, perspective, depth, color, recognizably human features. In his work, the human form comes warmly to life, especially through his use of color. As Julia Kristeva once noted, Giotto fragments color, links it to the body so that light becomes not merely perception but emotion, desire, joy, delight.[124] By breaking light's "undifferentiated unicity" through color, Kris-

---

120. Aquinas held that sacraments are not "internal states" or mere "mental realities" but external, visible, sensible activities that engage embodied human beings fully in word and deed. See *Summa Theologiae* IIa IIae, Q. 111, art. 1, corpus: *Signa . . . exteriora non solum sunt verba, sed etiam facta* ("the external signs are not only words but deeds").

121. *De latere Christi dormientis in cruce fluxerunt sacramenta, idest sanguis et aqua, quibus est Ecclesia instituta* (*Summa Theologiae* Ia, Q. 92, art. 3, corpus).

122. Rahner and Vorgrimler, *Theological Dictionary*, 200, s.v. "Heaven."

123. Ibid., 407-8, s.v., "Resurrection (of Christ)."

124. See Julia Kristeva, "Giotto's Joy," in *Desire in Language*, ed. Leon Roudiez, trans. T. Gora, A.

teva notes, Giotto opened a flood of colored surfaces and created an art that contested every "rigid, unitary theology, arrested in the dazzling whiteness of meaning."[125]

When the Second Vatican Council mandated liturgical reform and renewal, it sought to do in our time what painters like Giotto, Ghirlandaio, and Caravaggio had done in theirs. It sought our direct, public engagement in worship that moves beyond the self, safely ensconced in its private autonomy and interiority, into the "mean streets" of history. Giotto and Caravaggio boldly rewrote the icons of Christ, Mary, and the saints, so that, through the "harsh vernaculars" of poor pilgrims with dirty feet, we could come to see in the body the privileged site of God's self-communication. Thus too, the council called Christians to active participation; to a vernacular liturgy; to worship that is unafraid of affirming the "qualities and talents" of diverse cultures; to ritual that is at home with the body and comfortable in its own skin.

QUESTIONS FOR REFLECTION

1. Do you agree or disagree with Louis-Marie Chauvet's "short definition" of a Christian sacrament as "God's Word at the mercy of the body"?
2. "The flesh is the hinge on which salvation depends" (Tertullian). How has the history of Christian attitudes toward human bodiliness shaped our understanding and experience of liturgical prayer?
3. The Second Vatican Council's Pastoral Constitution on the Church in the Modern World (*Gaudium et Spes* 22) affirms that "by his incarnation, the Son of God has united himself in some fashion with every human being." In response, Jacques Dupuis comments that while the incarnation is surely central to our faith, it is a mystery that leaves open a "space for an illuminating and salvific action of the Word as such, both *before* the incarnation and *after* the resurrection of Jesus Christ" (p. 160 above; my emphasis here). What are the implications of these two affirmations for understanding the relation between Christian liturgy and worship in other religious traditions?
4. How can art (e.g., the paintings of Caravaggio [pp. 169-72 above]) help us understand the essentially *embodied* character of Christian liturgy?
5. "Easter says not only that 'Jesus is risen,' but that through the Spirit's power *the body of Christ has become a people*" (p. 176 above). How and why can liturgy be described as *corporate action by God's people, Christ's body*?

Jardine, and L. Rudiez (New York: Columbia University Press, 1980), 219; cf. 223. See also Carl A. Raschke, *Fire and Roses: Postmodernity and the Thought of the Body* (Albany: State University of New York Press, 1996), 12-13.

125. Kristeva, "Giotto's Joy," 222.

SUGGESTIONS FOR FURTHER READING

Ackerman, Diane. *A Natural History of the Senses.* New York: Vintage Books, 1991. A fascinating study of the body's five senses, drawing on works of science and literature to elucidate our experience of the world.

Bell, Catherine. *Ritual Theory, Ritual Practice.* New York: Oxford University Press, 1992. One of the most important recent studies of ritual in all its aspects, written primarily for a scholarly audience.

Brown, Peter. *The Body and Society: Men, Women, and Sexual Renunciation in Early Christianity.* New York: Columbia University Press, 1988. A seminal study of how Christians view the body, especially in relation to social and ecclesial structures.

Dupuis, Jacques. *Christianity and the Religions: From Confrontation to Dialogue.* Translated by Philip Berryman. Maryknoll, N.Y.: Orbis Books, 2003. An important study of how Christians understand the mystery of the incarnation in light of dialogue with members of other world religions.

Keenan, James F. "Current Theology Note: Christian Perspectives on the Human Body." *Theological Studies* 55 (1994): 330-46. This valuable article provides succinct summaries and references that will help students understand how theologians today interpret human bodiliness.

6

Ritual Speech
and the Logic of Metaphor

I N CHAPTER 5, WE DISCUSSED the first and most obvious of liturgy's native languages, the language of the body. To act ritually or sacramentally requires fluency in the body's speech. Moreover, the body itself is a polyglot. We noted this in our previous chapter's discussion of the body as "narrative," as both story and source of stories. Similarly, chapters 3 and 4 spoke about ritual as a parabolic discourse designed to jolt us out of the familiar and move us toward "the Land of Unlikeness," toward a realm Jesus called "the kingdom or reign of God."[1] In chapter 6, we will explore another of liturgy's "native tongues:" the ritual logic of metaphor.

HOW LITURGY USES LANGUAGE

Surprising as it may seem, humanity's natural speech is not prose but poetry. If you recorded all your internal monologues and interpersonal communications during the course of a single day, you would discover that your speech patterns are not logical, rationally crafted paragraphs but cascading torrents, rapid outbursts of interjection and image. The enduring popularity of *The Cat in the Hat* and other favorites from Dr. Seuss is in part related to the fact that we teach children to speak and read primarily through poetry. And it is surely no accident that advertisers use rhyming jingles to market their wares. Jingles not only sell products; they're memorable. Whether they urge us to "fly the friendly skies" or munch the chocolates that "melt in your mouth, not in your hand," advertising slogans stay with us long after the products have been revamped or disappeared. In music, rappers have created a repertoire that is pure poetry—chanted recitative, rhythm, and rhyme. And should anyone

---

1. The phrase "Land of Unlikeness" is taken from W. H. Auden, "For the Time Being: A Christmas Oratorio; The Massacre of the Innocents; IV," in *Collected Poems*, ed. Edward Mendelson (New York: Vintage Books, 1991), 400.

doubt that rap or rock-n-roll doesn't qualify as serious poetry, consider that the distinguished critic Christopher Ricks has recently written a full-length study of Bob Dylan's lyrics.[2] So while ours is an age often classified as anti-ritual and unpoetic, neither charge is true. Ritual flourishes everywhere, from impromptu memorials to the dead (recall Ground Zero after 9/11) to shopping malls and amateur sports. Poetry pours from your iPod every second. Our waking hours are awash in ceremony and incantation. We say hellos and goodbyes, meet and make love, in rhythmic, alliterative, imagistic bursts of speech that are incantatory and ritualistic in character.

American poet Donald Hall remarks that poetry starts in the crib, in the infant's "mouth-pleasure in gurgle and shriek," and hence, "the body is poetry's door; the sounds of words—throbbing in legs and arms, rich in the mouth—let us into the house."[3] Try reciting aloud these lines from Walt Whitman's short poem "A Farm Picture":

> Through the ample open door of the peaceful country barn,
> A sunlit pasture field with cattle and horses fading,
> And haze and vista, and the far horizon fading away.[4]

If you read the poem several times aloud, you'll begin to feel its natural rhythm, its pattern of stressed and unstressed syllables. Each line has roughly the same number of syllables—fourteen in the first two lines; fifteen in the third. You may notice, too, that even though Whitman was writing "blank verse," the rhythm of his first line is interrupted by a slight breath or pause (indicated by the slash mark): "Through the AMple Open DOOR / of the PEACEful COUNtry BARN." Each half of the line contains three natural stresses (indicated by the underlined syllables in caps).[5] The pattern of the second line is similar: "a SUNlit PASture FIELD / with CATtle and HORSes FADing." If all three lines of the poem had kept the rhythm unaltered, the poem might seem boring, so Whitman *adds* a syllable to the final line that disrupts the meter just enough to get the reader's attention: "And HAZE and VISta, / and the FAR hoRIzon FADing aWAY." As Donald Hall points out, the speech of Whitman's final line slows, stretches in a "slow sensuous attentiveness," while the reader's mouth lingers "in luxury on the three long ays of the last line:" hAze . . . fAding . . . awAy.[6]

---

2. See Christopher Ricks, *Dylan's Visions of Sin* (New York: Ecco/HarperCollins, 2004).

3. Donald Hall, *Poetry: The Unsayable Said* (Port Townsend, Wa.: Copper Canyon Press, 1993), 1, 2.

4. Walt Whitman, *Leaves of Grass and Other Writings*, ed. Michael Moon (Norton Critical Editions; New York. W. W. Norton, 2002), 230.

5. The line admits of alternate scansions as well, for example: "Through the AMPle open DOOR / of the PEACEful country BARN," which has more the feel of an anapestic rhythm.

6. Hall, *Poetry: The Unsayable Said*, 3.

Short as it is, Whitman's poem is a rather complex work of art. It has not only rhythm and pitch; it has song—a music composed of languid vowels and diphthongs that let you loll among the words like a lazy sunbather. Ordinarily, of course, we don't analyze such features of speech; we simply *feel* them as bodily sensations. The poem also has a tiny bomb ticking within it. Repeat the word "peaceful" in the first line, and remember that Whitman first published this poem just as the Civil War was ending in 1865.[7] Whitman himself had not only witnessed the war, but had nursed wounded soldiers from both South and North in Washington, D.C.'s tent-hospitals. So what does that word "peaceful" signify? A prayer? A hope? Death? An ironic contrast to war and violence that had convulsed a nation? The poem's forms and images are pastoral, but its larger, looming resonance is parabolic.

There is something else about this brief poem. In three short lines, Whitman provokes a range of emotions for which we may not be able to give a logical, rational account. "And haze and vista, and the far horizon fading away." The scene is resolutely rural, bucolic. It evokes a kind of *Sehnsucht*, a nostalgic longing for—*what*? A way of life that has vanished? A simpler, quieter time in human history? An era when our responses to nature were direct and immediate, an epoch ended by the brutal technologies of war and industry? Is Whitman's poem a social commentary? Does he appeal to an early, innocent America? Perhaps. But the thing to notice is that *no paraphrase of Whitman's poem will be as emotionally exact as Whitman's own words are*. Great poetry resists paraphrase. As Hall comments,

> Feeling bodily pleasure and fulfillment, feeling rightness beyond reason, feeling contentment or even bliss—we cannot account for the extremity of our satisfaction. By its art of saying the unsayable, poetry produces a reponse in excess of the discernible stimulus.
>
> The unsayable builds a secret room . . . which shows in the excess of feeling over paraphrase. This room is not a Hidden Meaning, to be paraphrased by the intellect. . . . The secret room is something to acknowledge, accept, and honor in a silence of assent; the secret room is where the unsayable gathers, and it is poetry's uniqueness.[8]

Review the images in Whitman's poem. They are not abstract ideas; they are commonplace *things*. A barn door, open. A pasture lit by the sun. A field alive with cattle and horses. Haze . . . vista . . . horizon. All these are very simple yet specific objects and experiences. We don't have to ask—indeed, it would be useless to ask—what do "country barn" or "sunlit pasture" *mean*?

---

7. Whitman, *Leaves of Grass and Other Writings*, 230 n. 7.
8. Hall, *Poetry: The Unsayable Said*, 4.

They "mean" themselves, even as they evoke emotions that lie beyond the reach of speech.

Now read these three lines from a poem of Thomas Hardy:

> And the fair girl long ago
> Whom I often tried to know
> May be entering this rose.[9]

In these lines, two sorts of literalness seem to compete. We hear Hardy allude to the girl's molecular survival; particles of her (now dead) body become botanical nutrients to enrich the soil.[10] But the literalness of dissolution (the girl's body, buried, dissolving) is matched by the literalness of life and growth. The young woman's molecules and atoms "*enter* the rose as a living woman might walk through the portals of a church."[11] These images meet, as the poem attempts to "say the unsayable," to convey the hope and emotion of watching life come from death, growth from decay. So the reader of the poem feels, simultaneously, both the *literal* level of biological and molecular change (a rotting corpse, a living rose), and the *imaginative* level of ritual, "liturgical" gesture, and movement: the poem performs a procession, exits the world of daily action and observation (the "said") and enters a world of mysterious revelations (the "unsayable").

These examples from the poetry of Walt Whitman and Thomas Hardy reveal that language is not simply a tool (for communication), but a performance (like music, like liturgy). Words not only say, tell, or describe something; they *do* something—they move, create, cause. Consider this passage from the memoir *Brown*, by Richard Rodriguez:

> I write of a color that is not a singular color, not a strict recipe, not an expected result, but a color produced by careless desire, even by accident; by two or several. I write of blood that is blended. I write of brown as complete freedom of substance and narrative. I extol impurity. . . .
>
> I write about race in America in hopes of undermining the notion of race in America.
>
> Brown bleeds through the straight line, unstaunchable—the line separating black from white, for example. Brown confuses. Brown forms at the border of contradiction (the ability of language to express two or several thing at once, the ability of bodies to experience two or several things at once.[12]

---

9. Thomas Hardy, "Transformations," in *The Complete Poems*, ed. James Gibson (New York: Palgrave, 2001), no. 410, p. 472.

10. See discussion in Hall, *Poetry: The Unsayable Said*, 5.

11. Ibid.

12. Richard Rodriguez, *Brown: The Last Discovery of America* (New York: Viking, 2002), xi.

Because this passage opens *Brown*'s "Preface," readers expect the author to follow convention—to introduce himself, to tell us what he's about to do, to say why he wrote what he wrote. But the "Preface" composed by Rodriguez bends the genre. He does not "define" brown, but chooses intsead "to write brownly" and to "defy anyone who tries to unblend me." Behind these words we can, of course, hear the echoes of the author's biography. We sense that Rodriguez is an accomplished writer, and that his ethnic heritage is not Anglo. Or we can "Google" his name and listen to him tell us, more literally, who he is. "Just look at me," he writes in a 1997 interview:

> I come from another part of the world. I come from South of the border. My parents are Mexican immigrants and this is who I am. This man who has an Indian face and a Spanish surname and an Anglo first name, Richard, who carries the voice that was given to me, shoved down my throat actually by Irish nuns, who taught me unsentimentally, the Queen's English. You should wonder about the complexity that creates Richard Rodriguez, the centuries that have made this complexity. I am not, in any simple sense, the creature of multiculturalism. I am the creature of something much more radical and that's the penetration of one culture by another, one race by another. And so I stand here today, and I don't know which part is the Indian part speaking to you. Which leg is my Indian leg? Which leg is my Spanish leg?[13]

This too is powerful writing; but it follows familiar narrative conventions. It's first-person autobiography. It's Richard Rodriguez talking *about* himself. But the preface to *Brown* is quite different. True, the writer speaks in the first person—"*I* eulogize a literature that is suffused with brown"—but the opening page of his preface is not autobiography in any ordinary sense. Rodriguez is not writing "about" himself or even about "being brown"; he is "*writing brownly*" with "allusion, irony, paradox—ha!—pleasure."[14] The writer doesn't simply say "brown" or describe brown or call himself brown; he *does* brown, performs it. The reader is drawn directly into the "border of contradiction," into the power of language to express "several things at once," into a *real participation* in "brown." As Rodriguez warns us, "You will often find brown in this book as the cement between leaves of paradox. You may not want paradox in a book. In which case, you had better seek a pure author."[15]

We come to poetry both for the pleasure it gives the body and for its punch—its paradox, its uncanny accuracy in naming and illumining our emo-

---

13. "Remarks of Richard Rodriguez, Journalist and Author" (May 23, 1997), 1; at http://www .library.ca.gov/LDS/convo/convoc21.html. Accessed January 4, 2006.

14. Rodriguez, *Brown*, xi (emphasis added).

15. Ibid., xi-xii.

tions. Earlier I said that poetry is the native speech of human beings. As far as we can tell, every culture—oral, literate, archaic, industrialized—produces poetry and passes it from one generation to the next. "Poetry is the only art that uses as its material something that everyone practices," writes Donald Hall.[16] Still, poetry isn't just talk; it may sound like everyday noise, but poetry is "talk altered into art, speech slowed down and attended to, words arranged for the reader who contracts to read them for their whole heft of association and noise."[17] This is true whether the altered "talk" is a rap, a Bob Dylan lyric, or a poem by Emily Dickinson.

Poetry is talk altered into art, and art always deals in surplus, excess. As I've already suggested, art is irreducible. It cannot be shrunk to a "core," an "essence," or a single, quintessential significance. The harder one tries to pin down a poem's "exact meanings," the more elusive they become. Analysis only *multiplies* those meanings, to such a degree that when the analyzing ends, there is actually more to the poem than when one started. That is why I drew attention to the excess or surplus that spills over when talk is altered to art. Read this short poem of Whitman's aloud several times, and you'll begin to sense something of a poem's "irreducible plenitude":

> This is thy hour O Soul, thy free flight into the wordless,
> Away from books, away from art, the day erased, the lesson
>   done,
> Thee fully forth emerging, silent, gazing, pondering the
>   themes thou lovest best,
> Night, sleep, death and the stars.[18]

The poem's language is ordinary, its tone quiet. Whitman called it "A Clear Midnight," so the poem's "action" ("free flight . . . away . . . fully forth emerging . . . gazing . . . pondering") is imagined as happening while the world sleeps. The speaker (who?) recommends that the "Soul" (whose?) abandon art and learning ("away from books, away from art . . . the lesson done"), suspend time ("the day erased"), and venture forth in silence to ponder well-loved themes ("night, sleep, death, and the stars"). Is the poem prayer, supplication, aspiration, an encouragement to contemplation? Is it an open window on the poet's own "inner dialogue"? Does it implicitly criticize bookish folk who seek truth in study? Is the soul (or speaker) longing for death? for solitude? for wisdom? for transcendence? Is the poem a soliloquy by someone considering suicide? And upon what—or whom—is the soul "gazing"?

---

16. Hall, *Poetry: The Unsayable Said*, 8.
17. Ibid.
18. Whitman, *Leaves of Grass and Other Writings*, 408.

IN THE BEGINNING WAS THE METAPHOR

None of these questions can be answered with unequivocal certainty, yet it is impossible to say that poems like "A Farm Picture" or "A Clear Midnight" are absurd, incommunicable, or *meaningless*. On the contrary, they expose us to an experience—speech altered to art—that signifies and communicates, opaquely yet powerfully, without "meaning" any one thing in particular. We meet an experience, an art, that conveys truth only through indirection and significance only through an indefinable surplus. At the same time, readers of these poems recognize that to say the poems lack "a single meaning" is not to say they can be interpreted as meaning *anything*. Clearly, they cannot. The poem imposes its own internal limitations on our ability to say—or unsay—its meanings.[19] In short, poems are self-limiting. The poem itself has the last word.

This kind of allusive, elusive speech is native not only to poetry but to Christian ritual, liturgy, and sacrament as well. At the heart of such speech lies metaphor, which might be defined as putting two things together that seem *not* to belong together. "The moon's my mother." Well, not *really*—yet to identify moon and mother is to express a truth that transcends the metaphor's literal falsehood. So a metaphor can tell the truth only by *lying*. Christian worship is a veritable jungle of such metaphoric speech, for liturgy loves to call people names. It calls God king, lord, rock, hiding place, shepherd, father, mother, savior, redeemer, and a host of other things. It calls both the worshiping assembly and the consecrated eucharistic bread "the body of Christ." It calls the *lay* baptized assembly a *royal priesthood*.

Nor are liturgical metaphors always verbal. The *activity of worship* is evoked in metaphors of "sacrifice," "thanksgiving," "doxology," "service," "liturgy (public work)." Moreover, the *space* where the worshiping community gathers is a visual metaphor. In the first centuries of the Common Era, that space may have been the dining room of a private home, a renovated synagogue, a public hall (basilica), a martyr's tomb. The *gestures* that enact liturgical rites are embodied metaphors that borrow the grammar of everyday life to express what exceeds (and may subvert) the quotidian. Thus, in an earlier chapter, we saw how Israel's rites of offering the firstfruits of flock and fields

---

19. One could not plausibly argue, for instance, that "A Clear Midnight" reduces the human person to the sum total of his or her material parts (since the poem's "dialogue with the soul" clearly implies a spiritual faculty native to humans). At the same time, one could not legitimately claim that Whitman's poem inculcates a particular theological or philosophical doctrine (e.g., the "immortality of the soul").

are metaphoric acts that embody *possession* (of land, identity, mission) only through deeds of *surrender* and *dispossession*. Israel does not "take" its land or "take on" its identity; these are *given to her* from an Other. To "possess" is to *receive*; to "give" is to *be given*. Hence, God's people can be faithful to what they *receive* only by *giving it all away* (in "the liturgy of the neighbor").

Liturgy's metaphors are thus multiple: verbal and non-verbal, sensory and gestural, spatial and visual, architectural and musical, legal and political. It is important to notice that metaphors are not mere colorful speech or imaginative turns of phrase. What has been said of symbols may be applied to metaphors as well: both are "good to think with." Thinking begins when the mind recognizes polarity and *difference*: self—other; this—not that; one—many. Cognition and language struggle to make sense of these differences. The adjective, in fact, was born of such a struggle, for adjectives let us claim sameness (I see two cats) while affirming difference (one is grey, the other orange). Adjectives thus help us deal with real difference while maintaining the fiction that the two animals are simply "identical." Metaphors "up the ante" further by letting us take the "white lies" of language to new levels; we can claim that "this" (moon) which is not "that" (mother) really *is* "that." Why? Because metaphor's conflict—caused by putting two things together that don't belong—cannot be resolved at the literal level (not even Harry Potter can literally make the moon our mother). We are thus compelled to imagine a new possibility—something *true* that *differs* from both moon and mother, yet illumines the significance of both.

Linguists thus like to imagine metaphor as a mode of semantic "motion." This means that metaphor is heuristic, it launches us on a path of discovery—a point Thomas Aquinas recognized when he wrote that "signs" (both verbal and nonverbal) are a distinctively human way of moving from what we know to what we don't know.[20] The semantic motion of metaphor takes us (1) from the level of *perception and observation* ("Aha! that light I see must be the sun"), (2) to the level of *description* (e.g., Homer's favorite compound adjective for dawn, "rosy-fingered"), (3) to the level of *discourse* (saying something to someone about something), and finally, (4) to the still more complex level of metaphor (putting two things together that appear not to belong together). Metaphor's first movement always appears to be a *mistake*, a *transgression* within speech: "This can't be right; there must be some mistake!" In short, metaphor commits us to a journey we had never planned to take.

That is why metaphor could be defined as a "close encounter with *difference*, with *otherness*." From the get-go, there is something uncanny, perhaps

---

20. See *Summa Theologiae* IIIa Pars, Q. 60, art. 2, corpus.

even numinous, about metaphor. It strikes us as strange, weird, a surprise that may arouse many reactions at once—laughter, curiosity, disbelief, dread, delight, awe. Metaphors simultaneously attract and repel us. This power both to draw near while establishing distance (difference, otherness) reveals that metaphor's roots are prerational, preconscious. Those roots are buried deeply in our brains and bodies—in our primal instincts to "fight or flee"—and metaphors might thus be more aptly described as a way to "think with the skin." Or to put it another way, *metaphor is the body thinking about difference, about otherness*. It is the body coming to the recognition that nearness is possible only in distance and distance possible only in nearness.

We can now begin to see why the embodied language of metaphor is so closely linked to Christian liturgy, ritual, and sacrament. The God of faith is, after all, One who "makes a difference to all things and to whom all things make a difference"; One who remains incomprehensible while drawing incomprehensibly near, invading our embraces, encamping among our heartbeats. Most forms of human discourse seek closure; they try to "come to rest." When our intent is to simply to transmit information, for example, we unload or download the data, and that's that. When giving testimony at a trial, we answer questions posed by the prosecution or the defense; then, on cue, "step down" (even if one of the attorneys reserves the right to call us back to the stand later). But metaphor resists closure; it seeks to remain forever in motion. To use categories formulated by American philosopher Philip Wheelwright, metaphoric discourse "tweaks" the relation between "V[ehicle]" and "T[enor]," between "carrier" (words, speech) and "content" (message) in the linguistic event. Metaphor keeps the relation between V (carrier) and T (content) mobile, interactive—each redefining the other without ever coming to "the end." That is one reason why the language of public prayer may *pause* from time to time, but never really ends, even after the assembly is dismissed. For at the beginning of every eucharistic prayer we ask to be joined to those whose praise of God is unending, is still going on, always and everywhere: When we "enter" the liturgy, we in fact join a "program already in progress":

> Everywhere we proclaim your mighty works
> for you have called us out of darkness
> into your own wonderful light.
> And so, with all the choirs of angels in heaven
> We proclaim your glory
> And join in their unending hymn of praise:
> Holy, holy, holy . . .[21]

---

21. Preface I for Sundays in Ordinary Time.

Metaphor is not only the body *thinking* about difference (in speech); it is the body *interpreting* that otherness (in both words and gestures). Such a view of metaphor helps us see why Christian teachers like St. Augustine spoke of sacrament as *verbum visibile* (visible word). Note the inherent ambiguity of this metaphor. We think of words as *acoustic* events, not visual ones. To put *verbum* ("word") and *visibile* ("visible") together seems transgressive, a mistake. Augustine's decision to define "sacrament" as "visible word" embodies a metaphoric collision. It suggests that "sacrament" is a ritual experience through which we learn to "*see* with our *ears*" and to "*hear* with our *eyes*." If the root of sacrament is metaphor, then a new possibility is opened up for us: we may perceive the audible as visible and the visible as audible.[22]

THE HUMAN METAPHOR

In the previous paragraph, I proposed that we define metaphor as "body thinking about difference and interpreting that difference (or *otherness*) in words and gestures." I have emphasized the body as "thinker" for a very specific reason. Most Westerners assume that human thought is essentially "immaterial," disembodied. At least since Descartes, if not earlier, Western thinking has been dominated by a "cognitive apartheid" that not only separates mind from matter, *thought* from *action*, but makes thinking the core of human existence and identity. "I think therefore I am," was Descartes' famous formula. Whether he intended it or not, Descartes' *distinction* has become a *dichotomy*. Cognition (the reasoning mind) rules sensation (bodily life and action). The goal of Descartes' thinking, autonomous subject is "clear and distinct" ideas; the power of cognitive analysis; the precision and elegance of mathematical proof. Cognitive science is thus perceived as innately superior to knowledge born of the body.

The old Zen proverb—"there are some things that can be known only by rubbing two people together"—would thus puzzle a devout Cartesian. Yet metaphor is not a refusal to *think*. It is, as Elizabeth Sewell says, thinking

---

22. Augustine invokes the notion of sacrament as "visible word" in the commentary on John's Gospel (Tractate 80.3). It is in this same context that he speaks about the essential relation between "material elements" and "Word of God" in sacramental celebrations: *accedit verbum ad elementum et fit sacramentum* ("the word comes to the material element and a sacrament begins to be"). Still more complex, metaphorically, is Augustine's view that *sacrificium visibile invisibilis sacrificii sacramentum est* ("visible sacrifice is a sacrament of an invisible sacrifice") (*City of God* 10.5, 6). Aquinas makes use of this Augustinian understanding in his treatise on the eucharist in *Summa Theologiae* IIIa Pars, Quaestio 82, articulus 4, corpus.

with the whole self. This includes using . . . mind and body, as part of the metaphor and method. It also includes . . . use of the specifically human forms of living experience—love, suffering the consciousness of failure or of mortality, for example—as metaphors, with power of interpretation beyond themselves.[23]

Metaphor is a kind of embodied "divination," a half-conscious groping or "guessing" (the French verb *deviner* means "to guess") that—in spite of its imprecision, incompleteness, inexactness—nevertheless represents progress toward knowledge that is real and human. As a matter of fact, this "groping after" not only characterizes theological and liturgical language; it also shapes a good deal of modern scientific thought, as Michael Polanyi and others have shown.

Metaphor thus offers its own kind of precision, one that arises more from its *methods* than from its meanings.[24] Walt Whitman's poem "A Clear Midnight," analyzed earlier in this chapter, certainly conveys wisdom and insight into the human condition (e.g., our relation to larger, natural rhythms such as "night, sleep, death, and the stars"). But what may go unnoticed is how Whitman transmits his insight. The poem is metaphoric not simply at the level of word and meaning but at the level of method. It offers *itself* as an instrument of divination, an invitation to redefine the *human* in terms of the *cosmic*. In the reader's hand, the poem becomes a key for unlocking the doors of perception, for suspending time and embarking on a "free flight" beyond the everyday (books, art, lessons) to the limitless reaches of the universe (the stars). "A Clear Midnight" is ambiguous in its images, but precise in its method. It dares the reader to let *otherness* (night, sleep, death, the stars—forces that surpass human control) define the human and determine the course of its freedom (its "free flight into the wordless").

We are now in a better position to understand how and why liturgical language is metaphoric. It is not the case that that every word we utter in worship is "chock-full of metaphors." Take the liturgy for the Midnight Mass of Christmas, for example. The opening prayer and the first reading (Isa 9:1-6) certainly *do* make use of evocative metaphors. "Father, you make this holy night radiant with the splendor of *Jesus Christ our light*," says the opening prayer. "A *child* is born to us," says the first reading, "they name him *Wonder-Counselor, God-Hero, Father-Forever, Prince of Peace*." But the second reading (Titus 2:11-14) focuses less on image than on ethical exhortation, while the

---

23. Elizabeth Sewell, *The Human Metaphor* (Notre Dame, Ind.: University of Notre Dame Press, 1966), 12.

24. Iibd., 68.

Gospel (Luke 2:1-14) narrates events surrounding Jesus' birth. Yet even when the liturgy's prayers and texts are not littered with metaphors, liturgy's *method* is metaphoric. Metaphor, Gail Ramshaw argues,

> is the distinctive characteristic of the working human mind. To see something newly; to suggest that it is as it is not and in the suggestion to make it so for the community; to expand human imagination by the layering of what is with what was not: this is the process of human thought and the vehicle of human communication. Although some speech is more obviously metaphoric than other, all extension of thought and all accumulation of imagination are at root metaphoric endeavors. We recognize this use of the mind when the three-year-old after a long bath looks in dismay at her toes and cries out, "I got raisin feet!"; when scientists call something . . . a black hole.[25]

Because it is the basic strategy for shaping and nurturing communal meaning, metaphor has always found a home in Christian liturgy. It constitutes the indispensable method of all liturgical language, verbal and nonverbal—even when no explicit "figure of speech" is involved:

> To say the unknowable God and to describe mercy, the community relies on metaphor. "May God's face shine upon you," we say. Of course, God has no face. But we give God a face as part of the way we say mercy. May it "shine": another metaphor. The Church is continuously cultivating its garden of metaphors. . . . The hope is that with all the metaphors thriving, meaning will abound for all the faithful.[26]

METAPHOR MEETS MYSTERY

Metaphor is, then, the renewable linguistic resource by which a liturgical community renegotiates, from one generation to the next, its layered relationships to Mystery and manners, God and culture, the world of nature and the work of human hands. Metaphors are not fixed points on a compass—eternal, inert, immutable—but "working points" (as Elizabeth Sewell says), a "flexible net of relations which the mind establishes or perceives between the two universes, inner and outer, for the purpose of interpreting each."[27]

---

25. Gail Ramshaw, *Liturgical Language: Keeping It Metaphoric, Making It Inclusive* (American Essays in Liturgy; Collegeville, Minn.: Liturgical Press, 1996), 9.
26. Ibid.
27. Sewell, *Human Metaphor*, 109.

> For all are Men in Eternity. Rivers Mountains Cities Villages.
> All are Human & when you enter into their Bosoms you walk
> In Heavens & Earths; as in your own Bosom you bear your Heaven
> And Earth, & all you behold, tho it appears Without it is Within
> In your Imagination of which this World of Mortality is but a Shadow.[28]

If liturgy's principal aim is to know and name the connections between God, world, and humankind, then metaphoric speech provides us with the method to meet that goal. In the rituals of worship, God, world, and people engage one other in a perpetual process of redefinition. Only metaphor's method lets the celebrating assembly recognize the "body of Christ" as simultaneously "on" and "at" the table. Only metaphor leads it to affirm God as simultaneously "incomprehensible" yet "incomprehensibly near." And only metaphor lets us say that "Rivers Mountains Cities Villages" are eternally human and that when you enter them, "you walk in Heavens & Earths, as in your own Bosom you bear your Heaven and Earth." Or as George Herbert wrote in his famous poem "Prayer,"

> PRAYER the Churches banquet, Angels age,
> Gods breath in man returning to his birth,
> The soul in paraphrase, heart in pilgrimage,
> The Christian plummet sounding heav'n and earth ;
>
> Engine against th' Almightie, sinner's towre,
> Reversed thunder, Christ-side-piercing spear,
> The six daies world-transposing in an houre,
> A kinde of tune, which all things heare and fear ;
>
> Softnesse, and peace, and joy, and love, and blisse,
> Exalted Manna, gladnesse of the best,
> Heaven in ordinarie, man well drest,
> The milkie way, the bird of Paradise,
>
> Church-bels beyond the stars heard, the souls bloud,
> The land of spices, something understood.[29]

---

28. William Blake, *Jerusalem*, section 71, lines 15-19, edited by Morton D. Paley; vol. 1 of *Blake's Illuminated Books* (Princeton: Princeton University Press, 1991), 247.

29. *The Poetical Works of George Herbert* (New York: D. Appleton, 1857), 61-62.

Putting together "worlds" that seem *not* to belong together, metaphor gives Christian liturgy the method it needs to arrive at an astonishing conclusion: namely, that *God, world, and people share a human face*. As I've noted earlier in this book, one of liturgy's basic strategies is to "defy the space that separates," to shrink the space that divides "signified" from "signifier." Christ is at the center of Christian worship precisely because in him signifier and signified meet and marry—making the world a wedding and showing us "Heaven in ordinarie, man well drest / The milkie way, the bird of paradise."

But what does it mean to say that in Christ, "signifier and signified meet and marry"? And how can this be said to happen in liturgy, in sacramental celebration? To clarify this point, it may help to turn, in the five points that follow, to the work of postmodern theologians such as Jean-Luc Marion and Catherine Pickstock.

1. *Thinkers like Marion may remind some readers of the great twentieth-century Protestant theologian Karl Barth (1886-1968).* Barth defended God's absolute sovereignty over all things human, insisting that God's supremacy and transcendence are not merely matters of "divine preeminence." On the contrary, God's *difference*—God's utter *otherness* from all that is created or human—is so profound that it can never be grasped by human reason. In short, "theology," in any positivistic sense, is *impossible*. Because the Fall has darkened the human heart and mind, reason is no longer reliable. Theology cannot be constructed, then, either on the basis of "nature" (a "natural theology," based on God's self-revelation in creation) or on the basis of human experience. God is revealed *only* in Jesus Christ—and this Word is the only one God speaks to and for humanity. All other things (including humanity's cultural achievements), Barth reasoned, are rooted in sin and thus cannot possess ultimate value.

With Barth's perspective in mind, we may approach some of Marion's theological concerns. First, Marion argues that no *theo*logy can be authentic unless and until it breaks with theo*logy*. In other words, theology must renounce its pretense of speaking "truly and accurately" about God. "Only God can speak well of God," says Marion, quoting Pascal.[30] What makes Christian theology distinctive is not the singularity of its "insights" and meanings, but what *authorizes* their singularity. Christian theology speaks of *Christ*. But Christ does not speak words "about" God or even words "inspired by" God. Rather, Christ erases the gap—shrinks the space—between speaker and speech, between speaker and sign. Christ himself, argues Marion, does not say a (or "the") word; rather, "He says *himself*—the Word." Christ deliv-

---

30. Jean-Luc Marion, *God without Being*, trans. Thomas A. Carlson (Chicago: University of Chicago Press, 1983), 139 and 223 n. 1.

ers no "message" different from himself; in him, uniquely, *speaker*, *sign* (i.e., word, speech) and *reference* (i.e., "meaning") coincide. When Christ "is said . . . all is said: all is accomplished in this word that performs, in speaking, the statement that 'the Word pitched its tent among us' (John 1:14)." As God's Word in person, Christ performs—in speech made flesh—all that is God. So Marion concludes,

> The Word, as Said of God, no man can hear or understand adequately, so that the more men hear him speak their own words, the less their understanding grasps what the said words nevertheless say as clear as day. In return, men cannot render the Word the homage of an adequate denomination [naming]; if they can—by exceptional grace—sometimes confess him as "Son of God," they do not manage (nor ever will manage) to say him as he says himself. The Word is not said in any tongue, since he transgresses language itself, seeing that, Word in flesh and bone, he is given as indissolubly speaker, sign, and referent.[31]

2. *Theology thus becomes as "impossible" for Marion as it was for Karl Barth.* Still, readers may have noticed that theologians *do* keep talking and theological books *do* keep getting written and published. So how, then, does an "impossible" theological discourse become "possible"? Or should theology be dismissed as prattle and idolatrous nonsense? "To justify its Christianity," writes Marion, "a theology must be conceived as a logos of the Logos, a word of the Word, a said of the Said." This can happen only if theologians understand language *not* as something they control but as something by which they are governed, something to which they must surrender.

> To do theology is not to speak the language of gods or of "Gød," but to let the Word speak us . . . for in order to say Gød one first must let oneself be said by him to the point that, by this docile abandon, Gød speaks in our speech, just as in the words of the Word sounded the unspeakable Word of his Father.[32]

The theologian's task is not to speak about God but to let him- or herself "be said by the Word"—just as the Word let itself be said by the Father. The theologian's first task is surrender, not control. She or he must first be spoken by God in human speech, for God speaks *all* our names in the Word.[33] And

---

31. Ibid., 140-41.
32. Ibid., 143. The diagonal line through the *o* of the word "God" (represented in the English of Marion's printed text as an *X*) is meant to show that the *word* "God" is precisely *not* God in any proper sense.
33. Ibid., 144.

where does that happen? Christian tradition, East and West, maintains that it is above all in liturgical prayer that God "calls each one by name." Hence, worship—doxology—is the premier site of theology.[34]

3. *"Impossible" theology thus becomes "possible" on condition that theologians let themselves be spoken by God's Word.* But if that is so, what would theology talk *about*? Does it have content, subject matter? If we look at the Christian Scriptures, we could say that the Word seems simply to transmit *words*—a *text*. But of course it is *event*—not text—that is central to revelation. God reveals not merely by talking but by acting. Indeed, God's speech is already action. So the question is: How do we retrieve those actions, those events? History can be neither reversed nor repeated. How, then, can one claim that liturgy somehow "puts us in touch" with real revealed events, rather than merely with the scriptural texts that record or remember those events? Jean-Luc Marion proposes a parallel between the way revelatory *events* leave their trace on the Gospel texts and the way

> a nuclear explosion leaves burns and shadows on the walls. . . . [T]he text does not coincide with the event or permit going back to it. . . . The shadow fixed by the flash of lightning does not reproduce the lightning, unless negatively. The text assures us a *negative* of the event that alone constitutes the original.[35]

Even in the Gospels, then, this gap between *text* and *event*—between *record* and *revelation*—remains.

Where does that leave us? Can the gap be bridged? If real events produced the text(s), can we return to those events without violating the trajectory of history? Simply reading or repeating the texts ritually will not do, because texts didn't produce the events—events produced *them*. Simply reading the Bible in public ritual will not reconstitute events or magically retrieve real moments in history. There is no magic bullet that suddenly makes us contemporary with the events of Jesus' passion, death, and resurrection. The gap between text and event remains insurmountable—and in that, Marion suggests, lies its ultimate *grace*. Easter is not an "interpretation" or a "meaning" or an "effect" (the fallout) of meaning, it is precisely an *event*, though not one limited by space and time, since by definition it occurs beyond the trajectory of history. (That is why the risen One appears in the postresurrection narra-

---

34. That is why liturgical theologians such as Aidan Kavanagh speak of the theology that arises directly from the experience of communal worship as *theologia prima*, as opposed to secondary, derivate, "systematic theology." See Aidan Kavanagh, *On Liturgical Theology* (New York: Pueblo, 1984), 73-95.

35. Marion, *God without Being*, 145 (emphasis added).

tives as *real* and connected to history—bearing in his body the marks of his wounds—yet as surpassing the conditions of history.) As Marianne Sawicki has pointed out, the event of Easter "deconstructs" time by refusing to consign the dead to the "past":

> [Jesus] *cannot be both past and risen*, for to be past means not to be active and available now. The canonical texts [i.e., the Gospels] decline to identify the Risen Lord as one who is available through stories as what is *past*. Rather, he is on the loose beyond the canonical texts. The name of Jesus, a text, attaches itself to *persons* and to experiences of *empowerment* that turn up day by day in the infinitely varying career of the church. The *referent* of the Gospel texts, so to speak, is toward versions of themselves being continually inscribed into human activities: that is, toward ongoing discoveries of the Risen Lord that they make possible.[36]

In other words, here is a case where the text's referent (the "thing signified") is *not* a *past* deed or event that can be encoded (hence confined) within *stories*, but a *future* that continues to unfold uncontrollably. That unfolding future inscribes itself sacramentally (i.e., in ritual symbols) on the bodies of believers—in the liturgies of Christian initiation, for example. In the event of Easter, Jesus did not become a story; he became our *future*. Like the Big Bang, Easter isn't "over" (i.e., its action is not completed and it cannot, therefore, belong to the past). Thus, even Easter has to keep "deconstructing" exploding. "The story of an event confined within the past, as Easter morning, falls apart," so "resurrection cannot have been an event in the past" and hence the only true "story" of Easter is one that unfolds into the future.[37]

This point becomes clearer if one compares it to the creation accounts in Genesis, where narratives that are ostensibly about *beginnings* are actually not *protologies* (explanations of origins) at all, but *eschatologies* (narratives about how humanity will be when it fully, freely, and finally surrenders to God). Similarly, Easter is not a Christian protology (a story about our origins in the historical past) but a Christian eschatology. It tells us not where humanity has been, but where it's going. Easter did not end with Jesus' emergence from the tomb; because it implicates all humankind (as Vatican II's *Gaudium et Spes* 22 clearly affirms), its action does not and will not end until all share Christ's resurrection destiny. Easter thus explodes all the structures that bind and restrict human availability. Jesus is now available *not* through stories of

---

36. Marianne Sawicki, *Seeing the Lord: Resurrection and Early Christian Practices* (Minneapolis: Fortress, 1994), 334 (some emphasis added).
37. See ibid., 334-35.

the past but through empowering activity in the *present* (*leitourgia* and *diakonia*, worship and service, cult and care) that propels us toward an open future. As Sawicki points out, sacramental liturgy (especially eucharist)

> is the means of crossing the eschatological frontier. It overcomes the opposition between what is "Jesus" and what is not. Sacramental liturgy is the means of assimilating to Jesus many persons, communities, and even material elements that, according to our accustomed narrative time line, could not possibly have supported any such connection.
>
> Resurrection, then, is "about" the availability of Jesus as Risen Lord in the activities of caring for the poor and celebrating the liturgy.[38]

In sum, liturgy—understood as both "cult" and "care," the "liturgy of the church" and the "liturgy of the neighbor"—is the place where the gap between event and text (deed and word) is overcome. Precisely because Easter—as *event*—remains beyond any "text" (i.e., cannot be reduced to a story because it is not yet completed), it can become the authorized interpreter of reality. The Emmaus story in Luke 24 is a case in point. There the dejected disciples remain clueless—the scriptural texts remain closed and unintelligible to them, and they fail to see what is plain and evident. But since the risen Jesus, as God's Word, is not simply a "story" (belonging to the past), he can become the authorized interpreter, the one who opens the eyes of the disciples. He is known to them not while reviewing the Scriptures (stories of past events), but precisely in a present action— the breaking of bread—an action that belongs not to the past but to the future the "Stranger" (the Risen Christ) has disclosed to the disciples. That is why Marion insists that "*the theologian must go beyond the text to the Word, interpreting it from the point of view of the Word.*"[39]

4. *Now we are in a better position to grasp how an "impossible" theology becomes possible.* Theology is possible only when its hermeneutic (its method of interpretation) is doxological, liturgical, "eucharistic." Think once more about the Emmaus story in Luke 24. In that narrative, Marion notes, "Eucharist accomplishes, as its central moment, the hermeneutic. . . . It alone allows the text to pass to its referent, recognized as the *non*textual Word of the words."[40] That is, eucharist keeps Easter *eschatological* and prevents it from becoming simply another story about the past. Hence the essential bond between Easter and eucharist; hence too the emphasis of early Chris-

---

38. Ibid., 335.
39. Marion, *God without Being*, 149.
40. Ibid., 150.

tian writers on Christian initiation (baptism and chrismation, culminating in the *repeatable* act of eucharist)—as "*paschal* sacraments." Hence also the reason why Aidan Kavanagh speaks of liturgy as "*theologia prima*," and Marion speaks of the "eucharistic site" of (*all*) theology. Eucharist is not simply "one source among many," one "place among many" where theology may begin. It is *the* theological site par excellence. Here is how Marion puts the matter:

> The Word intervenes in person in the Eucharist . . . to accomplish in this way the hermeneutic; the hermeneutic culminates in the Eucharist; the one assures the other its condition of possibility; the intervention in person of the referent of the text [Christ is the referent referred to] as center of its meaning. . . . If the Word intervenes in person only at the eucharistic moment, the hermeneutic (hence fundamental theology) will take place, will have its place, only in the Eucharist. . . . [Hence,] the theologian secures the place of his hermeneutic . . . only in the Eucharist, where the Word in person, silently, speaks and blesses, speaks to the extent that he blesses.[41]

In eucharist, therefore, *speaker* (signifier), *speech* (word), and *reference* (significance meaning)—all three—coincide in the person of God's Word, the risen Christ. The young British theologian Catherine Pickstock has advanced a similar argument in her book *After Writing*. In her preface to that work, Pickstock writes that doxology (ritual, the "embodied speech" of prayer, praise and worship) permits

> a co-primacy of sign and body. . . . [This] coincidence of sign and body is most manifest in the event of the Eucharist. Moreover, this event, by giving death as life, also overcomes the opposition of death to life . . .
>
> Not only is the Eucharist . . . an example of the coincidence of sign and body, death and life. It is . . . only a realistic construal of the event of the Eucharist [that] allows us to ground a view of language which does not evacuate the body, and does not give way to necrophilia. . . . Eucharist . . . grounds meaningful language as such. Indeed, . . . I suggest that liturgical language is [for Christians] the only language that really makes sense.[42]

Here Pickstock also echoes a position, articulated in slightly different terms, by Marion:

> The Christian assembly that celebrates the Eucharist unceasingly reproduces this hermeneutic site of theology. . . . [I]t hears the text, verbally

---

41. Ibid., 150-51.
42. Catherine Pickstock, *After Writing: On the Liturgical Consummation of Philosophy* (Oxford: Blackwell, 1998), xv.

passes through it in the direction of the referent Word, because the carnal Word comes to the community, and the community into him. The community therefore interprets the text in view of its referent [Christ] only to the strict degree that it lets itself be called together and assimilated, hence converted and interpreted by the Word, sacramentally and therefore actually. . . .[43]

5. *Two consequences flow from such analyses of how an "impossible" theology becomes possible when it becomes eucharistic.* The first is this: in sacramental liturgy (especially eucharist), the Word is boundless precisely because it is the *Easter* Word, the Word-made-flesh whose rising completes itself only when humanity and cosmos are transformed and "God is all in all" (cf. 1 Cor 15:28; Col 1:15-20). The Word (as "text") is no longer the product or possession of the human authors who wrote it down. It becomes, instead, the speech of the Word who (precisely as the risen One) cannot be confined to the "story" or bound to the past. Hence, as Marion suggests, "a sort of infinite text is composed," an "infinite surplus of meaning" that can never be plumbed or exhausted, and hence demands "an infinity of interpretations." "This endless fecundity," Marion goes on to say, "depends on the power of the Spirit that gives rise to the eucharistic attitudes" embodied in a celebrating assembly. For "a theology is celebrated before it is written—because 'before all things, and particularly before theology, one must begin by prayer'. . . . [H]ence an infinity of Eucharists, celebrated by an infinity of different communities, each of which leads a fragment of the words back to the Word. . . ."[44]

The second consequence is this: in a faith community such as the Roman Catholic Church, theology progresses *eucharistically*. Gathered around the Lord's table, the Sunday assembly itself is the site of *theologia prima*. Theology begins, then, *liturgically*—and not with authoritative pronouncements by church leadership. As Marion remarks,

Theology cannot aim at any other progress than its own conversion to the Word, the theologian . . . becoming bishop or else one of the poor believers, in the common Eucharist. . . . *[T]heo*logical progress [is] less an . . . ambiguous and sterile groping than the absolutely infinite unfolding of possibilities already realized in the Word but not yet in us and our words. . . . We are infinitely free in theology: we find all already given, gained, available. It only remains to understand, to say, and to celebrate. So much freedom frightens us, deservedly.[45]

---

43. Marion, *God without Being*, 152.
44. Ibid., 156, 157.
45. Ibid., 158.

Thus the impossibility of theology is overcome by the eucharistic assembly's ritual deeds and symbols. But this "progress" never goes forward in a perfectly linear, ever-rising path. At one level, liturgy too is an "impossibility." "[L]iturgy," writes Pickstock,

> is at once a gift from God and a sacrifice to God, a reciprocal exchange which shatters all ordinary positions of agency and reception. . . . Moreover, liturgical expression is made "impossible" by the breach which occurred at the Fall. This breach is the site of an apparent *aporia*, for it renders the human subject incapable of doxology, and yet, . . . the human subject is constituted . . . only in the dispossessing act of praise.[46]

Here we meet a theme already found in the sacramental theology of Louis-Marie Chauvet. The church can "offer" its gifts only in the mode of disappropriation, of dispossession. It can "give" only what it has received, and hence, as the Liturgy of St. John Chrysostom puts it, "We offer you your own, of what is your own, in all and for the sake of all."

DEFINED BY DOXOLOGY

I have been suggesting that the gap between event (the past) and text (story, record) can be overcome only when metaphor meets mystery and sacrament results. Now I hope to show how aspects of Catherine Pickstock's work may help close the gap between liturgy as "impossible task" and doxology as the definition of what it means to be human. For Pickstock, God's self and action—revealed in the life, death, and resurrection of Jesus—constitute a kind of *divine madness*. Yet God's folly is "wiser than human wisdom, and the weakness of God is stronger than human strength" (1 Cor 1:23-25). As Pickstock observes, the Christian creed (and Paul's short summary of it just cited) confronts us with "the insane figure of God incarnate [as] . . . the wisdom which [remains inscrutable, which] cannot be understood by empirical or 'logical' investigation, Christ made man, but seen by men as a madman."[47]

In the institution narrative of the eucharistic prayer, Pickstock argues, "the world is made to abase itself before this madness."[48] How so? The words of

---

46. Pickstock, *After Writing*, 176-77.

47. Catherine Pickstock, "Asyndeton: Syntax and Insanity: A Study of the Revision of the Nicene Creed," *Modern Theology* 10, no. 4 (October 1994): 337.

48. Ibid., 336.

Jesus inserted into the eucharistic prayer are basically "asyndetic";[49] they appear almost out of nowhere, with little preparation and with barely any connection to what precedes and follows. In the midst of a longer narrative that praises God's work in creation, among the people of Israel, and down to our own time, Jesus' words are inserted as a direct quotation, an *assertion* dropped into the midst of a lengthy *prayer* spoken by somebody else (the presider). This strategy is popular in postmodern literature, where authors use "asyndeton" (an absence of links, conjunctions, and cross-references) to convey a sense of uprootedness, flux, isolation, and estrangement. But such a strategy is rare indeed in traditional liturgical discourse, which usually tries to show how words, deeds, people, and events are *connected*.

Jesus' words, quoted in the middle of the eucharistic prayer, form a sudden intrusion from elsewhere—from someone *other* than the speaker (the presider) or the community (in whose name the prayer is being recited). To make the intrusion all the more dramatic, the prayer uses a rhetorical strategy known as "deceleration." (Scholars today distinguish between "decelerated" [slowed down] and "accelerated" [sped up] narratives. These contrasting terms point to "*how much* territory the text covers" and "*how long* it takes to cover it.") The Creed we recite at Mass, for example, is mostly *accelerated* narrative that covers a huge expanse of history (everything from creation to the "resurrection of the flesh and everlasting life") in a short span of time. Yet the Creed also *decelerates* when the mystery of the incarnation is described, and that slow-down is punctuated by a ritual gesture (a bow or a genuflection): "For us men and for our salvation he came down from heaven; by the power of the Holy Spirit he was born of the virgin Mary, and became man."

The eucharistic prayer also combines accelerated and decelerated narrative. From preface dialogue to doxology, the prayer moves at an accelerated pace, except for two slow-downs. The first occurs at the "Holy," which breaks the prayer's flow and speed with an outburst of adoration and praise by the people: "Holy, holy, holy, God of power and might. . . ." The second deceleration begins as the prayer describes, in some detail, Jesus' words and deeds at table on "the day before he suffered" (Eucharistic Prayer [EP] I). EP I—like its ancestor, the old Latin Roman canon—slows the narrative still more by adding rhetorical flourishes not found in Scripture: "The day before he suffered he took bread *in his sacred hands* (Latin: *in sanctas ac venerabiles manus suas*) and *looking up to heaven to you, his almighty Father* (Latin: *et elevatis oculis in caelum ad te Deum Patrem suum omnipotentem*). . . ." The italicized phrases

---

49. The term "asyndetic" is used in modern rhetoric to designate speech that resists the use of conjunctions, cross-references, or relative and subordinate clauses (clauses that indicate, for example, how several thoughts are distinct, coordinated, or codependent).

create a kind of halo around Jesus' actions that slows the narrative and heightens the difference between what precedes and follows the "institution narrative." Once that narrative ends (with the people's memorial acclamation), the prayer picks up speed in a rapid recitation that remembers Christ's death and resurrection, commends the church's offering (EP I: "we offer you, Father, this life-giving bread, this saving cup"), recalls the communion of saints, makes intercession for the living and the dead, and concludes with a doxology ("through him, with him, in him . . . ").

There is another point to be noticed in the way the eucharistic prayers of the Roman rite quote Jesus' words and deeds in the institution narrative. The traditional religious language that Jesus, a Jewish layman, knew and used belonged to a unified world of religious discourse where each symbol (e.g., "blood") resonated with every other use of that symbol. Thus, in the Hebrew Scriptures, references to the "blood" of the Temple sacrifices would have evoked every other mention of blood—e.g., the blood of Abel crying out from the earth after his death, the blood of the firstborn in Egypt, the (just barely) averted bloodshed in the story of the sacrifice of Isaac. Whether Jesus' death occurred in a "Passover context" or not, his mention of blood and covenant would have evoked a sweeping set of symbolic resonances.

But in the eucharistic prayer two things happen. First, Christ's words are removed from their Synoptic context (the passion narrative)—just as Paul had quoted them without that context in 1 Corinthians 11. Second, Jesus' words are asyndetic in relation to the rest of the prayer. They are not logically or structurally required by what precedes and follows them[50] and—more startling still—they are words that quite literally cannot come from either the presider or the rest of the assembly who "offer you, God of glory and majesty, this holy and perfect sacrifice." (Neither presiding priest nor people can say, literally, "this is my body . . . this is my blood"; these are *quotations*.) Christ's words, in short, drop unexpectedly into the prayer; appearing on the scene much as the Stranger did on the road to Emmaus, "out of nowhere." As quoted in the eucharistic prayer, therefore, Jesus' words—though still linked with the religious history of his people—are freed from any closed system of references that might be controlled by human thought, speech, or memory. Jesus' eucharistic words break with the logic and "rationality" not only of the world but also of religious tradition and prayer—including the eucharistic prayer itself!

---

50. We have examples of ancient eucharistic prayers that do not, in fact, contain an "institution narrative" at all. Perhaps the most famous of these is the "anaphora of Addai and Mari," which may be found, in English translation, in *Prayers of the Eucharist, Early and Reformed*, ed. R. C. D. Jasper and G. J. Cuming (2nd ed.; New York: Oxford University Press, 1980), 26-28.

That is why Jesus' words are, as Catherine Pickstock analyzes them, an example of "divine madness." They break with both human rationality *and* the conventional religious speech of his time—or ours. Jesus' words thus enter the timeless condition of "non-sense," of speech severed from the ordinary world of thought and analysis. "This is my body which is given for you. . . . This is my blood which is shed for you." Nothing in the Passover ritual or in the tradition of formal meals shared among friends and family would have made such a claim comprehensible. The words seem to be the disconnected (asyndetic) gibberish of a madman. "Christ's use of asyndeton at the Last Supper," Pickstock writes,

> is a reminder in every liturgical performance that human reason is incomplete, and that the work of praise is never finished. . . . The insanity of the Cross, the non-sense of sacrifice, was a wisdom which drowned in the "rationality" of the world, and revealed there its non-sense. By the asyndetic silence which binds his anamnetic utterances at the Last Supper, his speech opens a void, an arena of emptiness (fuller than fullness) which no words can "explain," for it is a mystery that can only be performed, received, and then repeated. These lacunae provoke a breach between human "rationality" and divine wisdom, where only God . . . can discern the "reason" in the non-sense.[51]

The eucharistic actions of Christians—like the eucharistic words of Jesus—are, therefore, profoundly unsettling. They assault both secular and religious rationality and affirm, as Pickstock suggests, that *to be* is to worship, that human existence is itself doxological. Yet Jesus' words also reveal that worship remains, at some level, "impossible," and that divine wisdom, embodied in Christ's broken body and shed blood, reveals itself to us as folly, as divine madness. Nevertheless, Pickstock concludes, doxology is what makes our existence as human subjects possible. The desire to be a "self," a "subject," is not an autonomous project—we do not, in fact, "invent" ourselves. The human subject is constituted not by self-possession, but by self-*dis*possession. We become real persons, we "come to" ourselves, only in the kenotic (self-emptying) act of praising God.

Pickstock observes that such an idea is not new in Western thought. Plato recognized that speech has a fundamentally "doxological" character, and hence liturgical poetry—hymns to the gods, songs in praise of the good—was

---

51. Pickstock, "Asyndeton: Syntax and Insanity," 335. Pickstock does not delve into the sticky exegetical problem of whether or not the eucharistic words of Jesus (in the Synoptics and in Paul) actually represent *ipsissima verba Jesu* ("the exact words of Jesus himself").

not excluded from his *Republic* (though most other forms of poetry were). Plato recognized that speech signals not only temporality—since human utterance means one syllable must die before the next one can be born—but openness to the "other." He assumed that language has a transcendent nature, that is, "language exists primarily, and in the end only has meaning as, the praise of the divine." Thus, doxological expression unites "the one who gives praise, the object of praise, and all those who share in its expression" in a single, transparent act in which "nothing can be held back or veiled." Liturgical action does not simply represent something or someone as praiseworthy, but "constitutes a whole way of life. To give praise to what is praise-worthy [*sic*] by definition involves participation in it, just as emulation . . . of the transcendent good must perforce involve *methexis* [sharing, participation] in the good." As a result, doxology is not an occasional function of speech but a mode of life that "constitutes the supreme ethic" and makes the speaker a subject, that is, a person who is "fully central to himself at the very moment that he is fully committed to the object of his praise." Seen from this angle, Plato's understanding of human speech sees liturgy, doxology, as the "highest form of language, that which both expresses and performs shared values of what is praiseworthy."[52]

Pickstock's analysis of Plato's doxological theory of speech and human speakers helps explain why modern writers like the philosopher Josef Pieper could consider affirmation—saying yes to all that is—as the source of Christian celebration and festivity.[53] It is also the reason why Aidan Kavanagh could affirm that liturgical acts, *doxological* acts, are always *rite*:

Rite can be called a whole style of Christian living found in the myriad particularities of worship, of laws . . . of ascetical and monastic structures, of evangelical and catechetical endeavors. . . . A liturgical act concretizes all these and in doing so makes them accessible to the community assembled in a given time and place before the living God for the life of the world. Rite in this Christian sense is generated and sustained in this regular meeting of faithful people in whose presence and through whose deeds the vertiginous Source of the cosmos itself is pleased to settle down freely and abide as among friends. A liturgy of Christians is thus nothing less than the way a redeemed world is, so to speak, done.[54]

---

52. Pickstock, *After Writing*, xiii-xiv, 37, 39, 40.
53. See Josef Pieper, *In Tune with the World: A Theory of Festivity*, trans. Richard Winston and Clara Winston (Chicago: Franciscan Herald Press, 1973).
54. Kavanagh, *On Liturgical Theology*, 100.

LITURGY: DOXOLOGY OR PRODUCTION?

To argue that we humans are defined by doxology and to say that Christian liturgy is "the way a redeemed world is . . . done" is to embrace the "whole style of Christian living" that constitutes *rite*, our meeting with that "vertiginous Source of the cosmos" who settles among us as friends. Yet, true as these things may be, they are hardly self-evident—especially in "capitalist, conquering" postmodern societies dominated by notions of "economic, technological, and political progress" and bent on "the conquest and subjugation of what is other."[55] Earlier in this book I referred to Laurence Paul Hemming's essay "The Subject of Prayer: Unwilling Words in the Postmodern Access to God." In it, Hemming makes a perceptive comment about the experience of worship in late-capitalist, technologically advanced Western cultures of the twenty-first century. "We are no longer constituted liturgically in prayer," he writes; "we constitute for ourselves the liturgy that best expresses our interior psychic life. Liturgy becomes style. It does not produce me; I produce it. In consequence, when I say that it 'feels right' I am saying that it fits an interior disposition I already have—if I think about it at all."[56] For many, "liturgy no longer makes *us*; *we* make the liturgy." It is *our* property: *we* plan it, produce it, and perform it. As a result, liturgy is increasingly perceived as a locally grown, home-made commodity rather than a selfless act of surrender to the One whose glory, in Isaiah's vision, filled the earth, shook the door frames, and filled the Temple with smoke (Isa 6:1-4).

In saying this I do not mean to suggest that postconciliar worship has "lost its sense of the sacred," that it lacks order and decorum, or that it exalts the celebrating assembly above the awesomeness of God. As I noted in the introduction to this book, responsible postconciliar liturgists have consistently avoided choosing between transcendence and community—recognizing, instead, that each always implies the other. In worship we acknowledge *both* God *and* assembly as awesome yet homely, homely yet awesome. Richard Gaillardetz is surely correct, therefore, to argue that a fully renewed liturgy requires the retrieval of the "trinitarian and eucharistic foundations of Christian community." For liturgy celebrates the unity of "communion with God

---

55. For the assessment of (modern American) culture as "capitalist, conquering," see Michel de Certeau, *The Practice of Everyday Life*, trans. Steven Rendall (Berkeley: University of California Press, 1984), 136. The other quotations in this sentence are from Graham Ward, "Postmodern Theology," in *The Modern Theologians*, ed. David F. Ford (2nd ed.; Oxford: Blackwell, 1997), 595.

56. Laurence Paul Hemming, "The Subject of Prayer: Unwilling Words in the Postmodern Access to God" in *The Blackwell Companion to Postmodern Theology*, ed. Graham Ward (Oxford: Blackwell, 2001), 444-57.

and communion with one another,"[57] just as Jesus insisted we must know and name *God's* love in the neighbor.

It is thus false to claim that American Catholics must choose between an "awe-inspiring, liturgical celebration which transports one into another spiritual realm, or a warm and informal gathering of pseudo-intimates."[58] The fact is that human connectedness—which is as real when welcoming strangers as it is when greeting friends—is itself the icon of God's own interpersonal life of communion. Christians believe that God is a village, a communion of persons—Father, Son, and Spirit—whose personhood emerges *precisely from the act of giving themselves to each other*. God's inner life is *kenōsis* (self-emptying self-surrender), and hence in the mystery of God, persons are forever "caught in the act" of *giving* themselves. God is "altogether gift," donation.[59] To confess the Trinity is to affirm God as Given—given to, given for, given up, given over, given away. Each person pours itself out utterly to and for the others. In God's life, "possession" of personhood happens only in the act of *dis*possession. Hence Aquinas could characterize the Trinity as a personal community of "subsistent *relations*." In sum, God is a communion of persons poured out for each other and for us. God's personhood is self-bestowal, mutual given-ness. As a result, every liturgical celebration is "the privileged ritual expression of what is in fact true every moment of our lives: every authentic act of human communion is by that fact communion with God."[60]

LITURGY AND "CONSUMER RELIGION"

Still, it is unquestionably true that postmodern consumerist cultures (such as twenty-first-century American society) tend to see liturgy as a "production," the result of self-conscious planning and effort. Catholics who favor a return to the preconciliar liturgy (the Latin Tridentine Mass) might be surprised to learn that their own sensibility is in fact "deeply contemporary."[61] As Vincent J. Miller has recently written,

---

57. Richard R. Gaillardetz, "North American Culture and the Liturgical Life of the Church: The Separation of the Quests for Transcendence and Community," *Worship* 68, no. 5 (September 1994): 403-16, esp. 413.

58. Ibid., 416.

59. See Michael Downey, *Altogether Gift: A Trinitarian Spirituality* (Maryknoll, N.Y.: Orbis Books, 2000).

60. Gaillardetz, "North American Culture and the Liturgical Life of the Church," 416.

61. Vincent J. Miller, *Consuming Religion: Christian Faith and Practice in a Consumer Culture* (New York: Continuum, 2004), 81.

Neotraditionalist forms of Catholicism that repudiate the Second Vatican Council seem almost perfect illustrations of commodified nostalgia. Rejecting the council's attempts to engage modernity critically, they dwell in the Catholicism of the recent past, revering its practices, beliefs, décor, and costume. Such nostalgic retrievals inevitably idealize the past by abstracting it from the particularities that created it and sunder it from any organic relation to the present.... Inevitably, such "traditionalist" retrievals are not only innovative but also deeply contemporary. Fundamentalism is a thoroughly modern phenomenon.[62]

Consumer religion (whether of the "right" or of the "left") is inevitably linked to consumer culture, which, like many phenomena of the postmodern world, offers both good news and bad. First, the good news. Consumer culture, as Miller observes, "is experienced by most people as a liberation." Like modern technology, it frees people from burdens our forebears took for granted. A century ago, for example, many Catholics in the United States were European immigrants whose lives unfolded in "closed cultures," small, close-knit communities that had "tightly scripted class, gender, and social roles" and were firmly under the control of "local authorities such as parents, teachers, pastors, bishops, and even spouses, friends, and fellow parishioners."[63] Liberties we take for granted today—for example, the freedom to choose a marriage partner without undue family interference; the freedom of married couples to regulate family planning despite the 1968 papal ban on artificial contraception—were virtually impossible in the urban communities of Catholic immigrants a century ago.

Now for the bad news. A consumerist paradise produces

> a situation where culture is deprived of political friction, where each individual is free to pursue his or her own religious synthesis, whether ingenious and inspired, or banal and conforming— . . . all of these . . . *imprisoned in the private realm of individual insight, while globalizing capitalism goes about its business unopposed.*[64]

Unregulated consumerism, for example, blesses the conspicuous consumption that lets Americans drive gas-guzzling SUVs in blissful disregard of the planet's future or the fate of nations whose oil is needed to fuel them. Moreover, consumerism produces a twin—*commodification*, a social process in which the habits, practices, and attitudes learned from buying and consum-

---

62. Ibid., 80-81.
63. Ibid., 228.
64. Ibid. (emphasis added).

ing products carry over into our relationships with *all* other persons, places, and things. Among those "persons, places, and things" is liturgy. It too becomes a commodity in a production economy. No wonder Benedictine Fr. Virgil Michel, an American liturgical pioneer who launched the journal *Orate Fratres* (now *Worship*) in 1926, recognized that the renewal of liturgy must begin with economic and social renewal.

When consumerism teams up with commodification, the result is a culture based on "market value," a culture where everything—including Christians and their liturgies—belongs to an economy of production, cost-calculation, and profit. Money and market value invade all areas of life, and liturgy falls very naturally into the pattern of a late-capitalist "service economy." Vincent Miller notes that when the "rhetoric of *things*" (buying and consuming them) colonizes ever greater areas of our experience, two results follow.[65] First, the meaning of value itself changes; it ceases to be an intrinsic quality and becomes an arbitrary, extrinsic "price." Lacking significance of its own, value then serves merely as image or "stand-in" for something else, even if the "something else" is a fantasy (like winning the lottery). Under such conditions, value becomes purely inflationary—an image without any "original," a pretense, a make-believe. Second, the goods and products to which "value" is attached are themselves transformed into imaginary acts—a "style," window dressing, props for an imaginary life. In sum, "consumption becomes an imaginary activity whose object is *the advertisement as much as the product itself.* This, one might say, is Victoria's *real* Secret."[66]

In brief, consumerist cultures that view liturgy as "production" or "style" resist ritual's metaphoric logic. That logic, as I've tried to show in this chapter, relocates meaning and value by placing them beyond human economies of value and consumption. Metaphor is, after all, a *transgression.* It puts together things that don't belong together—meat and cheese, leper and village, lion and lamb, Jew and Gentile, slave and free, haves and have-nots, the quick and the dead. Every metaphor breaks boundaries, risks disorder, threatens chaos, drives us toward the margins of "respectable" society. As Gail Ramshaw says of liturgy, metaphor is its method and inclusivity is its goal: "To see something newly; . . . to expand human imagination by the layering of what is with what was not. . . . Such creativity of the mind shaping and nurturing communal meaning is what Genesis means by 'the image of God.' *The divine has burst out from the natural; meaning has been created.*"[67]

---

65. Ibid., 57.
66. Ibid.
67. Ramshaw, *Liturgical Language*, 9.

Ritual's metaphoric logic aims to let us "see reality anew," to move beyond culture-bound categories of gender, economic status, and social rank. Liturgy's metaphors rehearse that inclusive "logic of God's kingdom" where the least and littlest have the first seats at table, and all are fed. Metaphor is, simply, the condition of possibility for *shared* meaning, the native speech of an assembly that welcomes the stranger and makes room for the outcast.

But can Christians in postmodern, Western, consumerist cultures still hear ritual's native speech (metaphor) or understand its logic? Certainly, our age is as voluble as any other. Despite their longstanding apophatic tradition (God is inexpressible and thus unnamable), Christians rarely seem to be tongue-tied at worship. On the contrary, history is littered with liturgical texts that witness to our fondness for calling the unnamable God names. But what about the *liturgical act itself*, which is not only verbal but nonverbal, embracing both the *audible words* of song and speech and the *visible words* of sacrament and ritual gesture? How do Christians defend their preposterous claim that liturgical speech, verbal and nonverbal, *may*, and under certain circumstances—the cry of the poor, the warning of a prophet, the word of forgiveness—*must* be heard as *God's Word*? And how can we have the audacity to assert that this happens preeminently within the liturgical assembly?

To answer these questions, it will be necessary to take a closer look at some of the reasons why liturgy has become not something we *do* (i.e., deeds inscribed on human bodies), but something we *think* about, discuss, plan, and then "produce." We will need to examine what the late Jesuit social scientist Michel de Certeau called "recited societies." In Certeau's analysis, a "capitalist conquering" culture like that of the United States is one "defined by stories (*récits*, the fables constituted by our advertising and informational media), by *citations* of stories, and by the interminable *recitation* of stories. These narrations have the twofold and strange power of transforming seeing into believing, and of fabricating realities out of appearances."[68] As Graham Ward comments, we often know that our media-generated stories are fables (hence false) and that the "realities" they claim to disclose are mere simulacra—but never mind, we believe them anyway. We embrace an "objectless credibility," based on "citing the authority of others." Thus, Ward notes, we create fables and pretenses (shams, simulacra) whose purpose is to "make people believe that others believe" in them, "but without providing any believable object."[69] The result is a culture full of "faith" and full of the loud, public, politicized rhetoric of faith, that actually believes in nothing. It is, Certeau argued, a soci-

68. Certeau, *Practice of Everyday Life*, 186.
69. Graham Ward, "Introduction," in *Blackwell Companion to Postmodern Theology*, xxii.

ety of "pseudo-believers" bolstered by a "culture of deferral, credit, and accreditation," a culture of the "virtually real."[70]

CALLING GOD NAMES

So what are the liturgy's chances in postmodern "recited societies"? As I noted above, liturgy today is often perceived as production, a homemade fabrication whose main purpose is to express our "interior" beliefs and convictions. Yet historically, Roman Catholics and other Christians who regularly use prescribed ritual forms have thought of liturgy not as the words *we* give to *worship* but as the words *worship* gives to *us*. We participate in the liturgy on someone else's passport, using someone else's speech. Liturgy is less our act of naming God than God's act of naming us.

Despite all that, liturgy—whatever the source of its speech—*does* love to call God names. Now it is true that calling God names—"holy, strong, undying, unnamable"—is not quite the same thing as *naming* God. Jean-Luc Marion reminds us that "the Name ['God'] does not name God as an essence; it designates what passes beyond every name. The Name designates what one does *not* name and says that *one does not name it*." God's Name, understood this way, does not "inscribe God with the . . . horizon of our predication [i.e., within our human system of affirmation and denial]," but rather "inscribes us . . . in the very horizon of God." The liturgical naming of God is thus not so much our attempt to "tell God who he is," but our surrender to the name *God* gives *us*. "This is exactly," writes Marion, "what baptism accomplishes when, far from our attributing to God a name that is intelligible to us, we enter *into* God's unpronounceable Name" and thereby "receive our own." For that reason, liturgy is "never a matter of our speaking *of* God, but of speaking *to* God in the words of the Word."[71] Liturgy, in short, is prayer, and prayer embodies the fundamentally liturgical function of *all* theological discourse (much as, in Plato's view, doxology defines the human as "being-in-relation-to-the-divine").

But if liturgy—public prayer—is the final destination of all theological discourse, and if liturgy speaks the "words of the Word" by which *God* names *us*, how can liturgical language be in "crisis"? From quarrels about the accuracy of translations from the Latin *typica* (official editions of liturgical books)

---

70. Michel de Certeau, in *On Signs*, ed. Marshall Blonsky (Oxford: Blackwell, 1987), 202.

71. Jean-Luc Marion, *In Excess: Studies of Saturated Phenomena*, trans. Robyn Horner and Vincent Berraud (New York: Fordham University Press, 2002), 157.

to complaints about prayer texts that lack "decorum and dignity," the language of Roman Catholic worship seems to have become a casualty of the "culture-and-liturgy wars." This crisis, I suggest, actually stems from two distinct sources, one *biblical*, the other *philosophical*. Those sources, in turn, are rendered more complex by the conditions of postmodern "recited societies," about which I will say more in a few pages.

First, let us consider the *biblical* source of this crisis. Irenaeus of Lyons (d. ca. 200 C.E.) once said that Christ's coming "brought us all possible newness by bringing us himself. For Christ was announced in advance, and what was announced was precisely this: that Newness in person would come to renew and quicken humankind" (*Adversus Haereses* 4.34.1).[72] If Easter embodies Christ's radical *newness*, we might expect that it would also bring about a more immediate and palpable presence of God within the world—an experience of God's incomprehensible nearness in the risen body of Jesus. But as we have seen earlier in this book, that is not the story the Bible tells. A careful reading of the Christian Scriptures suggests that Easter produces not a more certain conviction of God's presence but a heightened awareness of distance and *absence*. The risen Jesus' advice to Mary Magdalen is "Back off! Don't touch!" (John 20:17). And even if, later in John's Gospel, the tardy twin Thomas *is* invited to put his finger into the nail prints and his hand into the wounded side, Jesus chides his weak faith and implies that faith *in the absence of bodily evidence* is better (John 20:27-29). No matter where one turns in the Gospel literature, the language surrounding Easter is ominously empty and distant, like voices ricocheting in empty rooms. John and the Synoptics speak of young men or announcing angels whose terrible message confirms that "He is *not here!*" (John 20; Matt 28:6; Mark 16:6; Luke 24:6). *Not here!* The *empty* tomb has become a void, a vacancy, an icon-in-stone of *loss* and *absence*.

Luke's Gospel confronts us with a similar surprise. The disciples on the road to Emmaus meet not a familiar face but a chatty Stranger who, when finally *recognized in the breaking of bread*, instantly "*vanishes* from their sight" (Luke 24:31). *Aphantos egeneto*, says the Greek text of Luke 24:30; "He became *invisible*." Nor does the ascension scene in Acts offer us much consolation. Far from confirming that heaven is a blissful "place of presence," Acts 1:9 tells us that "a cloud *took* [Jesus] from their sight," *seized* him, *concealed* him, *swallowed him whole*. This is not the "little cloud that could" but a

---

72. See Adelin Rousseau et al., eds., Irénée de Lyon: *Contre les Hérésies*, Livre IV (Sources chretiennes 100 pt. 2; Paris: Cerf, 1965), pp. 846-49. The translation is based on that given in Jean-Luc Marion, "The Gift of a Presence," in *Prologomena to Charity*, trans. Stephen Lewis (New York: Fordham University Press, 2002), 124.

cloud that *can't* and *won't*; it snatches the risen One away, abducts him, erases the evidence, and exchanges Christ's *body* for a void. The ascension produces not presence but disappearance. *Aphantos egeneto*: "he became invisible."

Paradoxically, then, the Easter mystery intensifies—it does not eliminate—the problem of presence. Wolfhart Pannenberg once wrote that in the Easter mystery, "the Revealer of the eschatological will of God became the very *incarnation* of [that] eschatological reality itself."[73] That is certainly an apt description of what Christians *believe*. But at the very moment when God's eschatological promise to humanity is, presumably, embodied and fulfilled in Jesus' rising from the dead, our immediate *access* to that presence is cut off. *Aphantos egeneto*: "he became invisible." Strange as it may seem, the eschatological reality that embodies God's decision to abide forever with us in the risen flesh of Christ is translated, in the Christian Scriptures, *not as a discourse of proximity and presence, but as a discourse of absence*, disappearance, distance, and invisibility. As the first chapter of Acts suggests, Easter and its aftermath end with Jesus *going away*, and with the disciples standing speechless, looking up into an empty sky.

So the first source of the postmodern crisis in liturgical language is biblical; it flows from the Easter narrative itself. If God's ultimate (eschatological) will and presence are revealed in the person and work of Jesus—if they abide forever in the glorified flesh of the risen One and are embodied in the ritual repertoire of Christ's body the church—why do the Christian Scriptures speak a post-Easter discourse of *disappearance, distance,* and *absence*? In a nutshell, what if "the words of the Word" (the source of liturgy's speech) speak of absence? Why does Jesus need to "go away" in order to be present? Already on the pages of the Gospels, the Easter *mystery* has become a *message* and Christ's risen *body* an inscribed *text*, a topic of ongoing debate and discussion. The Emmaus story may reach its climax in a *"request for presence"* ("Stay with us, sir, for it is almost evening"), but it begins and ends with gossip. Which is, of course, a short definition of Christian worship itself: the liturgy *is* the church's public gossip about God, its rumors about One whose *presence* can be discerned, named, and known only as an *absence*.

The second source of our postmodern discomfort with liturgical language is philosophical, and its modern origins can be traced back to the thought of seventeenth-century philosopher René Descartes. Two points about Descartes' understanding of selfhood and God are relevant here.

The first concerns Descartes' understanding of the human subject, the "self." Descartes' *Ego* is constituted by thought and autonomy, interiority and isola-

---

73. Wolfhart Pannenberg, *Jesus, God and Man*, trans. Lewis L. Wilkins and Duane A Priebe (Philadelphia: Westminster, 1977), 367 (text slightly modified; emphasis added).

tion. In a very real sense, the Cartesian optic sees the self as self-made. "*I* think, therefore *I* am." The human self emerges *not* from dialogue with *otherness* (with other persons or *the* Other, who is God), but from a wholly *internal* dialogue. Thus, Descartes' famous formula focuses on the autonomous, thinking "I": *Cogito, ergo sum; I think, therefore I am.* (Note that the formula uses the *first person singular.*)

The second point concerns Descartes' view of God as a clear and distinct idea whose reality is "eminent" (i.e., more "real" than us or the physical world at large). "By 'God,'" Descartes tells us, "I mean a substance that's infinite, independent, supremely intelligent, and supremely powerful—the thing from which I and everything else that may exist derive our existence. The more I consider these attributes, the less it seems that they could have come from me alone. So I must conclude that God necessarily exists."[74] The logic seems flawless, yet there's a fly in the ointment. Descartes protests that the idea of God is *completely clear and distinct* and contains more subjective reality than any other idea. But this creates a problem, not a solution. God morphs into an *idea*—and that idea remains, finally, a *conclusion* reached by *autonomous, thinking subjects.* God is met, Descartes implies, not in the body, not in the world and its history, but within the self's isolating *interiority.*

These, in my estimation, are the biblical and philosophical sources for the crisis that besets liturgical language today. For us heirs of Descartes' *Third Meditation,* prayer of *every* kind (public or private, individual or social) belongs to the *interior* world of thought and ideas. It is an internalized, autonomous production, a psychological act, something *we* intend and do. God is met mainly within the theater of my own selfhood, my autonomous subjectivity—and not, as the Hebrew Bible suggests, in the disruptive mode of revelation, in the tumult of bodies creating history together. Descartes' God is an *inference,* a conclusion we arrive at through reason and cognition—*not* the sudden, unexpected *eruption* who leaps from the pages of the Hebrew Bible, flashing flames of fire, shaking the wilderness of Kadesh, and cleansing the prophet's lips with a burning coal—while ever replenishing the widow's cruse of oil and breathing gently on the back of Elijah's neck. Of course, if God is an "inference made by the thinking, autonomous, human self" rather than an "eruption from elsewhere," the very nature of public prayer changes. Liturgy becomes a function of the *meanings, choices,* and *intentions* that "I" and "you" (another solitary "I") bring to the act. It becomes an *intentional project,* a *production,* a style through which we solitaries express

---

74. René Descartes, *Meditations on First Philosophy,* trans. George Heffernan (Notre Dame, Ind.: University of Notre Dame Press, 1992), 48.

our interiority. It is no longer the prayer of the body, and its language is derived not from our bodily inscription into God's Word, but from the interiority and autonomy of the thinking *self.*

REDISCOVERING LITURGY'S NATIVE SPEECH

So where does that leave us? Are we postmoderns still capable of learning how to speak "liturgy," or is it, like Latin, a dead language? As we have seen earlier in this book, postmodern thought is typically "rhizomal," characterized by an endless multiplicity of connections. In contrast, liturgy's speech—if it is "the words of the Word," as Marion suggests—seems flat and one-dimensional, terminally boring. Moreover, while *modernity* in the West was defined by the *emergence* of Descartes' autonomous self, with its preference for rigorous scientific method and "clear and distinct ideas," the complex polyphony of *postmodernism* is much more difficult to decode. Some prefer to distinguish *postmodernity* (as a term describing culture) from *postmodernism* (a dominant philosophy, theology, or worldview). But many would agree with Michel de Certeau, that capitalist conquering Western cultures have become "*recited societies,*" that is, societies defined by their *stories,* especially those fables repeated by marketers, spin doctors, and peddlers of information technology—stories cited and *re*cited as "gospel truth," especially in the media. As Graham Ward puts it, people in recited societies "believe what they *see,* and what they see is *produced for* them," largely through televised images.[75] And because ours is a world of technologized images; because our images are produced on screens; and because there is not necessarily any "original" behind or beyond those screens, it is very difficult for us to distinguish fiction from fact (hence that oxymoronic phenomenon known as "reality TV"). We install "authorities" (news anchors, politicians, radio talk-show hosts, Internet blogs) to tell us the difference. The challenges "recited societies" pose for the metaphoric logic of liturgical language are fairly obvious. Meeting them will require at least two distinct strategies. First, liturgy needs to retrieve its native tongue, its primary speech—which is *the language of the body itself.* The "words of the Word" are the words of the *Word made flesh,* the words of a Word whose body is a *human* body—a body that, even on the other side of Easter, does not lose its links to history and the world. This, of course, is a hard saying for us "Cartesian Christians," who tend to privilege mind over matter and thought over action. And yet Christian worship will have a future only if it can find

---

75. Ward, "Introduction," in *Blackwell Companion to Postmodern Theology*, xxii.

its way back to the body as the premier site of ritual, of liturgical celebration. The ancient Christian ritual instinct was, I suspect, the right one: *our bodies make our prayers.* We pray as a body through the gestures, postures, and shared exertions of singing, responding, processing, lifting, moving, touching, tasting, saying, seeing, hearing. If liturgy is the church's gossip; our bodies are the church's best and most reliable grapevine. After all, the mind will say anything one wants to hear; the body never lies. Liturgy speaks a language whose primary story—whose native narrative or *text*—is the *body itself.* Our bodies, moreover, are not images but *icons.* Images invite voyeurism (they beg to be looked at). But icons are different. We do not look at icons; they look at us. It is significant that the Letter to the Colossians celebrates Jesus as *eikōn tou Theou aoratou,* "the image of the invisible God, firstborn of all creation . . . head of the body, the church . . . the beginning . . . the firstborn from the dead" (Col 1:15-18).

How do we go about learning the body's iconic language? A good place to begin might be Ivan Illich's fascinating commentary on Hugh of St. Victor's *Didascalion.* Illich notes that throughout much of the first millennium, Christian readers experienced written pages as tablature, notation, a performance piece, a musical *score* for mumblers. The words painted on a page were meant to be *mouthed, read aloud,* their meanings *tasted* and absorbed by the body.[76] That is why Augustine was amazed (and perhaps annoyed) to see his mentor, Bishop Ambrose of Milan, reading *with his eyes only.* In the ancient world, reading was done "out loud," by munching the words, by a devout chewing that made *the body itself* the principal text, interpreter, and language of the liturgy. Liturgical reading was emphatically not the self's withdrawal into Cartesian "interiority." The book was a body, the body a book. Hence, in the liturgy, both bodies and the written pages of Gospel books were encircled by light and bathed in smoky fragrance. Reading and chanting *aloud* kept alive the *critical social connection* that bound the reader's *body* to God's Word, that linked person to person in a democracy of reading that created a community of devout "munchers" who understood that human speech is, above all, a desire to touch, to connect; that mouth and tongue embody "the innate imperfection of [all] human [striving]. . . ambition, and anxiety."[77] To read aloud was to feel in one's flesh both the wonder and the woundedness of words.

Liturgical assemblies might thus be called "recited societies" in reverse, where reading is not the assertion of a controlling autonomy (by the interi-

---

76. Ivan Illich, *In the Vineyard of the Text: A Commentary to Hugh's Didascalion* (Chicago: University of Chicago Press, 1993), 2.

77. W. S. Merwin, *The Ends of the Earth* (Washington, D.C.: Shoemaker & Hoard, 2004), 151.

orized self), but a *kenotic* experience in which God's Word, painted on pages and chanted in human speech and song, is reinscribed onto human bodies. Liturgy is never a homemade celebrity spectacle, nor is it a self-indulgent celebration of a closed community's interests, power, or prestige. On the contrary, liturgy *embodies* emptiness, powerlessness—that "*absence*" in human life where *God's* Word and *ours* are surrendered into mutual presence that creates *communion* without suffering *confinement*. Worship is inescapably embodied and iconic; it makes us—we don't make it. Why? Because liturgy is the moment when God's own Word places itself at the mercy of the body, at the mercy of human flesh. In liturgy, God's Word surrenders to world, to history, and to bodies. That is what is means to say that "God *names us*" in the act of Christian worship.

CONCLUSION

Chapter 6 has focused on another voice that is heard within liturgy's rich, polyphonic texture: the language and logic of metaphor. As we saw, metaphor's logic leads us to truth by way of "transgression" and "indirection," by "putting things together that appear not to belong together." Metaphor confronts us with *otherness* and *difference* (rather than sameness and familiarity) as ways of grasping multiple truths simultaneously—truths that may, on the surface, seem to challenge and even contradict each other. Metaphors are, I suggested, "the body thinking about difference and interpreting that difference (or *otherness*) in words and gestures." That is one reason why St. Augustine could define sacrament as "visible word," embodied word.

Perhaps the best image of Christian worship as "metaphor" comes from the story of an anonymous woman in Luke 7:36-50. Like God, this woman is nameless. A stranger (and hence, by definition, dangerous), she enters the house of Simon the Pharisee to anoint the feet of Jesus. Namelessly, wordlessly, her own body enacts a kind of eucharist. She *takes* her costly jar of perfume, *breaks* it open, and *gives* it as balm and blessing. She takes, breaks, gives, blesses: in these four actions, this nameless woman *names* Jesus, names him truly as God's *Christos*, Anointed One. *Her* body, broken open in love and tears, meets *his* body, broken open to receive her hospitality. Together, Jesus and this woman, form an embodied, eucharistic icon of Savior and Saved. Christ is anointed for his mission (culminating in the cross) and the woman is released into freedom and forgiveness. Luke's story begins with name-calling, but it ends with God's Word surrendered, as love and forgiveness, to the mercy of the body.

The point of Luke's story is, I think, deliberately shocking and subversive. It tells us that *God's own Word is wounded.* Just as Jesus' body opened to that woman's tears, love, oil, and perfume, so his own body, hung like a criminal's on a tree, opened to the spit, the shame, the hammered nail, the thrust of the spear. Note well. God's Word was "kenotic," self-surrendering, not only on the cross but from the very *beginning*—and *before.* From everlasting to everlasting, God's Word is speech *given to, handed over,* in that communion of Persons who are not "discrete, individuated, interiorized centers of consciousness" (as we are), but *givenness* so utter and so complete that it makes them who they are. That is why I insisted, earlier in this chapter, that God's tripersonal life is kenotic; that personhood in God is constituted by self-emptying, mutual self-surrender. God's Persons *possess* themselves precisely by *dispossessing* themselves.

Every liturgical act is an attempt to inscribe that trinitarian *dis*possession onto human bodies. That is why, in this chapter, I have described ritual's logic as metaphor and its native speech as iconic. That is also why I have said that worship is God's Word at the mercy of the body. A theology of liturgical language must therefore appeal to the voice of an Other, to the Word's own cry of dereliction on the cross, to the loud voice of Jesus' blood. On the cross, *crucified speech* at last learns the obedience of worship. On the cross, the human tongue was at last loosed and began to sing the great, unending hymn of the liturgy, a hymn sung "by all, and for the sake of all." On the cross, our crucified speech, silenced by sin and death, at last finds its voice. That is why we can accept the invitation to join the company of saints and angels and peoples of all times and places in that "unending hymn of praise." We can do this because those persons whose communion constitutes the blissful life of God open up a space, in the crucified Word, to receive our wounded speech into their own life, making it their own. We may, at last, hear human speech as God's Word.

QUESTIONS FOR REFLECTION

1. "Allusive, elusive speech is native not only to poetry, but to Christian ritual, liturgy, and sacrament as well. At the heart of such speech lies metaphor, which might be defined as putting two things together that seem *not* to belong together" (p. 195 above). Why does liturgical language *have* to be "metaphoric"?

2. "If liturgy's principal aim is to know and name the connections between God, world, and humankind, then metaphoric speech provides us with the method to meet that goal" (p. 201 above). What would you describe as liturgy's "principal aim"?

3. "In a faith-community such as the Roman Catholic Church, theology progresses *eucharistically*. Gathered around the Lord's table, the Sunday assembly itself is the site of *theologia prima*" (p. 208 above). True or not? Why?

4. "Liturgical action does not simply represent something or someone as praiseworthy, but 'constitutes a whole way of life.' . . . As a result, doxology is not an occasional function of speech but a mode of life that 'constitutes the supreme ethic' and makes the speaker a subject, that is, a person who is 'fully central to himself at the very moment that he is fully committed to the object of his praise'" (p. 213 above). In what ways are human beings "defined by doxology"? How does doxology as "the supreme ethic" link (or fail to link) to the notion that Christian liturgy must always be verified in the "liturgy of the neighbor"?

5. In what ways does "consumer religion" lead to the perception and experience of Christian liturgy as a "production"?

SUGGESTIONS FOR FURTHER READING

Hall, Donald. *Poetry: The Unsayable Said.* Port Townsend, Wa.: Copper Canyon Press, 1993. A short introduction, by an important American poet, on the nature of poetic language and of metaphor.

Kavanagh, Aidan. *On Liturgical Theology.* Collegeville, Minn.: Liturgical Press/A Pueblo Book, 1984/1992. Examines the relation between doctrine (as formulated within the church and interpreted by theologians) and doxology (faith as grasped and celebrated in the church's public liturgy).

Ramshaw, Gail. *Liturgical Language: Keeping It Metaphoric, Making It Inclusive.* American Essays in Liturgy. Collegeville, Minn.: Liturgical Press, 1996. A short introduction to the nature of liturgical language.

Sawicki, Marianne. *Seeing the Lord: Resurrection and Early Christian Practices.* Minneapolis: Fortress, 1994. A study of the way Christians have access to the risen Lord in the diverse practices of pastoral care and public cult (liturgy).

Ward, Graham, ed. *The Blackwell Companion to Postmodern Theology.* Oxford: Blackwell, 2001. A comprehensive introduction to the postmodern Christian thought and the thinkers who are contributing to it.

7

Parts and Participation

Ministry, Assembly, and Sacrament

CHRISTIAN LITURGY not only speaks the languages of bodily action and ritual metaphor; it also speaks service and ministry, assembly and sacrament. While worship is undeniably the public praise and adoration of God, it is, just as undeniably, an act of pastoral care, of interpersonal, face-to-face ministry among people. It is not only God's dignity that the liturgy proclaims. As Pope Leo the Great knew, faith and worship also proclaim the God-given dignity of each person within the Christian assembly: "Acknowledge, Christian, your dignity! You have become a participant in the divine nature. . . . Recall of whose head and of whose body you are a member!"[1] As "participants in the divine nature" and "members of one body whose head is Christ," Christians are equipped to act as ministers, to offer the Father a "sacrifice of praise and thanksgiving."

Christians can hardly be said, however, to have a monopoly on ministry. In actual practice, most (though not all) communities of faith are served by persons especially designated—by birth, vocation, or election—for tasks of cultic leadership and/or pastoral ministry. In ancient Israel, for example, the priesthood that served local sanctuaries (e.g., Bethel, Shechem) and, later, the centralized Temple in Jerusalem, was largely a matter of genealogy; one became a "priest" by birth and inheritance, not by vocation or choice.[2] During the period of the Second Temple, after the Jewish people had returned from exile, priestly clans and families—such as that of Zechariah, the father of John the Baptist—served in Jerusalem on a rotating basis, and some of their most solemn duties were assigned by lot. Thus, Luke's Gospel tells us that Zechariah was "chosen by lot according to the custom of the priesthood,

---

1. Leo the Great, Sermon I on the Lord's Nativity; Latin text in *Patrologiae cursus completus: Series latina,* ed. J. P. Migne (221 vols.; Paris, 1844-64), 54:192-93; my translation.

2. On the early Israelite sanctuaries, the centralization of worship in the Jerusalem Temple, and the evolution of the Jewish priesthood, see Roland de Vaux, *Ancient Israel: Its Life and Institutions* (New York: McGraw-Hill, 1965), 271-405. On the hereditary priesthood, see p. 359.

to enter the sanctuary of the Lord and offer incense" (Luke 1:9). It was there
and then that he had his famous vision of an "angel of the Lord" who fore-
told the Baptist's birth (see Luke 1:11-23).

Other world religions also recognize persons especially equipped to teach,
to interpret sacred literature, and/or to conduct holy rites. In Hinduism, for
example, spiritual teachers may sometimes be accorded divine status. For in
the Hindu tradition, writes Vasudha Narayanan, "deities descend to the earth
as human beings ascend to a divine status. Salvific truth is said to be mediated by these holy persons. . . . In many Hindu communities, the sacred
teacher is considered to be as important as the deity and is venerated, and
even worshipped."[3] This is an ancient tradition, one reflected in both the
sacred texts and ritual practice of millions of Hindus. An eleventh-century
C.E. text, *Acharya devo bhava* [Consider Your Teacher as God], reads in part:

> I bow to the lineage of teachers (*gurus*)
> which begins with the Lord of Lakshmi,
> with Nathamuni and Yamuna in the middle;
> I take refuge with my teacher![4]

This text, celebrating the long lineage of holy men and women is "recited by
Sri Vaishnava Hindus at the beginning of all ritual prayer; it recognizes
Lakshmi as one of the first teachers. . . . Nathamuni and Yamuna are seen to
be in the 'middle' of the spiritual chain.'"[5]

As Narayanan remarks, this intense devotion to religious teachers is not
surprising, because "perhaps more than any other religious tradition, Hinduism recognizes divinity in human beings. . . . For some disciples, the teachers are even more important than God. The Upanishadic dictum (*Taittiriya
Upanishad*) to treat your teacher as God is well known to millions of Hindus." Respect and reverence for the teacher are reflected, too, in Hinduism's
devotion toward sacred spaces. The map of India is dotted with holy places
and crisscrossed with pilgrimage routes. But it is not only public shrines that
are considered sacred. "The human body itself is sometimes spoken of as the
'temple of the supreme being.' . . . In one song, the eighth-century C.E. poet
Periyalvar declared: 'Build a temple in your heart. Install the Lord Krishna in

---

3. Vasudha Narayanan, "Hinduism," in *Eastern Religions: Hinduism, Buddhism, Taoism, Confucian-ism, Shinto*, ed. Michael D. Coogan (New York: Oxford University Press, 2005), 53. Narayanan goes on to point out, however, that not all Hindu communities consider their teachers so significant.
4. Ibid., 58. The term *guru* is probably familiar to many readers. Like related terms such as *swami* and *acharya*, it designates a teacher who initiates disciples into a religious movement—though tech-nically, *acharya* denotes "the formal head of a monastery" (p. 54).
5. Ibid., 59.

it; Offer him the flower of love."[6] Holy teachers, sacred spaces, the human body itself: all are sites where the divine may manifest itself. And this conviction, held by many Hindus, is one many Christians may also share.

Thus, for example, *Sacrosanctum Concilium*, the Second Vatican Council's Constitution on the Sacred Liturgy (no. 14) speaks of the celebrating assembly as "a chosen race, a royal priesthood, a holy nation, a redeemed people," and insists that when it comes to liturgy, "full and active participation by all the people is the aim to be considered before all else, for it is the primary and indispensable source from which the faithful are to derive the true Christian spirit." Pastoral ministry exists in the church for this reason and this reason only: to assist God's "royal priesthood" toward "full, active participation" in a liturgy that rehearses God's deepest plan for humankind—a festive banquet where all human hungers are satisfied and no one is sent away empty. Chapter 7 will focus on two principal themes. In the first part we explore "service in a servant church," and in the second part we take up the relation between *assembly*—as "community of the forgiven" and "sacrament of the world"—and *sacrament*, "the language of God's giving."[7]

SERVICE IN A SERVANT CHURCH

Since the early twentieth century, biblical and liturgical scholars have noted how the Synoptic accounts of Jesus' actions at the farewell meal he shared with his disciples on the night before he died have shaped our eucharistic traditions. Jesus, we are told, *took* bread, *blessed* it, *broke* it, and *gave* it to those with him at table. These four verbs—four familiar actions—established what Dom Gregory Dix famously called "the shape of the liturgy":

> With absolute unanimity the liturgical tradition reproduces these . . . actions as four: (1) The offertory [i.e., preparation of gifts]; bread and wine are "taken" and placed on the table together. ["took"] (2) The prayer; the president gives thanks to God over bread and wine together. ["blessed"] (3) The fraction; the bread is broken. ["broke"] (4) The communion; the bread and wine are distributed together. ["gave"]
>
> In that form and in that order these four actions constituted the absolutely invariable nucleus of every eucharistic rite known to us from antiquity from the Euphrates to Gaul.[8]

---

6. Ibid., 59, 70-71.

7. This phrase is the subtitle of David Power's fine study, *Sacrament: The Language of God's Giving* (New York: Crossroad, 1999).

8. Gregory Dix, *The Shape of the Liturgy*, rev. ed. with notes by Paul V. Marshall (New York: Seabury Press, 1982), 48.

Taking, blessing, breaking, giving: If Paul's account in 1 Corinthians 11 is any guide, the first generation of Christians already believed that to participate in the Lord's Supper (1 Cor 11:20) was to experience the "continued empowering presence" of Jesus himself—"the continued presence of absolutely the same Jesus in an absolutely different [i.e., a new and *risen*] mode of existence."[9] Jesus' table practice—taking, blessing, breaking, giving—thus survived his death and became, after Easter, the focal point for gatherings of people who believed his message about God's eschatological arrival, about God's reign or kingdom breaking into human history. As I noted earlier in this book, Jesus' table fellowship "with tax collectors and sinners" was so "meaningful to his followers and . . . offensive to his critics," that it became the most direct link between the community life of Christians and the "pre-Easter fellowship of Jesus and his disciples."[10]

Joyful companionship at table was thus the pivotal link connecting the Jesus of history with the Jesus Christians recognized as risen, forever alive in God's presence and accessible in both *cult* (sacramental liturgy) and *care* (pastoral service of the "little ones," the "least" and most vulnerable). Jesus the bread breaker had become Jesus the bread broken—and now the reality of God's kingdom was accessible in cult *and* care, in liturgy *and* service, in the assembly's worship *and* its pastoral ministry. The root of these realities was Jesus' own preaching about the reign or kingdom of God. As John Dominic Crossan points out, the kingdom that Jesus proclaimed was not a geopolitical reality and hence was not based on any secular model of rulership. "The Kingdom movement," Crossan writes,

> was an empowering rather than a dominating one. The historical Jesus . . . told [his disciples] they could do just what he was doing. They could heal one another, share their food together, and thereby bring the Kingdom into their midst. The God of that Kingdom was one who empowered people, unlike Caesar, whose kingdom dominated people. . . . When [Jesus] was executed, those with him lost their nerve and fled. They did not lose their faith and quit. What they found, even after his execution, was that the empowering Kingdom was still present, was still operative, was still there. . . . Jesus' presence was still experienced as empowerment, not only by those who had known him before, but by others hearing about him now for the first time.[11]

---

9. John D. Crossan, *Who Killed Jesus?* (San Francisco: Harper, 1995), 210.
10. Norman Perrin, *Rediscovering the Teaching of Jesus* (New York: Harper & Row, 1967), 102, 107.
11. Crossan, *Who Killed Jesus?* 209.

A New Map for the Table

Christian faith is thus empowerment, not the power to coerce or dominate others. And this faith—whose icon is Easter and whose cultic expression is eucharist—started long before the spice-bearing women made their astonishing discovery at the empty tomb. Christian faith started around those open, inclusive tables where Jesus proposed an entirely new map to chart the relationships between person and person—and between people and God. Two things about Jesus' table ministry appear to have been distinctive. First, there was the radical way in which *Jesus' meals differed from those of his surrounding culture*. Typically, in the ancient world (and perhaps in our own as well), a meal was a synopsis of social preferences. Besides satisfying hunger, a meal's chief purpose was to reflect and reinforce the stratified "social geography" of the diners—their socioeconomic status and rank; their gender, race, and political affiliation. Who ate what with whom—and in what order—made a huge difference in first-century Mediterranean cultures. But as we've seen earlier, Jesus challenged these customs and redrew meals' maps. Indeed, he seemed to invite *any*one to eat *any*thing with *any*one else at *any* time. In short, Jesus spread a table where all are welcome and no one is excluded on the basis of gender, race, socioeconomic status or (most shocking of all) "moral condition." Jesus claimed a right to eat and drink with sinners. He advocated "an open commensality, an eating together without using table as a miniature map of society's vertical discriminations and lateral separations."[12]

The *second* distinctive thing about Jesus' table ministry was how dramatically it departed from the religious culture of his contemporaries. Other Jewish reform movements of the period—the Essene community at Qumran, for instance—also stressed the important of shared ritual meals. *But the meals at Qumran emphasized order, dignity, precedence, rank, and hierarchy*—not the inclusive egalitarianism apparently favored by Jesus. The Qumran *Rule of the Congregation* insists that at "the common table," no one can bless the "first-fruits of bread and wine before the Priest." After the Priest, the "Messiah of Israel shall extend his hand over the bread"; then each member of the congregation—"in the order of his dignity"—utters a blessing.[13]

But Jesus emphasized not the ritual prerogatives of a few but the feeding of the many: "*Take, bless, break, give.*" Crossan points out that these verbs sug-

---

12. John Dominic Crossan, *Jesus: A Revolutionary Biography* (San Francisco: HarperCollins, 1994), 69.

13. Geza Vermes, *The Dead Sea Scrolls in English* (New York: Penguin, 1962), 121.

gest "a process of *equal sharing*, whereby whatever food is there is distributed alike to all."[14] As many scholars have observed, the first two verbs—*take* and *bless*—are actions of a leader, of a host, someone "in charge of the proceedings." But the second two verbs—*break* and *give*—are actions of a servant, someone whose job is to see that others' needs are met. Crossan comments: "Jesus, as master and host, performs the role of servant, and all share the same food as equals." More startling still, by taking on the role of a *servant*, Jesus assumed the role of a *woman*—for in both the religious and secular meals of his world, women usually did not recline equally with men at table; they ministered by serving food, clearing tables, or providing post-prandial entertainment. So "Jesus took on himself the role not only of servant but of female. . . . Far from reclining and being served, Jesus himself serves, like any housewife, the same meal to all, including himself."[15]

A New Map for Ministry

The four verbs that formed the ritual shape of Christian table liturgy thus present not only a challenging theology of eucharist but an even more challenging theology of ministry. Recall, for a moment, the story of the anonymous woman who crashes Simon's dinner party in Mark 14:3-9. Preachers often assume (on the basis of a similar story in Luke 7:36-50[16]) that this woman was a "sinner" and that her "sin" was sexual. In fact, Mark says nothing of the kind. Instead, he says—in language whose *eucharistic* resonances are loud and clear—that this woman brought a costly "alabaster jar of perfumed oil," broke it open, and poured it over Jesus' head. The precious perfume became a blessing for Jesus, anointing his head and perhaps running down his beard "like the dew of Hermon that falls on the heights of Sion" (Ps 133:3). Note the woman's actions: she *took*, *broke*, *blessed*, and *gave*. In effect, she and Jesus became a "eucharistic team" at that table in Simon's house. And the story's conclusion is even more startling. "Amen I say to you," Jesus cries, "wherever the gospel is proclaimed to the whole world, what she has done will be told *in memory of her*" (Mark 14:9). Just as, by combining the deeds of a host (*take, bless*) with those of a (female) servant (*break, give*), Jesus' eucharistic actions model a new map for meals, so this woman's actions model a new map for ministry. And while Luke (22:19) and Paul (1 Cor 11:24, 25)

---

14. Crossan, *Jesus: A Revolutionary Biography*, 181.
15. Ibid.
16. For comments on Luke's version of this story, see the "Conclusion" section of chapter 6 above.

attach the "command to repeat" ("Do this in memory of me") to Jesus' own deeds, Mark omits any such command in his account of the Supper (Mark 14:22-26). Instead, it is the woman's generous act of care and service—her anointing of Jesus' feet—that will be repeated "in memory of her" (Mark 14:9)—just as John implies that Jesus' meal is "re-membered" in acts of mutual service.

Perhaps this helps explain why in John's Gospel the eucharistic narrative (as enshrined in Paul and the Synoptics) is eclipsed altogether, replaced by Jesus' act of washing his disciples' feet. Feet figure prominently in both Mark 14 and John 13, and in both texts they direct us into the path of a new map of ministry. In John, Jesus the "master" does for his own "servants" what the woman in Mark did for him—and the table becomes *not* the place where "rank" is displayed or "power" is demonstrated, but the place where selfless acts of service—washing, anointing—are brought into direct relation to the food and drink of the table.

Ministry thus becomes key to the meaning of eucharist, and eucharist becomes the meaning of ministry. The content of what Jesus did by taking, blessing, breaking, and giving bread and wine is directly mirrored by what the unnamed woman in Mark's story did when she took, broke, and blessed Jesus' body with precious, perfumed oil—not counting the cost. Each act invites the other.

Vatican II's New Map for Ordained Ministry

The new maps for meal and ministry that emerge from the Gospels are an important biblical source for the renewal of American Catholic parish life that has taken shape over the past forty-plus years since the appearance of Vatican II's *Sacrosanctum Concilium*. While traditional vocations to priesthood and religious life have declined, *nonordained* vocations—evident in lay liturgical leadership at the local level—have blossomed. Nor has this been a matter of lay volunteers performing tasks that priests no longer have the time or the will to do. In virtually every area of liturgical life—from greeting parishioners and reading Scripture to leading music and serving as ministers of communion—competent lay ministers can be seen every Sunday serving the assembly's public prayer.[17]

Since Vatican II, lay liturgical ministries have developed and matured. In

---

17. For a recent theological assessment of newly emergent (and still emerging) lay ministries and their relation to ordained ministers, see Edward P. Hahnenberg, *Ministries: A Relational Appproach* (New York: Crossroad/A Herder & Herder Book, 2003).

his 1997 pastoral letter *Gather Faithfully Together*, Cardinal Roger Mahoney noted that this lay involvement in Sunday worship "is an area where the churches in our country have taken the renewal of Vatican II to heart. It is clear that many ministries are best done by members of the assembly who have the talents and training to do them well."[18] The heart of these emerging liturgical ministries, Mahoney observed, is *the assembly itself*. Whoever serves the people at prayer must first of all participate *in* and *with* the assembly fully, consciously, and actively. Such ministers

> understand what it means to step forward and proclaim a reading, minister holy communion or sing in the choir. Parishes might set a limit on the number of years a person serves in a ministry, asking that each person take off a year after four or five years in a single ministry. This limit would refresh people in their primary role as assembly members.[19]

Cardinal Mahoney's letter draws attention to an important development in the postconciliar theology of ministry. The gathered assembly is the primary *subject* (agent) of liturgical action and is not only the "object" or passive recipient of ministry from the ordained. Mary Alice Piil has shown how this conciliar theology of the assembly as subject of liturgical acts developed over the course of the twentieth century.[20] The theological seeds were already sown in two great encyclicals of Pius XII, *Mystici Corporis* (1943) and *Mediator Dei* (1947). In them, the pope began to expand the range of Roman Catholic ecclesiology. The church, Pius XII insisted, is not merely a hierarchical, juridical-social organism; it is also a *faithful people*, an *assembly* of grace, faith, and love; a *congregation* gathered by the Spirit. At the liturgy (and more specifically, at *eucharist*) the priest acts "in the person of *both* Christ *and* the church. The faithful offer because they pray with and through the priest."

Still, in Pius XII's view, "*direct* participation in the liturgical act is reserved to the priest" *alone*.

> The priest alone is necessary for the completion of this [liturgical, eucharistic] act. Pius XII does indicate, however, that the faithful should be encouraged to participate actively in the Mass. The value of this participation of the faithful lies in its pastoral effectiveness for the individual and is in no way necessary for the offering of the eucharist. However, Pius

---

18. Cardinal Roger Mahoney, *Gather Faithfully Together: Guide for Sunday Mass* (Chicago: Liturgy Training Publications, 1997), 31.
19. Ibid.
20. See Mary Alice Piil, "The Local Church as the Subject of the Action of the Eucharist," in *Shaping English Liturgy*, ed. Peter Finn and James Schellman (Washington, D.C.: Pastoral Press, 1990), 173-96.

XII does leave the way open for further development of the role of the faithful in the liturgical act.[21]

Because the pope's conclusions about the precise relationship between the roles of assembly and priest in the liturgy were somewhat open-ended, the bishops at the Second Vatican Council revisited the issue. As I will explain in the paragraphs that follow, *Sacrosanctum Concilium* (SC) did not raise and resolve all the questions that lingered about the nature of this relationship; but what it proposed went several steps beyond the conclusions reached by Pius XII in *Mystici Corporis* and *Mediator Dei*.

1. SC 14 recognized the priesthood of all believers not simply as a biblical image but as a *theological principle*—rooted in the nature of the liturgy itself—that *requires* popular participation as an *essential* (not an "optional") dimension of Christian worship. In Christian worship, the presence and participation of the people is no more "optional" than the presence of the ordained presider is.

2. SC 2, 7, and 41-42 recognized that the *local* church is really and truly a *church*. The celebrating assembly, gathered around its bishop for eucharist, is in fact the *praecipua manifestatio* ("principal manifestation") of the church. The council thereby gave us the seeds of an ecclesiology derived from *eucharist* rather than from juridical or hierarchical categories.

3. SC 14 recognized that participation by the people in the liturgy is rooted in the theology of baptism, and so it concluded that "in the restoration and promotion of the liturgy *the full and active participation by all the people is the aim to be considered before all else.*"

4. In a much-quoted phrase, SC 48 insisted that the Christian people should be present at the liturgy not "as strangers or silent spectators" but as real, active agents who truly offer "the immaculate victim, *not only through the hands of the priest but also together with him.*" The Latin of this passage was very precise: . . . *immaculatam hostiam, non tantum per sacerdotis manus, sed etiam una cum ipso offerentes*. This suggests, of course, that people and presider *each* have a unique, distinctive, and essential contribution to make to the eucharistic offering. *Together*, each in their own manner, people and priest celebrate the liturgy. The assembly—in its own way, distinct from that of the priest—is the *subject* of the liturgical act.

This was the fundamental theology that shaped the *General Instruction of the Roman Missal* (GIRM), which stresses that "the entire local assembly

21. Ibid., 175-76.

gathered for eucharist is the *subject* of the official liturgical act." Earlier, in traditional scholastic theology, the *priest alone* was understood to be the "immediate subject of the official ritual offering of the eucharistic sacrifice."[22] Both GIRM and SC moved beyond the old scholastic formulas, though they are somewhat ambiguous about "the specific manner in which priest/presider, priest/concelebrant, and other members of the assembly participate in the local Church's eucharist."[23] In our postconciliar era, therefore, concludes Mary Alice Piil,

> Two ecclesiologies, two eucharistic theologies, continue to exist side by side. When the congregation gathered for Sunday Mass truly understands that the eucharist is Christ's gift to the Church, that is, the local Church assembled under the leadership of the priest, presiding in the person of Christ, then the local Church will be seen to be the immediate subject of the action of the eucharist. In contrast, when the faithful attend Sunday Mass with the understanding that the priest acts for them, then no matter how many ritual changes there are, the laity will continue to see themselves as passive recipients of the eucharistic action.[24]

Unresolved Issues

It might be said, then, that Vatican II and the liturgical reforms that followed it managed both to clarify and to cloud the presider's role at eucharist. A brief historical review will reveal how and why "two ecclesiologies" and "two eucharistic theologies" continue to compete within the Catholic community.

Today, those who think reform should cease and the liturgy be "re-Catholicized" often appeal to SC 38, which speaks of "the *substantial unity of the Roman Rite.*" Behind this language lurks a powerful myth. The myth arises from an uncritical assumption that the Roman liturgy has had, from time immemorial, an unbroken history of invariable rites and rubrics, texts and gestures, that everyone recognizes as *Roman* in origin, *Roman* in content, and *Roman* in structure. Yet even the mildest acquaintance with Western liturgical history will expose this myth as little more than wishful thinking or euphoric recall. It is probably more accurate to say that a *single* "Roman rite" has more in common with fiction than with fact.

This should not surprise us. More than forty years ago, the research of

---

22. Piil, "Local Church as the Subject of the Action of the Eucharist," 191.
23. Ibid., 195.
24. Ibid.

Stephen van Dijk and Joan Hazelden Walker revealed that during the seventh century, the Roman rite was revolutionized by the "dramatic influx into Rome of Eastern monks and clerics, refugees from Arab invasion and Monothelite persecution."[25] These refugees became so numerous and influential that they actually came "to dominate the councils of the papacy and swamp the native element of the Roman clergy."[26] They brought with them not only Greek language, liturgies, and customs but new fashions in ecclesiastical art and architecture as well. In fact, "a lavish programme of painting, ornamentation and elaboration . . . undertaken by refugee Eastern artists" transformed many Roman churches into "not-so-Roman" sacred spaces. We may recall, too, that even Gregory the Great, who died at the beginning of the seventh century (604 C.E.), had already been accused of "Byzantinizing" or "Greek-izing" the Roman rite—a charge he hotly denied.[27]

There can be little doubt, then, that during the seventh century, especially, what we call "the Roman rite" was altered (in some cases dramatically) by the assimilation of imported Greek Byzantine culture. In fact, Stephen van Dijk specifically mentions *Ordo Romanus Primus* (OR I, the "First Roman Order of Service") as one of two "outstanding documents of Roman ecclesiastical High Society" which show the degree to which, especially during the pontificate of Pope Vitalian (657-672 C.E.), "imitation of Byzantine ideas and culture" shaped the liturgy of the papal court.[28] A look at the communion rite in OR I will illustrate this point. In early centuries, the act of distributing communion in both kinds to participants in the eucharist was ritually straightforward and simple. For example, the *First Apology* of Justin Martyr (ca. 150 C.E.), describes the distribution of communion in this way:

> And when the president [i.e., the one presiding at eucharist] has given thanks and all the people have assented, those whom we call deacons give to each one present a portion of the bread and wine and water over which thanks have been given, and take them to those who are not present.[29]

---

25. See J. Richards, *Consul of God: The Life and Time of Gregory the Great* (London: Routledge, 1980), 121; see also S. J. P. van Dijk, "The Urban and Papal Rites in Seventh and Eighth-Century Rome," *Sacris Erudiri* 12 (1961): 411-87.

26. Richards, *Consul of God,* 121.

27. See Gregory's letter to John, bishop of Syracuse, in Dag Norberg, ed., *S. Gregorii Magni Registrum Epistolarum,* vol. 2, *Libri viii-xiv* (Corpus Cristianorum 140A; Turnholt: Brepols, 1982), 586-87 (IX, 26).

28. Van Dijk, "Urban and Papal Rites," 467. OR I was probably compiled around the year 700 C.E. For an English translation of its description of the rituals used in a papal Mass (as celebrated in one of the Roman parish churches), see *Prayers of the Eucharist, Early and Reformed,* ed. R. C. D. Jasper and G. J. Cuming (2nd ed.; New York: Oxford University Press, 1980), 125-29.

29. English translation from Jasper and Cuming, *Prayers of the Eucharist Early and Reformed,* 19.

In Justin's description there is no evidence that the deacons use elaborate ceremonial when delivering the eucharistic elements to the people. The elements are affirmed as "the flesh and blood of the incarnate Jesus," but their reception is not highly ritualized.[30]

But the communion rite in OR I is quite a different story. Once the eucharistic prayer had ended (with the people's "Great Amen") and the Our Father and its embolism had been recited, a virtual army of ministers began the distribution of communion:

> The pope comes down from his seat with the chancellor and the chief counselor, to administer [communion] to those in the senatorial area, after which the archdeacon communicates them. After the archdeacon the bishops give the communion, the deacons administering after them. For (when) the pope came to give the communion, an acolyte went before him with a linen cloth hanging round his neck, with which he held the paten with the host. Likewise they [that is probably to say, the acolytes] go after the deacons also with ewers and bowls, pouring the wine into gemellions [basins] for the communion to the people. . . . When the chancellor nods, the presbyters, by command of the pope communicate the people in both kinds.
>
> Now as soon as the pope begins to give the communion in the senatorial area, the choir at once begin the communion antiphon by turns with the subdeacons, and *sing until all the people have been communicated*, and the pope nods for them to say *Glory be to the Father;* and then, when they have repeated the verse, they fall silent.
>
> The pope, as soon as he has communicated those on the women's side, returns to his seat and communicates the district officials in order as they stand in line. . . . When all have communicated, the pope sits down and washes his hands.[31]

Even a brief glance at this text in OR I reveals how ceremonially complex the communion rite had become. In Justin's description, ritual attention is focused on the deacons' ministry and the people's communion. In OR I, attention shifts from communion as a corporate act by the assembly to the *elaborate ritual choreography* now required for administering the sacrament in a socially stratified community (note the mention of the "senatorial area," the separate area for women, the ministry of archdeacon, deacons, subdeacons, acolytes, etc.) . The basic outline and sequence of events mentioned by Justin

---

30. Ibid.
31. Ibid., 127-29.

Martyr are still visible—gifts are brought, the presider utters a great thanks-giving prayer, consecrated bread and wine are shared among all present and taken to those absent—but the degree of ceremonial elaboration in OR I is astonishing when compared to the simplicity of Justin's rite.

Quite clearly, the seventh-century Roman liturgy had experienced a major and momentous Byzantine-based *reinculturation* that continues to shape our worship down to the present day. This reinculturation resulted, above all, in the introduction of a new *papal* liturgy, one "modeled on Byzantine ecclesi-astical and court ceremonial," a rite that differed dramatically from the old urban liturgy (and music) used by Christians in the Roman parish churches.[32] This new papal rite (as opposed to the older Roman parish liturgy) resulted from what van Dijk called "the spectacular growth of the pontiff's household and the parallel evolution of the station services" (visible, certainly, in the communion rite of OR I). The new shape given to the liturgy of the papal court and household was a consequence of imported Byzantine culture. "In its caesaropapism," writes van Dijk, "this [liturgy] had become a wonderland of unlimited treasure."[33]

"Caesaropapist magnificence": that phrase expresses, in a nutshell, the direction the Roman rite was to take over the next several centuries. In Jesus' meal ministry, eucharist was a ritual whose purpose was to establish commu-nion between people and God by establishing communion (through the reception of common food and drink) among participants. The source of that communion was Jesus' own sacrifice "for you and for all." Such a purpose is still plainly visible in Justin Martyr's *First Apology*, but it is far less apparent in OR I, where the communion rite has become a complex choreography that focuses not on the holy assembly—the *communio sanctorum* (the "communion of saints") whose *communicatio in sacris* ("participation in holy things") creates a *sacra communio* ("a holy communion")—but upon *the presiding celebrity, the pope*. The Roman liturgy was rapidly becoming a "celebrity rite," with the pope (or his surrogate) at its center. Increasingly, the *papal* liturgy (which slowly displaced the old Roman parish rite) required the services of skilled experts, especially for performance of its musical repertoire—trained singers whose presence constituted "at once, a political and artistic event, symboliz-ing and ensuring the pontiff's supremacy in the West."[34] Because of its sheer ceremonial complexity, this new papal rite tended to make the people passive spectators and listeners—a ritual role far different from the one the assembly

---

32. See Richards, *God's Consul*, 121.
33. Van Dijk, "Urban and Papal Rites," 467.
34. Ibid., 468.

played in the old Roman *urban* rite, whose distinguishing feature had been active "participation in the ritual by the congregation as well as the clergy."[35]

The fallout from this seventh- and eighth-century Byzantinization of the Roman rite was enormous. For as Roman liturgical forms evolved during the medieval era, they became populist in their rhetoric, but aristocratic and papal in their ritual structure. It was a liturgy designed to highlight the prestige of the papal household and especially the person of the pope himself. It was a liturgy organized around a "cult of personality" that promoted the parallels between papal and imperial power. And it relied on what van Dijk called "an ideal . . . which admitted no improvisation in its unapproachable and rigid etiquette."[36]

In sum, it was a liturgy that represented and reinforced the prestige of the papacy and the personality of the presider. This was "the" Roman rite whose "substantial unity" survived in the medieval *ordines* ("orders of service") of the papal court; that was diffused throughout Europe (especially through the activity and influence of the mendicant friars); that served as the basis for the "Tridentine" missal of 1570; and that continued in use until Vatican II (1962-65). It was entirely predictable that, when the Missal of Paul VI appeared in 1970, presiders would continue to behave as though *they* were the center of liturgical gravity, so to speak—simply because the very history of the Roman rite favors such a "celebrity model" for presiding at eucharist and at all forms of liturgical prayer. This model has been justly criticized by liturgists on both the left and the right, but it is still quite visible in papal and parish Masses celebrated throughout the world. To this day, Roman Catholics have a liturgy "for the people" that is still dominated by a disproportionate focus on the *presider.*

The Liturgical Role of the Ordained

Given this history, it is not suprising that the relation between ordained ministers and the assembly as primary agent or "subject" of the liturgical action (discussed above) remains a neuralgic issue in the Latin West. Sixteen centuries ago, St. Augustine spoke about his own service to the North African people of Hippo in these terms:

The Lord Jesus would not call any burden his own unless he carried it along with the one who bore it. You also: sustain me so that together,

35. Richards, *God's Consul*, 121.
36. Van Dijk, "Urban and Papal Rites," 467.

according to the apostle's command, we may bear one another's burdens and so fulfill the law of Christ. Unless he shoulders the load with us, we stumble; unless he carries us, we fall. When I am frightened by what I am for you, then I am consoled by what I am with you. For you I am a bishop; with you I am a Christian. The first is an office assumed, the second a grace bestowed; the first is dangerous, the second brings salvation. (*Sermon* 340.1)[37]

Augustine was well aware that the ordained presider at Sunday Mass is always, first, a member of the assembly. He understood the Catholic tradition that insists on a real, flesh-and-blood connection between clergy and local congregation. Nobody is ever ordained "at large." One must actually be connected, in service, to a place and a people, to a concrete, particular community—even if (as is the case with some titular bishops) that place is an ancient city now submerged under the Mediterranean! In Augustine's time, the bishop, as pastor of the local church, was the ordinary presider at eucharist. In our own day, the one who presides at Sunday Mass is usually a presbyter. Still, as Cardinal Mahoney writes in his pastoral letter *Gather Faithfully Together,*

the one who is called by the church to the order of priest is to be in the local parish community as the presence of the bishop. . . . On Sunday, the one who presides, the ordained priest, comes not only as other ministers do, from the assembly, but comes as the one who "orders" this assembly, who relates this assembly to the bishop and to the larger church. True to our Catholic soul, we understand our church bonds to be more flesh and blood than theory and theology. Here, in this human being, is our bond with the bishop and with the other communities throughout the world and the centuries. (32-33)

Clearly, the Catholic tradition recognizes an ancient and enduring *difference* between the ministries of the ordained and the nonordained within the Sunday assembly. No one denies this. Roman documents of the past decade, however, have emphasized this difference to an extraordinary (perhaps exaggerated) degree. For example, the Vatican document entitled "Some Questions Regarding Collaboration of Non-Ordained Faithful in Priests' Sacred Ministry" seems quite nervous about what it perceives as unwarranted intrusions by laypersons into ministry traditionally assigned to ordained clergy.[38]

---

37. Latin text in Marcella Recchia, ed., *Sant'Agostino, Discorsi*, Vol. V (Rome: Città Nuova Editrice, 1966), 995; my translation. Augustine's text is also cited in Vatican II's Dogmatic Constitution on the Church, *Lumen Gentium* 32.

38. This document was issued by the prefects of the Vatican congregations for Clergy, Laity, Evangelization, Bishops, Consecrated Life, Worship, and Doctrine of the Faith on August 15, 1997.

A similar disquiet is evident in *Sacramentum Redemptionis*, which seeks to limit and rein in lay ministers (such as those who serve as extraordinary ministers of the eucharist at Sunday Mass).[39]

Yet anyone who thinks the lay ministries that have blossomed since the end of the Second Vatican Council are meant to offer "competition" to the clergy has scant understanding of pastoral conditions in a global church. As the great theologian of interreligious dialogue, Jacques Dupuis, wrote,

> The real ecclesiological problem . . . consists less in defining the laity's place in the Church than in determining the function in it of the hierarchical priesthood . . . and in showing how it is related to the basic priestly reality of the People of God. Does not in the last analysis the priest's function in the Church community raise a more difficult question than does simply being a member of God's People? And has not our own time been marked by an identity crisis of priests rather than of lay people?[40]

Dupuis's point is well made. As Edward Hahnenberg comments, "The first question to ask about ministry today is not: Which tasks are proper to the clergy and which are proper to the laity? The important question is: How are the many ministries alive today to be ordered within the baptismal community?"[41] Laypeople who minister have neither the desire nor the intention of taking over the ordained priest's functions. They instinctively understand the difference between what *they* do and what *he* does. Most lay Catholics who minister at Sunday eucharist do so with dignity and gratitude. They are grateful to "stand in God's presence and serve," grateful for God's gracious initiative that calls them to faith and ministry; grateful for Jesus' lively presence in Word, prayer, and song, in gathered people, in bread and wine; grateful to *all* who minister (clergy included; see SC 7). They understand in their bones that what binds us together is more important than what separates or divides.

Still, for the past half-century or more, church authorities have emphasized a theological formula that stresses the *essential difference* between laity and clergy. The ordained priesthood, it is said, differs "*in essence and not merely in degree*" from the baptismal priesthood common to all Christians. But this phrase—foreshadowed in Pius XII's 1947 encyclical *Mediator Dei* (38-48), used at Vatican II in *Lumen Gentium* (10), and repeated in the *Catechism of the Catholic Church* (1992)—may easily be misinterpreted. It is often taken to

---

39. Issued by Cardinal Francis Arinze, Prefect of the Congregation for Divine Worship, on March 25, 2004.

40. Jacques Dupuis, "Lay People in Church and World: The Contribution of Recent Literature to a Synodal Theme," *Gregorianum* 68 (1987): 389-90.

41. Hahnenberg, *Ministries*, 209.

mean that the ordained clergy constitute an elite corps of ministers who are ontologically superior to all other Christians. This, as British theologian Michael Richards notes, is precisely what the phrase does *not* mean. When Vatican II asserted an "essential difference" between the ordained and the common priesthood of the baptized, it affirmed "essence" and set "degree" aside. The council was saying, writes Richards, "that if you want to understand what difference ordination makes, you must look for an *essential* difference, a difference *in kind* not a mere difference of degree."[42]

In short, by setting aside "degree," the council deliberately eliminated those associations we commonly attach to the word "hierarchy" (coercive power, rank, privilege, membership in an elitist corps of officers with its own internal order of importance). After carefully analyzing the Latin phrases used in *Lumen Gentium*, Richards reaches this conclusion:

> In this formal declaration of the mind of the Church, [hierarchy] can only be interpreted as a particular application of the teaching given by Christ to his Apostles. When they asked . . . 'Who is the greatest among them?' he told them that whoever wanted to be first must make himself the last and the servant of all: in other words, a person without rank, a non-hierarchical person, in the customary meaning of that word. . . .
>
> In seems abundantly clear that when the Second Vatican Council wanted to emphasise the special gift that is conferred by ordination and makes the priesthood of the ordained different in kind from the priesthood of the non-ordained, and chose to define it [by] the word "hierarchical," it did not thereby intend to say that the special gift is superiority in rank. It did not declare that bishops, presbyters and deacons are superior to the rest of us in the Church, and that this superiority constitutes the essence of their priesthood.[43]

"Worthy to Stand in Your Presence and Serve"

The council's teaching means, therefore, that we cannot use *secular* models of power to understand the difference between the ordained and the non-ordained in the assembly gathered for worship. Each kind of service is distinctive—and none is based on "rank" or "superior degree." Like baptism itself, ordination is neither a "promotion" nor a coronation. Both sacraments

---

42. Michael Richards, "Hierarchy and Priesthood," *Priests & People* 8, no. 6 (June 1994): 228-32, here 229 (emphasis added).
43. Ibid., 229 -30.

commit the Christian to "kitchen duty" in the kingdom of God—peeling potatoes, cooking, cleaning, serving, making sure that the least and the littlest are cared for. The ordained "teach," therefore, by washing feet; they "sanctify" by showing how God's power works as empowerment that heals and forgives; they "govern" by giving themselves away, after the example of Jesus who gave himself away at table and on the cross. Jesuit Gary Smith, whose principal pastoral ministry is among the poor and homeless of Portland, Oregon, describes a Holy Thursday celebration that illustrates how ordained ministry differs in "kind" but not in "rank" from laypersons in the church.

> Tonight at the Holy Thursday liturgy, many of the poor were present, having their feet gently washed. . . . When I saw it all in front of me—the poor, the washing basins, the awkwardness of the washers, the faces of the silent and reverent congregation—I realized once again what the sanctity of service is. . . .
>
> I remember thinking . . . that if I had to choose some relic of the Passion, I wouldn't pick up a scourge or a spear, but that round bowl of dirty water. And I would want to go around the world with that receptacle under my arm, looking only at people's feet; and for each one I'd tie a towel around me, bend down, and never raise my eyes higher than their ankles, so as not to distinguish friends from enemies. I'd wash the feet of atheists, drug addicts, arms dealers, murderers, pimps, abusers of all kinds—and all in silence, until they understood.[44]

What unites ordained and nonordained ministry is that "bowl of dirty water." As an icon of selfless service, foot washing not only molded the Last Supper narrative in John's Gospel; it also shaped the liturgy of Christian baptism in many Western Christian churches. As Ambrose, bishop of Milan (d. 397 C.E.), told the newly baptized, foot washing belongs essentially to the mystery of baptism; it

> consists in the very act of humble service, for Christ says: "If I, your Lord and Master, have washed your feet; how much more ought you to wash each other's feet?" For, since the very source of salvation has redeemed us through his obedience, how much more should we, his servants, offer the service of our humility and obedience? (*De mysteriis* 6.33; my translation)

Foot washing as an integral part of the liturgy of baptism did not disappear after Ambrose. Exhortations recalling Christ's action in John's Gospel as the warrant for baptismal foot washing are also found in many eighth-

---

44. Gary Smith, *Radical Compassion: Finding Christ in the Heart of the Poor* (Chicago: Loyola Press, 2002), 115-16.

century Gallican, Frankish, Spanish, and Italian sacramentaries.[45] For example: "The Lord and Savior Jesus Christ washed the feet of his disciples. I [the
priest or bishop] now wash your feet, so that you may do likewise to pilgrims
and strangers. If you do this, you will have lasting life for ever and ever."[46]

It is thus the theology of Christian initiation, rooted in Christ's own act of
foot washing, that illumines and defines the significance of *all* service in the
church, whether it is performed by lay ministers or by ordained bishops,
priests, and deacons. As Thomas Aquinas knew, the one and only priesthood
that exists among Christians is that of Christ, whose passion began with acts
of foot washing and feeding at the Supper and was completed on the cross.[47]
Sacramental initiation—baptism, chrismation ("confirmation"), eucharist—is
the radical source of all Christian participation in that priesthood, whether by
laypersons or by the ordained. Such participation, Aquinas explained, defines
what Christians mean by sacramental "character."[48] Character is not an
object, a thing, or (as the *Baltimore Catechism* used to say) an "indelible mark,"
but a *relationship*, a God-given empowerment that connects Christians per-
manently to the priesthood of Christ and so to membership in the church
and participation in its liturgy.[49] That is precisely why SC 14 linked "full,
conscious, active participation in liturgical celebrations" to the "royal priesthood" that is ours "by reason of baptism," the root sacrament that renders
Christians "ready for ritual," ready to take their places at the Lord's table.[50]

---

45. Ironically, perhaps, it was the Roman church—among the many Latin churches of Western
Christianity—that omitted the baptismal foot washing. Ambrose alludes to this anomaly in his mys-
tagogic catecheses *De sacramentis* 3.5-6. See Edward Yarnold, *The Awe-Inspiring Rites of Initiation:
Baptismal Homilies of the Fourth Century* (Slough, UK: St. Paul Publications, 1972), 122-23.

46. The Latin text of this prayer may be found in *Missale Gallicanum Vetus*, ed. Leo Cunibert
Mohlberg (Rerum eccesiasticarum documenta, series maior, Fontes III; Rome: Herder, 1958), no.
176, p. 42; my translation.

47. See Thomas Aquinas, *Summa Theologiae* IIIa Pars, Q. 35, art. 7, corpus.

48. As Eliseo Ruffini noted in an essay entitled "Character as a Concrete Visible Element of the
Sacrament in Relation to the Church" (in *The Sacraments in General: A New Perspective*, ed. E. Schillebeeckx and B. Willems [Concilium 31; New York: Paulist Press, 1968], 101-14), medieval theologians
in the century before Aquinas correctly discerned the sacramental structure of "character" (i.e., they
saw that while the baptismal rite is transitory, the condition of baptism itself remains), but they perhaps forgot the Augustinian doctrine that was based on "a clear perception of the ecclesial dimension
of baptism. For Augustine, baptism . . . was primarily the act of definitive aggregation to the community of salvation; hence, character was in a certain manner the visible prolongation of the baptismal
act itself." In their concern for baptism as "purificatory" (it wipes out "original sin"), the early scholas-
tics may have overlooked the essentially ecclesial significance of the sacrament (pp. 104-5). Meanwhile, in the thirteenth century, Aquinas's doctrine of character, rooted in the Christian's participation
in Christ's priesthood, represented a "notable turn" because it stressed the baptized person's empowerment to worship—"not to private and subjective worship but to the worship which continues that
of Christ the priest and finds its realization in the visible cultic activity of the church" (ibid., 106).

49. Thomas Aquinas, *Summa Theologiae* IIIa Pars, Q. 63, art. 1, corpus; art. 5, corpus; see also IIIa
Pars, Q. 64, art. 1, corpus.

50. On the use of the image of "royal priesthood" by Christian writers (e.g., 1 Pet 2.9), see my
study *Mission and Ministry: History and Theology in the Sacrament of Order* (Wilmington, Del.:
Michael Glazier, 1982), 283-84.

That is also why, according to the ancient *Ordo Romanus* XI (describing the liturgy of baptism), newly baptized and chrismated Christians were vested in stole and chasuble (*stola, casula*) for presentation to the bishop, who "confirmed them with an invocation of the sevenfold grace of the Holy Spirit."[51] Investiture with stole and chasuble reflected the initiands' new priestly relation to Christ and community.

There is thus no "two-track" system of priesthood in the church, for the simple reason that, as Aquinas put it, "The whole ritual structure of the Christian religion is derived from the priesthood of Christ. It is obvious, therefore, that when we speak of 'sacramental character,' we are speaking of Christ's own priestly power, to which the faithful are configured through sacraments."[52] The root of all priesthood in the church—that of the baptized individual, that of the celebrating assembly, that of the ordained—is *relational*. That relation exists, always and only, for the sake of *communion*; and that communion exists not in some "divinized . . . abstract universal" unity but, as Vatican II saw it, in *concrete local communities*:[53]

> This church of Christ is really present in all legitimately organized local groups of the faithful, which, in so far as they are united to their pastors, are also quite appropriately called Churches in the New Testament. For these are in fact, in their own localities, the new people called by God, in the power of the Holy Spirit and as the result of full conviction (cf. 1 Thes 1:5). In them the faithful are gathered together through the preaching of the Gospel of Christ, and the mystery of the Lord's Supper is celebrated "so that, by means of the flesh and blood of the Lord the whole membership of the Body may be welded together. In any community existing around an altar, under the bishop's sacred ministry, a manifest symbol is to

---

51. See texts in E. C. Whitaker, *Documents of the Baptismal Liturgy*, revised and expanded by Maxwell E. Johnson (Collegeville, Minn.: Liturgical Press, 2003), 244-51, here, 251. *Ordo Romanus* XI probably reflects usages from about the year 700 C.E., but its manuscript witnesses date from a later period (the ninth century), and it is unclear whether OR XI represents "purely Roman practice" or Roman customs as revised by Frankish editors.

52. Thomas Aquinas, *Summa Theologiae* IIIa Pars, Q. 63, art. 3, corpus.

53. In 1992, the Congregation for the Doctrine of the Faith (CDF) issued a document ("Some Aspects of the Church Understood as Communion") which attempted "to counter approaches to [ecclesial] communion that overemphasize the local church" (see Hahnenberg, *Ministries*, 119). The CDF insisted that the "essential mystery" of the church is "a reality ontologically and temporally prior to every individual particular church." While it is certainly true that Vatican II spoke in *Lumen Gentium* of the "mystery of the church," and while it linked that mystery to God's one, eternal plan to invite all humanity into communion with "his own divine life" (LG 1, 2), it also linked that mystery to the concrete history of salvation, to God's historical action in and among people. Thus, LG 2 argues that the church could be said to exist from "the time of Adam, 'from Abel, the just one, to the last of the elect,'" whom God will gather when the world ends and history is consummated (LG 2). In short, "mystery" cannot be separated from "history." There can be no "church" apart from the people God calls to share the divine life. That is why LG follows its first chapter, on the "mystery" of the church, with a second, "on the pilgrim people of God."

be seen of the charity and unity of the mystical body. . . . In these communities, though they may often be small and poor, or existing in the diaspora, Christ is present through whose power and influence the One, Holy, Catholic and Apostolic Church is constituted" (LG 26).

This text makes it clear that communion is not something the clergy produce for the people; it is, rather, the result of God's own "calling a new people in the power of the Spirit," gathering them "through the preaching of the gospel," and leading them to "the mystery of the Lord's Supper" whose goal is always (as Aquinas, quoting Augustine, recognized), "the church's unity."[54] The ordained minister to that process; they do not create it. As my teacher Aidan Kavanagh used to say, Christ died, rose, and became a people. That is the source of Christian service and ministry; that is the source of priesthood in the church; and that is the source of the church's communion in faith, life, and sacrament:

> Baptism and eucharist are really one corporate person dying and rising. That is a lot to load onto simple things like water and oil, bread and wine. But they never complain. They have never sinned either. They are faithful and close to God in their original innocence, . . . to a degree that staggers one's imagination. To become like them is what he came to show us. They are superb as God meant us to be. To get that way is a passion for us who have fallen, as it were, into reason.[55]

The point here is not that baptized laypersons and ordained ministers have "competing" priesthoods. It is a mistake to interpret the "royal priesthood" of the laity by using the sacrament of holy orders as a model. Baptism should not be construed as an "ordination," even though *Ordo Romanus* XI and Aquinas's theology *do* insist—the one by ritual gesture, the other by theological argument—that baptismal participation in *Christ's* priesthood empowers and equips Christians for liturgy. Nor, as Hahnenberg points out, is priesthood a "metaphor for ministry."[56] Instead, "the foundation upon which the communication of sacerdotality rests," for the baptized as well as for the ordained, "is primarily communion with Christ in his Church rather than the sacramental acts of baptism or holy orders taken in themselves and abstracted

---

54. Thomas Aquinas, *Summa Theologiae* IIIa Pars, Q. 22, art. 6, ad 2um. Aquinas understood that the purpose of Christ's real presence in the eucharistic elements was precisely "the unity of the body that is the church.""The sacrament of the eucharist ," wrote Thomas, "pertains especially to love [*caritatem*]: for it is the sacrament of the church's unity [*cum sit sacramentum ecclesiasticae unionis*], containing the very One in whom the whole church is united and strengthened—namely, Christ himself. Therefore the eucharist is the very origin or bond of love [*eucharistia est quasiquadam caritatis origo sive vinculum*]" (*Summa Theologiae*, Suppl. Q. 71, art. 9, corpus; ad 3um).
55. Aidan Kavanagh, "Initiation: Baptism and Confirmation," *Worship* 46 (1972): 270.
56. Hahnenberg, *Ministries*, 175.

apart from this same communion."[57] Thus, whatever its form—ordained or nonordained—Christian ministry leads not to the arrogance of power, but to the humble prayer that we become worthy "to stand in Your presence and serve You." We pray to become worthy of water and oil, bread and wine—elements innocent, faithful, close to God. We pray to become superb as God meant us to be. We pray to become worthy of the poor, of the people we serve.

Touched by Fire: Becoming a Liturgical Assembly

Thus, as Kavanagh remarks, the church

> baptizes to priesthood: it ordains only to executive exercise of that priesthood in the major orders of ministry. . . . Nor does sacerdotality come upon one for the first time . . . at one's ordination. In constant genesis in the font, the Church is born there as a sacerdotal assembly by the Spirit of the Anointed One himself.[58]

Ordination does not mean, therefore, that one forfeits either baptism or membership in the assembly. All who minister liturgically in the church serve from within the assembly. But who or what is that assembly?

In the late 1930s, the distinguished German theologian Romano Guardini wrote a series of meditations later published under the title *Meditations before Mass*. Speaking about the significance of the liturgical assembly, Guardini commented that the Christian congregation is not simply a voluntary association of like-minded people; it comes to exist when the "living Christ" in their midst (Matt 18:20) leads them before the face of the Father in the power of the Holy Spirit. The congregation is called forth by God's initiative, but that call—as divine invitation *and* response of faith—is *contingent on the presence of justice.* Only when "the injustice that isolates has been overcome" can the congregation come to be. The liturgical assembly is thus born of the communion that follows *forgiveness.* It is a community of the forgiven, and hence forgiveness belongs to its very definition. Forgiveness, Guardini notes, is neither prudence ("we'd better hedge our bets"), indifference ("it doesn't matter anyway"), false friendliness ("inverted hostility"), or cowardice ("better flee than fight").[59] What is given in forgiveness is not simply the cancel-

---

57. Aidan Kavanagh, "Unfinished and Unbegun Revisited: The Rite of Christian Initiation of Adults," *Worship* 53 (1979): 338.

58. Ibid., 335-36.

59. Romano Guardini, *Preparing Yourself for Mass*, foreword by Henri J. M. Nouwen (Manchester, N.H.: Sophia Institute Press, 1993), 96-98. This English edition of Guardini's work was originally published by the Newman Press in 1956, under the title, *Meditations before Mass.*

lation of debts or absolution from sin and error, but God's own self. Forgiveness, as Thomas Sheehan writes, is nothing less than *God, given-for:* "the arrival of God in the present, his superabundant gift of himself to his people."[60]

Forgiveness is thus not our work for God, but God's action on our behalf, God doing for us what we cannot do for ourselves. Rectifying injustice—the "condition of possibility" for a Christian congregation, a liturgical assembly—does not result from human willingness and labor alone. Guardini sums it up well:

> The commandment to forgive one's enemies might have been expressed: "Know that you can forgive your enemy because Christ on the Cross forgave his; it is he who effects forgiveness in you." . . .
>
>   The forgiveness of Christ . . . means that divine love gains a footing in us, creating that new order which is meant to reign among the sons and daughters of God.[61]

So the liturgical assembly does not invent or constitute itself. It can exist only when injustice is overcome, and that can happen only through God's forgiveness. Injustice isolates, divides, drives people apart, and hence, before there can be feast, there has to be forgiveness. Daniel Berrigan has made this point powerfully in a commentary on the cleansing of the prophet Isaiah's lips, "touched with fire" (Isa 6:1-13). The work of justice and forgiveness—*God's* work—demands a truthfulness, Berrigan notes, that lies quite "beyond our own capacity, which leans entirely toward self-deception." Justice and forgiveness require lips and lives "touched by fire," because "the truth of our condition, verified on every hand," is that we are "blind, deaf, and worst of all heartless. Our depredations, the stench of blood, are evident across the world." And so, what happened to the prophet Isaiah—who was touched by a purifying fire that burnt up his past—has to happen to us if we are to become "a liturgical assembly." A "community, a circle about the fire, is not merely warmed by the fire, but touched by the fire, marked indelibly"; and hence, writes Berrigan, "going through the motions of this or that desultory liturgy" will only convict us of appeasement and bad faith.[62]

No one understood better than the prophet Isaiah the futility of making a liturgy a "hideout," a place of refuge for those whose practice of injustice puts

---

60. Thomas Sheehan, *The First Coming: How the Kingdom of God Became Christianity* (1986; New York: Random House Vintage Books, 1988), 66.

61. Guardini, *Meditations before Mass*, 98.

62. Daniel Berrigan, *Isaiah: Spirit of Courage, Gift of Tears* (Minneapolis: Fortress Press, 1996), 27-35, esp. 33.

them at risk. Here, says Isaiah (in the poetic paraphrase of David Rosenberg), is God's reaction to *that* little scheme:

> Look up from the self-indulgence
> of gilt-edged prayers
> the sentimental eyewash
> of the time you "sacrifice"
> the money of your ritual donations
> to make yourself feel better . . .
> I've seen enough
> of your distracted meditation and mysteries.
> [I'm tired, God thunders, of your]
> trampling through my sanctuary . . .
> with your precious albums
> your unreal books
> your desperate fantasy of prayer
> I want no more sacred mirrors
> of yourselves
> the microphones of your empty voices . . .
> I can't stand your weird impersonations
> of spiritual beings / your minutes of meditation
> and Sundays off
> I hate that cheap
> indulgence of spirit . . .
> your hands are full of blood.[63]

Isaiah's admonitions about a God who cannot abide injustice and loathes "cheap indulgence of spirit" are not mere rhetorical flourishes. The "great feast" (Isa 26:6-8) truly *is* the divine plan for all humanity, but the God who sets the table is a "consuming fire" (Isa 33:14) that sears what it touches. God's arrival as forgiveness—God's coming as One who reverses injustice— is what makes a community of life and liturgy possible. God's justice rains food and drink, but not before it rains righteousness (another word for "judgment"). Most of us, of course, want no such thing. We prefer to jail peacemakers and declare unpatriotic those who question war. Meanwhile, we train "death squad leaders" whose "curriculum includes modes of torture." We prefer "the fictions of the powerful," whose "measured responses" and "high-level decisions" are described as "doing God's work."[64]

---

63. David Rosenberg, *A Poet's Bible: Rediscovering the Voices of the Original Text* (New York: Hyperion, 1991), 228-30 (material in brackets added).

64. Berrigan, *Isaiah*, 84.

Against all such moral numbness stands the "just one" of Isaiah's prophecy, who "refuses to listen to plans involving bloodshed" and promises life renewed in "the city of our feasts," home to a community of the forgiven (Isa 33:15, 20, 24; *New Jerusalem Bible* translation). Jesus' command to "go first and be reconciled" (Matt 5:24) is thus firmly rooted in ancient Jewish prophecy like Isaiah's. If bread and feasting are the chief icons of God's gathered community—and if bread is always about bodies—then the conclusion is inescapable: there can be no true liturgical assembly in the absence of justice. When Christians gather for Sunday worship, they assemble as a community of the forgiven, of the repentant who "dance in the fiery knot of [God's] judgment." In that dance, they discover "a great mercy":

> To judge . . . is not to condemn.
> To judge is not to condone.
> To judge is to announce God the merciful, not God
>   the neutral.
> To be judged is not to be condemned.
> To be judged is not to be condoned.
> To be judged is to undergo God the merciful, not God
>   the neutral.
>   Finally, to be judged is to hearken and submit to the voice
> of community. This judgment is rendered active and merciful, both an acceptance and an invitation to conversion.[65]

FROM ASSEMBLY TO SACRAMENT

Because it is a baptized community of the forgiven—of the repentant, the always converting—the ecclesial assembly's own identity is sacramental in structure. This point was clearly recognized in the documents of the Second Vatican Council, especially the Dogmatic Constitution on the Church (*Lumen Gentium*) and the Pastoral Constitution on the Church in the Modern World (*Gaudium et Spes*). The ecclesiology contained in *Lumen Gentium* and *Gaudium et Spes* considerably broadened our understanding of how God, church, and world are interrelated. For starters, the council stressed the single, "all-embracing divine salvation" that has existed from the very "beginning of human history, even when there was not yet . . . a community of believers gathered on the basis of a special revelation."[66] The "utterly gratuitous and

---

65. Ibid., 88-89.
66. Jan Groot, "The Church as Sacrament of the World," in *The Sacraments in General: A New*

mysterious design" of God's "wisdom and goodness created the whole universe and chose to raise up men and women to share in his own divine life" (LG 2). God's gracious design thus embraces everything and everyone—and predates the historical revelations found in the history of Israel and in the mystery of the Word made flesh. Both *Lumen Gentium* and *Gaudium et Spes* could thus speak of the church's role as a *sacramentum mundi* ("sacrament of the world"), the visible sign of the "saving unity" that embodies God's will and intention not only for humankind but for creation itself.[67]

By invoking the language of sacrament in order to describe its relation to world, history, humanity, and cosmos, the church acknowledged that *it* is not the center of the universe. In the documents of Vatican II, Groot states, the church began to see itself as "no longer the real center round which the whole of human history circles," even as it recognized the "special and important function" that it is destined "to fulfill in that history." In short, the church began to acknowledge its sacramental character as "sign and instrument" of that "salvation, justice and peace" that God wills for all humanity, all history, and the entire created cosmos.[68] God's Wisdom, Word, and Spirit, the council affirmed, speak and work through the length and breadth of human history in what Karl Rahner named "the liturgy of the world" and in what Jewish philosopher Emmanuel Levinas called "the liturgy of the neighbor." As Jacques Dupuis has pointed out, this conciliar sacramental ecclesiology forms a new context for understanding how Christians are related to a world characterized by a "pluralism of cultures and of religious traditions," each of which has a "right to its own difference." Hence, writes Dupuis,

> the one divine plan of salvation for all peoples embraces the whole universe. The mission of the Church has to be understood within the context of this plan. The Church does not monopolize God's action in the universe. While it is aware of a special mission of God in the world, it has to be attentive to God's action in the world, as manifested also in the other religions. . . . While proclamation is the expression of its awareness of being in mission, dialogue is the expression of its awareness of presence and action outside its boundaries.[69]

Perspective, ed. Edward Schillebeeckx and Boniface Willems (Concilium 31; New York: Paulist Press, 1968), 51-66, here, 51.

67. See LG 9: "that for each and for all she [the church] may be the visible sacrament of saving unity." LG 1 and GS 42: "the church, in Christ, is . . . sacrament—sign and instrument—of communion with God and unity among all peoples." Cf. Col 1:19-20: "In him all the fullness was pleased to dwell, and through him to reconcile all things for him, making peace by the blood of the cross, whether those on earth or those in heaven."

68. Groot, "Church as Sacrament of the World," 52.

69. Jacques Dupuis, "The Church's Evangelising Mission in the Context of Religious Pluralism," *Pastoral Review* (online edition, March 2005): I.2.

Like the church itself, Christian liturgy exists not for its own sake but for the *world's* sake; it exists to point to the liturgy of the world, the liturgy of the neighbor. That is why Vatican II's Declaration on the Relation of the Church to Non-Christian Religions (*Nostra Aetate* [NA; 1965]) spoke about what is "true and holy" in other religions (NA 2). It acknowledged Christianity's special relationship to Judaism and also affirmed the "spiritual and moral truths" found in the prayer, teaching, ritual, social life, and culture of world faiths such as Hinduism, Buddhism, and Islam. At the same time, *Nostra Aetate* utterly rejected as contrary to human dignity "any discrimination against people or any harassment of them on the basis of their race, color, condition in life or religion" (NA 5). In a nutshell, like the "option for the poor," the Christian commitment to interreligious dialogue is not a "take-it-or-leave-it" matter; it is a theological and pastoral necessity, especially in a post–9/11 world.

Nostra Aetate's affirmation of interreligious dialogue as belonging essentially to the sacramental structure of the church (its condition as "sign and instrument of the world's unity") has also served to broaden our understanding of sacraments generally three theological principles support this more inclusive understanding of sacrament:

Principle 1. The "mystery of unity." Gaudium et Spes not only insisted that the church is a *sacramentum mundi*, but that all humanity has *one* vocation, rooted in our origins and our destiny, a point powerfully made in GS 22. *"Since Christ died for all human beings,"* that paragraph tells us, *"and since all humans are in fact called to one and the same destiny, which is divine, we must hold that the Holy Spirit—in a manner known to God alone—offers to every person the possibility of being made partner in the paschal mystery."* We thus believe —and our church teaches—that God has a single plan of salvation in which all human persons are invited to participate. This is not, of course, a new belief; but what is new is the insistence of *Gaudium et Spes* that all peoples are called to become "partners in the paschal mystery" by *"the Holy Spirit . . . in a way known to God alone."* The council thereby affirmed that all women and men *do* share a common vocation, a common destiny, although they do not necessarily share it the same way. As Dupuis said, in a world of diverse cultures and religious traditions, each has a "right to its own difference."[70]

Principle 2. The universal action of God's Spirit in the world. A second principle that has helped to broaden the notion of sacramentality was developed especially by Pope John Paul II, who affirmed *the active presence of God's Spirit in the religious traditions of other peoples*, especially *in their life of prayer*. Just as God's Word spoke *before* and *during, after* and *beyond*, Jesus' life, min-

---

70. Ibid., first paragraph.

istry, passion, death, and rising, so too God's Spirit worked *before* and *during*, *after* and *beyond*, that same life of Jesus.[71] The Spirit's "presence and activity are universal," wrote John Paul II in his 1990 encyclical *Redemptoris Missio*; that activity affects "not only individuals but also society and history, peoples, cultures, and religions" (28). In short, God's "Spirit of truth operates outside the visible confines of [Christ's] Mystical Body" (*Redemptor Hominis* 6)[72] and thus the *differences* that exist between religions are, to quote this same pope's words, "a less important element than the[ir] unity which, by contrast, is radical, basic, and decisive."[73] In short, the culture and religions of other peoples are not "pitiful aberrations" but places where Christians are called to recognize the real presence and activity of God's Spirit.[74] And just as God's Spirit-filled action does not cancel the church's mission to proclaim the gospel, so the church's mission does not cancel the Spirit's presence in the faith, prayer, culture, and religious practice of other peoples.

Principle 3. The universality of God's reign. Jesus' own image for humanity's final destiny was the reign or rule or "kingdom" of God. As I have mentioned several times in this book, God's plan for all peoples can be summarized in a single word—*dinner*. God's reign, as Jesus saw it, was neither a place nor a program, but a meal to which all peoples in all times and places are called to participate, and during the course of which it is the task of Christians not to preside grandly but to be the kitchen help, the servers, the guys with bowls of dirty water in their hands. The sacramental structure of the church thus points to a common sacramental destiny—a universal feasting in the presence of God that signals the arrival of justice, peace, and unity for humankind, history, world, and cosmos.

Entering Other Worlds: Letting Oneself Be Changed

The church's commitment to interreligious dialogue, affirmed in principle in *Nostra Aetate*, thus flows from its own sacramental structure and from the sacramental destiny of human persons and their history. But how, concretely,

---

71. See Jacques Dupuis, *Christianity and the Religions: From Confrontation to Dialogue* (Maryknoll, N.Y.: Orbis Books, 2003), 110-13, 156-61.

72. Cited in Dupuis, "Church's Evangelising Mission," 8.

73. John Paul II, Speech to members of the Roman curia (December 22, 1986); cited in Dupuis, "Church's Evangelising Mission," 8.

74. In speaking of the prophet Muhammad, Jacques Dupuis cites R. C. Zaehner's opinion that "it is impossible to read the two books [Hebrew Bible and the Qurʾan] without concluding that it is the same God who speaks in both." Thus it is increasingly common among Christian theologians to acknowledge "Muhammad as a genuine prophet of God" and the Qurʾan as a holy book which, while "not without error" contains "divine truth" that is a "word of God uttered through the prophet." See Dupuis, *Christianity and the Religions*, 126.

is such dialogue done? Perhaps the best model comes from Jesus' own prophetic and pastoral activity. Recall the story found in Mark (7:25-30) and Matthew (15:21-28) about the "Syrophoenician woman" who comes to Jesus asking help for her daughter. As scholars note, the story is potentially explosive, even scandalous, because the woman is "doubly marginal": she is (1) "a woman alone in a man's world," and (2) a gentile whom devout Jews would avoid as "unclean."[75] In other words, both the woman's religion and her ethnicity were suspect in Jesus' world. She prays, but her prayers aren't those of Jewish Scripture and liturgy. Her prayer is her desperation; her prayer is her body and her boldness; her prayer is her daughter's need. At first Jesus is put off by her "otherness," her difference: "It isn't right," he says, "to take the children's food (i.e., the gifts God gave the Jewish people) and throw it to the dogs" (Mark 7:27). Quicker than lightning, the woman picks up Jesus' image and turns it to her own advantage. "Well, right," she says; "but even the puppies under the table eat the children's crumbs" (Mark 7:28). Jesus appears to have been stunned. And more shocking still, *he lets himself be changed by this pagan woman's attitude.* Indeed, by story's end, *both* Jesus *and* the woman are changed by the encounter. Neither converts to the other's religion—Jesus remains a Jew, the woman remains a gentile—but each of them enters more deeply into the mystery of God's plan for humankind, a plan that embraces all persons. The woman's faith (it's *real* faith, even if it isn't *Jewish* faith) leaves Jesus awestruck: "Woman," he says, "your faith is great; let it be done for you as you wish" (Matt 15:28).

The story of Jesus and the Syrophoenician woman makes a further point: Jesus changes precisely because this pagan woman helps him *imagine* God's action in the world in a new way; helps him see the sheer wideness of God's mercy, the breathtaking scope of God's plan to save all peoples. *Imagination* is key. If we want to enter another's religious world—to learn how, what, and why that person believes—we have to break free of business as usual. As Judith Berling has written, commenting on the pedagogical model developed by Maxine Greene, imagination

> is not just the isolated ability to envision bits and pieces of the as-yet unthought, but is rather the faculty that expands our horizons beyond "the givens" and opens up a vast realm of alternatives and possibilities. Imagination has an ethical and social dimension; it opens up . . . alternative[s] . . . [it creates] new possibilities for human community.[76]

---

75. See Benedict Viviano, "Matthew," in *The New Jerome Biblical Commentary*, ed. Raymond E. Brown et al. (Englewood Cliffs, N.J.: Prentice-Hall, 1990), 42:100 (p. 658).

76. Judith A. Berling, *Understanding Other Religious Worlds: A Guide for Interreligious Education* (Maryknoll, N.Y.: Orbis Books, 2004), 27.

Perhaps the best way to prepare ourselves for the expanded vision of sacramentality that interreligious dialogue requires is to visit an art gallery or to accompany your kids to their school art class. Art is not simply about seeing; it is about what was never seen before, about seeing *differently*. That is why art moves and disturbs us, propels us toward change. What the Syrophoenician woman did for Jesus was verbal art, repartee: she picked up his image and threw it back in his face with a twist so novel that it almost gave him whiplash. That is what it means to "learn through imagination"; to enter another's world.

Finally, an expanded understanding of sacrament invites us to affirm faith while engaging otherness. As Berling notes, "Serious bilateral dialogue, if its goal is genuine understanding, profoundly engages difference and constrains any rush to identify similarities."[77] If we are to speak of church as *sacramentum mundi* or to affirm the common "sacramental destiny" of humankind, we have to *let others be other*. Interreligious dialogue is not an excuse for treating other religious traditions as "anonymously Christian" or pretending that unity has arrived when none exists. To come to a deep and reverent appreciation of how and why others believe as they do requires patience, openness, a mutually critical "give-and-take," the willingness to affirm not only similarities but real differences. As Pope Benedict XVI commented in a homily on the day after his election, our mission as servants of the gospel is to reach out to "everybody, even those who follow other religions or who simply look for an answer to life's fundamental questions and still haven't found it."[78]

Rewriting Sacrament

The challenge to broaden our notions of sacramentality arises not only from conciliar ecclesiology and the demands of interreligious dialogue, but from within the Catholic theological tradition itself. In an intriguing article, "Ritual and Text in the Renaissance," Thomas M. Greene analyzes a pattern of *reinterpreting* sacrament that had already begun in the late medieval period in the West. Greene points to what he calls "the waning of the ceremonial sign," an "incipient, massive, slow, uneven, almost invisible process" that was already under way in Dante's *Commedia* and reached a literary climax in the work of Cervantes and Shakespeare.[79] Greene attributes this decline to early moder-

---

77. Ibid., 55.

78. Reported on the front page of the *New York Times*, Wednesday, April 20, 2005.

79. Thomas M. Greene, "Ritual and Text in the Renaissance," *Canadian Review of Comparative Literature/Revue Canadienne de Littérature Comparée* 15 (June-September 1991): 179-97. Greene

nity's repudiation of the medieval view that ritual is "life-defining," that its symbols create a sacred canopy under which all aspects of public life find meaning and coherence. "The repeated, symbolic, communal, formal, efficacious act," Greene writes, "not only focused and defined the life of the church but also the life of the court, the city, the guild, the confraternity, the law court, the university, the aristocratic house and manor, the rustic countryside."[80] It would not strain credulity, Greene concludes, to argue that "each medieval individual" was "endowed with a ceremonial identity" acquired through repeated participation in the church's sacramental liturgy.[81] True, the medieval period had its fair share of doubters and debunkers; France had its Cathars and Albigensians, and later, England had its Lollards. All these groups disputed or denied the "ceremonial identity" bestowed by symbol and sacrament; but in the main, medieval Christians in Western Europe appear to have affirmed both the appropriateness and the efficacy of liturgy's ritual discourse.[82]

Slowly, however, this medieval consensus about the efficacy of ritual symbols began to erode and dissolve. The medieval church's reliance on what Greene calls "apotropaic" semiotics gave way to early modernity's "disjunctive semiotics," a denial of any real relation between representation and referent, sign and signified, symbol and subject. Greene believes that this erasure of medieval convictions about the liturgy's ritual efficacy led not only to a "crisis" in the publicly shared, performative sign, but to a transference of its power from *sacerdotium* to *imperium*, from church to court. The creation of symbolic unity in the body politic—a task late medieval Christians assigned to the liturgy (and especially, to the eucharist) —had now migrated into the hands of monarchs and magistrates. "Arguably . . . ," Greene writes,

> the sixteenth century provided more ritual and ceremonial occasions than any other century. . . . The newly powerful, centralized monarchies of the sixteenth century learned how to use ceremonial occasions brilliantly in order to aggrandize their prestige. The medieval solemnity of the royal entry into a city received a new éclat; chivalric contests like the tilt and the joust were perpetuated; *mascarades* . . . celebrated monarch and court with

---

notes the "uncertain statue of ceremony" in Shakespeare, whose plays are "rich in experimentiation with ceremonial symbolism and parody" (pp. 192-94). He observes that Shakespeare presents the coronation scene in *Richard II* as a "ritual in reverse," a "public de-coronation." Cervantes, for his part, *seems* bent on demystifying ceremony, reducing it to brute realism and transparence. But as Greene deftly shows, Cervantes' travesty is a trap, for his ultimate intention is to *remystify* ceremony in a *secular* mode that is anti-institutional and tragic (pp. 194-95).

80. Ibid., 179-80.

81. Ibid., 180.

82. It was the liturgy's symbolic discourse that provided a framework for the innovative art and spirituality of women like Hildegard of Bingen and Mechtilde of Magdeburg. See my essay, "The Struggle of Religious Women for Eucharist," *Benedictines* 52, no. 2 (Winter 1999): 12-25.

lavish splendor. But these brilliant fetes heightened a manipulative element which had doubtless always been present. Despite their brilliance, we can no longer speak of the society of 1600 as we could in 1200 as a basically ceremonial society. In a growing sector of this society, we can no longer speak of ceremonial identity. During the religious wars in France, partisan mobs used ceremonial forms for their own brutal purposes, in what Natalie Davis has called "rites of violence." The traditional performative sign was called into question. . . . *[W]e are compelled to recognize . . . a profound reversal in human techniques of signification.*[83]

Greene's thesis is echoed in Edward Muir's more recent, book-length study, entitled *Ritual in Early Modern Europe*.[84] The Reformation of the sixteenth century is best understood, Muir argues, as "a revolution in ritual theory."[85] In support of his position, Muir notes that late-medieval lay Catholics based their religious practice on three assumptions: First, that ritual deeds, words, and objects (relics, for example, or the words of consecration, or the eucharistic Host) create *a real, physical bond* between people and God; second, that human interaction with these objects is primarily sensual and aesthetic rather than cognitive or rational; and third, that matter gives access to mystery, perceived *in* and *as* manners. "Late medieval Christians," Muir writes,

> expected to find the sacred manifest itself in material objects that could be seen, touched, smelled, tasted, and ingested. As the codification of a ritual system, the official sacraments and semi-official sacramentals depended upon the assumption that divine and saintly beings would make themselves present in material objects in response to the supplications of humans. These contractual, aesthetic, and sensual characteristics meant that Christian ritual demanded the presence of human and divine bodies to work its wonders.[86]

Although erudite dissenters like Wyclif and Hus had challenged all these assumptions in the fourteenth and fifteenth centuries, a full-blown "crisis of the communal, performative sign" finally erupted in the sixteenth century, as Reformers sought to create (in Muir's words) "a new theological metaphysics by drawing precise boundaries between the spiritual and material worlds, breaking the deeply mysterious connections between the two made evident in traditional rituals."[87]

In formulating his theory about the Reformation as a "revolution in ritual

83. Greene, "Ritual and Text in the Renaissance," 182-83 (emphasis added).
84. Edward Muir, *Ritual in Early Modern Europe* (New York: Cambridge University Press, 1997).
85. Ibid., 155-81.
86. Ibid., 157.
87. Ibid., 181.

theory" that results from a crisis in the "performative sign,"[88] Muir acknowledges his debt to the research of two scholars, Miri Rubin and Virginia Reinburg. Rubin's study *Corpus Christi: The Eucharist in Late Medieval Culture*
offers illumination to anyone seeking to understand Western Christian ritual
discourse as it was evolving early in the second millennium. From about the
year 1100 onward, Rubin argues, "the language of religion provided a language of social relations, and of a cosmic order; it described and explained the
interweaving of natural and supernatural with human action in a paradigm
which . . . was one of sacramentality, with the eucharist at its heart."[89]

In a nutshell, ritual symbols had become social currency; to perform them
was to negotiate social power and social control. This is no new insight, but
what *was* new in the eleventh and twelfth centuries was the strategic reposi-
tioning of Western Christianity's central liturgical symbol—the eucharist. As
Rubin observes, celebration of the Lord's Supper had long been a vital symbol among Christian communities,

> but it was *refigured* in the eleventh and twelfth centuries to create a new
> structure of relations, *thus modifying the symbolic order, and the social rela-
> tions and political claims which could be attached to it.* In this new order we
> witness the raising of a fragile, white, wheaten little disc to amazing
> prominence, and fallible, sometimes ill-lettered, men to the status of medi-
> ator between Christians and the supernatural. The eucharist emerged as a
> unifying symbol for a complex world, as a symbol unburdened by local
> voices and regional associations.[90]

In short, a world that lacked any single, unifying political or social authority—a world deeply divided by *local* fiefdoms, *local* allegiances, and *locally constructed* identities—sought and found a "super-authority" in a sacramental
system that made the eucharist its efficacious center and ordained clerics its
frontline ritual negotiators.

Still, even though medieval "lay participants experienced a Mass monop-
olized by the clergy, they did not, it appears, feel hopelessly alienated from its
rituals."[91] As Reinburg argues, late medieval lay participation in the eucharist
was *not* radically "impoverished." If art and contemporary accounts are any
guide, those present at a medieval Mass found there a familiar, comfortable,

---

88. Muir's "crisis in the performative sign" may be compared to Greene's "decline of the ceremonial sign." In each case the result is similar, a "disjunctive semiotics" that subverts or denies any real
relation between *signum* and *signatum*.

89. Miri Rubin, *Corpus Christi: The Eucharist in Late Medieval Culture* (New York: Cambridge
University Press, 1991), 1.

90. Ibid., 347 (emphasis added).

91. Muir, *Ritual in Early Modern Europe*, 164.

"communal rite of greeting, sharing, giving, receiving, and making peace"; they found it an effective means of uniting themselves "with God, . . . Church, and each other." While they may have been mystified by the Latin language (as the clergy themselves often were; hence our English "hocus-pocus"), medieval laity "understood" the liturgy primarily with their skins, their *bodies*. Their connection to liturgy thus flowed from "a rich layering of associations, of social relationships and rituals expressing those relationships." This point is confirmed, Reinburg notes, by the many medieval illustrations that show a strong *gestural* kinship between the liturgy and the rituals of secular life. "[T]he late medieval liturgy," Reinburg concludes, "can be viewed as the establishment of social and spiritual solidarity among God, the Church['s leadership], and the lay community."[92] In sum: *Medieval layfolk participated in the Mass precisely by deploying the ritual repertoire they learned from their culture* —from ceremonies inscribed on their bodies by city, court, and commerce, in alleys, streets, inns, and pubs, in home and hearth. In a word, layfolk learned how to participate in religious ritual by participating in the "liturgy of the world."

Reinburg's argument thus resonates with a position taken by Catherine Pickstock, who writes that "the liturgy of the Middle Ages, *unlike the liturgy of today*, was embedded in a *culture* which was ritual in character." One reason why Pickstock believes the Roman Catholic liturgical reforms that followed Vatican II have faltered is because they did not accurately read the cultural context of worship today. Because they neglected to see the liturgy as a comprehensive cultural and ethical system, the postconciliar reforms have (in Pickstock's words) "failed to challenge those structures of the modern secular world which are wholly inimical to liturgical purpose: those structures . . . which perpetuate a separation of everyday life from liturgical enactment." The result, she argues, has a been a kind of "conciliar fundamentalism" that is even more pernicious than the conservative nostalgia of those who have continued to resist the conciliar reforms in the name of "ritual tradition" or "decorum and good taste." "A successful liturgical revision," Pickstock concludes, "would have to involve a revolutionary re-invention of language and practice which would challenge the structures of our modern world, and only thereby restore real language and action as liturgy."[93]

---

92. See Virginia Reinburg, "Liturgy and the Laity in Late Medieval and Reformation France," *Sixteenth Century Journal* 33, no. 3 (1992): 526-47, here 527, 532, 541, 542. On medieval lay participation at Mass, see also Eamon Duffy, *The Stripping of the Altars: Traditional Religion in England 1400-1580* (New Haven: Yale University Press, 1992), 91-130, 295-98.

93. Catherine Pickstock, "A Short Essay on the Reform of the Liturgy," *New Blackfriars* 78 (1997): 56 (emphasis added), 57. I have discussed Pickstock's views at greater length in the new edition of my book *Real Presence: The Work of Eucharist* (new and expanded ed.; Chicago: Liturgy Training Publications, 2001), 129-44.

Although I do not subscribe to Pickstock's analysis of the postconciliar
Roman Catholic liturgy, her challenge to "reinvent" language and practice
opens an opportunity. In the paragraphs that follow, I will show how three
very different thinkers have attempted to rewrite or "transcribe" the sacramental principle that lies so close not only to the heart of Christian worship,
but to its mission in a world of religious pluralism and cultural diversity. Each
of these attempts offers an innovative approach to Western Christianity's tradition about the efficacy of the ritual symbol, the "performative ceremonial
sign." Looking briefly at each of them will help us better understand how
liturgical symbol and sacrament work.

Aquinas: Persons and World as "Real" and "Sayable"

The first "transcription" of sacrament that concerns us was developed in
the mid-thirteenth century by Thomas Aquinas, who used Aristotelian language in order to give a *non*-Aristotelian account of how ritual symbols work,
especially in the sacrament of the eucharist.[94] Three short but crucial texts
from the *Summa Theologiae* and its Supplement epitomize Aquinas's thought
about those ritual symbols we call sacraments:

- *Summa Theologiae* IIIa Pars, Q. 75, art. 1, ad 3: *Sacramentum est in genere
  signi* ("a sacrament belongs to the category of sign")[95]
- *Summa Theologiae* IIIa Pars, Q. 60, art. 2, corpus: *Signa dantur hominibus
  quorum est per nota ad ignota pervenire* ("signs give human beings the
  ability to advance [to go, to proceed] from the known to the unknown").
  One of the consequences of Aquinas's argument in this question will be
  that because of the essentially "human orientation" of sacramental signs,
  something more is required of sacraments than merely the "natural

---

94. On the innovative character of Aquinas's theory of sacrament (as expressed in his eucharistic
theology), see Herbert McCabe, O.P., "The Eucharist as Language," *Modern Theology* 15 (1999): 131-
41.

95. As David Bourke notes, "In the present treatise [*Summa Theologiae* IIIa, 60 ff] St Thomas is
reverting to the approach of St Augustine by regarding them [the sacraments] initially and primarily
as signs—further prolongations, that is to say, of the divine gesture of the Incarnation, the mode in
which God, in his mysterious plan and counsel, chooses to present himself to man as an object of faith
and worship as well as a bringer of redemptive grace" (St. Thomas Aquinas, *Summa Theologiae*, vol.
56, *The Sacraments* [3a.60-65], trans. David Bourke [New York: McGraw-Hill/Blackfriars, 1975], 2-
3, note b). In his introduction to *Summa Theologiae* IIIa, 60, Aquinas explicitly cites Augustine's short
definition of sacrament (*signum rei sacrae*). Further, like many of his contemporaries, Aquinas had earlier "approached the sacraments . . . as efficient causes of grace" (Bourke). This shift (from "efficient
cause" to "sign" as the central way of understanding both the structure and the signifying power/effects
of sacraments) was a momentous one. See also Louis-Marie Chauvet, *Symbol and Sacrament: A Sacramental Reinterpretation of Christian Existence*, trans. Patrick Madigan and Madeleine Beaumont (Collegeville, Minn.: Liturgical Press, 1995), 9-21.

similitude of an effect to its cause."[96] The sacrament embodies "a *willed* meaning, corresponding to that of a physical gesture and given further precision by the words accompanying it."[97] In short, sacraments confront us with a world of "willed" [or determined, discovered, assigned] meanings, rather than with a world of [merely] natural resemblances.

- *Summa Theologiae* IIIa Pars Suppl., Q. 29, art. 2, corpus: *Sacramentum significando causat* ("a sacrament [i.e., an efficacious ritual symbol] functions—it works, produces, gives, accomplishes, effects—by the very act of signifying").[98]

These three texts point to one luminous fact: both human beings and the signifying world they inhabit are "real" and "sayable." People and world "say" each other; they are literally "co-efficient," and this real, mutual "sayability" lies at the heart of Aquinas's thinking about how the liturgy's ritual symbols work. (The mutual "sayability" of person and world is also a central theme in Virginia Woolf's astonishing, modernist novel *The Waves*.) Both human persons and their signs "say" and "show"; indeed, they "show" by saying and "say" by showing. Through the world of ritual symbols, Aquinas suggests, human beings discover how to *hear* with their eyes and how to *see* with their ears.

As Aquinas sees it, then, to say that sacraments "cause" (*sacramentum significando causa*) is to argue that sacramental signification results from human immersion in—and interaction with—thick linguistic systems that are simultaneously verbal and gestural.[99] Effective signification (i.e., signification that really "works") thus belongs to the relational world of intelligibility, for intelligibility arises neither from subjects alone nor from signs alone but from the complex interplay between them—subject and sign, the speaking human agent and the speaking symbol. (What is *un*intelligible cannot signify precisely because this essential, interactive relation between sign and subject is absent or blocked.)

For Aquinas, then, signification is inevitably relational and intelligible. Moreover, this signifying intelligibility is also and always *intentional*: speaking subjects "intend" symbols, and speaking symbols "intend" subjects. Perhaps that is why Aquinas trusted the axiom *sacramenta (sunt) propter homines*

---

96. Bourke, *Sacraments*, 8-9, note c.

97. Ibid.

98. See also *Summa Theologiae* Suppl., Q. 30, art. 2, sed contra (*sacramenta significando efficiunt*; the language is Lombard's, the sacrament being discussed is extreme unction); *Summa Theologiae*, Suppl., Q. 45, art. 3, corpus (*causae sacramentales significando efficiunt*; the sacrament being discussed is matrimony).

99. Aquinas held that sacraments are not "internal states" or mere "mental realities" but external, visible, sensible activities that engage human beings fully at the level of both word and deed. See *Summa Theologiae*, Pars IIa IIae, Q. 111, art. 1, corpus: *Signa . . . exteriora non solum sunt verba, sed etiam facta* ("external signs are not only words but also deeds").

(i.e., "ritual symbols ['sacraments'] exist for the sake of human beings"); they achieve their finality (their completion and proper "end") when joined to human subjects. The relation between subject and symbol points to a teleology that works simultaneously in two directions, from subject to sign and sign to subject. And this suggests, further, that *both* human subjectivity *and* the power of signification are "transcendental," that is, they are constituted by an "excess" that, in source and power, surpasses them both.[100]

For this reason as well, Aquinas affirmed that the "causality" of sacraments—their ability not only to "show and say" but to *do* something decisively new—is at once human and divine. Ultimately, it is not the *intentionality* of sign or subject that produces the ritual symbol's effect. Rather *the inexhaustible horizon—the "excess"—is itself causal*—that is, it is God's gracious work in Christ, who causes the sacrament's efficacy precisely by causing the whole range of human and natural deeds and results that constitute "signification." We call these deeds and results "history" and "creation"; Aquinas would have called them "instrumental causes," as distinguished from God, the primary, ultimate, or final cause.[101] Thus Aquinas insists: *Consecratio sacramentorum est ab ipso Deo* ("God determines what sacraments do or cause"),[102] or again, *De latere Christi dormientis in cruce fluxerunt sacramenta* ("From the side of Christ asleep on the cross the sacraments flow") (*Summa Theologiae* Ia, Q. 92, art. 3, corpus).

At first, it sounds as though Aquinas's transcription of sacrament is simply a *deus ex machina*, a bald request that God come and colonize human causes, making of them something we know they are *not*. But one must remember that, for Aquinas, God's causality does not overwhelm the human ("instrumental causality") any more than grace destroys nature. On the contrary, Aquinas's view of the structure of sacramental signification presupposes the radiant, ineradicable scandal of the incarnation, which the contemporary theologian Xavier John Seubert has expressed this way:

---

100. In my view, it is this aspect of Aquinas's thought that allows him to escape the "trap" that many postmodern theologians, especially those, like Jean-Luc Marion, who work from a phenomenological perspective, find in scholastic sacramental theology. The "trap," of course, is the implication (possible, I would argue, but not necessary) that the "subject" somehow constitutes (by intentionality) the sign. Marion and others would want to say that the sign (as saturated phenomenon) constitutes the subject.

101. See *Summa Theologiae* Suppl., Q. 45, art. 1, ad 1: *Sacramentorum prima causa est virtus divina, sed causae secundae instrumentales sunt materiales operationes ex divina institutione habent efficaciam* ("The first cause of sacraments is divine power, but the secondary instrumental causes are material actions that have their efficacy from God's own determination").

102. *Summa Theologiae* IIIa, Q. 83, art. 3, ad 8; cf. *Summa Theologiae*, Suppl., Q. 25, art. 2, ad 1: *Sacramentorum effectus non sunt determinati ab homine, sed a Deo* ("The effects of sacraments are not determined by human beings but by God").

[I]n Jesus God has become a human being and will remain human forever. The logical consequence of this is that, in becoming irrevocably connected to the human bodiliness of Jesus, God is irrevocably particular in a human way. . . .

Incarnation is the irrevocable choice of particularity within space and time as a mode of God's being: the material, historical and particular will be forever a place of God's substantial relationality.[103]

Thus Aquinas's transcription calls for a radical rereading of ritual symbols. What is at stake in sacramental signification, he held, is not the relation between "representation and referent," sign and signified, but the relations between God and world, God and history, God and humans. Thomas's citation of a medieval commonplace in Question 92, article 3 of the Ia Pars of the *Summa Theologiae* ("From the side of Christ asleep on the cross flowed water and blood, the sacraments through which the church was instituted") means that *God's being is irrevocably connected to the human bodiliness of Jesus,* the only source of the church's life and liturgy. For Aquinas, then—though commentators rarely notice it—metaphysics is already a profoundly "compromised" term. What Aquinas gives is not so much a metaphysics of being — where "being" implicitly subordinates the infinite to the finite[104]—as what one might call an "infraphysics of enfleshment." In short, the embarrassingly crass, clumsy causes of this world have become "necessary angels," the essential occasions within which the divine is disclosed, known, and named. God's being can no longer be divorced from historical process, and thus the human intelligibility of sacrament becomes a privileged site of our meeting with irreducible Mystery.

Paradoxically, perhaps, the Reformers of the sixteenth century implicitly affirmed Aquinas's transcription of sacrament by insisting that worship be intelligible and that people have "cognitive access" to the mystery of Christ— a doctrinally informed participation nurtured by the Word purely proclaimed and preached in their own language. More astonishing still, the Council of Trent also embraced Aquinas's "modernity," arguing that the Mass should be intelligible, and that pastors should "explain frequently during the celebration of the Mass" the mysteries being sacramentally celebrated.[105] Given this background, Vatican II's call for intelligible ritual symbols[106] was less a capit-

103. Xavier John Seubert, "'But Do Not Use the Rotted Names': Theological Adequacy and Homosexuality," *Heythrop Journal* 40, no. 1 (January 1999): 75.

104. See Chauvet, *Symbol and Sacrament,* 24-25.

105. This was the conclusion the bishops reached at Trent's twenty-second session (September 17, 1562). See *The Canons and Decrees of the Council of Trent,* trans. H. J. Schroeder (1941; repr., Rockford, Ill.: Tan Books, 1978), 148.

106. See esp. SC 33-34: "In the revision of the liturgy the following general norms should be

ulation to Enlightenment rationalism than a (perhaps naive) reaffirmation of
Aquinas's transcribed sacramentalism.

David Jones: "*Making* This *Thing* Other"

Intelligibility and cognition have essential roles to play in Aquinas's view of
how ritual symbols work, a point subsequently affirmed by Reformers,
Catholic Counter-Reformers (at and after Trent), and the Second Vatican
Council. Thomas understood that human intellection is *embodied*, and his
point leads to my second example of rewriting sacrament—an *aesthetic* transcription proposed by the Welsh poet David Jones in a 1960 essay originally
entitled "Nor Fire nor Candle Light: Symbol and Sacrament under Technology."[107] Arguing that the rapid evolution of technology in the twentieth century brought not only benefit but deprivation and a curious disregard for the
body, Jones wrote:

> In contrast with some beliefs the belief of the Catholic Church commits
> its adherents, in a most inescapable manner, to the body and the embod-
> ied; hence to history, to locality, to epoch and site, to sense-perception, to
> the contactual, the known, the felt, the seen, the handled, the cared for, the
> tended, the conserved; to the qualitative and to the intimate.
>
> All of which, and more especially the two last, precludes the ersatz, and
> tends to a certain mistrust of the unembodied concept.
>
> It commits its adherents also to the belief that things of all sort can, are,
> and should be given special significances, set aside, made other, raised
> above the utile to the status of *signa* and revered with corporeal, manual
> acts. It commits them to the "creaturely."[108]

Jones's reference to the Catholic habit of raising things of all sort "above
the utile to the status of *signa*" epitomizes his transcription of sacrament. Our
interaction with ritual symbols—and their power of signification—reminds
us, that the human person is *homo faber*, not merely the maker of tools and
artifacts (i.e., "technology") but "the maker, user and apprehender of signs."
Although art "'abides on the side of the mind,' its products are of the body."
And although, like birds and beavers, we build both nests and dams, "we have

---

observed. The rites should be distinguished by a noble simplicity. They should be short, clear, and
free from useless repetitions. They should be within the people's power of comprehension, and normally should not require much explanation."

107. Reprinted under the title "A Christmas Message 1960," in David Jones, *The Dying Gaul and
Other Writings*, ed. Harman Grisewood (London: Faber & Faber, 1978), 167-76.

108. Jones, "A Christmas Message 1960," 167.

from our ... beginnings been concerned with the extra-utile, with something I have termed a sign-making or a showing-forth."[109]

For Jones, then, ritual symbols are embodied technologies that "do" by "showing." In the human species, skill (Greek *technē*) and sign (Greek *sēmeion*) are mutually implicated. For this reason, he notes,

> the Incarnation and the Eucharist cannot be separated; the one thing being analogous to the other. If one binds us to the animalic the other binds us to artifacture and both bind us to *signa*, for both are a showing forth of the invisible under visible signs.
>
> The mewling babe in the ox-stall, the quasi-artifacts of bread and wine (products of tillage, of the oven, the vat) are to be regarded, so our religion demands, not as signs only but signs which are also the Thing signified, namely the Eternally Begotten Word, the Logos which gave *poiesis* to the expanding or contracting (whichever it should turn out to be) cosmos.[110]

Thus, Jones concludes, "the corporeal, the earthy, the earthly, the arti-facted, the creaturely"—indeed, *all* products of nature "pure" or technolo-gized—come to focus in the *signa* of eucharist, which then "images and incants a world very *other* than the world which you and I enjoy or suffer today and of which we are, willy-nilly, an integral part."[111] Ritual symbols thus constitute a "retechnologization" of human artifacts, a transformation of the merely "useful" into the sublimely "useless." One hears hints of this in a passage from Jones's long poem "The Anathemata," a reimagining of the old Roman Canon (Eucharistic Prayer I):

> We already and first of all discern him making this thing
>   other.
> His groping syntax, if we attend, already shapes:
>   "ADSCRIPTAM, RATAM, RATIONABILEM" ... and
> by pre-application and for them, under modes and patterns
> altogether theirs, the holy and venerable hands lift up an effi-
> cacious sign.
> These, at the sagging end and chapter's close, standing
> humbly before the tables spread, in the apsidal houses, who
> intend life:
>   between the sterile ornaments
>   under the pasteboard baldachins

---

109. Ibid., 169, 168.
110. Ibid., 171-72.
111. Ibid., 173 (emphasis added).

> as, in the young-time, in the sap-years:
>   between the living floriations
>   under the leaping arches.[112]

"Making *this* thing *other*." Ultimately, Jones believed, technology itself wants to become a sacrament, a transforming "remake" of creation. There are similarities between Jones's transcription of sacrament and the work of the contemporary German-American philosopher Albert Borgmann, who analyzes the modern conflict between what he calls technological *devices* and "*focal things*."[113] Technological devices are labor-saving tools that let users remain passive and uninvolved (think of a modern furnace as opposed to an old-fashioned fireplace). *Devices* commodify goods and practices; they ask very little engagement or interaction from us (if the furnace quits, you call the heating-and-cooling-systems experts, you don't dig up the back in search of a seam of coal). In contrast, according to Richard Gaillardetz, *focal practices* (e.g., growing your own garden or learning to play a violin) open up a "complex world of 'manifold engagement' . . . [a] multilayered web of relationships with the larger world" of nature, goods, and persons. Devices give "the goods without the practice," and under these conditions the character of the good itself changes. The good becomes a commodity—a site of commerce. Devices, in short, give us goods without context, "things" without my essential framework that reveals their value.[114] Focal practices, on the other hand, are "high maintenance"; they require constant attention, care, engagement, nurture, interaction.

Thus, in David Jones's transcription, ritual symbol and sacrament become "focal practices" that require engagement, attention. Sacrament is an act, not a thing; it is the placing of what we value most into the care of human practices. As Jones puts it in "The Anathemata,"

> The cult-man stands alone in Pellam's land:[115] more precariously than he knows he guards the *signa*: the pontifex among his house-treasures . . . he can fetch things new and old: the tokens, the matrices, the institutes, the ancilla, the fertile ashes— . . . the things come down from heaven together with the kept memorials, the things lifted up and the venerated trinkets.

---

112. David Jones, "The Anathemata: Rite and Fore-Time," in *Introducing David Jones: A Selection of His Writings,* ed. John Matthias (London: Faber & Faber, 1980), 139.

113. See Albert Borgmann, *Crossing the Postmodern Divide* (Chicago: University of Chicago Press, 1992).

114. Richard Gaillardetz, *Transforming Our Days: Spirituality, Community and Liturgy in Technological Culture* (New York: Crossroad, 2000), 19 (Gaillardetz is commenting upon Borgmann's distinction between devices and focal practices), 23, 51.

115. As Jones says in a note on this reference, "King Pellam in Malory's *Morte d'Arthur* is lord of the Waste Lands and the lord of the Two Lands" (*Introducing David Jones*, 177).

This man, so late in time, curiously surviving, shows courtesy to the objects when he moves among, handles or puts aside the name-bearing instruments, when he shows every day in his hand the salted cake given for this *gens* to savour all the *gentes*.[116]

In Christ, Jones concludes, the true cult-man cometh "under the sign of actual, visible flesh at an actual, identifiable site, at a very late date in the history of us sign-making and sign-comprehending mammalia." And the first to read this "ritual symbol" were the beasts. "Who were the first to cry: Noel? / Animals all as it befell." If we forget the animals, Jones warns,

> we are halfway to forgetting the creaturely in ourselves, and that in turn will impoverish the sacramental in us, for though the beasts knew nothing of sacrament we could know nothing of it either did we not share the bodily with them. No wonder the theologian most associated with the angelic hierarchies [Thomas Aquinas] should have declared that our having bodies is an advantage.[117]

Jean-Luc Marion: The Sacramental Gift

My third example of sacramental transcription is based on the work of the postmodern French Catholic theologian Jean-Luc Marion. Here, I will sketch three points about Marion's thought that may shed light on how ritual symbol and sacrament are related to what he calls "saturated phenomena."[118]

1. *"Suspended between two idolatries."* One of the common complaints of postmodern theology is that Western metaphysics, though it claims to assert the ultimacy of Being, in fact teeters on the brink of idolatry by assigning a human conceptual category ("being") to both God and creatures. The phrase "metaphysics of presence" epitomizes this problem, in part because the vocab-

---

116. Jones, "Anathemata," in *Introducing David Jones*, 140. Jones notes that his allusion to the "cult-man's" hand is an echo of a line from a medieval English poem entitled "Of a rose, a lovely rose," which speaks of the eucharist in these words: "Every day it shewit in prystes hond." Jones goes on to note that the salt cakes (*mola salsa*) were made by the Roman vestals as part of the purification of the daily sacrifices. Jones believed that Jesus' cryptic comment in Mark 9:49-50 may allude to a similar practice in the Jewish Temple cult. See *Introducing David Jones*, 177-78, nn. 6 and 7.

117. Jones, "A Christmas Message 1960," 175-76.

118. For a lengthier treatment of some aspects of Marion's work, see my *Real Presence: The Work of Eucharist* (new and expanded ed.), 107-46. See also Jean-Luc Marion, "In the Name: How to Avoid Speaking of 'Negative Theology,'" in *God, the Gift, and Postmodernism*, ed. John D. Caputo and Michael J. Scanlon (Bloomington: Indiana University Press, 1999), 20-53. This essay, in another translation, is included in Jean-Luc Marion, *In Excess: Studies of Saturated Phenomena*, trans. Robyn Horner and Vincent Berraud (New York: Fordham University Prress, 2002), 128-62.

ulary of presence plays such a decisive role in Western sacramental theology and practice. We speak, for example, of God's "presence" in the sacraments and of Christ's "real presence" in the consecrated eucharistic elements. Yet thinkers as early as Aquinas recognized the danger lurking in the language of presence. To speak of "making present" may simply mask *our desire to master things* through an explaining science or a calculating will."[119] Sacrament is above all an act of donation (God, giving; indeed, God giving what we cannot give), and hence the emphasis falls "not on the presence itself" but on "letting-enter-into-presence," on *"letting* the coming-into-presence." Thus, when Thomas asked in the *Summa Theologiae* whether Christ was present in the eucharistic species "as in a place" (*sicut in loco*), he answered no.[120] Localized presence—presence in the sense of "confinement" to *a* place—would, in Aquinas's view, reduce God's giving in the sacrament (the gift of the risen Christ's body and blood) to the status of a natural object within the natural world, a mere biochemical "fact" subject to the ordinary laws of nature and physics. Lost in such a perspective would be the otherness, the sheer givenness, the inexhaustible depth and "excess" of God's action—realities that are not limited by the natural laws of physics and chemistry.

Marion argues that much of today's thinking about sacrament is suspended between two idolatries. There is a *metaphysical* idolatry (popular among some traditionalist Catholics) that localizes presence in material signs (e.g., bread and wine), and there is a *psychological* idolatry (popular among progressives) that confines presence to a community's consciousness, its words, acts, and intentions. To Marion, both idolatries are equally odious, because they commodify presence, reducing it to the status of an "object" or "thing," removing presence from excess and donation (from God, giving).[121] These idolatries assign presence either to the world of natural objects (subject to the ordinary, this-worldly laws of physics and biochemistry) or to the

---

119. Chauvet, *Symbol and Sacrament*, 61.

120. For Aquinas's treatment of "local presence" in the eucharist, see *Summa Theologiae* IIIa, 75, 5 (*Utrum corpus Christi sit in hoc sacramento sicut in loco*). His response is: *Corpus Christi non est in hoc sacramento secundum proprium modum quantitatis dimensivae, sed magis secundum modum substantiae* ("The Body of Christ is not in this sacrament according to its own natural mode of quantitative dimension, but rather according to the mode of substance").

121. It should be pointed out that Marion's phenomenological philosophy stresses the "primacy of givenness" in our experience of phenomena, a givenness so inexhaustible ("excessive") that it requires a "radical rethinking both of the phenomenon itself and of the subject to whom it appears." See Shane Mackinlay, synopsis of his recently defended doctoral dissertation at the Catholic University of Louvain (June 6, 2005): http://www.kuleuven.be/doctoraatsverdediging/ (accessed July 26, 2005). "In place of phenomena appearing as objects or beings, within the limits of horizons imposed by a constituting subject" writes Mackinlay, "Marion envisages phenomena as appearing without condition or limits, given by themselves alone." The upshot, of course, is that the human subject is no longer a "sovereign ego that constitutes phenomena as objects; instead, the subject is the one on whom phenomena impose themselves."

world of aggrandizing, autonomous selves (communities, their plans and intentions). The result is a God held hostage by bread or by folk—that is, a God who no longer gives, freely, sovereignly, excessively, and inexhaustibly. In Marion's own words, "substantial presence . . . fixes and freezes the person in an available, permanent, handy, and delimited *thing*"; similarly, exaggerated attention to the assembly reduces presence to "liturgies where the community celebrates its own power . . . [to] collective self-satisfaction."[122]

In sum, the idolatrous impasse created by the metaphysics of presence results from our being caught between two traditional systems (or "ways") of predication, that is, of talk about God and God's relation to us: the way of *affirmation* (sometimes known as "cataphatic" or positive theology) and the way of *negation* (sometimes known as "apophatic" or negative theology). Neither of these ways works, Marion contends, and hence what is needed is a "third way," the way of "not-naming" ("de-nomination").[123] It is theology's task to "release" God from all naming, from systems that would simply affirm or deny God's action or "presence." The theologian seeks to "silence the Name" and so let *it* name *us*. As Marion puts it at the end of his essay "In the Name: How to Avoid Speaking of 'Negative Theology,'"

> The Name—it has to be dwelt in without saying it, but by letting it say, name, and call us. The Name is not said by us; it is the Name that calls us.
>
> And because nothing terrifies us more than this call, ". . . because we hold it [to] be a fearful task to name with our proper names the One" . . . to whom God has bestowed the gift of the name above all names.[124]

This is also the task of Christian prayer and praise. Because liturgy constantly "calls God names," it may seem as though it submits the Holy One to the metaphysics of presence. But Marion argues that the language of liturgy and sacrament is a language of "de-nomination." Its purpose, he writes, is not

> predicative (whether this means predicating an affirmation or a negation) but purely pragmatic. It is no longer a matter of naming or attributing something to something, but of aiming in the direction of . . . , of relating to . . . , of comporting oneself towards . . . of reckoning with . . . —in short of dealing with. . . . [P]rayer definitively marks the transgression of the predicative, nominative, and therefore metaphysical sense of language.[125]

---

122. Jean-Luc Marion, *God without Being*, trans. Thomas A. Carlson (Chicago: University of Chicago Press, 1991), 164.

123. Marion outlines the problems of positive and negative theologies and his own proposals for a "third way" in his essay "In the Name," in Caputo and Scanlon, *God, the Gift, and Postmodernism*, 24-42.

124. Ibid., 42; I have used the translation found in Marion, *In Excess*, 162.

125. Ibid., 30 (cf. *In Excess*, 144).

In liturgy and sacrament, naming is not "claiming" but *aiming*, a "gesturing toward." At worship we become "apostles of the impossible," an identity bestowed by the unnamable Name.[126] Thus, Marion argues, the risen Christ's command to "baptize them in the name" (Matt 28:19) is "not a predicate by which God's essence is inscribed within the horizon of our understanding, but rather that we are to be inscribed within God's un-nameable Name, that we are to be included in the clearing opened by that Name."[127]

2. *The "impossible logic" of the gift*: Marion's second concern relates to Jacques Derrida's "impossible logic" of the gift. As Aquinas, following Aristotle, says, "A gift is literally a giving that can have no return [*datio irreddibilis*], i.e., it is not given with repayment in mind."[128] Derrida has also read Aristotle, and so he argues that by definition a *gift* is *aneconomic;* that is, it does not participate in the "economy or circle of giving and return"[129] that characterize most forms of human exchange. Thus Derrida's syllogism: (a) A gift is a giving that can have no return; (b) but in our human experience, gifts imply exchange and restitution; hence (c) no real gift is possible. In Derrida's own words,

> For there to be a gift, there must be no reciprocity, return, exchange, countergift, or debt. If the other *gives* me back or owes me or has to give me *back* what I *give* him or her, there will not have been a gift, whether this restitution is immediate or whether it is programmed by a complex calculation of . . . long-term deferral or différance.[130]

The problem Derrida's views about gift seem to create for a theory of ritual symbol and sacrament is evident.[131] If, for example, eucharist "gives" but expects *gratitude* in "return," then the sacrament creates *obligation*, and neither the "giver," nor the "given," nor the "given to" is truly free. There can be

---

126. See John D. Caputo, "Apostles of the Impossible: On God and the Gift in Derrida and Marion," in Caputo and Scanlon, *God, the Gift and Postmodernism*, 185-222, here 193.

127. Ibid.

128. *Summa Theologiae* Ia Pars, Q. 38, art. 2, corpus. See *Summa Theologiae*, vol. 7, trans. T. C. O'Brien (London: Blackfriars Eyre and Spottiswoode, 1976), 94 (Latin), 95 (English).

129. Gerard Loughlin, *Telling God's Story: Bible, Church and Narrative Theology* (New York: Cambridge University Press, 1996), 226.

130. Jacques Derrida, *Given Time: I: Counterfeit Money*, trans. Peggy Kamuf (Chicago: University of Chicago Press, 1992), 7.

131. It should be noted that, despite the opinion of phenomenologist theologians like Marion, Derrida is not necessarily a critic of "gift," nor does he reject, without qualification, its possibility. See Caputo, "Apostles of the Impossible," 203-10. What "gift" raises for Derrida is the question of the "impossible" and its relation to deconstruction. As Caputo comments, the "impossible" is *the very condition of desire* for Derrida. "*The* impossible stirs our desire, feeds our faith, and nourishes our passion. . . . It is just when we see that it is *impossible* that our hearts are set afire and we are lifted up above the horizon of pedestrian possibility. For Derrida, we must not lose our faith in the impossible, which is also our hope, our love, our faith in the gift. The gift, *the* impossible, *viens, oui, oui!*" (Caputo, "Apostles of the Impossible," 205). It might perhaps be better to say that, for Derrida, it is not that "gift is impossible," but rather than the gift is "*the* impossible."

no gift, Derrida appears to argue, without a forgetting—indeed, an absolute forgetting, a "forgetting of forgetting."[132] But here too Christian theology hits a snag. Traditionally, symbol and sacrament are about "remembering." How can "memory" and "forgetting" coexist? To put it another way, how can one reconcile *anamnesis* (the Greek word for the kind of "remembering" Christians do in liturgy) with *amnesia* (forgetting)?

3. *"Time regained?" Anamnesis as amnesia; amnesia as anamnesis.* It seems, then, that the notions of "gift" and "remembering"—both of them mainstays of liturgical language—are incompatible, irreconcilable. Yet Marion would not see matters that way, in part because of his distinction between "presence" and "givenness." First of all, he would point out that our incomprehension of God flows not from "a lack of givenness" (not from a reluctance on God's part to give), "but from an excess in givenness, surplus." With all other reality and experience, Marion would argue, "we always mean or intend more than is actually given to us, and our experience is always forced to play catch-up with our intention. But with God, more is given to us than we can ever mean or say, so that words and concepts are always at a loss to express what has been given." The problem is not with our powers of comprehension, conceptualization, and signification as such, but with the sheer liberality of God's givenness, a givenness that overflows, saturates, surpasses all else. The distinction between "presence" and "givenness" provides Marion with a way to affirm God as "given" but not *present*, which means that "God gives himself in a way that exceeds our reach or our grasp, that God cannot be conceived according to the terms set by a metaphysical concept; it is to say that we are given access to God by God's own self-giving or givenness." In this way, Marion "keeps God's givenness safe from the 'metaphysics of presence.'"[133]

Seen from this angle, the distinction between "presence" and "givenness" redefines the notion of gift, removing it from "the economy or circle of giving and return," of reciprocity, debt, and obligation. Gifts, in Marion's view, lie "somewhere else," in a place where Derrida "did not think to look," *beyond* the horizon of economy—and hence "in the horizon of *donation*."[134] In this, of course, Marion is implicitly appealing to a very old idea in Catholic sacramental thought: viz., "*the appearing of the invisible in the visible.*"[135] In effect, what happens in ritual symbol and sacrament is that the "finite, visible, and

---

132. Derrida, *Given Time*, 17-18; see also Loughlin, *Telling God's Story*, 227-28.
133. See Caputo, "Apostles of the Impossible," 193-95.
134. Ibid., 203. As Caputo notes, however, it is possible that, especially in his earlier work, Marion misses the point of Derrida's analysis of the relation between the "gift" and "the impossible" (p. 205).
135. Ibid., 208. As Caputo notes, Marion seems to derive this position from the theological aesthetics of Hans Urs von Balthasar. It would mean, for example, that "the lover's invisible love shines through the visible gift of the ring, iconically, 'sacramentally.'"

present gift" (e.g., our gifts of bread and wine at eucharist) are *displaced*, and we are "saturated by the hyperpresence or hypergivenness of the gifting" in its "unlimited and invisible givenness."[136] Here, as John Caputo points out, "Marion's position is nourished by a Catholic theology of the sacraments, a notion of Christ as God's *icon*."[137]

Whatever his sources, Marion is clearly intent on "rescuing" the notion of gift, and to this end he proposes, first, to redefine time, and second, to show how *giving* has priority over *being*.[138] For if the gift comes *first*—prior to all being, subjectivity, or relationship—then "it is, and remains, pure gift."[139]

Marion first tackles time. Ordinarily, we define "past" and "future" *negatively*, in terms of the present. The past is what ends when the present begins; the future is what begins when the present ends. But as Marion points out, it is precisely the *present* that does not exist unless it is "given" by past and future. This, of course, implies a nonmetaphysical and nonchronological understanding of time. In this model, time is not *dur*ation but *cre*ation, not chronology but content. Time itself is gift—"that which *is* given, rather than . . . that which gives." The ordinary metaphysical conception of time tries to understand "the whole from the present," but a "gifted concept of time . . . understands the present from the whole."[140] In the eucharist, for example, Christ's passion, death, resurrection, ascension, and *parousia* are "remembered" not because somebody (we or God) might have forgotten, but *because these events do not cease to determine our present and our future.* So in a fundamental way, both past and future determine our present. The past makes the present memorial ("remembering") possible, just as the future determines its final trajectory, even though we are not yet able to know or face or figure it. As the French novelist Marcel Proust understood, the future may sometimes live in us without our knowing it.

So in ritual symbol and sacrament, paradoxically, "remembering" (past) and "excess" (future) combine to cause *amnesia*, the blissful "forgetting" that makes gift possible by removing it from the circle of debt, obligation, and economy. Remembered past and the already active-and-accumulating "excess" of the future take possession of the present redefining it not as duration[141] but as

---

136. Ibid., 209.

137. Ibid. It is for this reason, in part, that Marion's critics accuse him of posing as a philosopher-phenomenologist while behaving as a Catholic theologian who "smuggles" the invisible into the visible and imports transcendence into phenomenology. See Dominique Janicaud, "Veerings," in *Phenomenology and the "Theological Turn": The French Debate*, trans. Bernard Prusak (New York: Fordham University Press, 2000), 50-69.

138. See the analysis in Loughlin, *Telling God's Story*, 237-44, which I will follow closely in the paragraphs that follow.

139. Loughlin, *Telling God's Story*, 237.

140. Ibid., 238 (emphasis added), 239.

141. By definition, the "present" cannot be duration at all, since it is either "receding" into past or "advancing" into future. At best, "present" might be regarded as a *becoming*.

datio, giving. And because what is (always, already) "given" in the now-possible present is nothing else than God (the giving that *is* God), the ontological limits of the "impossible gift" are overcome and the conditions of an absolute amnesia (absolute forgetting) are fulfilled. In God all divisions between "giver," "gift," and "given *to*" are overcome. "When God gives, nothing passes from God to someone else; rather God draws near."[142] God's *giving* is, therefore, God's self-bestowal, God's utterly gratuitous (but not metaphysical) *presence* as *givenness*. As John Milbank says, "It is a gift *to* no-one, but rather establishes creatures as themselves gifts"; it is "absolute gratuity with absolute exchange."[143] For, writes Gerard Loughlin, "what is given absolutely is [already] an absolute return, for return to God is the being and beat of the human heart. We are made for God. And this is our possibility as free creatures . . . because of Jesus Christ who is the perfect return of God's gift."[144] Since we are baptized "in Christ," we *participate in* (indeed, we are *created by*) that "return" which is a never-ending relationship and exchange, the very conditions that constitute personhood in the mystery of God—and in us.

This is how Marion seeks to overcome Derrida's "impossible logic of the gift" and so lend legitimacy to ritual symbols that not only "say and show" but "do and give." The real problem, Marion suggests, is not that "gift" is impossible but that *God's* giving is inexhaustible excess—an excess that terrifies us. It creates (as Dostoevsky's "Grand Inquisitor" surely knew) an intolerable burden for guilt-ridden mortals. As T. S. Eliot puts it in the Pentecost lyric (section IV) of "Little Gidding,"

> Love is the unfamiliar Name
> Behind the hands that wove
> The intolerable shirt of flame
> Which human power cannot remove.
> > We only live, only suspire
> > Consumed by either fire or fire.[145]

---

142. Loughlin, *Telling God's Story*, 243.
143. John Milbank, "Can a Gift Be Given? Prolegomena to a Future Trinitarian Metaphysic," *Modern Theology* 11, no. 1 (January 1995): 119-61, here 135 (emphasis added). Milbank notes that in our usual human experience of giving, the gift has to travel some distance, passing through a kind of "neutral territory" where it (the gift) can be accepted or rejected, received or returned, abandoned (by the potential recipient) or retrieved (by the giver). In the case of divine giving (*datio*) these conditions do not apply. For one thing there is no "outside" (neutral space) for God to "give to" or "receive from." To say that God "gives" is thus to say that God "creates"—and God creates not by rearranging pre-existing "stuff," but precisely by bringing into existence what did not before exist. Classical theology refers to this as *creatio ex nihilo* ("creation out of nothing"). So when God "gives" *ad extra*, creation and creatures "happen."
144. Loughlin, *Telling God's Story*, 243.
145. T. S. Eliot, *Four Quartets* (New York: Harcourt Brace Jovanovich, 1971), 57.

In the mysteries of Easter and Pentecost, God has forever closed the distance—the "neutral territory"— that usually divides donor from receiver (and
vice versa). As *grace* (= self-bestowal, presence, immediacy), God's giving[146]
would seem to overcome Derrida's problematic (which requires distance, a
passageway, a "no-man's-land" between giver, gift, and receiver).[147] So the real
question, for thinkers like Marion, is whether we humans can endure "the
intolerable shirt of flame," those ritual symbols and sacraments that mediate—by the *appearing of the invisible in the visible*—God's inexhaustible *excess*.
Nicholas Lash has put this point powerfully in his book *Believing Three Ways
in One God*:

> We simply are not strong enough for this. To speak of "guilt" would not go
> deep enough. Beyond all moralizing, we are, surely, *crushed* beneath the
> weight of what [the Grand] . . . Inquisitor called these "terrible gifts."
> God's gift of life is more than human beings can bear; more than we can
> carry, more than we can bring to birth. The message . . . that God's life is
> carried in our hands, sounds most unlike good news. . . .
>
> [And yet,] God's utterance and outbreathing are eternal. The speak-
> ing of God's Word, and the engendering of God's delight, are never fin-
> ished. We should therefore exercise considerable caution in speaking of
> God's "donation" in the past tense. . . . God's giving never leaves God's
> hands, in which are held all things as ever "being-given."[148]

CONCLUSION

Chapter 7 has moved from a discussion of service and ministry within the
"royal priesthood" of the baptized to an examination of the bonds that connect the assembly, as a "community of the forgiven," to the structure of sacra-

---

146. Note that when we speak of God's grace as presence, immediacy, or self-bestowal, we are
removing it from the language (and the reality) of "spatialization" or "temporalization" (two coordi-
nates that would commodify or reify the notion of divine grace). In *Believing Three Ways in One God*
(Notre Dame, Ind.: University of Notre Dame Press, 1992), Nicholas Lash points out that by choosing the word "gift" as a "proper name" for the Spirit, Thomas Aquinas had already succeeded in avoid-
ing such spatializing, temporalizing commodifications (see *Summa Theologiae* Ia, 38, 2). Lash
summarizes Aquinas's argument in this way: "No one can give what is not theirs to give. To call the
Spirit 'gift,' therefore, relates gift given to the giver, names a relationship of origin. God gives, and
what God gives is nothing less than God. 'Gift,' then, may be taken as the nearest that we have to a
name distinctive of the Spirit of God's love, the gift that is the very 'being-given,' or givenness, of
God: God as 'donation.'"
147. Loughlin, *Telling God's Story*, 244. In the view of Marion and others, Derrida's position "spa-
tializes" gift (and so, at the same time, commodifies it). The view propounded by Marion, Milbank,
and Loughlin does not rely on such spatialization, but rather insists on the absolute *coincidence* of gift
and exchange, reception and return.
148. Lash, *Believing Three Ways in One God*, 105.

ment. We noted, among other things, an evolution within the church's teaching on the related roles of people and priest in the liturgy, starting with the encyclicals of Pope Pius XII (*Mystici Corporis* and *Mediator Dei*) and reaching a climax with Vatican II's Constitution on the Sacred Liturgy (*Sacrosanctum Concilium*), which affirmed that at Mass, the people "offer the immaculate victim. *not only through the hands of the priest but also together with him*" (SC 48). We explored in some detail what it means to be a "liturgical assembly," and why the practice of justice is essential to the definition of that assembly. We saw, too, how the church as a "sacrament of the world"—an icon of God's one plan for humankind—must be understood within the larger perspective of interreligious dialogue. For just as God's Word spoke *before* and *during, after* and *beyond,* Jesus' life, ministry, passion, death, and rising, so too God's Spirit continues to work, as Pope John Paul II put it, "not only in individuals but also in society and history, in peoples, cultures, and religions" across the ages, down to our own time.

Our discussion then moved, in the second part of the chapter, from the notion of church as "sacrament of the world" to those specific liturgical celebrations which Catholic tradition identifies as "sacraments." Three different ways of "transcribing" (reimagining, rewriting) sacrament were discussed: those of a medieval theologian (Thomas Aquinas), a twentieth-century poet (David Jones), and a contemporary postmodern phenomenologist (Jean-Luc Marion). Our chapter concluded with an analysis of the problematic of "gift" (an issue raised by the postmodern philosopher Jacques Derrida) and how sacrament might be aptly described as "the language of *God's* giving."

QUESTIONS FOR REFLECTION

1. "Joyful companionship at table was thus the pivotal link connecting the Jesus of history with the Jesus Christians recognized as risen, forever alive in God's presence and accessible in both *cult* (sacramental liturgy) and *care* (pastoral service of the 'little ones,' the 'least' and most vulnerable). Jesus the bread breaker had become Jesus the bread broken—and now the reality of God's kingdom was accessible in cult *and* care, in liturgy *and* service, in the assembly's worship *and* its pastoral ministry" (p. 231 above). How did Jesus'"new map for the table" give rise to a "new map for ministry"?
2. The four verbs *take, bless, break, give* "that formed the ritual shape of Christian table liturgy thus present not only a challenging theology of eucharist but an even more challenging theology of ministry" (p. 233 above). How is this basic ritual "shape of the liturgy" linked not only to the ordained (bishops, priests, deacons) but to the numerous lay ministers who have begun to serve in Christian parishes since the Second Vatican Council?

3. In what ways did the Second Vatican Council's Constitution on the Sacred Liturgy (*Sacrosanctum Concilium*) build upon and expand the theology of worship, church, and ministry found in Pope Pius XII's encyclicals *Mediator Dei* and *Mystici Corporis?*

4. Aidan Kavanagh remarks that the church "baptizes to priesthood: it ordains only to executive exercise of that priesthood in the major orders of ministry.... Nor does sacerdotality come upon one for the first time ... at one's ordination. In constant genesis in the font, the Church is born there as a sacerdotal assembly by the Spirit of the Anointed One himself" (p. 249 above). What is the "common ground" that unites God's priestly people (the liturgical assembly) and those who serve that people in the "ministerial (ordained)" priesthood?

5. Jean-Luc Marion "argues that much of today's thinking about sacrament is suspended between two idolatries. There is a *metaphysical* idolatry (popular among some traditionalist Catholics) that localizes presence in material signs (e.g., bread and wine), and there is a *psychological* idolatry (popular among progressives) that confines presence to a community's consciousness, its words, acts, and intentions" (p. 270 above). To avoid this dual danger—yet to respect Catholic tradition about sacraments and their significance—how can we interpret words like "gift" and "presence" as these are applied to ritual actions such as the eucharist?

SUGGESTIONS FOR FURTHER READING

Hahnenberg, Edward. *Ministries: A Relational Approach.* New York: Crossroad, 2003. Studies the relation between ordained and nonordained ministries in the church and presents an eloquent theology for lay ministers.

Mahoney, Roger. *Gather Faithfully Together: Guide for Sunday Mass.* Chicago: Liturgy Training Publications, 1997. A pastoral letter from the cardinal-archbishop of Los Angeles that presents a vivid liturgical theology of the Sunday assembly, with its richly diverse cultural settings and diverse ministries.

Martin, James, ed. *Celebrating Good Liturgy: A Guide to the Ministries of the Mass.* Chicago: Loyola Press, 2005. A series of succinct essays by leading American liturgical scholars on each part of the eucharistic liturgy and the ministries it requires.

Piil, Mary Alice. "The Local Church as the Subject of the Action of the Eucharist." In *Shaping English Liturgy,* edited by Peter Finn and James Schellman. Washington, D.C.: Pastoral Press, 1990. A short but important study of the Christian assembly as the active agent of the church's sacramental worship and not merely the passive recipient of ministry by the priest.

Smith, Gary. *Radical Compassion: Finding Christ in the Heart of the Poor.* Chicago: Loyola Press, 2002. Pastoral and theological reflections by a Jesuit priest whose principal parishioners are the homeless of Portland, Oregon.

Epilogue

T OWARD THE END OF THE PROLOGUE to this book, I mentioned that ritual is principally about *connections*, about discovering what links us to God, to one another, to space, time, and history, to world and planet, to memory, desire, and expectation. As our study of Christian ritual, liturgical prayer, and sacrament comes to a close, it is surely salutary to recall a point American writer Annie Dillard makes in her moving meditation *Holy the Firm*. The "high Christian churches," she writes, "come at God with an unwarranted air of professionalism, with authority and pomp, as though they knew what they were doing."[1] Public prayer, Dillard suggests, is not an assertion about what—or whom—we know, but the opening of a hospitable space to welcome the advent, the sudden arrival, of an Other (and indeed, *all* others). The words of worship are not polished, confident speeches given in God's presence by people "in the know." Rather, as Dillard puts it,

> the set pieces of liturgy [are] . . . words which people have successfully addressed to God without their getting killed. In the high churches they saunter through the liturgy like Mohawks along a strand of scaffolding who have long since forgotten their danger. If God were to blast such a service to bits, the congregation would be, I believe, genuinely shocked.[2]

As our chapter on the risks of ritual revealed, the meeting between God and people in liturgy may—and probably should—provoke discomfort. Rituals behave—as Jesus did in his ministry—*parabolically*, and hence worship is not a self-congratulatory exercise where we showcase "all the great stuff we're doing." The point of our coming together in prayer is not congratulation and comfort but challenge and change. Even when we arrive at the church doors aglow with prosperity and success, we enter only by "acknowledging our failures and asking the Lord for pardon and strength" (Order of Mass, Penitential Rite). We become a community of the forgiven. And even when we mourn and lament our loss, at the funeral of a loved one, we still accept the invitation to come before God "with praise and thanksgiving (Eucharistic Prayer I)," and to acknowledge that "*all* your actions show your wisdom and love" (Eucharistic Prayer IV).

---

1. Annie Dillard, *Holy the Firm* (New York: Bantam Books, 1979), 60.
2. Ibid.

As we saw, too (especially in chapter 5), our common prayer has less to do with thought, reason, speech, and texts than with the book of our bodies. "Body," in fact, could be a one-word definition of prayer. For as Jean-Louis Chrétien writes, whoever "turns toward the incorporeal does so corporeally, with all [the] body." The ritual act of opening space to welcome the arrival of an Other always puts our bodies on the line, "exposes [us] in every sense of the word *expose*, and with nothing held back." The "first voice" of prayer is always the body, for flesh is earlier than speech. "Prayer knows that it does not know how to pray, but it learns this only in praying,"[3] and it learns to pray only in the motion, tears, and gestures of the flesh. We inscribe the communal act of our appearing before the One we cannot see on our bodies.

Thus, the incarnate speech of the body is where liturgy and sacrament begin. It is also true, of course, that in ritual prayer flesh feels its way toward *speech*. Chapter 6 spoke, therefore, about liturgy and the logic of metaphor. There is, we saw, a transgressive aspect to liturgical language, since it seeks to make the unsayable said, the unthinkable thought. Thus the public language of our prayer always falls prey to the One whom we seek to address. For the logic of metaphor reminds us that our proudly confident language has "transgressed all measure, exceeded any ability to measure itself and know itself completely."[4] We talk, but like Peter at the Transfiguration, we don't know what we're saying (Luke 9:33). In our ordinary human experience, to speak is to seize, to grasp (an idea, an object, a reality, a truth); to name is to claim. But in the metaphoric language of liturgy, our words—like the words of lovers—lose themselves; they are "given to, given over." The gathered assembly calls upon One who has already heard our voice, our requests, our lamentation, praise, and thanksgiving. To be always, already heard by God literally *pre*-occupies our speech and cancels our right to "ownership" over what we say. "To be [always, already] heard by God is an ordeal," writes Chrétien, "speech being put to a test like no other; for our speech is exposed in all that it seeks to hide, excuse, justify, obtain"; our voices are "truly naked."[5]

Thus the reason why Isaiah's inaugural vision of God—a vision that happens in sacred space during liturgical prayer (Isa 6:1-13)—requires that the prophet's lips be "touched by fire." As Daniel Berrigan observes, "The Isaiah who speaks the words has first hearkened to them with all his heart. Had the message not first penetrated him, to make of him a truthful witness, of what worth were his words? He has kept on looking and has come to understand-

---

3. Jean-Louis Chrétien, "The Wounded Word: The Phenomenology of Prayer," in *Phenomenology and the "Theological Turn,"* trans. Bernard G. Prusak, Jeffrey L. Kosky, and Thomas A. Carlson (New York: Fordham University Press, 2000), 150, 160.
   4. Ibid., 161.
   5. Ibid.

ing." And because of that Isaiah can become an icon of what worship of God demands of a people who are "reduced to the state of moral zombies, sleep-walking the world. This is the truth of our condition, verified on every hand. Blind, deaf, and, worst of all, heartless. Our depredations, the stench of blood, are evident across the world."[6] Only fire can cleanse our lips (our speech) and waken the sleepwalker, and hence Isaiah, touched by flame from the altar's burning coals,

> becomes the measure of our own possibility of seeing, hearing, under-standing with the heart, of being healed. Against all odds, against the crushing odds death holds, the "holy" lives in Isaiah and in those who, like him, take the word of God seriously.
>
> The coal is lifted from the fire and held to his lips. Thus the fire of god-liness is passed on and on. A community, a circle about the fire, is not merely warmed by the fire, but touched by the fire, marked indelibly.[7]

Berrigan's words are an admirable synopsis of the trajectory traced by Christian liturgical prayer. "The fire of godliness is passed on and on," a "community . . . is . . . touched by the fire, marked indelibly." So touched, so marked, the community moves from fire to water, from the searing Word that pre-occupies all our words to the "bowl of dirty water" that Christians, kneel-ing like their Lord at the gnarly feet of all (including the unworthy and the ungrateful), hold in their hands—precious emblem of service and sacrament. At the end of the day, Jesus' words in John's Gospel tell us all we need to know about "worshipping in spirit and truth":

> Before the feast of Passover, Jesus knew that his hour had come to pass from this world to the Father. He loved his own in the world and he loved them to the end. . . . So, during supper, fully aware that the Father had put everything into his power and that he had come from God and was returning to God, he rose from supper . . . took a towel and tied it around his waist. Then he poured water into a basin and began to wash the dis-ciples' feet. (John 13:1-5)

To be continued . . .

---

6. Daniel Berrigan, *Isaiah: Spirit of Courage, Gift of Tears* (Minneapolis: Fortress, 1996), 33.
7. Ibid.

Index